Praise for *Vicksburg*

"In 1863 all across the Northern states life went on as normal, but not so for the people of the South. The agony of war was already well known in Dixie. The sufferings and struggles of the citizens and defenders of Vicksburg are emblematic of the agony endured by the Southern people. Sandy Mitcham's scholarly research brings the sounds of gunboats and siege artillery to life and reminds us that war is more than battles and leaders. *Vicksburg* demonstrates why invaded nations never forget."

—JAMES RONALD KENNEDY, bestselling author of *The South Was Right*

"Dr. Mitcham has written a very comprehensive work on Vicksburg during the War Between the States, the numerous campaigns against it by U.S. land and river forces, the Confederate defense against these campaigns, and interesting portraits of various commanders on both sides. He also includes throughout interesting vignettes of local interest during those times. In the end, Dr. Mitcham presents compelling evidence that exonerates Confederate General Pemberton—a Northerner by birth and in command at Vicksburg at the time of its fall—from much of the blame that was attributed to him by the people of the South. Not to be missed by any who wish to have a comprehensive account of the campaign from a different perspective."

—H. V. TRAYWICK JR., member of the Society of Independent Southern Historians and author of *Empire of the Owls: Reflections on the North's War against Southern Secession* and *Virginia Iliad: The Death and Destruction of 'The Mother of States and of Statesmen'*

Vicksburg

Vicksburg

The Bloody Siege that Turned the Tide of the Civil War

Samuel W. Mitcham Jr.

★≡

REGNERY
HISTORY

Regnery® is a registered trademark of Salem Communications Holding Corporation
Regnery History™ is a trademark of Salem Communications Holding Corporation

Cataloging-in-Publication data on file with the Library of Congress

ISBN 978-1-62157-639-6

Published in the United States by
Regnery History
An imprint of Regnery Publishing
A Division of Salem Media Group
300 New Jersey Ave NW
Washington, DC 20001
www.RegneryHistory.com

Manufactured in the United States of America

10 9 8 7 6 5 4 3 2 1

Books are available in quantity for promotional or premium use. For information on discounts and terms, please visit our website: www. Regnery.com.

This book is dedicated to my ancestors, Corporal Josephus McGough, Company H, 31st Louisiana Infantry, and Private Mark Meeks, 37th Arkansas Infantry, who gave his life for his country.

Contents

Introduction   xi

1   Vicksburg: The First Siege   1
2   John C. Pemberton   17
3   Northern Mississippi, 1862   33
4   Chickasaw Bluffs   53
5   The Canal, the Lake, and the River   75
6   The Yazoo Pass Expedition   87
7   The Steele's Bayou Expedition   99
8   To Grand Gulf   111
9   Port Gibson   137
10 Raymond   151
11 First Battle of Jackson   163
12 Champion Hill   175
13 The Big Black River   195
14 Into Vicksburg   203
15 The Assaults   219
16 Siege   243
17 The Surrender   293
18 Port Hudson   311
19 Aftermath   323
20 Conclusions   333
21 A Historical Footnote   339

Epilogue: What Happened to Them?   345
Notes   357
Bibliography   377
Order of Battle,
Army of Mississippi at Vicksburg   389
Index   393

INTRODUCTION

The two main purposes of this book are to describe the Vicksburg campaigns of the War of Southern Secession, primarily from the Confederate point of view, and to analyze the generalship of the Rebel commander, Lieutenant General John C. Pemberton.

It is my opinion that the Northern side of these campaigns (and especially the generalship of Ulysses S. Grant) has been well covered by several prominent historians, including Edwin C. Bearss, Major General J. F. C. Fuller, Terrence J. Winschel, and others. The Southern side has been neglected, relatively speaking. This book will do just the opposite. Here, the Rebel side will be told. The Union side will be covered only insofar as it reflects on the Confederate side, or on Southern civilians.

Certain readers will be distressed because this book is not "politically correct." I pray to God that I never write a book that is! Political correctness and historical objectivity cannot coexist in the same work. I believe political correctness and intellectual dishonesty are all too often synonymous. The politically correct party line is that the war was all about slavery. The selfless, valiant, and morally pristine Northern army, which was full of holy and righteous indignation, launched a holy crusade against the evil Southern slaveholders, and defeated them because of their superior military skills, selfless valor, and overwhelmingly great mental prowess. That would be funny if so many people didn't believe it. They have no idea that only 6 to 7 percent of the Confederate Army was made up of slaveholders. Even the undereducated who do not read but do watch television and have seen the movie *Gettysburg* should ask themselves, "Why would anybody go through that hell so somebody else could keep their slaves?" The inescapable conclusion is they would not. So why did the Southerner fight?

There were several major causes of the war, and the evil institution of slavery was one of them. But it certainly wasn't the only one. Money was a big one—and perhaps the most significant. There was no income tax in those days. The major source of revenue was the tariff. The Southern plantation owner and yeoman farmer produced more than 75 percent of the world's cotton. The South, which contained 30 percent of the nation's population, was paying more than 85 percent of its taxes. At the same time, around three-quarters of that money was being spent on internal improvements in the North. This is why, when asked why he didn't just let the South go, Lincoln cried, "Let the South go? Let the South go? From where then would we get our revenues?"

The self-ordained "politically correct" never mention the fact that the American slaves were originally enslaved by black Africans, not by white men on horseback who scooped up African warriors with giant butterfly or fish nets, as depicted in a certain movie. (If I wanted to commit suicide, trying to capture African warriors with a net would be a pretty good way to go about it.) They then sold them to Northern (or Arab [Muslim]) flesh peddlers. The slave fleets headquartered in Boston, Massachusetts, and Providence, Rhode Island, not in Charleston, New Orleans, and Savannah. Yankee flesh peddlers then transported them across the ocean and sold them to Southerners and various other Americans—or at least what was left of them. Of the twenty-four to twenty-five million slaves transported to the Western Hemisphere, only twenty million arrived alive. Four to five million died in what was called the "Middle Passage." (So much for Northern compassion.) Six percent of the survivors ended up in the colonies or the United States. It may surprise some readers to learn that the slave fleets continued to operate throughout the Civil War. They did not stop until 1885, when Brazil became the last country to outlaw the slave trade. But history is the most vulnerable field to those who want to dictate the present and control the future by changing the past. Today, the well-programmed "politically correct" (self-ordained) swell up in righteous indignation if you even bring up these inconvenient facts.

In addressing political correctness, famous Civil War historian Ludwell H. Johnson noted: "Nothing is too bizarre to be believed and taught as true when truth is just a matter of cultural or political preference." He went on to discuss a certain Northern curriculum which alleges that the Iroquois influenced Rousseau, Voltaire, Locke, Montesquieu, Jefferson, the Albany Confederation, the Articles of Confederation, and the U.S. Constitution. As he said, nothing is too bizarre for the politically correct. Now, even the Carpetbaggers are portrayed as wonderful people—they were, in fact, early civil rights workers. They certainly never stole anything and, even if they did, that was okay, because everybody else was doing it. So we must give them a pass—at least according to the "politically correct."

But everyone else was not doing it.

Although a study of the causes of the war is beyond the scope of this book, I feel compelled to note that most of the pain and suffering in world history and most of the wars are not a result of a conflict between good and evil, but a conflict between different ideas of good. For anyone interested in the reasons the Confederates fought, *The South Was Right* by Donald and Ronald Kennedy, *North Against South* by Ludwell H. Johnson, and H. W. Crocker, III's *The Politically Incorrect Guide to the Civil War* would be a good start. The Abbeville Institute website offers a superb free source of information about this and other issues.

I would like to thank George Bolm and Gordon Cotton of the McCardle Library in the Old Warren County Courthouse Museum in Vicksburg for providing a treasure trove of diaries and letters for this book. I would also like to thank Michael Fraering of the National Park Service's Port Hudson facility for his kind help, as well as the staff of the Vicksburg National Military Park for its assistance. Foremost of all, I would like to thank my wife Donna for all of her help and advice.

CHAPTER I

VICKSBURG: THE FIRST SIEGE

Vicksburg, in 1860, was one of the principal cities of the South. With six thousand people (including more than eleven hundred blacks), it was the second largest city in Mississippi. It was a major river port, with people entering its environs from every part of the world, and it had a progressive, cosmopolitan atmosphere. It featured six different newspapers (three of them dailies), each of a different political persuasion. There were plank sidewalks, four volunteer fire companies, five churches, two hospitals, several private schools, a large public school, many luxurious homes, several opulent hotels, and even an opera house. The Warren County Courthouse, which is now an excellent museum, was considered an awe-inspiring building when completed in 1860. It featured Greek Revival columns and was topped by a four-faced German clock and a cupola. There were many prosperous businesses in town, including several banks and tailor shops. But the city was also cursed by its geography, militarily speaking. It was located on 200-foot high bluffs, near where the Mississippi River doubles back on itself in a 180-degree horseshoe bend and was a half a mile across. Even a military illiterate could tell that this was a formidable position which would need to be taken to control the river.

Vicksburg, 1860. The courthouse is the most prominent building.

Such a person was Abraham Lincoln. His only military service was three months in the militia during the Black Hawk War, where all he accomplished was getting demoted from captain to private. He never saw action.[1] He did, however, have a healthy amount of common sense and, when the War Between the States began, even he declared that Vicksburg was the key. "The war can never be brought to a close until that key is in our pocket," he said. He went on to say that, as a young man, he had traveled down the Mississippi on flatboats, and he knew what he was talking about. And, this time, he was right.

Men who actually knew what they were doing concurred. General William T. Sherman, for example, said Vicksburg was "the strongest place I ever saw. . .No place on earth is favored by nature with natural defenses as Vicksburg."

As the war approached, Vicksburg was the most pro-Union city in Mississippi and most of its citizens were moderates. They opposed secession and, in the election of 1860, cast their ballots for John Bell, a former Whig senator from Tennessee and the head of the Constitutional Union

Map 1.1: Area of Operations

Party, which also opposed secession. This moderation did not change even after Lincoln was elected president in November. In December, Vicksburg voted 561 to 175 not to leave the Union. In January 1861, Vicksburg sent two anti-secessionist delegates to the secession convention, but the anti-secessionists were outvoted 84 to 15. Mississippi left the United States on January 9.

With secession an accomplished fact, many of its former opponents embraced the idea. Most Vicksburgians believed in states' rights and placed loyalty to the state above loyalty to the United States. (This was true throughout the South. Robert E. Lee, for example, opposed disbanding the Union, but went with Virginia when it seceded. Jefferson Davis also opposed secession but "went out" with Mississippi.) Vicksburg newspaper editor Marmaduke Shannon, formerly a staunch Unionist, wrote: "It is enough for us to know that Mississippi, our state, our government [,] has taken its position. We, too take our position by its side." Even so, the population of the city remained divided until April 15, 1861, when Lincoln called for 75,000 volunteers to suppress the "rebellion." This act convinced the holdouts that the "fire-eater" secessionists had been right all along, and the Republican Party was going to be as dictatorial and despotic as the fire-eaters had predicted.

The corner of Washington and Clay Streets, Vicksburg. This is still one of the most prominent intersections in the city.

The other side was also ready to go to war. Contrary to the simplistic and misleading view too often promulgated in schools, the Civil War was not just about slavery. There were other causes, including serious economic factors. One of these involved Midwesterners. They hated and deplored the fact that the Mississippi River was closed. For decades, they had used the river to transport their crops to market. Now they had to depend on the railroads, which were owned by greedy Northern robber barons, who charged them exorbitant fees and severely reduced the farmers' profit margins, if they didn't wipe them out altogether. The closing of the river placed many Midwestern farms in danger of bankruptcy and foreclosure. All of them were hurt economically. They had just emerged from the financial Panic of 1857 and, unless the Northern forces could reopen the river to commerce, Midwestern prosperity was at an end, and they faced a serious economic crisis and quite likely a regional depression. (By early 1863, this regional depression had arrived.) And so, for this reason, in addition to others including slavery, tariffs, and constitutional issues, Midwesterners joined General Grant's army in droves.

The first threat to Vicksburg came from the south. On April 28, 1862, Flag Officer David Farragut's fleet captured New Orleans. It then steamed up the river, easily occupied Baton Rouge and Natchez, and put in at Davis Bend, where its men captured Brierfield, Jefferson Davis' home, and Hurricane, the palatial mansion of his brother, Joseph Davis. Hurricane was so impressive that they assumed it must be the home of the president of the Confederacy, so they burned it. Brierfield they only looted. Continuing northward, they reached Vicksburg on May 18.

Farragut's force included five big warships and several transports, which carried fourteen hundred infantrymen under Brigadier General Thomas Williams. Commodore S. Phillips Lee, the commander of Farragut's Advance Naval Division, sent a note to "The Authorities at Vicksburg," demanding its surrender. Lieutenant Colonel James L. Autry, the military governor, wrote back: "Mississippians don't know, and refuse to learn, how to surrender to an enemy. If Commodore Farragut or Brigadier General Butler can teach them, let them come and try." Brigadier General Martin Luther Smith, the commandant of the Vicksburg defenses,[2] and Mayor Lazarus Lindsay sent similar messages. Lee responded that the bombardment would begin in twenty-four hours.

On May 18, Smith's infantry forces consisted of three Louisiana regiments, a Mississippi battalion, and a Louisiana battalion.[3] They were fresh troops but indifferently armed. All told, he had four thousand men.

The bombardment started during the afternoon of Sunday, May 25, when 166-pound shells exploded in the city. Citizens fled into the countryside while the men of the Confederate Army rushed into Vicksburg. Unfortunately for the Yankees, their ships' guns could not be elevated enough to destroy the Southern batteries on the bluff or even do maximum damage to the town. General Williams, meanwhile, declared that he could not storm the city unless the Rebel guns were silenced.

About four days later, Winchester Hall and his 3rd Louisiana Infantry Regiment marched into Vicksburg.[4] Colonel Hall recalled that it "looked as if the simoom of war already had swept over it . . . the city deserted by all who could leave, business houses that were not closed were barren of goods, beautiful homes, set in emerald lawns, embowered in magnolia, rose, myrtle and wild peach, and smiling with beautiful flowers, awaiting the coming of the spoiler."

But the spoiler didn't come. In the summer of 1862, Vicksburg first became a fortress, but there were growing pains. Many of the soldiers arrived without shelter. They knocked on doors and asked the citizens if they could sleep on their verandas, or even on their lawns. They were almost always accommodated. The ladies of Vicksburg in particular became known far and wide for their toughness, their courage, their indifference to enemy fire, and their selfless devotion to their Cause and their defenders. Normal life was now only a memory. Women and children were already growing vegetable gardens in their backyards, making coffee out of okra and acorns, and breaking out their grandmothers' old spinning wheels to make homespun clothing.

The garrison was soon joined by the 4th and 5th Louisiana under Colonel Henry Watkins Allen, who was only partially recovered from a wound suffered at Shiloh. General Smith also had three artillery batteries (eighteen guns) and the ingredients for three more heavy batteries. The big guns were sent to Vicksburg by Major General Mansfield Lovell, the commander at New Orleans, when he realized that city was doomed. Unfortunately, these heavy guns would have to be mounted, and now that would have to be done under enemy fire.

During the construction of one battery, Colonel Allen's men came under serious gunboat fire. They stopped working and ducked. Seeing this, Allen drew his revolver and shouted, "Soldiers, you came here to fight: you are ordered to build this Battery, and d—n me, if I don't shoot down the first of you that dodges from this work; by G-d, no soldier of mine shall dodge from his duty!" The proclamation had an "electric effect" on the men, who realized that the colonel was serious, and they soon completed the battery.

May 27 brought the heaviest shelling yet. Thirty-five enemy warships bombarded Vicksburg, "delivering broadside after broadside, firing shot, shell and grape, according to their distance from the city." The Rebel batteries replied in full force. "The roar of cannon was continuous and deafening," Sarah Dorsey recorded, "loud concussions shook the city to its foundations—shot and shell went hissing and tearing through trees, walls, houses, scattering fragments far and near . . . Men, women and children rushed into the streets and, amid the crash of falling houses, commenced a hasty flight into the country for safety." But, for all of the noise and destruction, not a single Confederate gun was destroyed or disabled.

One lady, the wife of a staff officer, came to Vicksburg during the first siege, to be near her husband. "How is it possible for you to live here?" she asked another lady.

"After one is accustomed to the change, we do not mind it," her friend replied, "but becoming accustomed, that is the trial."

The woman in question did become accustomed to it, more or less. "Still, resting in Vicksburg seemed like resting near a volcano," she concluded.

Meanwhile, more Rebel forces poured into the city and surrounding area. They included John C. Breckinridge's division with Brigadier General William Preston's, Brigadier General Benjamin H. Helm's, and Colonel Walter S. Statham's brigades,[5] as well as the 17th, 26th, and 27th Louisiana Infantry Regiments, the 3rd Mississippi, and Colonel Theo Withers' 1st Mississippi Light Artillery Regiment. They totaled more than five thousand men.

Just across the river lay the De Soto peninsula, extending opposite the city to the west. General Williams decided to dig a canal across the base of the peninsula, to divert the river and bypass the city. When completed, the De Soto peninsula would be an island and Vicksburg would be bypassed. But he needed laborers. Kate Stone, a resident of Madison Parish, Louisiana, recorded in her diary how the Federals impressed all of the local Negro men to work on the canal. Some went willingly and some went at gunpoint, but he eventually mustered thirty-two hundred men and more joined or were forced to join later.

Williams, Farragut, and their engineers calculated that they would require a ditch one-and-a-half miles long, forty feet wide, and fifteen feet deep. They would have to cut through a cypress swamp and heavy clay soil but, if successful, Vicksburg would be bypassed.

But they were not successful. Thousands of soldiers, slaves, and free blacks worked all day, every day, under the hot Louisiana sun. Mosquitoes were terrible in the swamps and they carried disease, and the snakes were poisonous. The heat was unbearable and the men were wet all of the time. They died by the dozens. And the underlying soil was much more difficult to shovel than they had anticipated. Progress was slow and hard, sickness took a heavy toll, and they needed more workers. They were down to less than one thousand laborers by July. Eventually, they had to give up, and the first Yankee attempt to capture Vicksburg had failed.

Midshipman Dabney Minor Scales of the *Arkansas* and a few of his colleagues inspected "Williams' Ditch" after the Northerners abandoned it. They found six hundred Union graves and five hundred live Negroes, most of whom were sick after being forced to work in mud and water for days on end. The bluecoats, Scales learned, tried to induce the sick blacks to leave. Healthy blacks who tried to escape were sometimes shot.

But for the North, help was on the way. Near the end of June, the U.S. fleet from Memphis, under the command of Flag Officer Charles H. Davis, arrived north of Vicksburg with forty gunboats, mortar boats, rams, and transports.

Unable to defeat the Rebels by bombardment, Farragut decided to run the batteries and join Flag Officer Davis' ironclads, north of the city. First, he wanted to suppress the Southern guns, insofar as was possible. He ordered his mortar boat commander, David Porter, to again bombard the city. He started at 4:00 a.m. on June 27 and continued until 10:00 p.m. Reverend C. K. Marshall watched the bombardment from a hilltop and wrote to his brother, "I was arrested by the magnificence of the view, the terrific roar, and the near approach of the shells to my locality . . . The shelling grew furious, and every moment seemed to carry many of the destroyers into the very ranks of our brave boys at the guns. Every bomb could be traced in its parabolic path by the fierce burning fuse; and at times there seemed to be twenty or thirty sweeping the heavens at once." He noted that many of the Union shells did not explode, but when one did "it would seem as if the whole country trembled under our feet." He seemed surprised, however, that the damage to the city was "comparatively trifling."[6]

In the pre-dawn darkness of June 28, about 3:30 a.m., Farragut ran the batteries with three of his five ocean-going warships and eight smaller gunboats. To keep the Rebels' heads down, every ship from both fleets pounded the bluffs and the city. "It was perfectly terrific," Rev. Marshall wrote. "The earth shuddered. The forest trembled. The buildings rattled as if smitten by a hurricane. There was not now a moment's cessation in the crash and roar for nearly three hours." Running against the current, progress was slow and damage was heavy. One of the warships did not follow the fleet and most of them suffered considerable damage. Two of the gunboats sank.

There was panic in the city. Rev. Marshall noted that the roads "were crowded with the flying citizens in the utmost confusion and alarm."

Hundreds of poor families took to the woods and fields, while others occupied cow-sheds, carriage houses, and shanties out of the range of Northern artillery. Hundreds made tents out of blankets, quilts, and sheets, because that was all they had.

Inside Vicksburg, citizens jammed every passway. Marshall wrote of "Women terror-stricken . . . the children were screaming and crying, separated from their parents, and lost in the mass, the clouds of dust and general confusion . . . while dogs, horses, mules and cows ran in all directions."

After the firing ceased, Rev. Marshall went to the Rebel forts, expecting to view a scene like Shiloh or Manassas. He asked the first officer he saw: "What of our boys?"

"All right," was the reply.

"Did they stand to their guns?"

"Men never behaved better."

"What casualties?" the preacher asked.

"One man killed and seven wounded," the artilleryman answered.

The Reverend was stunned there were so few. After the other forts reported, it was learned that the South lost two men killed and nine or ten wounded. Also dead, Marshall recalled, was Mrs. Gamble, "one of our most excellent women." She was a widow and left behind several small children.

Meanwhile, the Union fleets linked up. Exactly what the Federals accomplished by this maneuver is unclear, but they lost sixteen killed and forty-five wounded, and they were now no closer to capturing Vicksburg than they had been the previous week.

Meanwhile, the Rebels built an ironclad.

Except for the postmaster general, Confederate Secretary of War Stephen Mallory was the only member of Jefferson Davis' cabinet to hold his post throughout the war. A former U.S. senator who spent years on the naval affairs committee, he was under no illusions. He knew that the South could never even come close to matching the United States in ship production, so he did not try. Instead, he focused on harbor defense and innovations, such as ironclads and torpedoes (mines).

Because rivers were the South's lifelines, Mallory authorized the construction of four large, shallow-draft ironclads on the Mississippi River: the *Louisiana*, the *Mississippi*, the *Tennessee*, and the *Arkansas*. The *Louisiana* and *Mississippi* were sunk in the Battle of New Orleans. The *Tennessee* was not completed when Memphis fell on June 6, so the Confederates scuttled it. The *Arkansas* they towed south and then northeast, sixty miles up the Yazoo River. It was here that forty-six-year-old Lieutenant Isaac Newton Brown assumed command on May 28.

At age seventeen, Brown joined the U.S. Navy as a midshipman in 1834. He fought in the Mexican War and made several trips around the world before resigning his commission when Tennessee seceded. When he found the *Arkansas*, it was an abandoned derelict. Her engines were scattered around in various pieces, her guns had no carriages, her hulk had been abandoned, and her armor was at the bottom of the river. Brown and his men fished out the armor and towed the boat to Yazoo City, where they set up a naval yard. He solicited help from locals and nearby plantation owners, who furnished 214 workers and fourteen blacksmith forges. Work progressed day and night. Brown needed tons of iron, which he mainly acquired from nearby railroads. His crew he recruited from local river men and about sixty Missouri infantrymen, which the army provided. By working around the clock, the lieutenant and his men had the *Arkansas* semi-battleworthy in five weeks. She was a formidable vessel, armed with two 8-inch Columbiads, two 9-inch Dahlgrens, four 6-inch rifled cannons and two 32-pounder smooth-bores—ten guns in all. She drew fourteen feet of water and had a maximum speed of six knots (about seven miles per hour). It was a rusty brown in color and looked like a raft with a big box in the middle.

Lieutenant Brown had done a remarkable job. He had created a functional ironclad in the backwoods of Mississippi, with two enemy fleets only fifty miles away. On July 14, in spite of her questionable engine, Brown declared the *Arkansas* ready and steamed down the Yazoo to attack the Union fleet. He had to. It was summer and the Yazoo River was falling. If he didn't leave his dock now, he ran the risk of having his ironclad stuck on dry land.

Coincidentally, the Yankees had learned of the existence of the Rebel boat. The ironclad *Carondelet,* the wooden gunboat *Tyler,* and the *Queen of the West* (now a ram)[7] entered the river in search of the *Arkansas.* The *Carondelet* led the way.

The *Carondelet's* captain was Henry Walke, a friend of Brown from the old Navy. They had even been messmates on Commodore Matthew Perry's famous voyage to Japan. The small flotilla was several miles from the mouth of the Yazoo when Walke saw the *Arkansas.* He turned his ironclad around and fled. The *Arkansas* pursued it and was quick catching up. One of the shots from her bow guns damaged the *Carondelet's* steering. It made for shallow water, where the *Arkansas* hit it with a devastating close-range broadside, shattering its armor and almost causing it to roll over. Steam covered the badly damaged *Carondelet,* which was listing and helpless. It had suffered thirty-five casualties, killed, wounded, or scalded. If they had time, the Confederates could easily have taken her as a prize, but their commander had other items on his agenda.

Brown left the disabled ironclad behind and headed for the *Tyler* and the *Queen of the West,* both of which fled. A sharpshooter from the *Tyler* fired at Lieutenant Brown and hit him in the head, leaving a nasty gash. The running battle continued for ten miles, with the *Arkansas* pounding the two wooden Yankee vessels. Blood flowed freely on the *Tyler's* deck.

The Northern fleet watched with consternation as their two vessels entered the Mississippi, followed by the *Arkansas.* Because they were running short on fuel and were conserving their coal, none of the Union vessels was ready for action. But all of their sailors now scrambled to their guns.

Inside the *Arkansas'* engine room, the temperature reached 130 degrees Fahrenheit. New men had to be rotated in every fifteen minutes. The *Arkansas* now ran the gauntlet of the Union fleet, which was on both its starboard and port sides. Brown faced what he called "a forest of masts and smokestacks, sloops, rams, ironclads and other gunboats on the left side, and ordinary river steamboats and bomb-vessels on the right." There were so many ships and boats that any Yankee gunfire that missed the *Arkansas* was likely to hit a friendly vessel. Several of them took the chance and fired nonetheless.

The ironclad was hit by dozens of shells. One smashed the forward gunroom, killing or wounding sixteen men. A shell from an 11-inch gun killed or wounded every man at the gunboat's huge Columbiad gun.[8] Eight men were killed and seven wounded at the starboard broadside station. Her smokestack was riddled by sixty-eight shells, and she could barely make one knot, but she was helped by the river current. Even so, the gunboat fired back and hit several vessels. The *Hartford*, the *Iroquois,* and the *Benton* were all seriously damaged. The Union ram *Lancaster* came closest to sinking her, but a Southern cannon shot from one hundred yards out struck her boilers and covered the ram in steam. Much of her crew jumped into the river to avoid being scalded and she drifted out of control.[9]

After steaming all the way through both Union fleets, the *Arkansas* faced Commander Porter's mortar boats, which were no problem for it. The *Arkansas* ran one of them aground and the crew was forced to burn it, to keep it from being captured. The ironclad then limped to the east bank, where it was covered by the heavy guns on the Vicksburg bluffs. It was in bad shape. Its ramming beak had been broken, all of its lifeboats had been shot away, and it was a mechanical mess. It had lost ten killed outright and fifteen badly wounded,[10] and about thirty others were less seriously wounded. Total casualties amounted to more than half of the crew, and only forty-two crewmen were left to run the ship. The Union fleets lost forty-two killed and sixty-nine wounded, mostly aboard the *Carondelet.*

It was good for the South that the Yankees could not see inside the *Arkansas*, and thus could not tell how badly damaged it was, or they would have known it was unfit for action. Because they did not know this, all of the Union warships now had to keep up their steam, in case the *Arkansas* sallied out again. They were already short of coal. Soon they were dangerously low. They nevertheless continued their fruitless bombardment of the city.

The Arkansas *dueling with two Federal fleets.*

On July 27, Admiral Farragut had had enough. It was summer in Mississippi, the river was falling rapidly, and he was afraid his ocean-going vessels would soon be grounded. His ships weighed anchor and headed south, while Flag Officer Davis steamed north. Thus ended the second attempt to take or bypass the city, the first Siege of Vicksburg. It had featured a sixty-seven-day bombardment, in which twenty-five hundred shells fell on the city. They did little major damage. Only seven Confederate soldiers had been killed and twenty-five wounded, excluding the *Arkansas'* casualties. Only two civilians had died. One mother had been decapitated by a shell as she rushed her young son to safety, and a seven-year-old girl was killed by another shell.

Throughout the siege, Major General Earl Van Dorn, the commander of the Confederate Department of Mississippi and Eastern Louisiana as well as commander of the Army of the West, realized that Vicksburg was vulnerable from the land side. After Farragut left, Van Dorn began a defensive construction program. He made his wisest appointment ever when he placed Major Samuel H. Lockett in charge of it. Young Lockett was an 1859 West Point graduate, the chief engineer of the department, and a brilliant military engineer. When completed, the land side of Vicksburg featured a trench line eight and a fourth miles long. It included 172 artillery positions, redans, redoubts and other forts and strongholds, plus a continuous line of trenches designed to be manned by thirty thousand men. General Pemberton would make it even stronger.

Meanwhile, Van Dorn decided to recapture Baton Rouge. He selected Major General John C. Breckinridge, a former vice president of the United States, for this task. He also gave Breckinridge the *Arkansas*, to keep the heavy guns of the Federal gunboats out of the battle.

Lieutenant Brown had taken a short leave in Grenada, where he fell violently ill. In his absence, Van Dorn ordered the first officer, Lieutenant Harry K. Stevens, to command the ironclad during the assault. As soon as he heard the news, Brown jumped on a train for Vicksburg. He knew that the ship's engines were in no shape to go all the way to Baton Rouge. In addition, the crew was understrength and *Arkansas'* engineering officer had suffered a nervous breakdown. But Brown arrived too late. The *Arkansas* cast off on August 3. Shortly after it passed the Red River, it began to have engine troubles.

Breckinridge started on July 27 with five thousand men, but the railroad was in such bad shape that he could only carry the troops—not tents or other equipment. It started raining heavily. When he reached Baton Rouge on August 4, he had only three thousand combat effectives left. The other two thousand were sick from dysentery, pneumonia, and fevers caused by the rain, exposure, and extreme heat. When he attacked at dawn on August 5, he had only twenty-six hundred men. They faced twenty-five hundred Union defenders. The Union ground forces under General Williams were mauled and would have been destroyed had the *Arkansas'* engines not failed. As the Union gunboats closed in on her, Stevens set the boat on fire and scuttled it. Her combat career had lasted twenty-three days.

With the *Arkansas* burning, the heavy fire on the Union gunboats saved the Yankee ground forces. General Williams did not know it, however. He had been killed when a rifle ball struck him in the chest.

Breckinridge also lost some good men. Most prominent among them was Henry Watkins Allen, who commanded a brigade at Baton Rouge. Charging a Yankee battery, he was so badly crippled by a Union cannon that he could never walk again without the aid of crutches and was in constant pain for the rest of his life. Confederate General Benjamin Helm, Abraham Lincoln's brother-in-law, was severely injured when his horse was shot out from under him. Helm's aide, Lieutenant Todd, another brother-in-law of Lincoln, was killed.

Checked at Baton Rouge, General Breckinridge fell back to Port Hudson, about twenty-six miles north of the Louisiana capital, on August 12. This place was an excellent defensive position and could control traffic on the Mississippi. Now it became the southern anchor of the Confederate hold on the river. The three hundred river miles between Vicksburg and Port Hudson became the linchpin which held the two halves of the Confederacy together. It would hold for almost a year.

CHAPTER II

JOHN C. PEMBERTON

The first Siege of Vicksburg was a Southern victory, but elsewhere in the West things were not going well. U.S. General Grant took Forts Henry and Donelson (February 1862), General Buell captured Nashville (February 25, 1862), Grant beat back a Confederate counteroffensive at Shiloh (April 6–7, 1862), and Memphis fell (June 6, 1862) following the near annihilation of the Confederate River Defense Fleet.

Following Shiloh, the main Confederate army under General P. G. T. Beauregard slowly retreated to Corinth, which it abandoned on May 30. Here it was divided. Most of the men were assigned to General Braxton Bragg's Army of Mississippi (later called the Army of Tennessee), while twenty thousand troops under Earl Van Dorn were left to defend Vicksburg.[1] His forces were designated the Army of the West. About the same time, Lincoln also divided his much larger western army. Buell's Army of the Ohio was sent to eastern Tennessee, John Pope's Army of the Mississippi was ordered to defend Corinth, while Grant's Army of the Tennessee occupied Memphis and western Tennessee.

General Dabney H. Maury described Van Dorn as "The most remarkable man the state of Mississippi has ever known. He used to ride a beautiful bay Andalusian horse, and as he came galloping along the lines, with his yellow hair waving in the wind and his bright face lined with kindliness and courage, we all loved to see him.... [He] gave assurance of a man whom men could trust and follow."

Not everybody felt that way about General Van Dorn, however. He was bold, courageous, and gallant, to be sure, but he was also a drunkard, a whoremonger, and an adulterer. Born in Port Gibson, Mississippi, on September 17, 1820, he attended West Point and graduated fifty-second out of fifty-six—two spots above James Longstreet. He was short (five foot five), emotional, impulsive, and something of a party animal. He was an excellent combat officer at the regimental level. In Mexico, he was twice brevetted (to major) and was wounded twice in two days. Later, on the Western Frontier, he was wounded four times in actions against the Comanches. He resigned his commission in January 1861 and was immediately named brigadier general of the Mississippi State Troops. Two weeks after Mississippi seceded, he was named brigadier general in the state militia. The following month he was promoted to major general and commander, Mississippi State forces, replacing Jefferson Davis. A brigadier general in Confederate service from June 5, he was sent to Texas, and on September 19 was promoted to major general and transferred to Virginia, where he commanded a division. He was named commander of the Army of the West (then in the Trans-Mississippi Department) in January 1862.

Militarily Van Dorn was a good cavalry leader, but had been promoted above his ceiling as an army commander. His leadership was characterized by an appalling lack of attention to details and a failure to grasp what was possible. This led to his defeat at Pea Ridge (March 1862) and Corinth.

Van Dorn was always vain and could be jealous and petty. Nathan Bedford Forrest once said that he would like to cut his heart out.

Earl Van Dorn.

As Confederate commander in Mississippi, Van Dorn placed most of the state under martial law. He tossed many civilians into stockades and hanged six. He imposed price controls, restricted trade, shut down newspapers, and generally outraged the civilian population by his high-handed actions. The Confederate War Department in Richmond rescinded his martial law declaration, but the damage had been done. Then Van Dorn and his two deputies, Sterling Price and Mansfield Lovell, mishandled the Battles of Iuka (September 19) and Second Corinth (October 2–3) and almost got the Army of the West trapped. Jefferson Davis had had enough and replaced him with John C. Pemberton. Brigadier General John S. Bowen preferred charges against Van Dorn for neglect of duty and failure to care for his wounded after Corinth, but President Davis wanted to keep him as a cavalry commander, so he stacked the court with Van Dorn sympathizers[2] and he was acquitted.

John Clifford Pemberton was born into a family of Philadelphia Quakers. His father, John Pemberton (1783–1847) was a businessman, a land speculator, and a close friend of President Andrew Jackson, who named him collector for the port of Philadelphia. His mother, Rebecca Clifford Pemberton, was a tall, beautiful blonde. She bore thirteen children, ten of whom lived to adulthood. John C., who was born on August 10, 1814, was the second child. He grew up in Philadelphia and his best friend was George G. Meade, who later commanded the Union Army at Gettysburg. Another childhood playmate was George B. McClellan, who eventually directed the Army of the Potomac at Antietam.

Rebecca Pemberton—who was particularly close to her son—saw to it that he was well educated in the best private schools and had every advantage. He was an excellent linguist and was especially good at Greek and Latin, which he liked to read all of his life.

John Pemberton grew into a handsome young man. He was five foot ten and a half inches tall, at a time when the average man was five foot seven, and he was slender and erect until the day he died. He had dark brown (almost black) eyes and brown-black hair. He was also tough and in excellent physical condition. Later, in the army, Pemberton could march and ride with much younger troops and with the hardiest veterans. His close friends called him "Jack."

Pemberton was generally congenial but occasionally arrogant. He enjoyed hunting, fishing, and even participating in theatrical productions. He was also stubborn and seldom gave an inch if he thought he was right. He was slow to admit mistakes and was occasionally abrasive and quick-tempered.

Jack enrolled in the University of Pennsylvania in 1831 and ranked high in his class when he decided he wanted to be an engineer. The best engineering school in the Western Hemisphere at that time was the United States Military Academy at West Point. His father was reluctant to ask Andrew Jackson for a presidential appointment, but his mother had no such qualms, so she contacted the president directly, and Pemberton

received the appointment. During a trip to Philadelphia, the president
actually visited with Jack and gave him a pep talk about his future.

Pemberton entered West Point on July 1, 1833. Here his conduct took
a turn for the worse. He first got into trouble for throwing rolls in the
mess hall, for which he was arrested. He disliked the temperate nature
of the Academy and the food, which was both poor and monotonous
(mostly corn beef and potatoes). He took to drinking whiskey (sometimes to excess), smoking cigars, smoking a pipe, and even chewing
tobacco. He was a mediocre student, content with "C's." This attitude
cost him his dream of becoming an engineer, a distinction which was
reserved only for the top students. Even so, he liked West Point and
especially enjoyed camping. He faced graduation day with regret.

John Pemberton, date unknown.

Cadet Pemberton almost got expelled his senior year for having
liquor in his room. He was again arrested and forced to live in a local
boarding house until a court-martial was assembled, but he was
eventually allowed to graduate with his class (1837). His classmates

included future Confederate generals Robert Chilton (later Lee's chief of staff), Jubal Early, Arnold Elzey, William H. T. Walker, and Braxton Bragg, as well as future Union generals John Sedgwick, Joseph Hoover, and George Meade, who was Pemberton's roommate. He was close friends with William W. Mackall, later chief of staff to both Bragg and Joseph E. Johnston. Other future Civil War generals whom Pemberton got to know were lower classmen, including Henry Halleck, William Tecumseh Sherman, John Pope, George Thomas, P. G. T. Beauregard, Richard Ewell, and Lloyd Tilghman, who was a good friend at this time.

Pemberton's mediocre academic performance destroyed his dreams of becoming an engineer. He ranked twenty-seventh out of a class of fifty and was commissioned second lieutenant in the artillery. He had 163 accrued demerits, which was considered high. He was assigned to the 4th Artillery Regiment at Fort Columbia on Governors Island, where it guarded New York harbor, but he wasn't there long. He was sent to Florida to fight the Seminoles before the year was out.

Jack Pemberton had twenty duty stations over the next twenty-four years. He first saw action in the unsuccessful Battle of Loxahatchee, but he showed courage under fire. The following year, he was sent to western North Carolina, to chase Cherokees. That was followed by a posting to northern Maine, the scene of the bloodless Aroostook War, where a border dispute almost resulted in the United States coming to blows with the British Empire. By late 1838, he was back on Governors Island, but he was soon again in Florida.

As a cadet, Pemberton had met a girl, Angeline Stebbins of New York City, to whom he proposed after a very short courtship. His family did not approve of her. Now, in St. Augustine, Florida, John met another girl, which led to a broken engagement and almost to a duel with Angeline's brother. After that, Jack Pemberton had a series of shallow love affairs and drifted from girlfriend to girlfriend. Meanwhile, in the small peacetime army, Pemberton earned a solid reputation as an excellent administrative officer. There followed assignments to Fort Columbus; Camp Washington near Trenton, New Jersey, as a training officer; Detroit; Fort Mackinac on Mackinac Island, off the northern tip of the lower peninsula of Michigan; Fort Brady, at the eastern tip of the upper peninsula of Michigan; and Buffalo, New York, on the Niagara frontier, which Pemberton considered depressing. He was promoted to first lieutenant on March 19, 1842.

Pemberton spent the period 1842 to early 1846 in an alternating assignment between Carlisle Barracks, Pennsylvania, and Fort Monroe, Virginia. Here he met Martha "Pattie" or "Patty" Thompson, the daughter of William Henry Thompson, a prominent owner and operator of a line of cargo ships. She was a Virginia blueblood and related to Elbridge Gerry, a signer of the Declaration of Independence. Patty was five foot two, petite, with brown hair, striking gray-brown eyes, and fine teeth. A photograph of her later in life survives and there is no doubt about it—she was beautiful even then. She was also intelligent, had a dry sense of humor, and a head for finance, which John did not. He had met the love of his life. He proposed and she accepted, but his family again objected. This time it did not matter. He wanted to marry her very quickly but the needs of the service intervened, and Lieutenant Pemberton was packed off to Texas, just in time for the Mexican War.

John Pemberton was later accused of being indecisive in battle, but he showed no sign of that in Florida, Texas, or Mexico. His first big battle was at Palo Alto, but he really distinguished himself at Resaca de la Palma, where seventeen hundred Americans badly defeated four thousand Mexicans. Pemberton was in the thick of the fight. When a captain was hit, he took charge of an infantry company and proved to be an excellent battlefield commander. His straw hat was shot off of his head. A soldier beside him was wounded and grabbed Pemberton's leg as he fell. The lieutenant dragged him out of the line of fire to a place of safety, but the man died later. In all, six men were killed in immediate proximity to him, but he showed neither fear nor the slightest indecision. Pemberton later declared that he was exhilarated by the battle.

Pattie Pemberton.

Lieutenant Pemberton impressed his division commander, Brigadier General William Jenkins Worth, who named him his aide-de-camp. John remained in this position for the rest of the war, and won a brevet (honorary) promotion to captain at Monterrey. He also took part in the battles of Churubusco and Molino del Rey, where he won a brevet to major.[3] He was wounded in the hand outside Mexico City, but suffered no permanent damage. Shortly after the war, the city of Philadelphia presented him with a sword for his gallantry during the conflict.

Brevet Major Pemberton could hardly wait to get back to the United States to be with Pattie. They were married at the Episcopal Christ Church in Norfolk, Virginia, on January 18, 1848. None of his family attended. The charming Southern belle eventually won all of them over, however.

One of the friends he made in Mexico was Captain Ulysses S. Grant. "A more conscientious, honorable man never lived," Grant said later. After the Civil War, the Northern general recalled an incident in Mexico. An order came down that no junior officers were to ride their horses during the march toward Mexico City. These men soon became footsore and riding was again permitted—but permission was only given verbally. The order was never officially revoked, but everyone remounted, except Pemberton. He insisted on walking. "This I thought of all the time he was in Vicksburg and I outside of it; and I knew he would hold on to the last," Grant recalled.

Pemberton and his wife were initially stationed at Old Point, near Norfolk, with the 4th Artillery. She was soon with child and she delivered near the end of the year. It was a bad pregnancy. She was unconscious for hours; meanwhile, her baby son died.

Despite her F.F.V. (First Family of Virginia) heritage, Pattie was a good army wife and took the hardships of isolated garrisons in stride. They spent 1849 in Fort Pickens and Fort Brooke, Tampa Bay, Florida. It was here, on January 14, 1850, that Pemberton's daughter Martha (also called Pattie) was born. She and her father immediately became and would always remain very close.

In 1850, Jack was stationed at Jackson Barracks, New Orleans; Pascagoula, Mississippi; and Fort Hamilton, New York. He was promoted to captain on September 27. The following year, he was stationed at Fort Washington, on the Potomac, just across the river from Mount Vernon. His second daughter, Mary, was born here on August 9. More children came quickly and they were born at various army posts: John Clifford, Jr. (January 1853); William P. (December 1853); and Francis Rawle (1856). Francis weighed twelve and a half pounds. Jack was not much on organized religion, but each delivery found him on his knees in prayer. It worked. There were no more infant deaths. Their seventh and last child, Anna P., was born in 1857, while John was in Utah, operating against the Mormons.

In early 1861, Captain Pemberton was at Fort Ridgely, Minnesota, when the order came: because of the Fort Sumter crisis, the 4th Artillery Regiment was recalled to the Washington, D.C., area, in case it was needed to help suppress the "rebellion."

By now, Pemberton's personality was set. He had two sets of manners: one for the drawing room and one for the service. To his troops, he was aloof, cold, and formal—a stranger to the men he led. In social circles, however, he was relaxed, affable, congenial, and a pleasure to associate with. But he was rarely able to loosen up around his men, a fact which would hurt him and reduce his effectiveness in the years ahead—especially with informal Confederate volunteers.

Jack Pemberton underwent a great emotional struggle in the spring of 1861. On the one hand, he thought the South was right. He believed in the doctrines of states' rights and state sovereignty and opposed the overreach of the Federal government. On the other hand, he was never particularly political and had little to gain and everything to lose by joining the South. He would be throwing away twenty-eight years and a fine military career if he did. And he would be fighting against his own family. Two of his younger brothers, Andrew and Clifford, had joined the Union cavalry and his brother Henry (who hated horses) rode from Philadelphia to D.C. to talk him out of resigning. He was not blind or insensitive to the pain his joining the Confederacy would cause. But there was another family. After they left Minnesota, his wife and children moved on to Norfolk. She wrote him frequently, imploring him to join them as soon as possible.

On April 17, Virginia—his adopted state—seceded. Pemberton continued to struggle. Two days later, the 4th Artillery was ordered to seize all steamboats on the Potomac, to make sure that they did not fall into Confederate hands. He helped carry out this order. But a few days later, he made up his mind. He resigned his commission on April 24.

Winfield Scott, the general-in-chief of the U.S. Army, tried to talk him out of it. He called him in and offered him a colonelcy if he would stay. But he would not. He left for Richmond on April 26. Two days later, Governor John Letcher nominated him for the rank of lieutenant colonel, Virginia Volunteers. The legislature confirmed him as a lieutenant colonel of artillery, Provisional Army of Virginia, on May 8. His immediate superior was Brigadier General Joseph E. Johnston.

It is not known if Pemberton and Johnston met before this, but it is more than likely that they did, as they had both been members of the 4th Artillery. We do know that Johnston had set up three training/instructional camps and he was anxious for Pemberton to command one of them. He gave him the one near Norfolk and his family. Initially he was responsible for training artillery and cavalry; however, he soon turned his horsemen over to Jeb Stuart and concentrated on gunnery.

Meanwhile, the nation (or nations) barreled toward an armed clash. On June 15, 1861, Pemberton was transferred from state to Confederate service and was named major, Confederate States Army (C.S.A.) Artillery Corps. Two days later, he was promoted to brigadier general, bypassing the ranks of lieutenant colonel and colonel. He was given command of an artillery brigade in the Smithfield-Suffolk area, just west of Norfolk, where he engaged in training the raw volunteers and constructing shore batteries on the James River. His family moved into a house in Smithfield, to be near him. Here they remained until late November 1861, when he received orders to report to Robert E. Lee in Charleston, South Carolina. He did so on the morning of November 29.

Lee (then a major general) had been named commander of the Department of South Carolina, Georgia and Florida on November 5. His principal civilian counterpart was Governor Francis Pickens of South Carolina, who was a prickly sort.[4] He insisted that Lee should have brigadiers so, on November 29, Jefferson Davis sent him Nathan G. Evans and John C. Pemberton. Lee placed Pemberton in charge of District 4, the coastal area south of Charleston. He headquartered at Coosawhatchie, a railroad stop on the Charleston & Savannah Railroad, about halfway between the two cities. Here, Lee instituted one of his several brilliant military innovations: he used railroads to move units from place to place and take advantage of his interior lines to concentrate quickly, thus partially compensating for his numerical inferiority.

Robert E. Lee, Pemberton's commander in South Carolina.
Lee thought highly of Pemberton.

Pemberton fought only one significant engagement as a district commander and that was near Port Royal. The Union forces made an incursion up the Coosaw River on New Year's Day, 1862, which he beat back. He did so only with great difficulty, however, because the Union gunboats were able to silence his guns. This convinced Pemberton of the futility of trying to defend outlying areas with forts and batteries.

Robert E. Lee was not only a military genius—he was a consummate military diplomat as well. A Virginia aristocrat himself, he got along with the Old School Charlestonians who still ran South Carolina in 1861. They were an arrogant lot. In those days, people joked that there were two kinds of South Carolinians: those who had never worn shoes and those who made you feel as if you had never worn shoes. Charleston, it was said, is where the Ashley and Cooper Rivers join to form the Atlantic Ocean. Robert E. Lee managed to fit in with these high-toned and clannish people, as he did with everybody; this the Northern-born John C. Pemberton could never do. Also, Pemberton was a coolly impartial man. He treated the rich and famous exactly the same as he treated crackers. This contributed to his lack of popularity with Charleston's rich and famous.

Jefferson Davis had already earmarked Robert E. Lee for greater assignments. Davis had also known Pemberton for years; he was one of the president's favorites, and Davis wanted Pemberton to succeed Lee. He promoted him to major general on February 13, 1862, and to rank from January 14. On March 2, 1862, Jack Pemberton became commander of the Department of South Carolina, Georgia and Florida. He initially commanded about twenty-five thousand men, scattered along a 300-mile line of sea coast. He set up his headquarters at Pocotaligo Station, South Carolina, on the Charleston-Savannah line.

Before he left, Lee admonished Pemberton not to risk losing his army in order to defend a particular place. Pemberton took this advice to heart and was reluctant to commit his forces to an all-out defense of Charleston. Pickens wrote to Lee and objected to the very idea of losing the city. Lee straightened the matter out by writing Pemberton and suggesting that critical places like Charleston must be defended "street by street, house by house as long as we have a foot of ground to stand upon." Pemberton, who very much respected General Lee, took this advice as gospel as well. But Pickens now suspected

Pemberton might abandon Charleston, if the situation became dire. This suspicion increased after the general let it be known that he intended to reduce the forces at Fort Sumter because it had no defensive value.

Pemberton ignored civilian criticism and set about the task of defending his district. He assembled a staff which included John R. Waddy (adjutant and chief ordnance officer), Robert W. Memminger (assistant adjutant or AAG), and James H. Morrison and John C. Taylor (aides). Only Waddy had served with him before, when they were both in the 4th Artillery.[5] Because his staff lacked engineering expertise, Pemberton borrowed Colonel William Robinson Boggs, the state engineer of Georgia, from Governor Joseph E. Brown.[6] He and his staff then set out making the plans for defense of his department—especially Charleston—and constructing the defenses, including fortifications and gun positions. Their plans were good and later General Beauregard made only minor changes. In 1864, John B. Jones, a Rebel war clerk who did not like Pemberton, begrudgingly recalled, "Beauregard says Fort Wagner, which has made such a successful defense on Morris Island, was located by General Pemberton, and this is evidence of some military skill." In June 1862, Pemberton also laid out the defenses of James Island, where the Federals were checked in 1862, 1863, and 1864. Even after he had been reduced in rank to lieutenant colonel, Ambrosio Jose Gonzales, the chief of artillery for the Department of South Carolina, Georgia and Florida, wrote him and suggested that Charleston still stood only because of Pemberton and his policy of strengthening his interior positions.

Governor Pickens, Pemberton's nemesis in South Carolina. He gave the general as much trouble as did the Yankees.

Meanwhile, after the Confederate defeat at the Battle of Shiloh, Pemberton was ordered to send eight regiments to northern Mississippi. His army was reduced from 23,000 to 18,700 men. To partially compensate for this loss, Pemberton pulled the regular Confederate forces out of some of the outer defensive positions which he felt could no longer be successfully held, leaving behind only local militia. These included Cole's Island and Battery Island, southwest of Charleston. This was the heart of Pickens' problem with Pemberton. The general wanted to hold the defensible, interior lines, not the outlying areas, which the Yankees could easily overwhelm or smash with their heavy naval artillery. Pemberton, however, lacked Lee's diplomatic skills. The friction between the general and Pickens and his friends continued to grow throughout the summer.

Brigadier General Roswell S. Ripley commanded the Rebel defenses on Cole's Island, which controlled the entrance to the Stono River. Pemberton did not believe this forward position could be successfully defended, so on March 27, he ordered Ripley to withdraw his heavy artillery. Defense of the island would be left to sixteen hundred local defense troops. This was tantamount to abandoning the island. It was common knowledge that the militia, without heavy guns, could not hold the place against the United States Navy and regular Federal troops. The irascible Ripley—who never got along with any superior officer, including General Lee—objected. He felt that he could hold the island. Pemberton disagreed and, unable to gain cooperation, relieved Ripley of his command on May 26.[7]

Pemberton was no doubt right. Cole's Island was isolated and, because the South had no navy to speak of in South Carolina, its eventual loss was inevitable. Pemberton's decision nevertheless caused consternation and panic in Charleston. The defenses of the city, they cried, had been weakened! Tension between Pemberton and the South Carolina upper crust continued to mount.

The key to Charleston, according to Robert E. Lee, John C. Pemberton, and P. G. T. Beauregard, was James Island, just south of the city. The major battle fought in the state during Pemberton's time in command occurred here on June 16, 1862. Pemberton now only had about ten thousand men in his entire department, excluding local defense forces and militias, but he correctly deduced that the Yankees would try to land on James Island, then capture Secessionville.[8] They would be only eight miles from Charleston and would be in a position to threaten the harbor.

Because of their heavy naval guns, there was no way to prevent the Yankees from landing on James Island, which they did on June 2. But Pemberton had concentrated sixty-five hundred men on the island by the time the Northerners attacked on June 16. Sixty-five hundred Federals struck at 2:00 a.m., when only five hundred men garrisoned the town, but they were blasted by Confederate heavy guns. The fighting was soon hand-to-hand, but nearby Rebel reinforcements rushed to the threatened point and made the difference. The Yankees were repulsed and lost seven hundred men, against two hundred for the defenders. The bluecoats evacuated James Island a few days later—not that Pickens and his friends gave Pemberton any credit for the victory.

Meanwhile, Pattie became seriously ill. The attending physician was Dr. George Rhett of the Charleston Rhetts, a very prominent and influential family. During this time, General Pemberton ran into an old friend, an army doctor whom he trusted. Desperately concerned about his wife, Pemberton asked him to examine Pattie and see if he could do anything to save her, which the physician did. Dr. Rhett took instant offense and refused to have anything further to do with the case.

In the hot summer of 1862, ice was very scarce. Pemberton ordered the entire supply set aside and rationed for hospitals. He did, however, order that a small amount be sent to his home, to bring down Pattie's high fever. Another of the Rhetts owned a newspaper with a statewide circulation. Tipped off about Pemberton's order, he blasted the general in print for diverting ice to his own home, implying that it was for recreational use. He did not mention Pattie's illness.

Pemberton also placed an embargo on selling cotton to the enemy, which infuriated a number of the planters. He further annoyed many more of them by impressing some of their slaves as military laborers. The general also had to deal with a critical shortage of funds. He often had to choose between purchasing supplies and paying his men.

That summer, President Davis sent General Cooper to South Carolina to investigate the situation. He concluded that Pemberton had done all an intelligent officer could do under the circumstances. Even this failed to satisfy Pickens. In early July, Cooper signaled Pemberton to be prepared to come to Virginia. He was being replaced by Major General Gustav W. Smith. Pemberton was delighted, but the next day Smith reported himself unfit for duty.

On August 5, 1862, Governor Pickens wrote President Davis and asked that Pemberton be replaced by General Beauregard, who had now recovered his health. Davis pled for cooperation, but Pickens would have nothing to do with it. The South Carolina congressional delegation sided with the governor, so Davis relieved Jack Pemberton on August 29. He was summoned to Richmond for consultations. Beauregard assumed command on September 4.

Davis' high opinion of Pemberton was not lowered by his failure to get along with Pickens and, as we have seen, he did a good job militarily. Meanwhile, the situation in northern Mississippi, from the Confederate point of view, was a mess. On October 1, 1862, Pemberton received Special Orders Number 73 from Cooper, naming him commander of the Department of Mississippi and Eastern Louisiana.

CHAPTER III

NORTHERN MISSISSIPPI, 1862

John C. Pemberton and his staff arrived in Jackson, Mississippi on October 9 and immediately set up their headquarters.[1] The transition was much smoother than it had been in South Carolina for a number of reasons. First of all, Jefferson Davis of Mississippi wrote to John J. Pettus, the governor of Mississippi, and helped pave the way for Pemberton by commending him as an officer of "great merit."[2] Secondly, Pemberton impressed people with his appearance and military bearing. He *looked* like a soldier. One editor said he looked like a gladiator. He was tall, stood erect, was immaculate, and radiated dignity and calm determination. Finally, the department he took over was a mess and everybody knew it. In South Carolina, Pemberton replaced a very competent and admired commander in Robert E. Lee. Lee set high standards which Pemberton could never equal, at least in the eyes of the South Carolinians. Van Dorn, on the other hand, was in over his head—a fact that was obvious to all. They were glad when he was replaced by Pemberton and they received the Pennsylvanian with friendly enthusiasm.

John J. Pettus was a grim, quiet man with an abrupt manner and a fierce temper. After receiving the letter of endorsement from his old friend, Jefferson Davis, he welcomed Pemberton and the two established a cooperative working relationship, although they never quite became friends. Pettus, however, rendered every aid he could and helped Pemberton acquire materials, supplies, and slave labor for his fortification projects.

In Mississippi, Pemberton was better at public relations than he had been in South Carolina. His courtly manners helped dispel the suspicion of his Northern roots, and his gallant comportment was a welcome relief from the overbearing Van Dorn. The Mississippians (press and public) welcomed him with open arms. His work ethic also impressed them. *The Daily Mississippian* (Jackson, Miss.) wrote of him, "No officer ever devoted himself with greater assiduity to his duties. Late and early he is at this office, laboring incessantly."

When Pemberton arrived, the quartermaster, medical, commissary, engineer and ordnance corps were in complete disarray. But Pemberton had an aptitude for administration that Van Dorn did not. He reorganized his department, with special emphasis on the support services. He also broke his department into three territorial districts. The 1st District headquartered in Jackson and was directed by Brigadier General Daniel Ruggles. The 2nd District centered around Vicksburg under the command of Martin Luther Smith; and Brigadier General William N. R. Beall directed the 3rd District from Port Hudson, Louisiana. Beall was replaced in December by Franklin Gardner. Later, Pemberton established a 4th District under Brigadier General John Adams (also headquartered in Jackson) and a 5th District under Brigadier General James R. Chalmers in northern Mississippi and headquartered in Panola. Chalmers controlled little except Colonel Black Bob McCulloch's small cavalry brigade, Mississippi State Troops, and partisan rangers.[3]

Combat units with the main army were easier to reorganize. Pemberton broke the army into two corps: Van Dorn's I and Price's II. This left a senior major general, Mansfield Lovell, as present for duty but without a command. This organizational structure created yet another

issue, because Van Dorn and Lovell were senior to Pemberton, and neither was likely to waive his seniority. Jefferson Davis solved the problem
by promoting him to lieutenant general on October 13, to rank from
October 10. Lovell was the odd man out. He was sent home to await
orders which never came. He was not reemployed.[4]

Pemberton's force had previously been known as the Army of West
Tennessee and the Army of the West. Pemberton wanted to call it the
Army of Northern Mississippi, but the War Department designated it
the Army of Mississippi. In all, it had less than 24,000 men. In western
Tennessee, Grant had a field force of more than 60,000 men.

Pemberton was also not happy with the lackadaisical attitude of some
of his combat troops. He immediately ordered extra drills and tightened
discipline. The landward defenses of Vicksburg and Port Hudson failed
his inspection, so he had his engineers and garrison troops intensify work
on the perimeter defenses and fortifications, and put them to work making
abatis and clearing fields of fire. In addition, he fortified and garrisoned
Snyder's Bluff, at the mouth of the Yazoo, and Warrenton, ten miles south
of Vicksburg. In doing all this, he gained the begrudging respect of some
of his soldiers, most of whom disliked being under a Northerner.

It should be noted that discipline in the Confederate Army varied
considerably from regiment to regiment. Units elected their own officers
and, in some cases, even their own corporals. To a large extent, the
character of the unit determined the quality of the officers they elected
and their attitudes toward discipline. Applying the electoral system to
military formations was (is) not a good idea, but it did not produce the
disastrous results that some authors suppose. Private John Franklin of
a Texas cavalry regiment recalled, "It might seem that the necessity to
be elected by the men could give rise to a group of officers who would
be subservient to the men, but this was not the case. The men elected
the officers to lead them, and any officer who failed to lead would have
been deposed." He added, "I never wanted any man over me, but if I
had to have one, I wanted the hair on his chest as thick as pencil lead."

Discipline in the Confederate Army was enforced unevenly. Minor
infractions tended to be ignored but not always. Edward J. Dunn of the

1st Louisiana Heavy Artillery, who was evidently a good gunner, had a couple of brushes with Confederate law. He was promoted to corporal twice and was twice thrown in the brig for being AWOL and "busted" to private. Eventually promoted to sergeant, he was captured in the Second Battle of Jackson on July 17, 1863. He spent the rest of the war in Camp Morton, Indiana. He later told his family that he was treated far better in Federal prison than he ever was in a Confederate jail.

Some offenses were dealt with more harshly. A good example occurred on New Year's morning, 1863. Captain Rowling of the 56th Georgia woke up and could not find his boots. He ordered a thorough search of the regiment and found them, along with several other stolen items, in the possession of a young private named Rataree, who already had the reputation of being a rogue.

Rowling had Rataree's shirt taken off. He was then given 101 lashes on his back with a whip. The hair on one side of his head was shaved off, and he was forced to march, hat in hand, through the camp, to the tune of the "Rogue's March." He was then dishonorably discharged from Southern service.

From his scouts, Pemberton knew that Grant was building up for an advance several weeks before he moved out. Obviously, he was going to need help. He telegraphed Braxton Bragg and Theophilus Holmes for support.

Lieutenant General Theophilus Holmes was one of Robert E. Lee's rejects. A fifty-seven-year-old West Point graduate, he was slow, nearly deaf, envious, irascible, obstinate, and sometimes hateful. He performed poorly as a divisional commander during the Seven Days Campaign, and was severely criticized by D. H. Hill for his apathy at Malvern Hill. Afterwards, as an old friend of Jefferson Davis, he had been "kicked upstairs" to the command of the Trans-Mississippi Department (Arkansas, Louisiana, Texas, and Indian Territory). Here he was inefficient, jealous, resentful, and refused to cooperate with the Army of Mississippi in any way. Holmes believed Arkansas was being neglected by Richmond and, in retaliation, he refused to do anything to help his colleagues. He was especially jealous of Pemberton and Sterling Price. He answered Pemberton's request with a disrespectful dispatch, labeling him as a man who "has many ways of making people hate him, and none that inspire confidence."[5] Pemberton never did get much help from west of the Mississippi. Bragg was not prepared to send him any infantry either, although he did send a cavalry raid into Grant's rear after the offensive began (see below).

Meanwhile, Pemberton reviewed his troops. When he heard that Price and his Arkansas and Missouri troops were unhappy serving east of the Mississippi, he agreed to let them return to the Trans-Mississippi if Holmes would replace them with an equal number of troops. After he inspected them, however, he was impressed and changed his mind about giving them up. (Perhaps after corresponding with Holmes, he did not trust that general to send him units of equal caliber.) Eventually Price would return to Arkansas without his men.

On the other side of the lines, Southerners were not doing so well. Grant placed William T. Sherman in charge of Memphis. He abused his power over the defenseless civilians with his characteristic overbearing cruelty. When he entered the city and found it pretty much closed down, he ordered everything to begin operating immediately—or else. He ordered all churches to pray for Abraham Lincoln or they would be closed and their pastors arrested. He expelled the wives and families of Rebel soldiers from their homes. (Mrs. Luxton, Nathan Bedford Forrest's mother, was not disturbed. Her son was capturing too many Yankees and Sherman knew he would retaliate.) He arrested newspaper editors and reporters who displeased him, even Northern correspondents.

On September 24, 1862, Sherman ordered the town of Randolph, Tennessee, burned because somebody had fired on a Union gunboat. He ordered all houses, farms, and outbuildings on the Arkansas side of the Mississippi River across from Memphis burned for a distance of fifteen miles. He decreed that for every incident of sniper firing on a Yankee, ten families would be expelled from Memphis. Shortly afterward, forty families were expelled.

Grant joined the abuse by issuing orders that all people caught with contraband items were to be arrested. He was especially hard on Jews, whom he hated with a special hatred. "Jews should receive special attention," he commanded.

On December 17, 1862, Grant issued General Order No. 11. "The Jews, as a class having violated every regulation of trade established by the Treasury Department and also department orders, are hereby expelled from the department within twenty-four hours of the receipt of this order," he decreed, adding that no appeals were to be permitted.

Except for Andrew Jackson's Indian removals, this was the largest expulsion of a particular people in American history until the relocation of Japanese-Americans from the West Coast during World War II. Whole families were uprooted. Others who did not receive the order or who ignored it were arrested and tossed into one of Lincoln's dungeons.

The Jews protested to President Lincoln via telegram, but he ignored them. One of them, Cesar Kaskel, went to Washington and finally succeeded in getting an audience with Lincoln, who claimed to know nothing about it. Or at least that's what he said. He sent Kaskel to Halleck with a note, instructing Grant to cancel the order. "The President has no objection to your expelling traitors and Jew peddlers, which, I suppose, was the object of your order," Halleck wrote to Grant on January 4, 1863, "but as it proscribed an entire religious class, some of whom are fighting in our ranks, the President deemed it necessary to revoke it." But by this time, of course, many of the Jews had already been expelled.

Sherman continued his reign of terror until December 1862, when he boarded a ship bound for Chickasaw Bluffs (see below). He was succeeded by Major General Stephen Hurlbut, commander of the newly formed XVI Corps. Hurlbut was born and raised in South Carolina, but fled when he was twenty-three, in order to escape his creditors. He moved to Illinois, where he became a crony of a Springfield lawyer named Abraham Lincoln, whom he helped politically. He was rewarded with a brigadier generalcy. Despite a lack of military qualifications, he performed well at Shiloh, which led to his promotion. Although he was as anti-Semitic as Grant, he did not want to expel Jews—especially rich Jews—from Memphis. He wanted to arrest them, with or without cause, and hold them in a hellhole called Fort Putnam until their families coughed up a ransom. He did the same to rich Gentiles, whether they were loyal to the Confederacy or not. Corruption was rampant in Memphis in 1862.

On the Southern side, the opposite was true. Many citizens felt Earl Van Dorn was corrupt and overbearing (they hadn't met Sherman yet), and John C. Pemberton was like a breath of fresh air. Civilians praised him and local newspapers described him as selfless, tireless, and free from ostentation. He was also not a drunkard or a womanizer. They lauded him for never playing favorites. They liked the way he immersed himself in his work. He gained public confidence because of his seriousness and intensity, and the manner in which he worked with civil authorities. No doubt about it—Jack Pemberton had learned a lot in South Carolina and was correcting his mistakes. The general had great public relations until May 1863. Even in the summer of 1863, many Mississippians spoke highly of him. Shortly after Jackson fell (see Chapter XI), state Attorney General T. J. Wharton visited Richmond and met with his friend, Jefferson Davis. During the conversation, the president revealed that he had interviewed Generals Samuel Cooper and Robert E. Lee separately and asked each whom they would recommend for the Mississippi command. Both picked Pemberton.

Wharton told Davis that, as chief law enforcement officer of the state, he had frequently consulted with Pemberton. He commended the general for his "hearty co-operation" with the civil authorities, and added: "I had never seen a more laborious and painstaking officer," nor one who paid closer attention to detail.

It snowed on October 25, which was early for northern Mississippi, and there was much suffering among the troops. The logistical system was working better now, however, and food supplies and forage were adequate. Grant began his offensive on November 8 and his plan was obvious: he intended to drive two hundred miles from the Tennessee border, down the tracks of the Mississippi Central Railroad, straight south to Jackson, in the center of the state. Then he would turn west and capture Vicksburg.

Pemberton's scouts accurately estimated that Grant had sixty to seventy thousand men. Pemberton had twenty thousand in northern Mississippi. Outnumbered three to one, he fell back slowly and refused to engage in a lopsided battle; instead, he executed a prearranged retreat to Holly Springs, which fell after a brief skirmish on November 13. He retreated to Lumpkin's Mill, twelve miles to the south, then to Abbeville, thirteen miles south of that, just below the Tallahatchie River. Grant followed and, on November 20, Pemberton evacuated Abbeville (eleven miles north of Oxford), covered by Major General Dabney H. Maury's infantry division and four thousand cavalrymen under Van Dorn. Nine days later, he was forced to retreat again, closely pursued by the Yankees. "In Oxford, the scene almost beggared description," Sergeant William Henry Tunnard of the 3rd Louisiana Infantry Regiment recalled.[6] "Long columns of troops, tired, wet and soiled, poured through the town, accompanied by carriages, buggies, and even carts, filled with terror-stricken, delicate ladies—whole families carrying with them their household goods and negroes. The scene was one of indescribable confusion and excitement—one of the gloomy pictures of the war so distressing in all its circumstances."

After a brisk skirmish, Oxford fell on December 2. Some of the Rebels barely escaped. Dozens of sick and wounded soldiers were taken prisoner when the Confederate Hospital was captured, including thirty-four members of the 42nd Alabama. The retreat continued through cold, driving rainstorms through Water Valley, Spring Valley, and Coffeeville. Tunnard was pleased with his commanding general's performance so far. Instead of getting trapped, as Price had done at Iuka and Van Dorn had done after Corinth, Pemberton had "wisely" retreated deeper into Mississippi. He was heading for Grenada, a beautiful little town of two thousand, on the southern bank of the Yalobusha River, where the Mississippi & Tennessee

Railroad from the west met the Mississippi Central. But the ever-aggressive Grant was trying to steal a march on him. On December 3, the men of the 3rd Louisiana heard the thunder of artillery to the west. The Yankee cavalry was trying to reach Grenada before the Confederate Army could retreat through it. Pemberton, however, had sent a small, 1,200-man cavalry brigade under Lieutenant Colonel John S. Griffith to cover his left flank, in case of just such an eventuality.[7]

Thursday, December 3, was a "cool, pleasant day," according to Miss Emma Moore, a resident of Oakland, Mississippi. Just west of town, at a critical road junction, Griffith placed the 27th Texas Cavalry. North of the junction was the 3rd Texas Cavalry, while to the south, blocking the road to Charleston, lay Colonel Jack Wharton's 6th Texas Cavalry. Because of the poor condition of the road, Griffith had left his own artillery behind, but he was joined by a four-gun battery from Arkansas.

The battle began when the 1st Indiana Cavalry blundered into the Rebels. Much to the consternation of the Yankees, the Texans dismounted and fought as infantry. They counterattacked immediately and rapidly pushed the Northerners back. The Indiana commander was soon calling for help.

The Union commander at Oakland and the leader of the raid was Brigadier General Cadwallader Colden Washburn, a highly competent commander and future founder of General Mills. He was supported by an infantry brigade under Brigadier General Alvin P. Hovey. Together, they had ten thousand men. Washburn sent forward two lightweight mountain howitzers, which the Texans promptly captured. The Union forces now began to fan out left and right, while Griffith prepared to launch another attack. When he realized how many men Washburn had, however, he called off the advance and eventually retreated. The Yankees briefly occupied Oakland but, by this time, Confederate infantry was available and Washburn's raid had been blocked.

Grant made another effort to cut off Pemberton by getting behind his right flank. He sent a six-regiment cavalry brigade under Colonel T. Lyle Dickey to loop behind the retreating Southern columns and cut them off. Pemberton sent Brigadier General William E. Baldwin's Mississippi Brigade to block it, along with Colonel William H. "Red" Jackson's 7th Tennessee Cavalry and the 9th Arkansas Infantry and 3rd Kentucky Infantry Regiments of Brigadier General Albert Rust's Division. Brigadier General Lloyd Tilghman was in charge of this battle group.

On December 5, Tilghman set an ambush for the Yankees. His men hid on a wooded ridge alongside the Water Valley-Coffeeville Road. The Union vanguard was within fifty yards of Tilghman's position when the Rebel artillery opened up and the infantry fired in volleys. The Yankee cavalry promptly withdrew, leaving behind thirty-four dead, and forty-three missing. They also suffered 234 wounded, for a total of 311 casualties. Tilghman lost seven killed, forty-three wounded, and ten missing—sixty men in all.

In the meantime, the rest of the Army of Mississippi retreated behind the Yalobusha River, with a defensive line centered on Grenada, almost halfway between the state line and Jackson. It was a strong position. The army immediately began to dig in.

On December 7, Pemberton relieved Van Dorn as commander of the I Corps and replaced him with Major General W. W. Loring. He had another job for Earl Van Dorn.

Meanwhile, history of an entirely different kind was made on the Yazoo River.

Pemberton had stationed almost six thousand men at Vicksburg (many of them supply and support troops and heavy artillery units), plus another forty-five hundred at Port Hudson. Grant thought he might be able to capture Haines' Bluff (sometimes spelled Haynes' Bluff) on the Yazoo River, the northern anchor of the Chickasaw Hills position. If the Chickasaw Hills were captured, he would be able to take Vicksburg before Pemberton could react. For this purpose, he sent General William Tecumseh Sherman's entire XIII Corps (twenty-one thousand men) from Oxford back to Memphis, to prepare for an amphibious assault on Chickasaw Hills. In preparation for this offensive, the U.S. Navy sent the USS *Cairo* up the Yazoo, to clear away Confederate mines, which were called "torpedoes" in those days.

The *Cairo* was huge by the standards of the day. It displaced 521 tons, had a crew of 251, and was armed with three 8-inch smoothbores, three 42-pounder rifled cannons, six 32-pounder rifled cannons, a 30-pounder rifled cannon, and a 12-pounder.[8]

After the fall of New Orleans, Beverly Kennon, a Rebel naval lieutenant, arrived in Vicksburg. He was one of several innovative officers in Secretary Mallory's Naval Department, which was always looking for new and exciting ways to sink Yankee ships. He approached Lieutenant Isaac Brown, the former commander of the *Arkansas*, and they discussed Kennon's latest idea: an electronically detonated mine. Brown liked what he heard and decided to detonate it himself. He didn't have to wait long.

On December 12, the *Cairo* (pronounced KAY-ROW) steamed up the Yazoo. When her bow crossed over one of the five-gallon glass jugs which were filled with black powder, Brown detonated it. The explosion was so powerful that it literally lifted the huge warship out of the water. As soon as she came down, Brown detonated a second mine directly beneath her. Although no Northerners were killed or even seriously wounded, the *Cairo* sank in twelve minutes in thirty-six feet of water. She was the first ship in history to be sunk by an electrical underwater mine.[9]

The USS Cairo.

Meanwhile, on November 24, 1862, Jefferson Davis further confused an already flawed Confederate command structure. He created the Department of the West and placed it under the command of Joseph E. Johnston. It included the Army of Tennessee (Braxton Bragg); the Department of Eastern Tennessee (Edmund Kirby Smith); and the Department of Mississippi and Eastern Louisiana (Pemberton). It did not include the Trans-Mississippi Department, which operated much like an independent country.

Joseph E. Johnston had a distinguished pre-war career. He was born in Farmville, Virginia, in 1807 and graduated from West Point in 1829, in the same class in which Robert E. Lee finished second. Commissioned in the 4th Artillery, he served in the Black Hawk and Seminole Wars and in Mexico, where he was wounded five times and received three brevets. He was promoted to brigadier general and head of the U.S. Army's quartermaster department in 1860.

Although Johnston had been an outstanding junior officer when he was on Winfield Scott's staff, he was a timid and hesitant army commander. After the Confederate victory at the 1st Manassas (Bull Run), he did not want to pursue the Yankee army and take Washington, as Stonewall Jackson advocated. Jefferson Davis took Johnston's advice and did not pursue. The president later said that this was the worst mistake of his life.

Famous historian Douglas Southall Freeman[10] called Joseph E. Johnston "a generous superior, a carping equal, [and] an impossible subordinate." He was a very jealous kind of person. Winston Groom wrote that he was "difficult, condescending, and a prima donna." He did not want this position and accepted it only reluctantly. Johnston submitted his resignation twice during the first two months he was in his new job, but President Davis rejected it twice.

Braxton Bragg's invasion of Kentucky was defeated in October 1862, at least partially because there was no cooperation between Bragg's army and that of Edmund Kirby Smith. Apparently, Davis created Johnston's position so that he would obtain coordination between Bragg, Kirby Smith, and Pemberton. He did not realize that Johnston had no intention of coordinating anything, would be very uncooperative, and would favor the Army of Tennessee over the Army of Mississippi.

In 1861 and the first five months of 1862, Johnston had commanded what became the Army of Northern Virginia until he was wounded in the Southern defeat at Seven Pines. He may have expected to be restored to that command, but that was no longer possible; his successor, Robert E. Lee, had won too many victories.[11] This is not to suggest that President Davis wanted Johnston in Virginia—he didn't. The two men did not get along and Davis rightly looked upon Johnston as a political enemy. Perhaps for that reason, Davis instructed Pemberton to report to Richmond *and* Johnston. This further offended Johnston, who was easy to offend in the best of times. The Bible clearly states that "No man can serve two masters."[12] The Confederate high command made a serious mistake when it violated this axiom, and Pemberton made a serious mistake when he tried to serve two masters. But this is getting ahead of our story.

Joseph E. Johnston was petty, spiteful, resentful, jealous, and never blamed himself for anything. He was also more interested in not losing a battle than in winning one. Diarist Mary Chesnut told a story about the time Johnston and several other officers went pheasant hunting. All the other officers shot at the birds. Sometimes they hit them, sometimes they missed. Johnston—who was a crack shot—would not fire unless he was sure of killing something; consequently, he never fired. At the end of the day, he was the only man who did not miss all day long. He was also the only man who did not kill a bird that day. Unfortunately for the South, he approached his military duties with the same excessive caution. He was the kind of general who would give up key positions and even vital cities, rather than risk losing a battle. At heart, Johnston was a pessimist. He set up his headquarters at Chattanooga and neglected Pemberton's army, in favor of Bragg's Army of Tennessee.

In the meantime, Governor Pettus and C.S. Senator James Phelan of Mississippi urged President Davis to visit the state, in order to reassure the population. Davis agreed to do so and decided to visit Bragg's army as well.

Accompanied by Joe Johnston, Jefferson Davis inspected the Army of Tennessee in mid-December. He met with Johnston and Bragg at the latter's headquarters at Murfreesboro, thirty miles southeast of Nashville. While there, on December 19, Davis ordered Bragg to transfer Major General Carter Stevenson's infantry division to Pemberton. Johnston heatedly objected. Davis overruled him. Johnston sulked.

Stevenson's Division included Brigadier General Seth Barton's Brigade and Brigadier General Alfred Cumming's Brigade (both from Georgia); Brigadier General Edward D. Tracy's Alabama brigade; and Colonel Alfred J. Vaughn's Tennessee brigade. Most of its regiments were inexperienced and some of them were not especially good. It did, however, have the virtue of being full strength and numbered nine thousand men.[13]

Stevenson's regiments received their orders on December 19, and began departing for Mississippi the next day. The South's railroads, however, were generally poor, and her locomotives and rolling stock had received few spare parts in months because of the Union blockade. It was impossible for all of the regiments in the division to travel together. Some arrived quickly; others did not. The 56th Georgia, for example, could not leave Murfreesboro until December 24. It arrived in Chattanooga that night and rolled into Atlanta the day after Christmas. The men of the regiment off-loaded in Montgomery at 10:00 p.m. on December 28, and boarded a steamer on the Alabama River, which transferred them to Selma on December 29. That evening they got on another train, which carried them to Demopolis. Here, on December 30, they were met by a buffet of enormous size, compliments of the ladies of the town, who said they had been feeding Confederate soldiers for seven days, had provisions for seven more, and would continue to feed them as long as Demopolis had a pound of meat and a loaf of bread. Lieutenant Oscar Cantrell remembered the ladies as being "kind, beautiful, and patriotic."

At sunset on December 30, they boarded the steamboat *Marengo* on the Tombigbee River, which took them to McDowell's Landing. They made a short march to another train, which transported them to Meridian, Mississippi. They arrived at 9:00 p.m. on January 1, 1863. The 56th Georgia camped here until January 5, when another train arrived, to carry them to Jackson and Vicksburg. There was no longer any hurry, however, because the battle which they had been rushing to join was already over (see Chapter IV). They had been on the road for more than two weeks and were still one hundred miles from Vicksburg. Such was the state of Southern communications in early 1863. The regiment did not arrive in the "Confederate Gibraltar" until the evening of January 24.

Jefferson Davis' train—of course—had the highest priority and moved a lot faster. He left Bragg's Headquarters on December 20 and his next stop was Mississippi. Joseph Johnston didn't want to go. He had never visited his Mississippi army and did not intend to now. Requesting did not work and President Davis had to order him to accompany him to Vicksburg.

⌐

While Davis and Johnston were heading west to visit him, Pemberton was in the middle of a complex military campaign. At the moment, there was a lull. Grant had halted north of the Yalobusha, waiting for Sherman to attack Vicksburg before he resumed his offensive. Pemberton, however, had decided to preempt him. He had already asked Braxton Bragg for help. Bragg accommodated him by sending Nathan Bedford Forrest's cavalry division on a raid against the railroads in western Tennessee, and especially the one from Columbia, Kentucky, which supplied Grant's army. Forrest crossed the Tennessee River on December 15, diverting the attention of the Union generals from their front in northern Mississippi.

Even though he was acquitted, Earl Van Dorn had been humiliated by his court-martial of November 1862. He personally paid for one thousand copies of the court's findings to be distributed to Southern newspapers, but not everyone was convinced he should not have been convicted. The State of Mississippi, Senator Phelan wrote to Jefferson Davis in early December, was "dense with narratives of his negligence, whoring, and drunkenness," and the court of public opinion had not acquitted him of the charges.

Mid-nineteenth century Americans considered adultery to be a serious infraction; it was even considered a crime in 1862. Rumors circulated throughout the country that Van Dorn had fathered three illegitimate children in Texas before the war. And they were true. For his part, Van Dorn felt abused by the citizens of his home state. His defense against the charge of whoremongering was lame. In a letter to President Davis, he admitted that he was unfortunately not always a good Christian, but he asserted that "I have never had intercourse with any woman . . . who was not alike accessible to others." He asked to be transferred, but Davis refused to accommodate him.

Meanwhile, Colonel Griffith sent General Pemberton a letter, suggesting a raid against General Grant's main supply depot at Holly Springs, and he recommended Earl Van Dorn lead it. After due consideration, Pemberton decided this was a capital idea and sent for Van Dorn. After listening to Pemberton, the previously depressed general became excited. Here was his chance to redeem his reputation.

Major General Earl Van Dorn, who was known as the "Terror of Ugly Husbands." A notorious womanizer, he was unsuccessful as an army commander, but did much better commanding cavalry.

Colonel Griffith had suggested employing every available cavalry-man in the Army of Mississippi, of which Pemberton had some six thousand, including partisans. Van Dorn reduced the number to a division of twenty-five hundred hand-picked men, divided into three brigades under Griffith, Red Jackson, and Colonel Robert M. "Black Bob" McCulloch. He carried no wagons or artillery.

The men roared their approval when Van Dorn joined them at dawn on December 16. The raiders left Grenada immediately and headed east. It was rainy and very cold. The column was three miles long as they rode along the south bank of the Yalobusha. One member of Van Dorn's staff recalled him "sitting astride his horse like a knight, and looking every inch a soldier."

Using the route Van Dorn selected, it was just over one hundred miles from Grenada to Holly Springs; they made an excellent forty-six miles the first day and were thirty miles east of Grant's front. After a long, hard ride through bad weather and over terrible roads, the column reached Houston, Mississippi. After a brief rest, it turned due north and arrived in Pontotoc on the eighteenth. They were well fed by the citizens of the town. The men were tired, cold, and wet, but their enthusiasm was undiminished. They now turned west, toward Holly Springs, which was only thirty miles away. The troopers were so tired that some of them fell asleep in their saddles, but they kept riding. Map 3.1 shows Van Dorn's route.

Meanwhile, scouts and a slave tipped off Grant that there were Confederate raiders in his rear and moving north. Grant signaled Colonel Robert C. Murphy, the garrison commander at Holly Springs, as well as other outpost commanders, and ordered them to be alert. Inexplicably, Murphy failed to warn his troops and did not require his officers to be with their men. Most of them spent the night in private homes. About the only person who took the warning seriously was Julia Grant, the general's wife, who was in town visiting an old friend, the wife of a Confederate colonel. She hurriedly fled Holly Springs via railroad car on December 19, accompanied by only one of her slaves. After the war, the rumor spread that she was captured and quickly released by the Southern cavalrymen. This story was believed and repeated by a very prominent historian, but it was not true. The Rebels did capture her carriage, however.

By midnight, the Confederates closed in on the town. They captured three Yankee cotton speculators, took their clothes and their trading passes, and three Rebel spies went into Holly Springs to scout. They

Map 3.1: Van Dorn's Raid

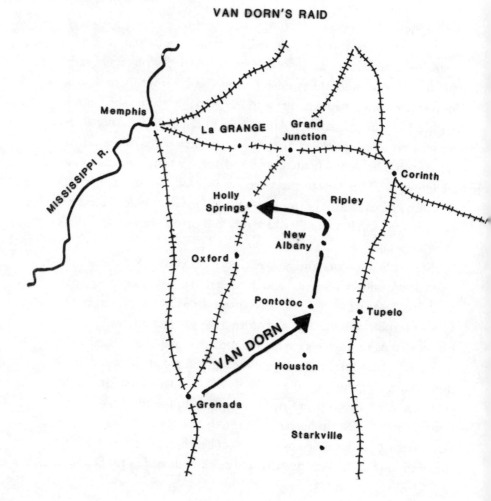

reported back that the town was asleep and no one suspected Van Dorn was anywhere close. The general ordered an attack for dawn.

Van Dorn roused his men just before daybreak on December 20. Survivors remembered how gallant and impressive he appeared that morning, sitting on his fine black mare, holding his hat above his head, ordering the charge. For suggesting the raid, Van Dorn rewarded Colonel Griffith with the honor of leading the attack. "I felt as if I could charge hell and capture the devil," Griffith recalled.

The Rebels poured into Holly Springs from several directions, catching the garrison flat-footed and, in most cases, asleep. There were four thousand Union soldiers in the vicinity of Holly Springs, but only fifteen hundred men in the town itself, and half of those were supply troops. Only a small Union cavalry detachment on the northern edge of town offered any resistance but, seeing everything fall apart, its commander wisely headed north and managed to escape with his men. No one else did. The battle was brief. Women in their sleeping clothes ran out into the streets, shedding tears of joy and cheering their heroes. Fifteen hundred Yankees were captured, including Colonel Murphy, who was in his nightshirt.[14] Van Dorn paroled the POWs and turned his attention to the supplies.

His men took everything they wanted and all they could carry, including carbines, whiskey bottles, cigars, and food. Many of them took Federal 6-shooters—some more than a dozen. They also captured a large number of horses from Northern corrals. They then burned a line of boxcars and several warehouses and buildings, filled with food, medicine, weapons, and ammunition. By midafternoon, Holly Springs and the surrounding area were covered in smoke.

Van Dorn remained in the area for a few days and then made good his escape, arriving back in Pemberton's camp on December 28, after having ridden five hundred miles. Meanwhile, Forrest wrecked the railroads of western Kentucky and western Tennessee so thoroughly that most of them could not be used for the rest of the war.

The Forrest and Van Dorn raids effectively neutralized Grant's army for the time being. He would not be able to resume his offensive in northern

Mississippi as planned. This meant he would not be able to assist Sherman, who was already steaming down the Mississippi to attack Vicksburg. Worse still, he could not communicate with his deputy to warn him that no help would be forthcoming.

CHAPTER IV

CHICKASAW BLUFFS

On December 21, 1862, Davis, Pemberton, and Johnston met in Vicksburg. They inspected Smith's troops and the defenses from Walnut Hills in the north to Warrenton in the south. General Johnston, of course, found fault with everything. He asserted that Pemberton's defensive plans were so extensive as to be worthless. (The Union soldiers who faced these defenses six months later used a lot of adjectives to describe them, but "worthless" was never one of them.)

Both Johnston and Pemberton urged Davis to transfer some of Holmes' troops to the Army of Mississippi. Davis wrote him and declared it seemed "clearly developed that the enemy has two principal objects in view, one to get control of the Miss. River, and the other to capture the capital of the Confederate States." He correctly stated that Lee's victory at Fredericksburg probably ended the Union plans to advance on Richmond that winter, but that to prevent "dismembering the Confederacy, we must mainly depend upon maintaining the points already occupied by defensive works: to wit, Vicksburg and Port Hudson." Holmes, who was not under any direct threat, had plenty of men.[1] An infusion of twenty thousand men, including cavalry units, would give Pemberton fifty thousand men—enough to meet Grant on nearly even terms. Nothing came of the suggestions, however. Holmes wouldn't agree. The secretary of war had already ordered him to join Pemberton with part of his command, but Holmes ignored him also. He did nothing.

Jefferson Davis was loyal to a fault. He should have fired Holmes immediately and replaced him with someone who would cooperate. But it would be four full months before he did. By then, it would be too late.

President Jefferson Davis.

After they finished inspecting the Vicksburg defenses, Davis, Pemberton, and the carping Johnston boarded a train and headed for Grenada. Meanwhile, 240 miles to the north, Sherman's infantrymen were boarding transports and preparing to attack the Confederate Gibraltar via the river route. On the way, Frederick Steele's division would join them at Helena, Arkansas. This would bring the size of Sherman's corps to thirty-three thousand men.

Vicksburg's northern flank consisted of high bluffs rising out of marshes and cypress swamps. Collectively, these positions on the south bank of the Yazoo were known as Walnut Hills or Chickasaw Bluffs. They began at the Mississippi and ranged up to Haines' Bluff, twelve miles to the northeast. Haines' Bluff and nearby Snyder's Mill were the anchors of the Confederate northern flank.

Even getting there would be difficult because the terrain between the Yazoo and the bluffs was an infantryman's nightmare: marshland, shallow lakes, bayous, and old-growth forests that had never known the axe. The undergrowth was dense, and there were plenty of thorns and brier patches. In places, a scout who knew the terrain or a veteran hunter might get through, but passage was simply impossible for large infantry formations; in fact, there were only five points where the Yankees could cross the swamp without pontoon bridges, and the Rebels knew where they were. The people who lived there resided along the roads or in the scattered plantations, which included slave cabins. No one lived in the interior. Sherman's plan was basically to bounce through the swamps before the Confederates could react.

Meanwhile, Davis and Johnston reviewed the troops at Grenada on Christmas Eve. Pemberton had by now gotten wind that something was up. Southern spies reported that the Yankees were preparing a large waterborne attack on Vicksburg. The fact that the USS *Cairo* had been sunk clearing mines on the Yazoo the week before lent credibility to these reports. Pemberton ordered a brigade from Grenada to go to Vicksburg and kept an eye to the west.

On Christmas Eve night, two Confederate officers formed a lonely outpost in a small building on a plantation more than twenty miles north of Vicksburg. It was cold and raining, so they remained inside, playing cards to relieve the boredom. Suddenly a young African American girl came in and announced that she had heard a steamboat coming. The officers were startled. There were no Confederate vessels north of them. This could only be the enemy! They went out to take a look. To their astonishment, a Union ironclad emerged out of the darkness. Then another appeared. Then a third. No doubt taking cover, they counted seven ironclads. Then transports began to show up. They counted fifty-nine steamers, all packed with Federal troops. The senior officer, Major

Lee L. Daniels, did not wait around to see the rest. Had he done so, he would have counted sixty-one more, with several tinclads intermixed.[2]

Daniels hopped on his horse and raced three miles to the south, where there was an unoccupied telegraph station. Daniels, a telegraph operator before the war, quickly pounded out a message to Colonel Philip H. Fall at De Soto Point. He informed the colonel that the river was full of boats, as far as the eye could see. Fall was incredulous until Daniels signaled: "Great God, Phil, eighty-one gunboats and transports have passed here tonight." He asked Fall to rush to Vicksburg and sound the alarm. Fall immediately boarded a skiff and crossed the Father of Waters, despite the danger from white caps, high wind, rain, and current. Only the reader who has seen the Mississippi in a storm can fully appreciate what an act of courage this was.

The officers of Martin Luther Smith's Vicksburg garrison were attending a Christmas Ball at the Balfour House, the home of Dr. William Balfour and his socialite wife, Emma. It was an elegant affair, with lavish refreshments, including fine wines and champagne. The Balfour House was also Smith's Headquarters. When the dripping wet colonel burst into the ballroom and walked across the dance floor, the music stopped and the revelers parted like the Red Sea. Fall gave the general Daniel's message. Smith turned pale. "This ball is at an end! The enemy is coming down the river!" the general shouted.

The Balfour House, 2017.

"All noncombatants leave the city!" He realized immediately the Yankees were probably heading for Chickasaw Bluffs, so he ordered every available man, cannon, and howitzer to head there. Gun crews scrambled to man the twenty-eight heavy guns in front of Vicksburg, as well as the thirty or so heavy guns along the twelve miles from Vicksburg to Snyder's Mill. Ammunition wagons were loaded and sent forward, and hospitals were made ready. General Smith declared martial law in the area and created a temporary (provisional) division under Brigadier General Stephen Dill Lee.

Stephen Dill Lee.

Lee was a young man. Born in Charleston, South Carolina, in 1833, he graduated from West Point in 1854 and was commissioned in the artillery. He resigned from the army in 1861 and was an aide to General Beauregard at Fort Sumter. He then transferred to the artillery and fought in all of Robert E. Lee's battles up through Sharpsburg (September 17, 1862), by which time he was a colonel. Promoted to brigadier general on November 6, he was sent to Vicksburg to become Pemberton's chief of artillery, but was named commander of a Louisiana/Mississippi brigade instead. Now he created three provisional brigades under Colonels William T. "Theo" Withers, Allen Thomas, and Edward Higgins and, well before dawn, marched them to the bluffs. He had three thousand men and ten guns. In all, excluding Lee's division, Smith had six thousand men and about sixty heavy guns to defend about twenty miles of river front, including the bluffs and the fortifications along the Mississippi. But help was on the way.

Sherman arrived off the mouth of the Yazoo early Christmas morning. He did not know that the Union plan had already misfired and that Grant was not going to be able to pin Pemberton down on the Yalobusha, so he decided to indulge in his passion for destruction and arson. He remained aboard the transports while one of his brigades landed on the Louisiana side, wrecked a few miles of railroad west of De Soto, and burned some houses. He wasted the entire day.

On the other side of the line, General Pemberton did not waste a minute. In Grenada, Major General Dabney Maury had just sat down to a magnificent Christmas dinner when an order from the Philadelphian arrived: take your entire division and, traveling by rail, reinforce Stephen D. Lee at Vicksburg at once! A disappointed and hungry General Maury left the table and went to work immediately.

Even as the reluctant general left his dinner uneaten, the 26th Louisiana arrived on what would be the field of battle. General Lee ordered it and other regiments to cover the road from Johnson's plantation on the Yazoo River to the bluffs. The 26th Louisiana's sector had no rifle pits (which today we would call "fox holes" or "trenches"), so they used swords and bayonets to dig shallow emplacements, because that was all they had.

General Pemberton and his guests entrained for Jackson on Christmas Day. Davis continued on to Richmond, Johnston remained at Pemberton's Headquarters at Jackson (probably so he wouldn't have to proceed with Davis) and Pemberton headed for Vicksburg. Meanwhile, the 26th Louisiana and the other regiments bivouacked near a position the Yankees would call "Fort Morgan," within two miles of the Yazoo, and awaited Sherman's next move.

Sherman's men began to off-load from the transports on the morning of December 26. His forces included sixty guns and four infantry divisions under Brigadier Generals A. J. Smith (ten regiments); Morgan L. Smith (eight regiments); G. W. Morgan's division (eight regiments) and Frederick Steele's oversized division (seventeen infantry regiments). They skirmished with the 26th Louisiana and pushed in its outposts. That night, the 26th was replaced by Colonel Robert Richardson's 17th Louisiana Infantry.

William Tecumseh Sherman spent the entire day uploading his troops and sorting out equipment. As Lee had predicted, the landings concentrated at Johnson's Plantation and at a nearby racetrack. Steele took the left flank and marched along the road to the east, north of Chickasaw Bayou. Andrew Jackson "Whiskey" Smith occupied the right, while George Washington Morgan and Morgan Smith landed in the center, near the ruins of the plantation house, which had been blown away by Union gunboats.

Joseph D. Alison of the 2nd Alabama recalled a flood of refugees "having been run out of their homes by the Yankees and their houses burnt." He recorded in his diary: "The river is full of boats, some say as many as 80 are ashore. There is one continuous line of smoke . . ."

Jack Pemberton arrived at Martin Luther Smith's headquarters late that night. He learned that Sherman's men had landed and were advancing on Walnut Hills. He promptly wired Grenada and ordered that Stevenson's Division (then en route to Jackson) be sent on to Vicksburg. He also telegraphed Jackson and ordered Colonel Waddy to facilitate the moving of troops through the Mississippi capital. He sent Johnston a telegram and asked him to assist in this work as well.

That night, General Maury arrived with the first four hundred men. He recalled, "The night was black as a wolf's mouth, a cold rain was falling, and all around us lay the dead and wounded, whose piteous moans went out for help to the surgeons and litter-bearers . . ."

Maury outranked Lee but, because he knew little about the situation, he asked Stephen Lee to retain command, which he did.

Several hours later, Colonel William T. S. Barry's 35th Mississippi and Captain Hiram M. Bledsoe, Jr.'s Missouri Battery arrived over what General Maury called "the very worst [railroad] line in the state."

Maury recalled that Barry and Bledsoe were "capital fellows" and good friends. Barry was especially congenial and well-liked, but he was not above playing an occasional practical joke. They rode in the same boxcar that night. The six-foot-three captain was a great artilleryman but a sloppy dresser. His huge boots, for example, had never been polished and were now yellow—the same color as the cowhide from which they were made. After Bledsoe took them off and went to sleep, the colonel called to a Negro and gave him a dollar to blacken and polish them. That was a lot of money in those days, and the African American did a good job. When the colonel woke him up and told him it was time to go, Bledsoe did not recognize his boots and looked all over the car for them. When he realized what had happened, Bledsoe was so furious that he challenged Barry to a duel. The colonel, however, refused to waive his rank, laughed it off, and there was no duel. Bledsoe eventually got over being the butt of the joke.

The battle began in earnest early on the morning of December 27. Richardson's 17th Louisiana, which was located several hundred yards in front of the main line, skirmished with the Yankees and delayed their progress.[3] Lieutenant Colonel Hall sent two companies of his 26th Louisiana to a patch of woods on Richardson's right. It was soon involved in the fighting. Colonel Withers, the provisional brigade commander and the ranking officer at the front,[4] organized an attack, but when he realized how strong the Yankees were, he canceled it.

During the day, the 17th Louisiana was relieved by the 28th Louisiana of Colonel Thomas' brigade[5] and the 46th Mississippi (formerly of Lee's brigade) joined the skirmishers in front of the bluffs.

Stephen Dill Lee later commented that, had Sherman launched an all-out attack on December 27 at the position called the Indian Mound, he probably could have taken Vicksburg. But Sherman wasted the 26th and devoted December 27 and 28 to off-loading and reconnaissance. He found that he had essentially occupied an island, bound on the south and west by the Mississippi, on the north by the Yazoo, and on the east by Chickasaw Bayou. To make matters worse, the already swampy ground had been saturated by recent rains. Only one Southern regiment opposed

Morgan Smith's entire division, but it only demonstrated against the Rebels. Smith himself was so badly wounded in a skirmish that he could not return to active duty for almost a year. Sherman temporarily placed his division (on the Confederate left) under the command of Whiskey Smith.

Sherman was now basically in a tactical cul-de-sac. The terrain, rivers, bayous, and ponds channelized the Union advance like a funnel. As we have seen, there were only five places where Sherman could cross the swamps without having to build a bridge, including the bridge over Chickasaw Bayou, two miles from the Yazoo River. There was also a good road running along this stream. This road led to Vicksburg and this is where Sherman decided to make his main attack, with Morgan Smith's division against the Confederate right. Steele's Division on Sherman's far north (left) flank was of no use at all. It became so mired in mud, swamp, and quicksand that it could not reach the bluffs, even though it was unopposed. Steele was forced to retreat back to the Yazoo, where his division reembarked on steamboats. They transported it farther south, where it again off-loaded and redeployed.

On December 27, the U.S. Navy tried to divert the Rebels away from the bluffs by sending the USS *Benton* up the Yazoo, to feign an attack on Snyder's Mill and possibly destroy the Confederate heavy guns there. This sector was commanded by Colonel Edward Higgins, who normally directed the 22nd Louisiana Infantry Regiment.[6] Why this regiment was called "infantry" is a mystery, because it was really a heavy artillery unit with a few infantry components. Higgins himself had served fourteen years as a naval officer and was an expert heavy artillery commander. His well-trained men poured at least thirty shells through the *Benton's* portholes alone. The *Benton's* young captain, Lieutenant Commander William Gwin, was considered one of the most promising officers in the Union Navy and was highly thought of by both Porter and Grant. One of the Rebel shells ripped off his right arm and split him open, exposing his lungs. The Yankee doctors did everything they could to save him, but he died aboard a hospital ship on January 3, 1863. The *Benton's* demonstration accomplished nothing.

Colonel Edward Higgins, shown here after his promotion to brigadier general. A heavy artillery expert, Higgins commanded the northern anchor at Chickasaw Bluffs and the water batteries and most of the heavy artillery during the Siege of Vicksburg.

On December 28, the Yankees pushed Thomas' brigade back, which put the 26th Louisiana in a bad way. The Northerners took the woods to the Louisianan's right, where their sharpshooters opened up with enfilading fire. But behind the Rebels lay an open field sloping upward to the bluffs. A retreat would expose them from head to toe, so Colonel Hall's men remained in their rifle pits (i.e., trenches). The colonel recalled, "It seemed the night would never come. I wished for it as heartily as Wellington wished for night or Blucher at Waterloo." The regimental battle flag was penetrated by forty bullets that day. Lieutenant Lee, a cousin of General Stephen Lee and an officer on his staff, galloped up with an order for Colonel Hall. He galloped back with a finger in his mouth. A bullet had carried away a joint from his right forefinger. Remarkably, only seven Louisianans were killed that day, although several were wounded.

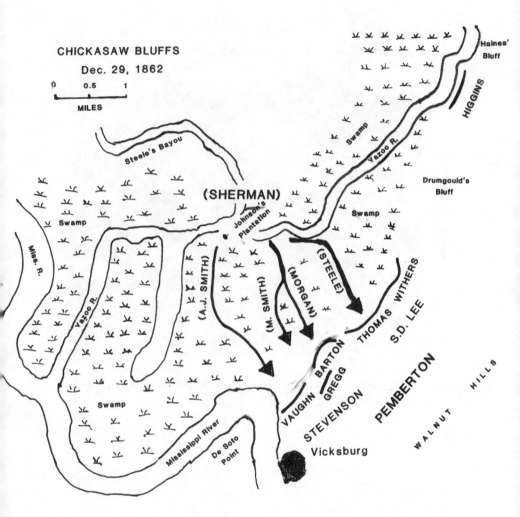

CHICKASAW BLUFFS

Dec. 29, 1862

0   0.5   1

MILES

Steele's Bayou

Haines' Bluff

HIGGINS

Swamp

Yazoo R.

Drumgould's Bluff

(SHERMAN)

Johnson's Plantation

Miss. R.

Swamp

Swamp

(A.J. SMITH)

Yazoo R.

(M. SMITH)

(MORGAN)

(STEELE)

THOMAS WITHERS

S.D. LEE

VAUGHN

BARTON

GREGG

STEVENSON

PEMBERTON

WALNUT HILLS

Swamp

Mississippi River

De Soto Point

Vicksburg

Map 4.1: The Battle of Chickasaw Bluffs

Rebel snipers were also giving the Yankees trouble. To their surprise, one of the bravest and most dangerous was a black Confederate soldier. Thomas Knox, a reporter for the *New York Herald*, who witnessed the action, wrote, "He mounts a breastwork regardless of all danger, and getting sight of a Federal soldier, draws up his musket at arm's length and fires, never failing of hitting his mark . . . It is certain that Negroes are fighting here [for the Confederacy] . . ." This disconcerted some of the less experienced Northerners, who had assumed that all African Americans supported the Union.[7] Most of them did, but certainly not all.[8]

Part of the 5ᵗʰ Georgia's "Clinch Rifles," a Confederate combat infantry unit which fought on the Western Front. Note the third man from the left.

General Lee and his staff, along with several ladies of Vicksburg, watched the battle from the bluffs, behind the 26ᵗʰ Louisiana. When night came, Lee ordered the regiment to withdraw.

At dawn on December 29, Sherman's front was much shorter. But Lee's front was also much thicker. Now that the Federals had committed themselves to battle at Chickasaw Bluffs, Smith's Division could safely be moved from Vicksburg and take positions on the Confederate left.

Harper's Weekly, *January 10, 1863, issue, showing two black Confederate pickets.*

By dawn, the Rebels' dispositions were complete. Left to right lay Brigadier General John C. Vaughn's Tennessee Brigade; Brigadier General John Gregg's Tennessee Brigade; and Brigadier General Seth Barton's Georgia Brigade and the 31st Louisiana Infantry Regiment which defended the critical Indian Mound. To Barton's right lay Lee's Provisional Division, with Thomas', Withers', and Higgins' provisional brigades. Lee now had ten thousand men and an ample quantity of artillery. Map 4.1 shows Pemberton's dispositions and Sherman's attacks.

Sherman's plans called for one division on each flank to launch a heavy diversion against the Rebels, while the main attack broke through the Confederate center. The spearhead was Sherman's 3rd Division, which was commanded by George Washington Morgan, a West Point dropout.

The Union infantry formed in full view of the Confederates and without one hundred yards of Company B/26th Louisiana. Although they had been instructed not to fire until ordered, "the temptation was too great for the naughty boys," Colonel Hall reported later. He again ordered them to cease fire, while the more astute Yankees ducked out of sight. Still the firing continued. After a sergeant from Company A fired against orders, the colonel ran over to him and gave him a "smart rap" on the back with the flat of his saber. Hall then posted himself in front of the regiment, cocked his revolver, and declared that he would shoot the next man who fired. To keep them occupied, he called them to attention and put them through the manual of arms, as if they were on parade—in full view of the enemy! When a no-doubt astonished General Lee rode up to observe this remarkable sight, they presented arms to him. He ordered the regiment to fall back a short distance to a place of safety.

The Northerners never fired on them. They were probably too shocked.

During the night of December 28–29, the Union engineers bridged the bayou to their front. When the cold, gray, overcast dawn broke, however, they realized that they had bridged the wrong stream. Also, they had expected to hear the sound of Grant's advancing army, but the only sound they heard was locomotives: the trains were carrying Pemberton's reinforcements.

General Morgan ordered the engineers to place the bridge in the correct spot, but it was too late. The Rebel sharpshooters drove the engineers back into the woods. Sherman ordered Morgan to advance anyway. They were going to have to suffer five thousand casualties to take Vicksburg and they might as well take them here, Sherman said. Morgan replied that Sherman's entire army could not take the position to his front, and the greater the number of men he sent in, the more men they would lose. Sherman commanded him to attack anyway.

Like several other Confederate regiments, the 60th Tennessee of Vaughn's Brigade was a recently formed unit which had never seen combat. It was placed in reserve, in a cotton field, when the Yankees started shelling it. The first shells overshot them by a wide margin, and the inexperienced Rebels laughed at the poor Northern marksmanship. They did not realize that the Union artillerists were ranging them. "In a little time the merriment ceased," Private Robert Bachman of Company G recalled, "for a shell fell in our company, passed directly through one man, then exploded wounding four others, one of whom died on the field." A fragment of the same shell knocked the bottom out of a soldier's tin cup and broke his bayonet in its scabbard. The Tennesseans promptly scampered for cover. "This was the first time we were under fire," Bachman recalled.[9]

After a fierce preliminary bombardment, Morgan struck across Chickasaw Bayou with three brigades abreast. Jared Young Sanders of the 26th Louisiana recalled, ". . . our infantry opened fire upon them & our cannon belched forth a perfect stream of lead and iron . . . Peal after peal from our batteries and the continued rattle of our rifles, mingled with shouts of men created a most 'indescribable confusion.'" Morgan reported that his men ran into "a perfect hail of artillery and rifle fire." Sherman later reported that his force "met so withering a fire from the rifle-pits, and cross-fire of grape and canister, that the column faltered and finally fell back, leaving many dead, wounded and prisoners in the hands of the enemy." Part of Colonel John F. De Courcy's Union brigade made it across the Bayou, but two Louisiana regiments were waiting on it. "I could see men falling by crowds—officers tumbling from their horses & horses dashing over the field," a soldier from the 26th Louisiana recalled, "and then our brave men began to fire in such volleys upon them that they could advance no further but turned about & made off 'at a run.'"

It was the same story all up and down the line. Brigadier General Francis P. Blair's brigade ran into Tennessee and Louisiana Regiments, which threw it back across the bayou. It left behind one hundred dead and more than five hundred wounded or captured. Morgan alone reported losing 1,652 killed, wounded, or missing.

Confederate veterans at a 1907 reunion.

As the Yankees advanced, the Confederates committed their reserves. Among others, Colonel John Crawford's 60th Tennessee Infantry Regiment rushed to the front line at double-quick time. A Union battery spotted them and opened up. "Shot and shell fell thick and fast among us," Private Bachman recalled. But the regiment arrived in time to help check the Northern assault.

The 6th (U.S.) Missouri managed to cross the bayou and pressed to the base of the Indian Mound, but there they ran into Barton's Georgians. The Yankees were pinned down and unable to move forward or backwards. They ended up scooping out dirt at the base of the hill with their bare hands, creating caves to give themselves some protection. The Rebels, right above their heads, held their muskets over the edge and fired vertically downward, without aiming, so they only exposed their arms, and then only briefly.

Colonel Hall of the 26th Louisiana recalled that the Union line of battle was formed and advanced at 10:00 a.m.

> A terrific storm of shot and shell now burst upon us, in its fury it seemed as if no living thing about us could escape . . . Under cover of shot and shell, the enemy advanced, with a force quite sufficient to carry our weak lines . . . every weapon on our side was warm, and every man was doing his best. Some approached within fifty yards of our line, but it was their last assault. Soon the line wavers and breaks, and confusedly attempts to retire. Many prefer surrender rather than being one of a mass our rifles could hardly miss . . .

After the assault failed, General Lee ordered the 26th to advance and secure whatever prisoners they could. But shortly thereafter, the Yankees seemed to be preparing for a second attack. Lee ordered his men to hold their fire until the bluecoats were within one hundred yards of the line. Captain Paul Hamilton, General Lee's adjutant, was killed, but the attack choked on its own blood. "Many of the wounded begged for water," the commander of the 26th Louisiana recalled. "I ordered water given to them, and their canteens filled."

As the Battle of Chickasaw Bluffs reached its climax, General Pemberton received an incredible dispatch from Joseph Johnston. Major General Carter Stevenson's division, sent by General Bragg pursuant to Jefferson Davis' orders, had arrived in Jackson. Did Pemberton want them forwarded to Vicksburg, or did he want to keep them in Jackson as a reserve? Johnston recommended the latter course. Pemberton was incredulous. "Yes, I want all the troops I can get," he responded. Stevenson's division began to arrive by train at the Vicksburg railroad depot just before nightfall. The noise of the locomotives and the cheers of the Confederates carried all the way to Northern lines, which did not make them feel any better.

As night descended, a cold, hard rain began to fall. "We bivouacked on the field," Robert Bachman of the 60th Tennessee recalled. "A tremendous rain fall. As I sat by a little tree, with my blanket wrapped about me, I could feel the water running down my back, and the ground upon which I sat was literally saturated." The Federals were particularly demoralized. In the darkness, the Yankees trapped at the base of the bluffs escaped, but only one at a time.

It was a miserable night for all concerned. A private in the 26th Louisiana recalled lying on a few rails to keep out of the mud, but he could not sleep. "I could hear the groans & piteous moans of the wounded & dying . . ." he recalled. "You cannot imagine how pitiful their cries did sound. They would cry out 'Oh boys! Come & help me' 'O God, I am dying' & all such exclamations that would make one's blood run cold."

The Union losses at Chickasaw Bluffs on December 29 were reported at 1,779 killed, wounded, captured, or missing, but were probably higher. Pemberton lost 187.

Sherman was not ready to give up. He was now low in ammunition, so he had to ask Admiral Porter to send a transport back to Memphis and bring back four hundred thousand rounds.[10] Morgan wanted to send out a delegation to the Confederates, asking to be allowed to retrieve his wounded. Sherman refused. Dozens of wounded Yankees suffered in the cold, rain, and wind. They agonized throughout the day on December 30, and many of them died. About the only action that took place this day was a foray from the 26th Louisiana. They quietly went forward and destroyed a bridge between the lines, in order to prevent the Yankees from bringing up artillery to support another charge.

Sherman finally relented after noon on December 31, when he sent a note to Carter Stevenson (who had superseded Stephen Lee and now commanded the Confederate defenses) and asked for a truce. Stevenson agreed and the Union medical corps went out to tend to the wounded and bury its dead. Even after the truce ended four hours later, at sundown, they continued their work. Neither side fired a shot.

During the night of December 29–30, Sherman decided that Snyder's Bluff (also known as Haines' Bluff) was the key to the Yazoo Valley. If it could be taken, his army could move up the Yazoo, land wherever they wished, cut Pemberton's rail line, and turn on Vicksburg and invest it. If he knew that the Rebels had erected a solidly constructed log boom (raft) across the river which completely blocked the stream, he did not act like it. He also planned to launch another attack against Chickasaw Bluffs on December 31, but his army was no longer up to it, so it never took place.

Sherman planned a night attack on December 31, 1862–January 1, 1863, in order to secure Haines' Bluff. His transports went forward, supported by a dozen of Porter's gunboats. But the fog and rain fouled up everything. Visibility dropped to less than ten feet and the steamers could not navigate or see Confederate mines. In addition, the aborted attempt drained the operation of the element of surprise.

New Years' Day, 1863, broke cold and wet. The Yankees could see increasing numbers of Rebels on top of the bluffs. No one wanted to try it again.

During the lull, General Lee invited Lieutenant Colonel Winchester Hall of the 26th Louisiana to his headquarters and fed him some cake and wine, compliments of the ladies of Vicksburg. He informed him that his promotion to colonel had been approved, so Hall received his third star.[11]

By now, the fourth Yankee attempt to capture Vicksburg had clearly failed. They disappeared on January 2. General Sherman did not withdraw to Memphis and rejoin Grant, as many people expected; instead, he went to the Louisiana side and established more or less permanent bases at Young's Point, Milliken's Bend, and Lake Providence.

The 17th and 26th Louisiana Infantry Regiments trudged back to their tents near the Vicksburg Cemetery in a driving rain. General Lee rode with the 26th Louisiana and awarded it "the post of honor" for the battle. (This was a strictly intangible honor.)

General Pemberton was less reticent on paper than in speech. He addressed his men in a letter, expressing his gratitude for their victories:

> The Lieutenant-General commanding the Department
> desires to express to the troops of his command his high

appreciation of their recent gallant defense of this important position. All praise is due them, not alone for so bravely repulsing the renewed assaults of an enemy vastly superior in numbers, but equally for the cheerful and patient endurance with which they have submitted to the hardships and exposure incident to ten successive days and nights of watchfulness in the trenches, rendered imperatively necessary by the close proximity of the opposed armies. While all have performed their duties with benefit to their country and honor to themselves, still, as must ever be the case in war, fortune has bestowed her opportunities unequally—to those who, by Her favor, held the posts of honor, and by their own resolute courage availed themselves of their opportunities, especial thanks are due; and it will be the pride and agreeable duty of the Lieutenant-General commanding to claim for them from their country the distinction and honor they have so justly deserved.

J. C. Pemberton

Lieutenant-General Commanding

Back in camp, Private Sanders of the 26th Louisiana wrote to a friend: "Since I wrote to you last I have seen the roughest side of a poor soldier's life. I have marched through rain & mud, passed sleepless nights in the hardest of weather, with nothing above me but the drenching clouds & beneath me—a wet blanket spread in the mud, upon a few sticks or bushes, perhaps to keep out of a mud-&-water bed. I have met the enemy; fought them, & seen the wounded, the bleeding & the dying upon two bloody fields."

Sherman selected George W. Morgan as the scapegoat for his failure at Chickasaw Bluffs and stopped just short of calling him a coward. Eventually a disgusted Morgan submitted his resignation. He was later elected to Congress from Ohio as a Democrat.

The city of Vicksburg, in the meantime, had already been transformed by the war. Rations were poor. Lieutenant Cantrell recorded that the 56th Georgia received "beef of the poorest quality, corn meal of the coarsest quality, black molasses, peas and sugar."

A soldier could supplement his rations by purchasing food in town, if he could afford it. Prices were high. A dozen biscuits cost $1 to $2, chickens ran $2 each, a dozen eggs cost $2, butter was $2 a pound, a gallon of milk sold for $2, and shoes were $15 a pair. A Confederate private was paid $13 a month—if the pay arrived. Often it did not.

General Joseph E. Johnston.

Meanwhile, an event occurred which would eventually prove devastating—and perhaps fatal—to the Southern Confederacy. Angry that Davis had taken Stevenson's infantry division from Braxton Bragg's Army of Tennessee, Joseph E. Johnston took Van Dorn's cavalry away from Pemberton and gave it to Bragg. These six thousand horsemen represented more than three quarters of the cavalry of the Army of Mississippi and included its best units. All of Pemberton's efforts to get it back or get it replaced were in vain. From early January 1863 on, Pemberton would be as blind as Lee was during the Gettysburg campaign.

CHAPTER V

THE CANAL, THE LAKE, AND THE RIVER

It had been proven that ironclads could successfully run the Confederate batteries at Vicksburg at night, but it was also known that transports and wooden cargo ships would be torn to pieces. If a canal could be dug across De Soto Point, they could pass without danger and Vicksburg would be bypassed and effectively neutralized. General Williams had begun such a project in 1862, but had to stop because he did not have enough men to complete it. But General Grant did—or so it was thought.

Ulysses S. Grant did not know much about the proposed canal, but Abraham Lincoln was enthusiastic about the idea and asked about it often, so Grant ordered General McClernand to look into it. McClernand passed the order on down to General Sherman.

Thousands of soldiers and contrabands went to work on the canal. (A contraband was the Federal name for a freed Negro who was not in the Union Army.) At one time or another, more than half of McClernand's and Sherman's XIII Corps was at work on the canal. The winter rains were heavy and the troops lacked shelter. Tents were not issued because they were within range of the Rebel guns at Vicksburg, and white tents made perfect targets. Some of the men dug holes in the levee and covered them with their black rubber slickers. It rained incessantly, the men were constantly cold and wet, and the river rose eight feet. Smallpox broke out, and hospital tents soon lined the back of the levee. Thousands were sick and hundreds died.

Grant's Canal, as it appears today.
Not much of the original canal remains.

The Yankees who were healthy and not digging made a nuisance of themselves. Stragglers and foraging parties ranged into the interior of Louisiana, and even General Sherman deplored the terrible misconduct of his soldiers. "Our armies are devastating the land," he wrote to his brother. "Farms disappear, houses are burned & plundered and every living animal is killed . . . Our soldiers are lawless . . ."

Major General Ethan Allen Hitchcock, the commissioner for prisoner exchange, agreed.[1] "Soldiers in plundering & burning make no discrimination between friends or foe," he wrote. "Even Negroes are plundered of their blankets, chickens, corn meal & their poorest garments." But little was done to discipline the looters.

Meanwhile, work on the canal continued. It was now sixty feet wide, thirteen feet deep, and more than a mile long. On Lincoln's personal orders, steam dredges and pumps were brought down from Cairo. Dams were constructed on either side to hold back the rising river. But General Grant was now in despair. Sylvanus Cadwallader recalled, "Our delay in completing the work had been so great that the Confederates had planted batteries on the opposite shore exactly opposite its mouth by which an enfilading fire could destroy vessels in the lower two-thirds of its length."

As the canal moved from the cypress swamp on the west to the low marsh near the river on the east, it came within range of the big guns of the 1st Louisiana Heavy Artillery Regiment. One gun in particular, an eighteen-pounder nicknamed "Whistling Dick" because of the sound of its incoming shells, blasted the workers and the steam dredges, which of course could not run, duck, or "hit the dirt."[2] Even so, Grant telegraphed General Halleck, the Union General-in-Chief, informing him that the canal was nearing completion, and he would be in Vicksburg within a month. As soon as this message went out, the northern dam collapsed and the Mississippi poured in on March 7 filling the canal with mud. The river still refused to be channeled into the canal, however. The Yankees who were still alive had to flee by steamboat to Milliken's Bend, twenty-five miles upriver.

This was the end of the fifth Federal attempt to take Vicksburg.

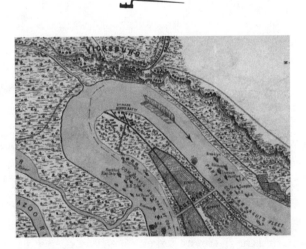

A Union Army map, showing the planned location for Grant's Canal.

In January 1863, there were thirty thousand Northern soldiers on the western (Louisiana) side of the Mississippi, from Young's Point (just opposite the Yazoo) to Milliken's Bend. Within a few weeks there were fifty thousand men, extending from Young's Point to Lake Providence, seventy miles north of Vicksburg.

Grant's army was between a river and a swamp. The sick roll was long. In addition to smallpox, men also contracted fatal cases of dysentery, typhoid, and measles. Then malaria broke out. The death toll averaged eighty-five per day. This was the equivalent of losing a regiment every ten days.

General Grant later claimed that he never had any faith in the canal project or the various bayou expeditions, but permitted them to go forward to exercise his men, so that they would be in good physical condition for the spring campaign. This statement must be taken with a pinch of salt. First of all, his correspondence at the time contradicts it. Secondly, the most incompetent second lieutenant in anybody's army could design a unit physical fitness program that would not kill eighty-five men per day—and Grant was not an incompetent officer. The reader, of course, must draw his or her own conclusions.

The North was understandably discouraged. Voluntary enlistments ceased. Grant felt that a withdrawal to a healthier climate would be interpreted as a defeat, so he refused to budge. Men were buried by the score.

Grant's next attempt to bypass Vicksburg involved connecting no less than five rivers and bayous, beginning with Lake Providence, a cut-off meander of the Mississippi, seventy miles north of the fortress, and ending with the Red River, which empties into the Mississippi, thirty miles above Port Hudson. The tortuous route was five hundred miles long but once completed, the Yankees could continue south and attack Port Hudson, or steam back 250 miles to the north, and attack Vicksburg from the south. To complete this ambitious project, the Northerners would have to take the following steps: blow the Mississippi River levee, which connected the river with Lake Providence; deepen Bayou Baxter, which would link Lake Providence with Bayou Macon; and then deepen

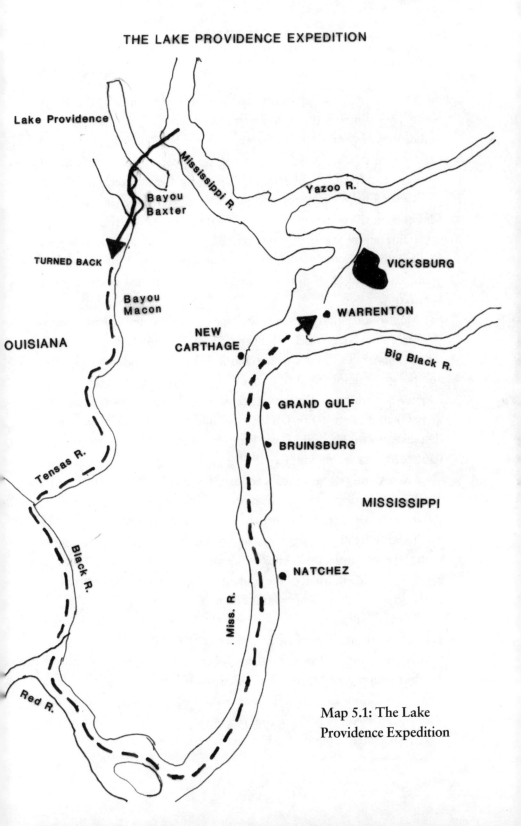

THE LAKE PROVIDENCE EXPEDITION

Lake Providence

Mississippi R.

Bayou Baxter

Yazoo R.

TURNED BACK

VICKSBURG

Bayou Macon

WARRENTON

NEW CARTHAGE

LOUISIANA

Big Black R.

GRAND GULF

Tensas R.

BRUINSBURG

MISSISSIPPI

Black R.

NATCHEZ

Miss. R.

Red R.

Map 5.1: The Lake Providence Expedition

most of the streams that connected Bayou Macon to the Mississippi River. To accomplish this, underwater snags would have to be identified and dealt with, and overhanging trees would have to be cut—many of them cypress trees, which are among the most difficult trees in the world to cut. Map 5.1 shows Grant's plan for the expedition.

To direct this operation, Grant selected Major General James B. McPherson, the commander of the XVII Corps. At age thirty-two, he was a fine engineer officer. Known to be very friendly, he was also very smart, and graduated first in his class at West Point. Both Grant and Sherman looked upon him as a possible future general-in-chief of the U.S. Army.

McPherson's first step was to impress slaves from nearby plantations to do the heavy work. McPherson himself commandeered Arlington, the home of a Confederate senator. It had an excellent wine cellar and the general and his staff had a fine time every night. They reportedly used the bottom floor as a stable and the upper rooms as living quarters and party central. They also had a steam tugboat in which they used to tool around Lake Providence every night, whilst being serenaded by a regimental band.

The general brought the steam dredges in from De Soto Point, and the War Department sent him a number of newly invented underwater steam saws. Unfortunately for the Yankees, Bayou Baxter was very small and ended up in a cypress swamp. The trees had to be cut almost to the level of the ground. The former slaves did most of the work and many of them died. Most of the soldiers occupied themselves by playing cards, shooting dice, fishing, and pitching horseshoes.

When Grant showed up to inspect the work, he was disappointed. There were so many narrow places along the route that even a small Confederate cavalry force could easily set ambushes, blast or capture and burn supply and transport vessels, block the route with logs, or create other kinds of havoc. He nevertheless allowed work to continue until the Mississippi fell, making the passage from the Mississippi to Lake Providence impossible. Then he abandoned the project altogether.

Thus ended the sixth Union attempt to take or neutralize Vicksburg.

To the shock and surprise of the Union Navy, the large riverboat *City of Vicksburg* steamed into the port of Vicksburg from the south, loaded with supplies, on February 1, 1863. It docked within sight of David D. Porter's flagship. The admiral was furious. The U.S. Army's ram fleet had just been placed under Navy command, despite the heated objections of Secretary of War Stanton, and Porter asked its commander, Colonel Charles R. Ellet, if he could sink the *City* with one of his rams. Ellet said that he could.

The next morning, Ellet moved down river with his best ram, the *Queen of the West*. It was loaded with two rows of cotton bales on the deck, to guard against Southern cannon fire. The *Queen* was supposed to ram the *City of Vicksburg* just aft of her wheel and then fire turpentine balls[3] into her to set her ablaze.

Porter ordered Ellet to launch a night attack, but he fooled around with preparations until after dawn. The *Queen* tried to ram the *City*, but an eddy in the river caught her at the last moment and her ram glanced off the boat. She fired her turpentine balls and set the steamboat on fire, but the Rebel guns blasted the Yankee ram and set her cotton bales aflame. "All hands on deck!" was called and the crew began tossing bales into the river, making themselves easy targets for the Confederate infantry. Still burning and under heavy fire, the *Queen* steamed to the west bank and the protection of Sherman's batteries. The damage, however, proved to be slight.

Porter now ordered the colonel downriver, to search for Rebel supply ships. Sherman gave him the unarmed river steamer *De Soto* as a support vessel. It wasn't long before the *Queen* captured the steamer *A. H. Baker*, which was carrying a typical load: one hundred and ten thousand pounds of barreled pork, five hundred live hogs, several tons of salt, and other supplies. Going down the Mississippi, Ellet captured several smaller supply vessels. He sent parties of "marines" ashore, to destroy wagons and burn plantation homes. For about two weeks the raid was very successful—until Ellet violated Porter's orders and steamed up the Red River, to capture a big Rebel gun which was rumored to be there. On the way, he captured another steamer, loaded with forty-five hundred bushels of corn. Eighty miles up the Red, he ran into an ambush. He found the big Rebel gun—and several others. Ellet tried to turn around but ran aground instead. He abandoned ship and he and his men were picked up by the *De Soto*, but it also ran aground. Again, they abandoned ship and escaped using the Confederate corn boat.

For two days, Ellet evaded Rebel steamers. He ran out of fuel and had to burn corn. Then they were rescued by the new ironclad *Indianola*, which Porter had sent downriver in case of just such an emergency.

CSS Queen of the West *and CSS* Webb *force the surrender of the* Indianola.

The captain of the *Indianola* hung around for two days. By now the Rebels had repaired the *Queen* and were joined by the *William H. Webb*, a converted steam ram. On the night of February 24, under a nearly full moon, the *Webb* and the *Queen* caught up with the *Indianola* and rammed her three times. She sank it in ten feet of water. The Southerners captured the crew.

The next day, Porter created a hoax ship, which appeared to be a large ironclad but was actually unarmed. They approached the *Indianola*, which the Rebels were in the process of salvaging. Thinking the hoax ship was a real ironclad, the Confederates blew up the *Indianola*.

Although the U.S. Navy got a great deal of satisfaction out of fooling the Rebels, this was certainly not a Union victory. The fleet had lost two of its strongest ironclads.

Meanwhile, the Yankees occupied the eastern parishes of north Louisiana.

Carroll,[4] Madison, Tensas, and Concordia Parishes were valued at $54.5 million in 1860, which was an astonishing amount for that day. Tensas, Carroll, and Concordia led the state in cotton production in 1859, and the value of their farms had increased from 600 to 700 percent between 1850 and 1860. The number of slaves increased proportionally. By 1860, 77 percent to 90 percent of the population in the four parishes was black.

Contrary to leftist mythology, the Northern soldiers were hard on Southern blacks. African American women frequently suffered violent rapes at the hands of their "liberators." Daughters were often raped in front of their mothers. U.S. Captain Eben F. Cutter, acting quartermaster of the "African Brigade" at Milliken's Bend, reported that he was "disturbed every night with complaints from black men that their wives were being ravished by white soldiers." Major Bryant of the 1st (U.S.) Mississippi Infantry Regiment, African Descent, testified that a dozen or more white soldiers had been arrested for attempted rape. Colonel Issac F. Shepard also reported rapes, as well as Negroes being robbed and their quarters ransacked and burned. God must weep, he wrote Grant, that such a "holy cause" as emancipation was being degraded by such "outrageous atrocities."[5]

Brigadier General Lorenzo Thomas, the U.S. adjutant general, however, saw a great deal of potential in the black population of the Louisiana and Mississippi Delta. He also formulated a plan to put the plantations on the west bank back into production. Of the roughly 150 plantations behind Union lines, most were now abandoned so that all but about ten were eligible for confiscation by the U.S. Army.

Thomas spoke to Union troops up and down the Mississippi about the idea of recruiting black soldiers. He correctly declared that, for every black regiment he raised, he freed a white regiment to fight the Confederates. For every black who stopped a bullet, there was a white man who didn't have to. Also, every former slave in the Union Army deprived the South of that much labor. The Rebels would need more white men at home to produce food.

Thomas succeeded impressively. He recruited seventy-six thousand men. This amounted to 40 percent of all African Americans who served in the U.S. Army during the Civil War. The Union high command did not view the new "African Descent" regiments Thomas organized as combat units, at least at first. (Later, several of them did see battle and some of them did very well.) They were primarily what the Germans in World War II called *Sicherung-Abteilungen* (security units). Their job was to secure the Union rear and to protect key installations from guerillas, partisan rangers, and Confederate raiders. By the end of the war, two-thirds of the forces guarding Union posts along the Mississippi River were black troops. (By then they were called "United States Colored Troops" or USCT.) They were, however, treated as second-class citizens by the Lincoln administration. The average black private, for example, was paid $10 per month, as opposed to $13 per month for the average white.[6] In addition, the white private received $3 per month clothing allowance. They deducted $3 per month from the black private's pay for the same purpose so, for all practical purposes, the white private received $16 per month, as opposed to $7 per month for the black. They were also given poor equipment and obsolete weaponry. Even worse, they usually received the least competent officers. This was certainly not always the case but, generally speaking, many of their commanders were men who could not gain promotion in white units. These incompetents got a great many former slaves killed in the years 1863 to 1865. During the Civil War, 14 percent of white Union soldiers died; the total in black units was 23 percent.

Thomas also leased a number of plantations to people who would later be called "Carpetbaggers." The Freemen on the plantations were paid $7 per month. Women received $5 per month, and children received half as much pay as adults. According to Private Samuel H. Glasgow of the 23rd Iowa, the new lessees did not have the best interests of the former slave at heart.[7] "Cotton closes their eyes to justice, just as it did in the case of the former slave masters," he wrote. Many blacks didn't find their situations on the leased plantations much better than slavery. They were often treated brutally and certainly were not allowed to leave. U.S. Brigadier General John P. Hawkins, the chief commissary of the XIII Corps, castigated the new lessees, and even suggested that, if better employers could not be found, the army should "send for their former masters and tell each one to claim his slaves, [because] his treatment of them was parental compared to what we now permit."

When it came to offenses against innocent Negroes, one of the worst offenders was Company A of the 10th Illinois Cavalry, which was supposed to be scouting for the African American regiments at Milliken's Bend. Its commander, Captain Christopher H. Anderson, admitted that half of his men viewed it as "a degradation to come in contact with Negro soldiers" and admitted that his men "abused Negroes."

Tensions came to a head on May 30, 1863, when two soldiers from the 10th Illinois Cavalry got drunk and wandered into the camp of the 1st Mississippi Infantry, African Descent. They found a black soldier tied to a tree, apparently as punishment for an infraction, and began to beat him. One of them kicked him so violently in the genitals that he was unable to work several days later. From there, they attacked Lizzie Briggs and her ten-year-old daughter. They forced the daughter to spread her legs, but Lizzie wrestled her away before they could rape her. The Yankees then threatened Lizzie with a hatchet. Lizzie's mother, who was very old, tried to save her daughter and granddaughter, but the bluecoats knocked her down and kicked her. Meanwhile, some more blacks appeared and tried to save the women. One Yankee knocked down a teenage boy and kicked him in the face, while the others ripped the clothes off of a Negro woman, but she managed to escape before they could rape her. More black men rushed to the aid of their women. The odds shifted, so the would-be rapists ran away, except for Private John O'Brien, who was captured.

Colonel Shepard, the commander of the 1st (U.S.) Mississippi Infantry Regiment, African Descent,[8] was a strong abolitionist. He ordered Private O'Brien whipped by members of his unit. Two white officers who witnessed the whipping found it inconsequential. The men used "twigs" that broke after a few blows, and one sergeant deemed the punishment "very light." The officers of the 10th Illinois Cavalry, however, flew into a rage, because a white soldier had been beaten by Negroes. They demanded Shepard apologize and resign. The enlisted men threatened to clean out "that damned nigger camp." Major Elvis P. Shaw of the 10th requested a court of inquiry.

In early June, Grant's inspector general, Brigadier General Jeremiah C. Sullivan, arrested Colonel Shepard. A court-martial was convened at Milliken's Bend on June 4. It met for ten days, interrupted by a Confederate attack. The court exonerated Shepard, on the grounds that too many abuses against black soldiers and their families had gone unpunished and ignored. It also pointed out that there had not been a single reported incident of abuse or attempted rape since O'Brien's "whipping."[9]

CHAPTER VI

THE YAZOO PASS
EXPEDITION

The Yazoo River and its tributaries offered several backdoor approaches to Vicksburg. One of these was via the Yazoo Pass, which was a bayou located five miles below Helena, Arkansas. It was fourteen miles long and had once emptied into the Mississippi, before the state sealed it off with a huge dike, one hundred feet wide and six feet high. Yazoo Pass now flowed into Moon Lake, then the Coldwater, Tallahatchie and Yazoo Rivers, which could be used to land troops behind Snyder's Bluff, which was 400 river miles away. Map 6.1 shows the Yazoo Pass Expedition as the Union commanders planned it in 1863.

Major General William Wing (W. W.) Loring took command of the 1st Division of the Army of Mississippi on January 2, 1863. Born in Wilmington, North Carolina, on December 14, 1818, his family moved to St. Augustine, Florida, in 1823, only two years after the United States acquired the territory from Spain. W. W. enlisted in the Florida Militia at age fourteen and was a sergeant three years later. He fought in the Great Seminole War of 1835–1842 and was promoted to second

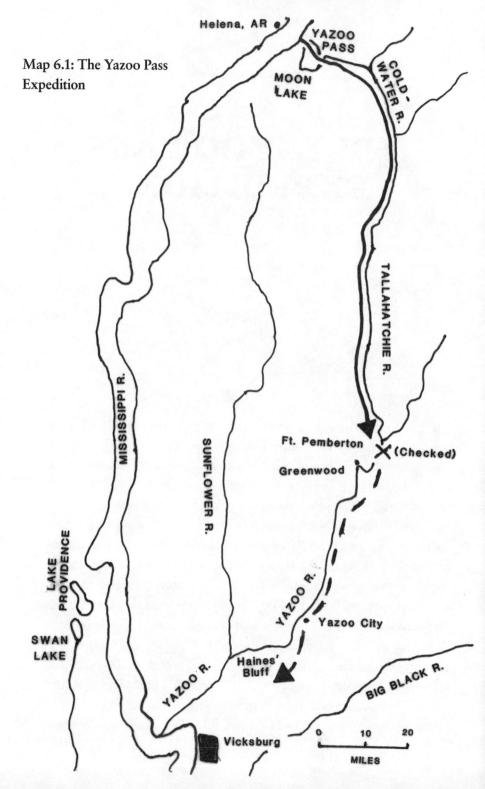

Map 6.1: The Yazoo Pass Expedition

lieutenant in 1837. He enrolled in Georgetown College in Virginia in 1839 but dropped out the following year in order to apprentice in the law office of Judge (later Governor) Robert R. Reid.

He became an associate of fire-eating Senator David Levy Yulee and was elected to the first Florida legislature in 1845.

When the Mexican War broke out in 1846, Senator Yulee secured for his young colleague a Regular Army commission as a captain in the Mounted Rifle Regiment. By 1847, he was a major. Loring fought at Vera Cruz, Contreras, and Churubusco, but his left arm was so badly shattered by a bullet at Chapultepec on September 13 that it had to be amputated. Loring, nevertheless, remained in the army and served mainly in the Mounted Rifles (later 3rd Cavalry) in the West and commanded the regiment from 1856 to 1861. He was the youngest old-line colonel in the army when the war began. He joined the Confederate Army in July 1861 as a brigadier general.

Loring had long experience on the frontier and was undoubtedly better suited to that duty than to higher command. He simply could not get along with his superiors. He was relieved by both Robert E. Lee and Stonewall Jackson, and Jackson would have court-martialed him had not Jefferson Davis blocked it. Instead, he was promoted to major general on February 15, 1862. Then, after briefly serving in the Suffolk area on the Virginia-North Carolina border, he was given command of the Department of Southwestern Virginia (later the Department of Western Virginia). Here he recaptured Charleston in September 1862, but was forced to abandon it the following month. A week later, General Cooper relieved Loring of his command as a result of a long-standing feud between W. W. and Governor Letcher. He was ordered to report to Jackson, Mississippi, as Lieutenant General Pemberton's second-in-command on November 27, 1862.

Predictably, Loring did not get along with Jack Pemberton, either. "I do not think much of the officer in charge [Pemberton]," he wrote to a friend on December 28. Pemberton nevertheless tried to get along with him and gave him command of the 1st Division.

W. W. Loring as a Confederate major general.

Loring's division including Brigadier General Lloyd Tilghman's Brigade, Colonel Albert Rust's Brigade and Colonel Thomas N. Waul's Texas Legion. Loring's Division remained at Grenada and held the Yalobusha River Line when General Pemberton went to Vicksburg during the victory at Chickasaw Bluffs.

Beginning on January 21, 1863, the Confederate outpost at Terrapin Neck on the Mississippi River, forty-six miles above Vicksburg, counted 107 steamboats and fifteen gunboats passing by in a seventy-two-hour period. They were heading for Helena and the Yazoo Pass.

The Yazoo Pass Expedition began on February 3, when the Federals blew up the Mississippi River dike at Yazoo Pass. The river at this point was nine feet higher than the countryside. By the next day, the gap in the levee was eighty yards wide. Colonel James H. Wilson, the Union engineer officer at the pass, called it "a perfect Niagara." Everyone headed for high ground, along with their livestock. The local plantation owners burned their cotton (if it wasn't already flooded) and warned the Rebels of the approach of the gunboats.

Because the Mississippi was higher than the water level in the pass, the Yankees had to wait four days, until they equalized. Then they entered the pass and the operation began in earnest. The naval contingent consisted

of two ironclads, five tinclads, and a tugboat. It was commanded by Lieutenant Commander Watson Smith, who was not healthy and was on the
verge of a nervous breakdown. Before he left Moon Lake, Smith was
reinforced with another gunboat and two rams. The army forces followed
with nine infantry regiments in thirteen transports, commanded by Brigadier General Leonard F. Ross. In all, he had forty-five hundred men.

Union progress was much slower than they anticipated. Moon Lake was
an oxbow lake (i.e., a former loop in the Mississippi that had been cut off when
the river changed course during geologic times). It was clogged with tangled
masses of trees, which had to be removed all along their route of advance.
Confederate engineers reacted quickly and made their tasks more difficult by
felling trees in front of the ironclads. They were joined by Black Bob McCulloch's 2nd Missouri Cavalry Regiment, which carried axes and sniper rifles.
Slaves from nearby plantations were commandeered by the Rebels and set to
work cutting trees. At one point, there were eighty fallen trees in a single mile
of river, and each one had to be removed singly. Sometimes they extended
from bank to bank. Union soldiers in parties of five hundred had to debark
from the transports and clear the trees from the river. It took the Yankees until
the end of February to navigate from Yazoo Pass (which the Federals called
Grant's Pass) to the Coldwater, a distance of only twelve miles.

Loring as a general in the Egyptian Army, 1873.

By mid-February, Pemberton had moved Waul's Legion to Yazoo City, forty-five miles north of Vicksburg. He met with Lieutenant Brown of the Confederate Navy and decided to construct a fort on a piece of dry land about a half a mile wide, just above Clayton's Bayou, with the Tallahatchie on the approaching side and the Yazoo on the other. He ordered eight guns, some of them big guns, to be hauled to the fort. On or about February 22, Pemberton ordered Loring to report to Yazoo City, where he placed him in charge of operations against Porter's flotilla. Loring hurried to Greenwood by boat, and then four miles to the west by water (two and a half miles by land) to the works, which he dubbed Fort Pemberton.

Because of the water obstructions, the Union campaign seemed to be moving in slow motion. They were also hampered by Commander Smith. He could only advance during hours of daylight, but he insisted on refueling during daylight hours. This wasted half a day every day. Smith also stopped about an hour every day for lunch. General Ross and Lieutenant Commander James P. Foster, the second-in-command of the naval task force, protested against this lack of urgency, but Smith ignored them. It was the beginning of March before Porter's boats entered the Tallahatchie. The going was much smoother now.

Fort Pemberton didn't look much like a fort. It was just above the surface of the water and was made out of three to five cotton bales stacked on top of one another, and layered four or five bales wide. The Rebels then threw dirt and sand on top of the bales, which were reinforced by logs. They built zig-zag breastworks in the fort and threw up fortifications on the right bank of the Yazoo, south of the fort. Their weapons included an excellent 6.4-inch Whitworth rifled cannon and a 32-pounder, which was much inferior to the 11-inch Dahlgrens on the ironclads. The garrison now consisted of about two thousand men, including the Texas Legion, the 2nd Texas, and 20th Mississippi Infantry, and the Pointe Coupee [Louisiana] Artillery, plus part of Loring's divisional artillery. To bolster the defenses, Loring ordered the USS *Star of the West*, a captured Yankee steamer, to be towed up the Tallahatchie to the fort, where it was swung squarely across the channel and sunk, blocking the only waterborne approach to the fort. Meanwhile, Tilgh-man's Brigade concentrated nearby at Yazoo City.

The Union flotilla approached Fort Pemberton on March 11. The defenders could see their black smoke when they were ten miles away. The large gunboat *Chillicothe*, commanded by Lieutenant Commander Watson Smith, led the way. The canal was so narrow that they could only advance with two boats at a time (i.e., with their boats in columns directly behind the lead two, instead of in line, which would have allowed them to bring multiple guns to bear.) The leading ironclads could not turn and could only use their bow guns against the fort. They could, however, still do damage. One shell from an 11-inch gun on the *Chillicothe* passed right through the parapet and ignited a powder magazine. Fifteen Louisiana artillerymen from the Pointe Coupee Battery were burned in the ensuing pyrotechnic eruption. Unfortunately for the Yankees, things began to come apart shortly thereafter. The Rebels opened up with five guns. A Southern shell flew straight into an open port and exploded, just as two big Union guns were about to fire. The explosion detonated two live shells inside the ironclad, killing or crippling fourteen men.[1] Commander Smith fainted. As soon as he revived, he ordered a retreat.

Meanwhile, the U.S. transports tied up well behind the gunboats at Shell Mound Plantation on the right bank. Indiana troops disembarked to probe against the Texas Legion, but the flooded terrain would not allow them to attack the enemy. Now the beauty of Pemberton's defensive position became evident: there was too much water for the Union soldiers to attack the fort or the Rebel infantry, but not enough for the Union Navy to launch a concentrated attack on either.

That afternoon, Federal scouts reported that the Rebels were driving their cattle and carrying equipment out of the fort—a sure sign they were about to abandon it. But it was a trick. The Rebels never intended to abandon the fort. The *Chillicothe*, with the ironclad *Baron De Kalb*, sallied forth again. The fort's guns opened up again and inflicted further damage. The ironclads withdrew after ten minutes.

At the same time, off the right flank of the fort, Lieutenant Henry of the 2nd Texas and his men were constructing canoes. They paddled over the river to spy on the Yankees but soon took to sniping. The gunboats responded by firing broadsides which "cut wagon roads through the canebrakes," as one Texan wrote, but it was a waste of ammunition. They didn't hit any Texans. The sniping continued.

About nightfall, the Union infantry landed a detachment at the edge of a piece of woods about seven hundred yards from the fort and brought ashore a 30-pounder Parrot. The next day, March 12, they placed another 30-pounder and a 12-pound howitzer.[2] They also converted three of their ironclads into "cottonclads." Meanwhile, elements of the 22nd Louisiana Infantry (a heavy artillery unit) arrived with another big gun.

A 12-pounder Confederate howitzer.

The third attack on Fort Pemberton began at 11:45 a.m. on March 13. The battle lasted five hours, with the three cottonclads and the shore battery firing dozens of rounds. The mortar boat *Lioness*, which had two hundred shells when it negotiated Grant's Pass, exhausted its ammunition on the fort. It did no good. The big naval projectiles bounced harmlessly off the breastworks, inflicting only minor damage here and there. Many of the shells simply buried themselves in the ground, while General Loring walked back and forth on top of the parapet, shouting:

"Give them a blizzard of shot, boys. Give them blizzards." From then on, his men called him "Old Blizzards."

Southern fire was somewhat more punishing. Thirty-eight Rebel shells hit the *Chillicothe* and caught the cotton bales on fire. Six sailors were wounded. The *Baron De Kalb* was hit six times, losing three killed and three wounded. Even inside an ironclad, men were killed or wounded by flying bolts and pieces of wood which were dislodged by Rebel shells and flew around the interior of the gunboat, like so many dangerous projectiles.

The USS Chillicothe.

The U.S. Navy licked its wounds on March 14 and 15, while the Confederates brought up an 8-inch naval gun from Yazoo City and mounted it. The Union infantry scoured the area for a viable approach to the fort but found none. The same water that flooded the countryside when the Yankees broke the Mississippi River levee now made it impossible to deploy the infantry against the fort.

The Northerners launched their fourth attack on March 16. They planned to push the cottonclads as close to the fort as possible and overwhelm it with shot and shell. But they could only get within eleven hundred yards of the fort, while Confederate gunners scored eight direct hits within fifteen minutes on the *Chillicothe*, sealing both forward gun ports so that they could not be opened. Commander Smith withdrew and then stepped down, handing command over to Commander Foster.

After this failure, the Union infantry spent March 16 through 20 trying to find an approach to the fort. After they failed, Foster and General Ross decided to retreat. As they withdrew, they ran into Brigadier General Isaac F. Quinby, the commander of the 7th Division, Army of the Tennessee, who ordered them to turn around. He was not convinced that the fort could not be taken and wanted to see for himself, so the Union expedition wearily turned about and tried again.

Meanwhile, someone suggested that another break in the Mississippi River levee might flood Fort Pemberton and drown Loring and his defenders. The break flooded more of the countryside, but not Fort Pemberton.

In the meantime, John C. Pemberton and W. W. Loring had several sharp exchanges. Loring wanted more troops and artillery. Pemberton tried to explain to him that there were no more troops available, Loring didn't need any more men or guns to turn back the Northerners, and even if he sent the requested reinforcements, Loring couldn't use them because of the limited dry ground available. (The second argument was true; the third argument appears to be inaccurate; and the first argument was subject to interpretation.) Pemberton did have almost twenty thousand men at Grenada, but he intended to use them against a possible Union invasion of northern Mississippi and to defend the northern approaches to Vicksburg. Loring disagreed with this strategy and openly and severely criticized his commander. Jack Pemberton's old friend, Brigadier General Lloyd Tilghman, allied with Loring.

Lloyd Tilghman was born in Maryland in 1816 and attended school in Baltimore. He entered West Point in 1831 at age 16 and graduated forty-sixth in his class. Commissioned in the dragoons, he resigned a few weeks after he matriculated and opted for a career as a civil engineer, mainly working for railroads. He returned to the army in 1846 to participate in the Mexican War, where he fought at Palo Alton and Resaca de la Palma. He was promoted to captain and commander of the Maryland and District of Columbia Volunteer Artillery. After the war,

Tilghman spent four years in Panama, building a railroad across the isthmus. Meanwhile, he and his wife had eight children, including three sons.

Tilghman settled in Paducah, Kentucky, and joined the State Guards. He was named commander of the 3rd Kentucky Volunteer Regiment in 1861 and on October 18 was promoted to brigadier general. Later that year, the Confederate secretary of war placed him in command of Forts Henry and Donelson.

General Grant landed on the east bank of the Tennessee River with twelve thousand men on February 6. Tilghman at Fort Henry had 2,610 men and eleven guns. He sent his infantry to Donelson and tried to hold against the Union gunboats, but surrendered ninety-four men (twelve of them in the hospital) after a two-hour engagement.

Tilghman spent the next six months as a prisoner of war at Fort Warren, Massachusetts. On August 5, 1862, he was traded for U.S. Brigadier General J. F. Reynolds, who had been captured by Lee's men at Gaines' Mill. The War Department sent him to Mississippi. He gave a speech at Clinton, after which Colonel McGavock remarked: "He is quite a demagogue—and lets off a great deal of gas."

He and Pemberton got along until the November retreat from northern Mississippi, during which Tilghman abandoned a number of large tents. For this act, he faced a court of inquiry, called by General Pemberton. Tilghman declared that, because the tents were wet and heavy, there was no time to load them on the wagons. The court cleared him, but it is obvious that Pemberton thought he acted improperly and should have been punished. The incident destroyed their friendship. Now he became one of Pemberton's more vocal detractors.

General Quinby, meanwhile, returned to the Fort Pemberton area and had no more luck than his predecessor. On March 23, the *Chillicothe* advanced again. The Confederates detonated a torpedo near her bow, causing her to withdraw. Quinby went ashore and established a headquarters in a farmhouse. He believed forces could be landed south of the fort and he could attack it from the rear, but he found that the Rebels had thrown up field works and were covered by artillery fire at the place where he intended to cross the river. His attempts to construct advanced artillery emplacements were hampered by flooding and heavy rains. Then, on March 29, Brigadier General Winfield Scott Featherson's Mississippi Brigade came up, as did Brigadier General John C. Moore's Texas Brigade. Pemberton had decided that an invasion of northern Mississippi was not in the offing and was clearly flooding the zone with soldiers. By April 1, Loring had more than seven thousand men.

On April 2, Major General Dabney H. Maury, who had arrived from Vicksburg the day before, probed Quinby's positions with the 37th Mississippi, the 1st Mississippi Sharpshooters, and the 2nd Texas Infantry. They were hampered by swarms of buffalo gnats.[3] Maury ordered his men to light fires so that the smoke might relieve them of the pests. Maury lost twenty-four mules that night because of the poisonous bites. But some of the Rebels reached the Tallahatchie and got behind the Yankee transports. The Northerners had to retreat rapidly. "Hit them on their way out!" Loring shouted. They were pursued by Brigadier General James Z. George's Mississippi State Troops, as well as the 26th Mississippi and 2nd Texas.[4] But the gunboats and transports made good their escape. The last one reentered the Mississippi by April 14. The seventh Federal attempt to capture Vicksburg had failed.

Ironically, the Yankees cut the Grand Levee of the Mississippi, causing the Yazoo to begin to rapidly rise on April 6. They intended to flood the Greenwood area, in order to prevent the Rebels from operating against their boats. The water forced Loring to temporarily evacuate Fort Pemberton on April 10, and the Yazoo River raft at Snyder's Mill was swept away on April 16.

CHAPTER VII

THE STEELE'S BAYOU EXPEDITION

General Ulysses S. Grant and Admiral David D. Porter were in the dark. They could not communicate with the Yazoo Pass Expedition, and they did not know that Generals Quinby and Ross had joined forces, or what had happened to them and the gunboats. They were understandably worried that the Expedition might have been cut off and was facing destruction. Admiral Porter therefore devised an innovative rescue scheme that would save Quinby and Ross and simultaneously bypass Fort Pemberton and open a back door to Vicksburg. Grant approved it immediately and named Sherman officer-in-charge of the Steele's Bayou Expedition (also known as the Deer Creek Expedition).

The plan, shown in Map 7.1, called for Porter to steam up the Mississippi River to Steele's Bayou. They would then proceed to Black Bayou, Deer Creek, Rolling Fork, the (Big) Sunflower River (twenty-five miles west of Fort Pemberton) and on to the Yazoo, twenty miles above the Confederate batteries at Haines' Bluff.

THE STEELE'S BAYOU EXPEDITION

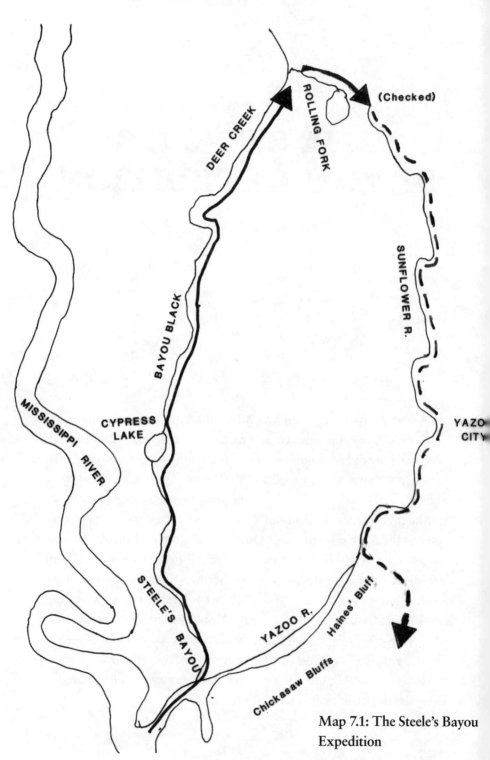

Map 7.1: The Steele's Bayou Expedition

Porter entered Steele's Bayou on March 14. The naval forces included five ironclads, four mortar boats, and four tugboats. They were followed by Sherman in the transports. He had seven thousand infantry.

Because of the high water caused by the levee cuts, the ironclads passed over drowned roads and houses. The water was at least fifteen feet deep. The gunboats only needed seven feet. But still there were serious problems. The streams were narrow and the higher trees swept away everything on deck, including the tall smokestacks, the pilothouses, and loading tackle.

Because of the flooding, varmints had climbed into trees to escape drowning. Every time a Yankee ship bumped a tree (which was often), a shower of snakes, raccoons, rats, mice, possums, lizards, roaches, and other insects poured onto the deck. Sometimes this menagerie included a wildcat or two. Water moccasins were the worst. Although rattlesnakes are more poisonous, they are generally not as dangerous, in my opinion. It is the instinct of the rattlesnake to flee, if possible. It is the instinct of the water moccasin to attack, whether flight is possible or not.

Navigation was obscured by the smoke of burning cotton. Wherever there was dry land, there seemed to be burning cotton. "Why did those fools set fire to that cotton?" Admiral Porter shouted to an old man.

"Because they didn't want you fools to have it," the Mississippian shouted back.

Steele's Bayou and Black Bayou were not too difficult to navigate and were behind them by the end of the second day, but Deer Creek was very tough for the sailors. It was only thirteen miles from the entry point at Black Bayou to the creek's exit point at Rolling Fork, if one went by land, but it was twenty-six miles by water. Porter's lead vessel was forty feet wide and the width of the stream was around forty-six feet. There were some six thousand bales of burning cotton on both sides of the stream. When a slave told him that the cotton would burn for three days, Porter decided that he could not wait. He forged ahead and barely made it through. The leading ironclad actually ran over a bridge. Because of the smoke from the burning cotton, it did not see it until it was too late.

Submerged vegetation was also an obstacle. Progress slowed to four miles a day.

The ironclads did not have tall masts like the transports, so they made better speed. Admiral Porter decided to leave the transports behind. That was a big mistake.

General Pemberton reacted quickly to the latest Yankee threat. He knew the local terrain much better than did Grant or Porter. He ordered his district commander, Carter L. Stevenson, and his divisional commander, Major General Dabney H. Maury,[1] to send Brigadier General Winfield S. Featherston's Mississippi Brigade to the junction of Deer Creek and Rolling Fork. Stephen Dill Lee at Fort Pemberton decided on his own to reinforce Featherston with one of his regiments.

The first Rebels to arrive in the sector were a battalion of infantry, six field pieces, and about fifty cavalry from Lee's brigade, all under the command of Lieutenant Colonel Samuel W. Ferguson. By now, the Confederates had perfected their techniques for dealing with Yankee gunboats. This time they did not cut down trees in front of the boats as before but now cut them down behind the gunboats. Porter forged ahead, oblivious to the fact that he was in a trap and pushing deeper into it with every mile he traveled.

On March 21, Porter reached Rolling Fork, the pass that would take the flotilla into the Sunflower River, which was wide and deep. There was a large patch of green vegetation in the way. Porter and all of his men thought it was some kind of pond scum, so they plowed into it. It was small willows. They stopped every boat in the fleet and held them. The Yankees tried to back out but could not do so, no matter how much steam they applied. They were stuck fast.

The sailors pulled out saws, cutlasses, axes, and anything else they had. When they cut some of the willows, others popped up. They simply could not free themselves or even move. Then they heard the boom of a Whitworth rifled gun. They knew that they were in serious trouble. Colonel Ferguson renewed his attack. The Rebels were closing in and Porter's men could not use their big guns, because the banks were too high and so close that they could not get the elevation they needed to fire. Rebel sharpshooters opened up from behind trees.

Fortunately for the Northerners, the four mortar boats were able to get the range and silence the Confederate guns, at least for the moment. But Porter knew that Pemberton would soon be sending more men and guns. His only hope was Sherman, who was back at Deer Creek. However, Sherman had no idea that the fleet was in danger.

During the lull, a slave offered to carry a message to General Sherman for $.50. Porter quickly paid the money and scribbled out a note on a piece of tissue paper. Sherman judged the note to be authentic, hurriedly off-loaded a rescue party, and sent it on a forced march to save Porter, who was thirty miles away.

Meanwhile, the admiral learned that two thousand Rebel infantrymen had landed up ahead at Rolling Fork. He believed he could hold off the Rebels, but was afraid they might be able to block Sherman and starve the gunboats into submission. He ordered everyone below, forbade anyone to go up on deck, and put everyone on half rations. He made plans to blow up his fleet and escape through the swamps, if necessary.

About that time, to Porter's great relief, Sherman's rescue party arrived. It included Colonel Giles Smith's 6th Missouri. It was enough of a force to protect the fleet for now, but not enough to drive off the Rebels. Smith reported that more than forty large trees had been cut behind the gunboats.

During the night of March 21–22, the water suddenly rose. No one knew it at the time, but this was caused by General Quinby's second levee cut. Porter was able to back out, although he lost all of his rudders. The next day, the crippled ironclads linked up with Sherman's infantry. They would not make it back to the Mississippi until March 27, after what Admiral Porter called "an eleven-day excursion into futility."

The eighth Northern attempt to take Vicksburg had failed.

If Pemberton had Van Dorn's cavalry, he might have succeeded in destroying most of Porter's fleet, including the seven gunboats. On March 21, from his headquarters in Jackson, Pemberton telegraphed Johnston in Tullahoma, Tennessee: "Have you separated the cavalry with Gen'l Van Dorn from my command entirely? If so, it very much diminishes my ability to defend the Northern portion of the State as the planting season comes on."

Until now, Pemberton had only mildly objected to Johnston's failure to return his cavalry. Apparently, he thought these six thousand horsemen would be sent back to him by spring. The protests grew much stronger from this point on, as it dawned on him that Johnston *never* intended to return his cavalry. He never did. On April 2, a frustrated General Pemberton went over General Johnston's head and wrote to Jefferson Davis: "It is indispensable that I have more cavalry." He made a similar request on April 10. Again, it did him no good.

Meanwhile Johnston, who clearly favored the Army of Tennessee, denied Pemberton's request for mounted troops. Instead, he was so pleased with Pemberton's victories that he asked him to return the nine thousand troops President Davis had transferred from Bragg's army in December. On April 13, Pemberton (who was always a team player) agreed to send him Rust's, Abraham Buford's and Tilghman's brigades to Tullahoma. This he did not do, however, because Ulysses S. Grant got in the way.

Meanwhile, on March 14, 1863, Admiral Farragut tried to run the batteries at Port Hudson.

Port Hudson had a natural bluff, 60–80 feet high. It had a steamboat landing, several warehouses, hotels, saloons, and a few other businesses. In 1862, President Davis decided to make it the southern bastion of his Mississippi River defenses. It was initially commanded by Brigadier General William N. R. Beall,[2] but he was superseded by General Gardner in December.

Franklin Gardner was born in New York City in 1823. He attended West Point, and graduated four places ahead of Ulysses S. Grant in 1843. He distinguished himself in Mexico and was appointed lieutenant colonel in the Confederate Army in March 1861. (He had married into the famous Mouton family of Louisiana.) He served in Tennessee and

Mississippi, and commanded a brigade of cavalry at Shiloh. Promoted to brigadier general on April 11, 1862, and to major general on December 13, he commanded a brigade in the Kentucky invasion before being sent to Louisiana.

Gardner was an excellent commander whose abilities have not been fully appreciated by Civil War historians. Immediately upon assuming command, he began to expand and improve the existing fortifications on both the land and river sides. When he finished, a two and a half mile stretch of river was defended by forty-three guns, varying in size from 6-pounder field guns to huge 10-inch Columbiads and 32-pounder rifles. To defend the land side, he had ten thousand men in March 1863.

Major General Franklin Gardner.

Gardner and Farragut both expected U.S. Major General Nathaniel P. Banks, the commander of the Army of the Gulf, to attack Port Hudson with fifteen thousand men. But Banks did nothing, so Farragut acted without him.

Farragut's fleet included three steam-screw[3] ocean-going ships of the line. They were the *Hartford* (the flagship), the *Monongahela*, and the *Richmond.* He also had the *Mississippi*, an older sidewheeler which had been Commodore Matthew Perry's flagship during his voyage to Japan.

Farragut also had four smaller gunboats and six mortar ships. In all, he had ninety-two guns. But running the Port Hudson batteries, he could only bring his starboard guns to bare, reducing his effective strength to forty-six guns. Worse still, he would be steaming against a five knot current, which gave him a forward speed of three knots (3.45 miles per hour). He would be in range of Southern guns for more than an hour. Also, the Rebel gunners on the bluff could use plunging fire on the ships, while Farragut's men would have trouble elevating their guns to the level of the highest Rebel batteries.

South of Port Hudson on the morning of March 14, the Northern fleet made their final preparations. They wrapped heavy chains around their starboard sides, to deflect Confederate shot, and they used cotton, boilerplate and anything else they could think of to protect vulnerable machinery. Three of the four smaller gunboats were lashed to the port (non-fighting) side of the big ships, to provide power in case their engines were damaged. This they could not do for the *Mississippi* because of its side paddle wheel.

All of the time they were being watched by Confederate outposts. There would be no surprise in the Northern attack. At 10:00 p.m., the signal was given. The *Hartford* went first, followed by the *Richmond*, the *Monongahela*, and the *Mississippi*.

The night was so black that some of the sailors thought the Rebels would not see them. This was wishful thinking. General Gardner was prepared for this. Suddenly, on the west bank, several huge bonfires leapt to life, illuminating the entire fleet. All of the Southern guns opened up at once. The *Hartford* was hulled several times. The Union guns fired back, and the Rebels fired at the flashes of the Yankee guns. One shell tore the leg off of the captain of the *Hartford*, Commander Cummings. He bled to death within a minute or so. Almost simultaneously, a solid shot ripped through the hull of *Richmond* and into the engine room, where it struck a main valve, sending scalding steam throughout the engine and steam rooms. The ship's steam pressure dropped to zero. Unable to make headway, even with the help of the small gunboat, the *Richmond* came about and retired. Unfortunately, the *Richmond's* gunners were working so hard and rapidly that they did not realize they were turning around. They fired on the *Mississippi*, scoring a number of direct hits on what they thought was a Confederate vessel. To avoid being sunk by the *Richmond*, the *Mississippi* turned abruptly and ran aground on a sandbar—directly under Rebel guns, which systematically blew her apart.

The USS Mississippi *(center).*

The commander of the *Mississippi* was Lieutenant (later Admiral) George Dewey, a brilliant naval officer who would later achieve international fame in the Battle of Manila Bay during the Spanish-American War. He recalled hearing the blood-curdling Rebel yells from above and thinking, "How they must hate us!" He organized a lifeboat relay and saved the lives of several of his wounded crewmen, but the ship was doomed. When the force of the river knocked it loose, there were only dead men on board. Engulfed by flames, it drifted south until the fire reached the magazines, and it disintegrated in a tremendous explosion.

The *Monongahela* was only just entering the combat zone when a Rebel shot jammed her rudder and she ran aground. The force of the grounding was so great that the lashed-on gunboat, the *Kineo*, ripped free and plowed deeply into the mud. The *Kineo* managed to free itself and then freed the *Monongahela* but in the process broke its crankshaft. It drifted south, out of the battle, while Confederate gunners pounded it until it was out of range. It lost twenty-seven crewmen killed or wounded.

The USS Hartford.

Only Admiral Farragut and the *Hartford* (along with its attached gunboat, the *Albatross*) successfully ran the batteries. The rest of the fleet turned about with heavy casualties, but the *Hartford* and *Albatross* continued north and ran by the Confederate defenders at Grand Gulf before they could fortify the place. They would soon be in a position to shell Vicksburg from the south.

The Union fleet running the batteries at Port Hudson.

Since he had tried every other direction, Grant decided to outflank Vicksburg to the south. He wanted to build a canal which would connect Duckport Landing on the Mississippi River with Walnut Bayou, allowing the Federals to reach New Carthage, Louisiana, by flatboat. This route could be used to supply an army on the east bank, south of the Confederate Gibraltar. But it turned out to be just one more futile attempt to undermine the Vicksburg defenses.

On March 31, six companies of Union engineers began to dig a canal seven feet deep, forty feet wide, and three miles long, connecting the Mississippi with Walnut Bayou at Cooper's Plantation. Progress was rapid and, at noon on April 13, they cut the levee, and four steam dredges entered the canal and began deepening the channel. Water levels in the bayou, however, did not rise as expected. Once again, the Mississippi River refused to cooperate. It started to fall and, by May 4, the Northern engineers gave up hope. Two dredges and twenty barges were marooned in the canal and in Walnut Bayou. Only one vessel, a tugboat, reached New Carthage.

The ninth Federal attempt to capture, bypass or weaken the Vicksburg defenses had failed. Grant would have to march across east-central Louisiana if he wanted to take Vicksburg via the southern route—which is exactly what he did.

CHAPTER VIII

TO GRAND GULF

A s the spring of 1863 approached, there was a considerable amount of frustration north of the Mason-Dixon line. The North appeared to be unable to take advantage of its vast numerical superiority. During the war, the U.S. put 2,672,314 men under arms, including 190,000 African Americans, 210,000 German mercenaries, 130,000 Irish mercenaries and 60,000 British and Canadian mercenaries. Southern manpower estimates are spotty because so many Confederate records were destroyed at the end of the war, but they fielded 750,000 to 900,000 soldiers and sailors. The figure 800,000 appears to be about right, giving the North an overall strength advantage of 3.34 to 1. Their superiority in armaments and manufacturing made the advantage even greater, and the South was never really able to compete with the North as a naval power. By the beginning of April 1863, the Union Army had more than 900,000 men under arms, while the South had fewer than 600,000. Yet little progress was being made.

In 1861, a frustrated Abraham Lincoln asked the first Union general-in-chief, Winfield Scott, how it was that he could take Mexico City with five thousand men, but could not take Richmond with one hundred thousand men?

"You want to know?" Scott replied. "I will tell you. The same men who took us into Mexico City are keeping us out of Richmond."

Lincoln fired Scott shortly thereafter. And he was just the first. Irwin McDowell, George C. McClellan, John C. Fremont, James Shields, John Pope, Ambrose Burnside, and Don Carlos Buell, among others, had been sacked or demoted—mostly Democrats. Lincoln's propensity to play political games with the army cost a great many men their lives in the 1861 to 1865 period. Lincoln and his advisors had not yet decided to fire Ulysses S. Grant, but he was definitely on a short leash in April 1863.

There can be no doubt that Grant was at a low point in his professional career. He had promised to be in Vicksburg by March, but was farther from the city now than he had been in December. He had made four attempts to take the city by military force, all of which had been defeated by John C. Pemberton: the winter offensive of 1862, which was ended by the Holly Springs Raid; Chickasaw Bluffs; the Yazoo Pass Expedition; and the Steele's Bayou Expedition. Grant's Canal had also been a Union defeat, although the Rebel artillery was not the decisive factor. He had also failed at Lake Providence and Duckport. Naval action against the Confederate Gibraltar was also singularly unsuccessful. All of this added up to too many failures. The press was after him. Secretary of War Stanton was so alarmed that he began drawing up orders replacing Grant with Benjamin Butler. General McClernand, an Illinois politician in civilian life, was plotting to have Grant replaced—with himself. He told his friend Lincoln that he was tired of supplying all the brains for the Army of the Tennessee. McClellan, Fremont, and David Hunter were also mentioned as possible replacements, in addition to Butler and McClernand. This was hardly an all-star lineup. Had Grant been sacked at this point and been replaced by one of these generals, the South would likely have won the war. Even Grant's friends, however, were beginning to turn on him. Brigadier General C. C. Washburn complained to his brother Elihu, one of Grant's sponsors, that the Vicksburg campaign was being "badly managed." He concluded: "I fear Grant won't do." Lincoln and General Henry Halleck, the general-in-chief who replaced McClellan, were showing signs of impatience. Public opinion had definitely turned against him.

Grant now decided to try to take Vicksburg from the south. It was, after all, the only point on the compass he had not tried. He knew that it would be his last attempt—one way or the other.

As spring approached, Lieutenant General John C. Pemberton was looking good. Despite the fact that he had no navy and was outnumbered more than two to one, he had checked Grant four times by military action (five if Grant's Canal is counted), and his forces had also smashed Farragut's fleet at Port Hudson and held the place against Banks' army. But Pemberton had his own problems. He had proven that he could hold Mississippi without a navy, but could he hold it without cavalry?

On March 21, he had asked that his horsemen be returned from the Army of Tennessee, but Johnston, who clearly favored that army, did nothing. He did not bother to reply himself but had his chief of staff, Colonel Benjamin S. Ewell, write Pemberton: "In the present aspect of affairs, General Van Dorn's cavalry is much more needed in this department [Tennessee] than in that of Mississippi and Eastern Louisiana, and cannot be sent back as long as this state of things exists. You have now in your department five brigades of the troops you most require, viz., infantry belonging to the Army of Tennessee. This is more than a compensation for the absence of General Van Dorn's cavalry command."[1]

Lieutenant General John C. Pemberton, early 1863.

This dispatch was untrue on a number of points. The cavalry *was* more needed in Mississippi, as General Pemberton foresaw and as we shall see. Pemberton most certainly did not need infantry more than cavalry. Even without Van Dorn's men, the Army of Tennessee still had Forrest's cavalry and that of Joseph Wheeler and John Hunt Morgan, so the cavalry could have been sent back. The infantry in question certainly did not compensate for the absence of cavalry. And the infantry in question (Stevenson's Division) did not belong to the Army of Tennessee. President Davis had transferred it to the Army of Mississippi over Johnston's heated objections. And here's the rub. Joseph E. Johnston was a petty and vindictive man. He did not accept the transfer as justified or permanent. In his mind, Stevenson's Division belonged to Bragg's Army of Tennessee. Now Pemberton had it. Very well. Now he would have to pay for the presidential override of Johnston's strategy by doing without cavalry.

On March 25, 1863, Pemberton advised Colonel Ewell that the dirt roads were drying and it would soon be practicable for Union artillery and wagons to use them. "I shall need all the cavalry force withdrawn from this department, under General Van Dorn, to cut his [Grant's] communications."

On April 20, he wrote Johnston again, stating that "Cavalry is indispensable to meet these expeditions [Union cavalry raids] . . . I have literally no cavalry from Grand Gulf to Yazoo City."

There were other instances of Pemberton begging Johnston for cavalry, but I don't see any reason to go into detail about them. The reader has gotten the point by now.

Johnston was not the only one Pemberton asked for horsemen, or at least for mounted help. On March 24 and later, he appealed to Major General Simon B. Buckner in Mobile, Alabama, and asked for the loan of a cavalry regiment. He was turned down. Buckner probably wondered, Why should I send Pemberton my cavalry? Johnston should take care of that![2]

The grave of Earl Van Dorn (right rear), Port Gibson, Mississippi. He is buried beside his father. His government marker is his footstone. For 150 years, historians have believed he was shot by a jealous husband on May 7, 1863. Bridget Smith of Raymond, Mississippi, however, has discovered the truth: although the general was having an affair with his wife, Dr. Peters did not shoot him for that. He shot Van Dorn because the general was fooling around with Peters's nineteen-year-old daughter, whom he impregnated. The entire story is told in Smith's Where Elephants Fought: The Murder of Confederate General Earl Van Dorn.

In March 1863, Jefferson Davis finally demoted the incompetent Theophilus Holmes, removing him from the command of the Trans-Mississippi Department. He replaced him with Edmund Kirby Smith.[3] Kirby Smith had proven in the Kentucky Campaign of 1862 that he was anything but a team player, but at least he didn't hate Pemberton personally, so the Philadelphian telegraphed him for help:

My cavalry is weak and wholly inadequate, either to cut the lines of communication of the enemy with the Mississippi River, or to guard and protect my own. Vicksburg (consequently the navigation of the Mississippi River) is the vital point indispensable to be held. Nothing can be done which might jeopardize it . . . You can contribute materially to the defence [sic] of Vicksburg, and the navigation of the Mississippi River, by a movement upon the line of communication of the enemy on the western side of the River. He derives his supplies and his re-enforcements, for the most part, by a route which leads from Milliken's Bend to New Carthage, La., a distance of some thirty-five or forty miles. To break this would render a most important service.

But Kirby Smith was no help either. He fell for a Union feint up the Red River and concentrated his meager forces for the defense of Shreveport. All he had left in northeast Louisiana was Colonel Frank A. Bartlett's 13th Louisiana Cavalry Battalion near Lake Providence and Major Isaac F. Harrison's 15th Louisiana Cavalry Battalion, operating out of Richmond, Louisiana.[4] Together these two battalions totaled only about five hundred men—hardly enough to make a difference.

Somewhat ironically, after he had failed to get any civilian cooperation in South Carolina, the only help Pemberton received in Mississippi was from John J. Pettus, the governor of Mississippi. He gave him mounted state troops, which Pemberton's officers organized into the 1st Mississippi Cavalry Regiment under the energetic William Wirt Adams.[5] Also, in spite of the growing opposition from Mississippi farmers, Pemberton continued to impress their horses to mount his infantry. It was not big enough to accomplish much, but it was better than nothing.

Pemberton began to pay for his lack of cavalry in April 1863. Grant summoned Colonel Benjamin Grierson to his headquarters and ordered him to ride into central Mississippi and do as much damage as he could.

Grierson was a thirty-seven-year-old Illinois music teacher who didn't like horses because a pony had kicked him in the face when he was a child.[6] He nevertheless became a cavalry brigade commander and, on April 17, rode out of the Union base at La Grange, Tennessee, with seventeen hundred men. He travelled light: five days' rations, six light artillery pieces and forty rounds of ammunition. Spies provided him with the locations of well-stocked warehouses and plantations.

Because of the absence of Confederate cavalry, Grierson advanced eighty miles in less than three days with almost no opposition. He captured Pontotoc, along with nearly two hundred sick or wounded Rebels, on April 20. The next day, he tore up the tracks of the Mobile & Ohio Railroad. On April 24, he captured the important supply point of Newton Station, halfway between Jackson and Meridian, and tore up the Southern Railroad of Mississippi. He blew up two locomotives and destroyed thirty-eight boxcars of supplies and ammunition bound for Bowen's forces at Grand Gulf, three hundred thousand percussion caps and thirty thousand pounds of gunpowder. The bluecoat cavalry continued south, tearing up bridges, freeing slaves, capturing isolated detachments, and generally creating panic and havoc throughout central Mississippi. Oddly enough, however, Grierson earned the nearly universal admiration of the people of Mississippi by his conduct. One lady, a Southern partisan, wrote: "Colonel Grierson was spoken of everywhere . . . as a gentleman who would not allow his men to treat any one with the slightest disrespect, or take the least article from a citizen's house; and they all treated ladies courteously. There was not one instance of unkindness to any human being, as far as I could learn."

Pemberton wanted to keep a strong force under Loring in the vicinity of Grenada, but, without cavalry, he was forced to use Loring's Division to counter Grierson, or at least to minimize further damage. He ordered Loring to Meridian with the 15th Mississippi, the 26th Mississippi, and part of the 14th Mississippi. Pemberton later wrote that Grierson's Raid "compelled me to divert Loring's entire Division to the line of the Mobile & Ohio, and other railroads, when I most needed the presence of this Division near Vicksburg."

Loring concentrated at Enterprise, in order to save the supply depot there. Grierson arrived outside the town on April 25 and demanded its surrender. Loring refused, so Grierson rode on. He was pursued by Adams' regiment, the small and poorly disciplined 1st Tennessee Partisan Ranger Regiment under Colonel Robert V. Richardson, and part of Loring's infantry division. None of these had any chance of bringing Grierson to heel. He took Hazelhurst, southeast of Grand Gulf, and captured a long train, including boxcars full of artillery shells, ammunition, and other stores, en route to Port Gibson and Grand Gulf. Shortly thereafter, he captured and burned a large wagon train near Hazelhurst. Colonel Grierson reached Union-held Baton Rouge on May 2, after a ride of six hundred miles.

Grierson's total casualties were three killed, seven wounded, and nine missing. Five soldiers too sick to finish the raid were captured, for a total of twenty-four casualties. He inflicted twenty times that number on the Confederates if Pontotoc is included. More importantly, he tied down an entire Confederate infantry division, part of which was engaged in a futile attempt to capture him and part of which successfully guarded most of Pemberton's supply depots and wagon trains—but none of which was available when Ulysses S. Grant crossed the Mississippi south of Vicksburg. The raid was also a portent of things to come. Up until this point in the war, all of the great mounted operations had been conducted by Confederates. This was the first successful Yankee cavalry raid of the war.

On April 27, Pemberton signaled Johnston,

> However necessary cavalry may be to the Army of Tennessee, it is indispensable to me to keep my communications. The enemy are to-day at Hazelhurst, on the New Orleans and Jackson Railroad. I cannot defend every station on the road with infantry. Am compelled to bring down cavalry from Northern Mississippi here, and the whole of that section is consequently left open. Further, these raids endanger my vital positions . . .

Johnston, however, considered Federal forays into northern Mississippi and the Grierson raid nothing more than "predatory incursions," not a prelude to bigger events. He finally promised to send Pemberton a cavalry brigade, but it never arrived.

It must be noted here that Pemberton was wrong to pursue Grierson with infantry. This was an overreaction, perhaps born out of frustration. He had no chance of capturing the Union horsemen with foot soldiers and, as a result, none of Loring's regiments were available to help Bowen in the Battle of Port Gibson—not that they would have changed the result of the battle. They would not have (see below).

Grant's strategy was to land the bulk of his army in northeastern Louisiana, march south along or near the west bank of the Mississippi to a point south of Vicksburg, and then cross the river. To facilitate this maneuver and to prevent Pemberton from concentrating against him, he created four diversions: 1) Grierson's Raid, 2) the Greenville Diversion, 3) the Sherman Diversion, and 4) the Hurlbut Diversion.

Grierson's raid was tremendously successful, as we have seen. The Greenville Diversion (April 2–25) was an operation directed by Major General Frederick Steele. His division was shifted from Young's Point, Louisiana, to Greenville, fifty miles north of Vicksburg. This move had two purposes: to destroy supplies along Deer Creek and around Greenville; and to help convince Pemberton and Johnston that Grant was moving away from Vicksburg. It was not as ambitious as the Grierson Raid and was not as devastating, although it did achieve some success.

The raid began on April 4, when the Yankees advanced southeast of Greenville, where they plundered and destroyed a great many farms and plantations, burned houses and other property, and carried off many African Americans. The area was a major source of supplies for the Army of Mississippi, and Pemberton had no choice but to react to it. He sent Stephen Dill Lee and his brigade to Deer Creek to counter it. They arrived on April 8 and checked the Yankee invaders, who retreated to Greenville on April 10. "The Yankees had no regard for honor, nor respect for human feelings," Lieutenant Cantrell of the 56th Georgia commented as he observed the desolated landscape.

Pemberton left Lee's Brigade in the area until April 28, "during which time our principal employment was fishing," one officer noted. This prevented the Northerners from sallying forth again, but of course it also meant that another brigade was not available south of Vicksburg.

The Deer Creek diversion succeeded in convincing Johnston that Grant was moving away from Vicksburg and that the Northerners had (at least temporarily) given up on taking the fortress, and that Grant was going to reinforce the Army of the Cumberland, which was operating against Bragg. As was typical, Johnston immediately began badgering Pemberton for reinforcements for his pet Army of Tennessee (although he later claimed this was Pemberton's idea), and on April 7 even President Davis asked Pemberton if he could send reinforcements to Bragg. And as was typical for Pemberton (the team player), he offered Johnston Brigadier General Abraham Buford's Brigade from Port Hudson (four thousand men), although he expressed no opinions as to what he thought were Grant's intentions. But Pemberton changed his mind on April 16 after his commander in northern Mississippi, General Chalmers, sent a dispatch stating that sixty-four steam boats had left Memphis, loaded with troops, "ostensibly to attack Vicksburg." Pemberton declared that there was evidence that "no large part of Grant's army would be sent away."

He was right.

Stationed in Memphis, western Tennessee, and northern Mississippi, Stephen Hurlbut's U.S. XVI Corps controlled twenty-five thousand men, including an entire cavalry division. Opposing him was Brigadier General James R. Chalmers, who commanded a small cavalry brigade of perhaps fifteen hundred men, plus a few state and local defense troops; and Brigadier General Daniel Ruggles, commanding the Subdistrict of

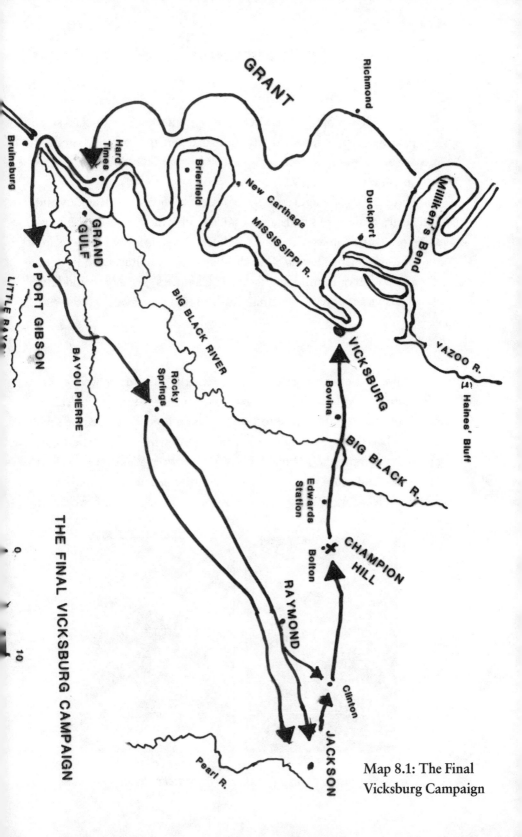

Map 8.1: The Final Vicksburg Campaign

Northeast Mississippi.[7] He had very little except some fourth-class state troops. Together, Chalmers and Ruggles had perhaps forty-five hundred men. It was absolutely necessary for Pemberton to hold northern Mississippi, in order to supply his army.

Hurlbut probed aggressively against Chalmers and Ruggles and launched a number of small cavalry raids against them, making it impossible for Pemberton to withdraw Chalmers' Brigade without sacrificing the food-producing regions of north Mississippi. Chalmers and Ruggles did a good job of minimizing damage. Chalmers' Brigade would later distinguish itself as part of Nathan Bedford Forrest's cavalry (1864–65).

Major General Carter Stevenson was the first to recognize that Vicksburg was vulnerable from the south, which constituted an Achilles heel. On March 5, he wrote to Pemberton and recommended he send Bowen's Division (with artillery) to Grand Gulf, which was the best port and thus the most likely Union landing site between Vicksburg and Port Hudson. Pemberton was also concerned that Grant might maneuver south of Vicksburg or succeed in bypassing it by establishing a workable canal.

Carter Stevenson, as a young U.S. Army officer and after the war.

To prevent this, he decided to establish a third fortress on the Mississippi. (Vicksburg and Port Hudson were the other two.) He decided to fortify Grand Gulf, at the mouth of the Big Black River, twenty-five land miles south of Vicksburg (fifty miles by river). On March 9, more than two thousand Missouri soldiers marched toward Grand Gulf. On March 11, he assigned the task of fortifying this position to Brigadier General Bowen. Map 8.1 shows Grand Gulf and Grant's subsequent moves which led to the Siege of Vicksburg.

Ephraim Anderson of the 1st Missouri Brigade recalled that the area was "beautiful and picturesque, though the town was now but a mass of ruins; the charred walls, blackened chimneys, and isolated pillars were all that was left, except two solitary houses, of that once flourishing little city, which contained probably two thousand inhabitants."

The man in charge of defending Grand Gulf, John Steven Bowen, was born in Georgia in 1829 into an upper middle-class family. He attended the prestigious Milledgeville Academy and then West Point.

He was suspended for a year for covering up for a classmate but graduated in 1853, thirteenth out of a class of fifty-two. The number one graduate was James B. McPherson, a close friend who later commanded the Lake Providence Expedition.

Major General John S. Bowen as a Missouri colonel before the war.

Lieutenant Bowen served as a training instructor at the Cavalry School at Carlisle Barracks, Pennsylvania, and at Jefferson Barracks, near St. Louis, Missouri, where he met and married the beautiful and feisty Mary Kennerly. In 1855, he joined the 1st U.S. Cavalry Regiment in west Texas, where he fought Comanches and Mescalero Apaches. Bowen resigned on May 1, 1856, returned to St. Louis, became an architect and lived in the affluent suburb of Carondelet. A former U.S. army captain named Ulysses S. Grant also lived in the area. Grant was at a low point in his life and was reduced to cutting firewood and selling and delivering it to more successful people. The "West Point Protective Association" (an unofficial group) is well known in today's army, but it also functioned very efficiently in the 1850s. Bowen bought his firewood exclusively from Grant (apparently including his architectural firm) and the two became friends.

Bowen became a lieutenant colonel in the Missouri Volunteer Militia in 1859. He organized and commanded a battalion on the Kansas frontier, guarding against abolitionist raids. He was captured in the Union surprise attack on the Missouri State Troops in Camp Jackson (near St. Louis) in 1861. Upon release, he visited Jefferson Davis in Richmond and received a colonel's commission in the Confederate Army. Bowen initially directed the 1st Missouri Infantry Regiment. A brigade commander by fall, he was promoted to brigadier general on March 14, 1862. Bowen distinguished himself at Shiloh, where he had two horses shot out from under him. Late in the afternoon of April 6, a shell exploded near him, killing his horse and throwing multiple fragments into his right shoulder, neck and side. It was thought that the wound was mortal, but he recovered in time to participate in the Battle of Corinth. Afterwards, he preferred charges against Earl Van Dorn for mishandling the battle, but the army commander was acquitted.

Bowen was undoubtedly the best of Pemberton's generals. He earned the sobriquet "the Stonewall of the West" and was so good that some historians have incorrectly referred to him as Pemberton's second-in-command. He was in fact outranked by Major Generals Loring, Stevenson, Smith, Maury, and John H. Forney, and some of the brigadiers as well. Pemberton described him as "one of the best soldiers in the

Confederate Army" and promoted him to divisional commander above a number of his contemporaries.[8]

In addition to being a fine architect and an excellent combat leader, John Bowen was a fine military engineer. To assist him, Pemberton sent Major Samuel H. Lockett, his best engineer. Grand Gulf was an excellent defensive position already, but Bowen and Lockett converted it into a maze of fortifications. They rounded up slaves from nearby Claiborne County plantations and put them to work, side by side with the Missouri infantry. Both black and white men worked day and night.

The northernmost defensive structure in Grand Gulf was Point of the Rock, where the Big Black emptied into the Mississippi. Here Bowen constructed Fort Cobun, which included big siege guns manned by Captain Henry Grayson's Company A, 1st Louisiana Heavy Artillery Regiment.

Bowen had the trenches covered by planks. They extended three-quarters of a mile along the base of the bluffs and on the east bank of the Mississippi, and featured a double-line of well-sited rifle pits. The Rebels constructed a southern anchor called Fort Wade. Bowen placed land mines along the river, in front of the earthworks. A second defensive position was built behind it, featuring infantry supported by field guns. Initially, only four 20-pounder Parrots under Colonel William Wade, Bowen's chief of artillery, protected the main fortifications.[9]

The only extant Confederate ambulance, Grand Gulf, Mississippi, 2017.

Because of the Confederate resistance during Farragut's attempt to capture Vicksburg in 1862, the Yankees destroyed the town of Grand Gulf. Only one or two houses survived.[10] This left plenty of bricks in the ruins. Bowen had them gathered up. He used them to construct two hot-shot furnaces, which were used to heat cannon balls, which would then perhaps set Union naval vessels on fire. Bowen also had his men scour the ruins of Grand Gulf for iron, iron bars, railroad spikes, nails, scrap iron, and Union shell fragments, which Colonel Wade converted into homemade canister.[11]

Bowen had to obstruct both the Big Black and Bayou Pierre, which entered the Mississippi just south of Grand Gulf. He blocked the bayou with trees, sent a battalion with two guns to Winkler's Bluff, and obstructed the river with trees cut by slaves. Four miles up the Big Black, at Thompson's Hill, he stationed Colonel Elijah Gates' 1st Missouri Cavalry (Dismounted)[12], as well as a battalion of Arkansas sharpshooters, to protect Grand Gulf's rear.

At daybreak on March 19, wooden Union warships suddenly appeared from the south and probed the defenses, but did nothing more. The next day, the CSS steamer *Anne Perette* (which had barely escaped on the nineteenth) boldly ducked out of the Big Black and entered Grand Gulf, where they offloaded four large-caliber guns with naval gun carriages. Pemberton, meanwhile, dispatched two more heavy guns from Vicksburg and detained three heavy guns intended for gunboats on the Trans-Mississippi and kept them in the fortress.

Throughout the department, logistics was a nightmare. Pemberton was supplying Vicksburg, Jackson, Port Hudson, Fort Pemberton, and Grand Gulf. With a shortage of rolling stock, and unable to obtain spare parts for locomotives because of the blockade, and badly damaged by Grierson's cavalry, the Mississippi railroads basically collapsed. The section of the Southern Railroad connecting Vicksburg to Jackson effectively ceased to function. Pemberton was now partially forced off the Mississippi by Porter and Farragut, so he had to rely on wagons. Labor continued at Grand Gulf, despite the fact that the troops had only cornbread to eat most days and not enough of that.

Shortly after 8:00 p.m. on March 31, Farragut attacked Grand Gulf with the *Hartford* and the *Albatross*. Bowen was taken by surprise. He had set up an outpost downriver at Hard Times Landing, but their signal rockets were defective. The Rebels nevertheless reacted quickly and got off a few cannon shots but without doing much damage.

One Confederate 20-pounder inside Fort Wade exploded, killing "a nice, intelligent Irishman" and wounding several other men. They were taken to Port Gibson, Private William L. Truman of Wade's Missouri Brigade recalled, where "they received royal attention and were soon back on duty." The garrison suffered more casualties when the 20-pounder exploded than it did from Yankee gunfire.

⌐⌐‾‾‾‾

The tenth Union attempt began in March 1863, when Ulysses S. Grant concentrated two of his corps at Milliken's Bend, Louisiana. He intended to drive south down the Louisiana side of the river, cross it at Warrenton, and take Vicksburg from the south. Grant's forces in Mississippi, Louisiana, western Tennessee and western Kentucky totaled one hundred and thirty thousand men, including more than fifty thousand in his field force. His main units included McClernand's XIII Corps (spearheading the advance); McPherson's XVII Corps (following McClernand); Sherman's XV Corps (northeast of Vicksburg, including elements at Greenville); and Stephen Hurlbut's XVI, a large corps of twenty-five thousand men (in reserve in and around Memphis).

Grant began his long march on March 29. It was a nightmare. Progress was slow because of the winter rains, which turned the dirt roads into ribbons of deep mud. The wagon road from Milliken's Bend to New Carthage was barely above water. Because of a levee break, a couple of miles of it was under water. As a result, Grant's vanguard did not reach New Carthage until April 6. The rest of the army was strung out for miles.

When Grant's army reached New Carthage, opposite Davis Bend and Brierfield, it could not occupy it because it was flooded, and only the roofs of the houses were visible. The Yankees continued marching south.

Major Isaac F. Harrison commanded the 15th Louisiana Cavalry Battalion. In early April, he spotted a large column of Federal infantry, cavalry, and artillery moving south from Milliken's Bend. Although part of the Trans-Mississippi Department, he took it upon himself to inform General Bowen of this development.

At first, Bowen thought it was a raid or a foraging party. But more Northerners appeared. Bowen now took the new developments more seriously and, early on April 4, wrote Pemberton and asked permission to send troops to eastern Louisiana to aid Major Harrison. Pemberton hesitated. He would be crossing the boundary line from his department to the Trans-Mississippi Department without informing General Kirby Smith, much less obtaining permission. Harrison continued to monitor the situation, continued to report to Bowen, and started conducting hit-and-run raids against the Yankees. Bowen now became more alarmed. This was not a foraging party!

When he did not hear from his commander by early afternoon on April 5, John Bowen sent the 2nd and 3rd Missouri Infantry Regiments (more than one thousand men) of Colonel Francis Cockrell's Missouri Brigade across the river without permission.[13] Later he sent two more regiments. He now had more than two thousand men in Louisiana.[14] They travelled by flatboats, propelled by oars. Bowen, who remained at Grand Gulf, now had less than one thousand men. He had plenty of artillery, but only the 6th Missouri Infantry Regiment. Pemberton did not officially grant him permission to cross the river until April 8.

On April 7, Bowen informed General Pemberton that McClernand's XIII Corps—fifteen thousand men—was north of Bayou Vidal, near Richmond, Louisiana. He speculated that they might be en route to Natchez. There was more or less constant skirmishing, but the Confederates were in delay mode only and refused to become decisively engaged. They did not have the men.

On April 14, while Grant continued to trudge south through Louisiana mud, Pemberton notified Johnston that, according to his scouts, Grant had ordered two hundred wagons down from Helena, Arkansas. He also forwarded Chalmers' reports that Union transports, loaded with troops, were steaming south. Grant's intentions were still unclear. Operating with hindsight, some historians have proclaimed that Pemberton should have realized that the main threat was south of Vicksburg and should have sent his entire strike force to Grand Gulf and Port Gibson. But Pemberton also had to take into account that Sherman was lurking just northeast of the city with an entire corps, and Hurlbut had another corps at Memphis which could easily be transported by river. President Davis had ordered Pemberton to hold Vicksburg at all hazards, and this was what he intended to do. If he had moved south, as they suggest he should have, Sherman and Hurlbut could easily have taken the city. This would have placed Pemberton between Grant and Sherman and without adequate means to resupply his army. This, of course, does not mean that Pemberton was entirely unaware of what Grant might be up to, but he simply could not defend everywhere and still hold Vicksburg.

Logistics was another restraining issue. In his brilliant reevaluation of Pemberton in the Vicksburg campaign, Major Malcolm G. Haynes of the U.S. Army's Command and General Staff College estimated that Pemberton needed a 2.5 to 1 attacker to defender ratio to check the Union advance. The U.S. advanced forces totaled about seventeen thousand men. Bowen would therefore need six thousand eight hundred men to check Grant. Naturally they would have to be fed. A division of six thousand men required eighteen thousand pounds of food per day—exclusive of ammunition, fodder and other supplies. Pemberton had no logistical bases or infrastructure in eastern Louisiana. He would therefore have to transport these supplies to Grand Gulf and then ship them across the river via steamboat. He had neither the wagons nor the boats to accomplish either task. ". . . supporting a division across the Mississippi was an unrealistic endeavor for Pemberton to undertake," Major Haynes concluded.[15]

It is obvious that Grant would need naval support to cross the Mississippi. The remnants of Farragut's fleet, which managed to run the guns at Port Hudson, would not get the job done. Help would have to be provided by Admiral Porter's fleet from the north.

On March 11, Pemberton telegraphed President Davis from Jackson and asked for more heavy guns. "If enemy increases his fleet you will have to increase my guns," he warned.

The Confederate River Defenses at Vicksburg were commanded by Colonel Higgins. The upper (northern) batteries were directed by Colonel Andrew Jackson, III, and consisted primarily of his own 1st Tennessee Heavy Artillery Regiment. The central command directed the guns along the city's waterfront and were commanded by Major Fred N. Ogden. The lower (southern) batteries were manned by Higgins' own 1st Louisiana Heavy Artillery Regiment, now directed by Lieutenant Colonel Daniel Beltzhoover. In all, Higgins had thirty-seven heavy guns in the Vicksburg sector, as well as thirteen field guns. The latter would be deadly if Grant launched an amphibious assault on the city, but useless against ironclads. All in all, the River Defenses presented a formidable lineup but hardly an overwhelming one.

Porter's fleet shoved off at 10:00 p.m. on April 16. It included the ironclads *Benton, Lafayette, Louisville, Mound City, Pittsburgh, Tuscumbia* and the now repaired *Carondelet*. Each had a large coal barge lashed to it. Logs, wet cotton and hay bales were placed on the port side to absorb Rebel shells. Three transports also accompanied the gunships.

The Yankees hoped to take the Rebels by surprise. That, of course, did not happen. The fire was terrific. One Northern newspaperman counted 525 discharges in an hour and a half. When the fleet reached the hairpin turn at the city, the Rebels set off a string of bonfires. Fortunately for the Yankees, the Confederates were using artillery fuses which had recently arrived from Richmond. They had not been tested and many were defective. This may have saved a good part of the Union fleet. All of the ironclads got through, although all sustained damage. Only one transport was sunk.

As soon as he learned that Porter had run the batteries, Pemberton knew that any hope he might have had about checking Grant in eastern Louisiana was dead. He ordered Bowen to withdraw his men from the Bayou State immediately. He had to move quickly, or Porter would cut him off. There was a wild race to the "mosquito fleet," as the civilian cargo vessels and flatboats which had transported Cockrell to Louisiana were called. Most of these boats only carried five or six passengers. Cockrell nevertheless won the race, but there was now nothing to slow Grant's march south except an understrength local cavalry battalion.

The vulnerable civilians on the west bank were subject to "general plunder and indiscriminate conflagration." Private Anderson of the 1st Missouri Brigade recalled that the residence of Dr. Bowey, "one of the handsomest of the many princely establishments in Louisiana, was burned by the Federals, with all its furniture . . . The usages of civilized war were utterly disregarded, and private property and the persons of non-combatants were subject, the one to destruction or appropriation, the other to insult and outrage."

Confederate Senator John Perkins knew that his plantation, "Somerset," was about to be captured, so he burned it himself, in order to deny the Yankees the satisfaction.[16] At a nearby plantation, the bluecoats stole $30,000 worth of silver. Every plantation in the area was sacked and most of them were burned.

Sarah Anne Dorsey left a record of how the Yankees broke into the house of Mr. K., a wealthy planter, who was not in the house at the time. They found his wife ill, with her three-day-old son lying by her side. They accosted and insulted her, and then grabbed her maid, a mulattress, threw her onto the bed, and ripped off her clothes. Mrs. K. begged, screamed, and tried to save her servant from the would-be rapists. "They replied with oaths and indecent ribaldry," Mrs. Dorsey recounted. Mrs. K. fainted. At that moment, Mr. K. returned and was so overcome by the scene that he had a seizure. This stopped the Northerners, who thought he was dead. They looted the house, swearing and cursing. After they left, Mr. K. gradually revived.

Meanwhile, Pemberton ordered Green and his Arkansas/Missouri brigade to Port Gibson, as well as the 6th Mississippi Infantry Regiment, the 1st Confederate Infantry Battalion, and the Virginia Battery. He signaled Kirby Smith and Major General Richard Taylor in Louisiana: "I cannot operate effectively on the west bank of the river; the enemy is now in force at New Carthage and Richmond. I beg your attention to this." He telegraphed Kirby Smith on April 18: "Without [your] co-operation it is impossible to oppose him [Grant]." He made a similar appeal on April 22. Even Joe Johnston signaled Kirby Smith and asked him to make a heavy demonstration with cavalry against Grant's line of communication.[17]

Now one of the flaws in the Confederate command system made itself apparent. The Trans-Mississippi Department was completely independent of Johnston's Department of the West. Johnston could request Kirby Smith's cooperation, but he couldn't order him to do anything. Despite the fact that the Trans-Mississippi had some of the best cavalry in the world, Kirby Smith did very little—and nothing until June, when it was too late.

Grant initially planned to land at Warrenton, ten miles south of Vicksburg. Once he got to the west bank opposite the town, however, he discovered that the current was unfavorable and it would take hours to launch a successful landing. In that time, Pemberton could rush heavy reinforcements to Warrenton and might wipe out the landing, so Grant changed the target to Grand Gulf. Because he was going to have to land farther south, he was going to need more supplies than initially planned; They would have to be delivered by river. A second running of the Vicksburg batteries would be necessary.

On April 22, six wooden transports and a dozen barges, all loaded with provisions, tried to run the batteries. One transport and half the barges were sunk, but five transports and six barges reached Grant. They carried one hundred thousand rations. Grant was now ready to cross the Mississippi.

Bowen was ready to try to stop him. He cut the levee north of Grand Gulf and flooded the entire area. Many potential landing sites were under water.

Pemberton was still checked by the XV Corps. Grant ordered Sherman to create a diversion and, on the morning of the twenty-seventh, he feinted an attack on Haines' Bluff. Pemberton later wrote: "Was not Sherman's large force—two-thirds of my entire strength—still at Haines' bluff on the city's very rim, prepared to march in if I marched out?" He did, however, send Brigadier General Edward D. Tracy's Alabama Brigade from Warrenton to Port Gibson.[18] They marched nonstop for twenty-seven hours to join Bowen. He also sent Brigadier General William E. Baldwin's Mississippi brigade, which marched rapidly toward Port Gibson.[19] But Pemberton was still not sure that Grant was desperate enough to risk his entire army by moving it along a single, vulnerable road, extending thirty-seven miles through the Louisiana swamplands.

Grant, however, was exactly that desperate.

From his outpost on Point of the Rock, Bowen could see Grant's assembly area at Hard Times Landing on the west bank through his binoculars. He signaled Pemberton that transports and barges were loaded down with troops. He estimated that he was facing almost thirty thousand men.

General Stevenson doubted this report. He was convinced Grant's drive south of Milliken's Bend was a feint. Sherman reinforced this false belief by moving up the Yazoo and demonstrating against Haines Bluff and Drumgould's Bluff on April 29 and 30. Pemberton, meanwhile, signaled back to Bowen: "Have you now force enough to hold your position? If not, give me the smallest additional number with which you can. My small cavalry force necessitates the use of infantry to protect important points."

Grant was confident that Grand Gulf "would fall easily." Porter agreed. His seven ironclads had eighty-four heavy naval guns, and he thought they could easily knock out the eight Rebel heavy guns. The fleet steamed toward the bluffs at 7:00 a.m.

Grant and Porter were wrong. The Rebels blasted Porter's flagship, the *Benton,* which was hit by hot shot and was soon on fire. Corporal

Leland of Wade's Missouri Battery was in charge of one of Captain Grayson's heavy siege guns because his field gun had been disabled earlier that day. Leland took aim at the *Tuscumbia* and turned to Private Dey. "Now, Frank, I have a good bead on that porthole of the gunboat, now fire!" Dey jerked the lanyard and the big shell flew straight through the porthole and exploded. In 1871, Seaman Harpell of the *Tuscumbia* told Dey that the explosion killed thirteen men, wounded many more, severely damaged its machinery, and pulverized one of its two engines. The *Tuscumbia* drifted downstream, out of the battle. All of the other ironclads were damaged to a lesser extent. Admiral Porter was on deck, encouraging his men. General Bowen recognized him and ordered his infantry not to fire on him.

The USS Benton.

Private Truman of Wade's Missouri Battery called his commanding officer, Lieutenant Richard C. Walsh, "a talented, brave, competent officer." He always stood with both feet far apart. On this day, a huge Union shell passed between his legs below the knee, inflicting a flesh wound on both limbs but doing no serious harm to the lucky lieutenant.

The Yankees managed to silence the big gun at Fort Wade and Colonel Wade's head was torn off by a shell, but the Southern artillery kept firing. The ironclads took two hundred hits. "Many projectiles were seen to hit the iron sides of the gunboats, then glance off and go shrieking across the Louisiana shore," a soldier with the 6th Missouri noted. But enough of them did damage to make a difference. Arkansas and Missouri sharpshooters were also active, firing into the open portals. They swept the decks clear of Union sailors. The ironclads fired more than twenty-five hundred rounds but could not knock out any more Rebel guns. One of the U.S. transports was sunk. The Rebels lost three men killed and eighteen wounded.

Shortly after 1:00 p.m., Grant boarded the *Benton* and was sickened by the sight of mangled, dead and dying men. He had had enough. He decided to cross the river farther south. Porter covered the transports, which ran past the guns. That evening, a happy Pemberton sent his congratulations and informed Bowen that he had recommended him for promotion to major general.

CHAPTER IX

PORT GIBSON

Grand Gulf was a Confederate victory, but only a minor one. It was impossible to defend the entire riverfront south of Grand Gulf, as well as Port Hudson, Jackson, Fort Pemberton, Snyder's Mill, Chickasaw Bluffs, the railroads, northern Mississippi, etc., against Grant, without ceding Vicksburg to Sherman. It was certainly not possible to check Grant at every potential landing point on the river.

Grant still wanted Grand Gulf as a port and supply base, but he could do without it for the time being. On April 30, he landed west of Bruinsburg, just below the mouth of Bayou Pierre.[1] A narrow dirt road led east to Port Gibson, ten miles away. The Union army spent the entire day crossing the Mississippi. By nightfall, there were twenty-two thousand Yankees on the east bank, with more arriving every hour.

Naturally, certain historians have criticized Pemberton for not having most of his army at Bruinsburg on April 30 where, they contend, he could have destroyed the Army of the Tennessee before it disembarked. They fail to ask a very important question: how could General

Pemberton have known that Grant was going to land at Bruinsburg? Grant himself did not know until April 29—the day before he landed. He had originally planned to come ashore at Warrenton and then Grand Gulf. Bruinsburg was his third choice. Had Pemberton concentrated there, would not Grant have made a fourth choice, rather than obligingly smash his army against fixed Confederate defenses, with a river to his back? I believe he would have selected a fourth option. In my opinion, Grand Gulf proves this. The man was not stupid, after all.

Bowen was also active on April 30. Because he had no cavalry, he sent General Green with 450 Arkansas infantrymen to reconnoiter the Bruinsburg Road on the north and the Rodney Road on the south. Anticipating Grant's landing, he ordered Green to block each road with several companies. Green concentrated on the Rodney Road because it offered a more direct route to Port Gibson than did the Bruinsburg Road.

To guard against Grierson's raiders, Tilghman had been posted at Edward's Station (between Vicksburg and Jackson) with two regiments. General Pemberton ordered Loring to join him, march to Port Gibson and assume command of that sector. The rest of Loring's division was to move from Jackson to Vicksburg. Pemberton signaled Stevenson: "Hurry reinforcements to Bowen tonight." He told Stevenson he was sending reinforcements from Jackson to Vicksburg to replace the troops sent to Bowen. He signaled Bowen that reinforcements were on the way and asked: "Can I do anything to assist you from Jackson?" He also contacted Johnston, Jefferson Davis, and Kirby Smith, pleading for help. He informed Richmond that, unless he was sent large reinforcements, Port Hudson and Grand Gulf should be evacuated. He also declared that he needed six thousand cavalry to prevent major cavalry raids and keep the railroads open.

President Davis promised to send two brigades (five thousand men) from Charleston, South Carolina, where General Beauregard had just turned back another Union attack. (Because of the dilapidated state of the Southern railroad system, they would take two weeks to arrive.) Johnston sent nothing except advice, while Kirby Smith did not even bother to reply.

Stevenson ordered Colonel Alexander W. Reynolds' Tennessee brigade to march for Port Gibson. Neither he nor Loring would arrive in time to be of any help to Bowen.

The Union infantry could not move far inland until they received three days' rations. Because of poor staff work, the food did not arrive until 4:00 p.m. on April 30. They moved out in the late afternoon. The countryside was beautiful. They soon came upon the Windsor Plantation, one of the loveliest plantations in the South. McClernand made it his headquarters. One Union soldier found the dirt road to Port Gibson beautiful and "romantic in the extreme." It soon became less so. Their vanguard ran into Green's brigade at 1:00 a.m. on May 1—the first clash of the final Vicksburg campaign. Heavy skirmishing became general and Confederate artillery joined in, and the Pettus Flying Artillery battery was particularly effective. The firing remained brisk until 3:00 a.m., when the moon set, and it became too dark to fight.

The terrain here was rough, tangled woodland. There was high ground in the vicinity of the Magnolia Church, but there were several ridges which formed excellent defensive positions. The key position was the junction of the Bruinsburg-Rodney Roads, about five miles from Port Gibson. As long as he held this position, Bowen could freely move his forces from one road to the other. This Grant could not easily do. McClernand divided his corps and sent half down each road.

The ruins of Windsor Plantation. Completed in 1861,
it was destroyed in a fire in 1931.

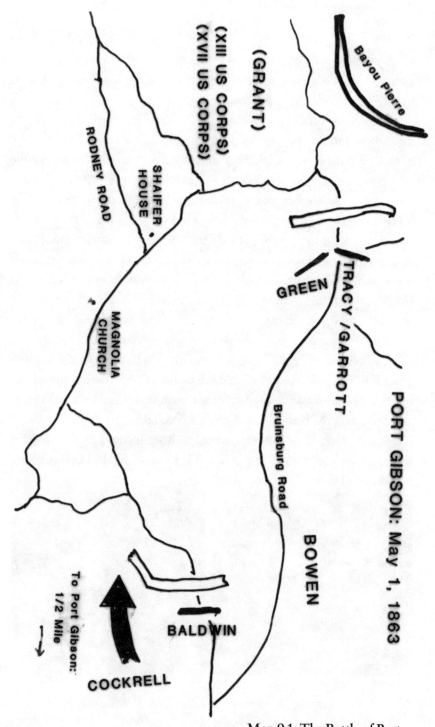

Map 9.1: The Battle of Port Gibson

Before dawn, Bowen telegraphed Pemberton, telling him that he had taken prisoners, and that they had informed him that three or four Union divisions had landed, and that McClernand was in command. Meanwhile, Tracy's Brigade marched forty miles in twenty-four hours in scorching weather over dusty roads. Its strength had dropped from twenty-two to fifteen hundred because of straggling. It arrived in the battle zone about 10:00 p.m. on April 30 and its men were ordered to rest. They would give a good account of themselves on May 1.

The battle began in earnest early that morning. The first shots were fired near the Shaifer House just off the Rodney Road. Here, Brigadier General Green rode into the yard of the house where terrified women were throwing their possessions into a wagon. Even while Green was assuring them there would be no Yankee advance, some bluecoats came up and fired at the wagon. The ladies leapt aboard and drove away as rapidly as they could. Map 9.1 shows the location of the Shaifer House and the subsequent Battle of Port Gibson.

As the Northerners pressed forward, Bowen deployed Tracy's Brigade on his right (northern) flank, astride the Bruinsville Road. General Green's men held the southern (left) flank and blocked the Rodney Road. With two brigades (about three thousand men), John Bowen held off three U.S. divisions (about twenty thousand men). Colonel Robert Lowry's 6th Mississippi Infantry Regiment of Green's brigade particularly distinguished itself.

General Bowen seemed to be everywhere. He behaved just as he did at Shiloh and took absolutely no interest in his own personal safety. He also looked a sight. His horse was hit in the thigh, and its switching tail covered the general in blood. Superior numbers told, however. Outnumbered five to one, Green's Brigade gave way and the Yankees captured Magnolia Church, along with two hundred men and a pair of howitzers, three caissons, and three wagons from the Botetourt (Virginia) Artillery. Bowen rallied the brigade and launched an immediate counterattack on the Federal right flank with the 23rd

Alabama, the 6th Mississippi, and the 12th Arkansas Sharpshooter Battalion.

They pushed back the surprised Yankees, recaptured the church, and overran several guns. The Northerners quickly recovered, however, attacked again, and took back their cannons. They did not push on toward Magnolia Church, however.

With the Yankees now on the defensive on his left flank, Bowen dashed to the rear, where Brigadier General William E. Baldwin's Louisiana/Mississippi brigade was coming up. Baldwin deployed his men along a ridge one and a half miles east of Magnolia Church. Bowen was so confident that Baldwin could hold that he transferred Green's entire brigade to the Bruinsburg Road (his right flank). He needed to. Tracy's Brigade was taking a beating. His first line could not hold and the Yankees overran the rest of the Botetourt Battery. Tracy fell back to his second line, which held.

Bowen knew before the battle began that he would need all the help he could get. Gambling that Grant and Porter would not attack Grand Gulf again, he stripped the fortress of its defenders and ordered them to join him at Port Gibson. Colonel Cockrell left only the 2nd Missouri Regiment, the 1st Confederate Battalion, and the immovable artillery at Grand Gulf and rushed to Bowen's aid with the Missouri Brigade. He arrived at noon with 1,259 men. Initially it was in reserve.

General Bowen now had four brigades and sixteen guns. He was fighting five divisions and about sixty guns. He was outnumbered twenty-five thousand to five thousand. Fortunately, the terrain was on his side. The tangled vegetation did not allow the Yankees to get a true reading as to his numbers, and Grant thought he had more men.

Shortly after noon, General Tracy was conversing with Sergeant Francis Obenchain of the Botetourt Battery when a minie ball struck him in the back of the neck. "Oh, Lord," were his last words. "He was dead when I stooped to him," the sergeant recalled. He was twenty-nine years old.

Brigadier General Edward D. Tracy

Louisiana historian W. H. Tunnard recalled that Tracy "was one of the most efficient brigade commanders in the army, and his loss was irreparable." He was succeeded by Colonel Isham W. Garrott, the commander of the 20th Alabama. A few days later, Stephen D. Lee, the erstwhile chief of artillery of the Army of Mississippi, was given command of the brigade.

Early in the afternoon, Bowen sent Colonel Eugene Erwin and his 6th Missouri to reinforce Tracy and Green on the right. Erwin launched a local counterattack and retook the Botetourt guns. The Northerners were soon attacking again, however. Their goal was the Bayou Pierre bridges—Bowen's only escape route. But the Alabama and Missouri infantry held.

Meanwhile, scouts reported that McClernand was massing twenty regiments to attack the weak Confederate center, which was just an infantry screen. Bowen knew that, if he allowed these Yankees to attack, they would finish him. So, he struck first. Using his interior lines, he brought up the 3rd and 5th Missouri of Cockrell's Brigade and the 4th

Mississippi Infantry Regiment of Baldwin's Brigade, and launched a very successful attack. The surprised Yankees were caught flatfooted in their assembly areas. The fighting was fierce. Four Union regiments were routed and their second line wavered and gave way, but their third line held. Bowen had four horses shot out from underneath him in the struggle. But the Union attack was spoiled. The day was very hot, both sides were exhausted, and, for the moment, neither side had much interest in renewing the struggle. By 3:00 p.m., the battle was a stalemate. The fighting resumed shortly thereafter and, at 5:00 p.m., the Yankees finally achieved their breakthrough.

Taking advantage of the dense vegetation, the Yankees brought up a six-gun battery of 12-pounders loaded with canister and pushed them by hand up a hill in the center of Baldwin's line. They blasted the position and surged forward with a reinforced infantry brigade. The Southerners retreated and their line remained intact, but Bowen had nothing in reserve, and he finally gave the order to retreat at 5:30 p.m., after some of the hardest fighting of the war. He had lost 787 men (60 killed, 340 wounded and 387 missing). Grant had lost 861, including 131 killed and 25 missing.

General Grant was highly complimentary of his opponent. Writing in 1886, he declared that Bowen's "defense was a very bold one and well carried out."

That evening, Bowen's Division crossed the Bayou Pierre suspension bridge about two miles northwest of Port Gibson. He deployed his men along the northern bank and dug in.

May 2 broke cloudless and warm. It would be hot before the sun set. Because of the recent rains, Bayou Pierre was a formidable obstacle, but Bowen knew he did not have enough men to hold it for long, and he also knew Pemberton's reinforcements were on their way. He decided to play for time and attempted to negotiate a twenty-four-hour ceasefire, for both sides to collect their dead. He met with General McPherson, a West

Point colleague and a man known for his compassion. They discussed yesterday's fighting like old friends and both of them told more than they should have. McPherson asked Bowen how many men he had during the battle. The Yankee general was stunned when Bowen said he only had five thousand. McPherson admitted to having more than twenty thousand.

McPherson took Bowen's truce proposal to Grant, who saw in a minute that Bowen was trying to gain time. He rejected the truce.

Pemberton's reinforcements were now arriving and, by midmorning, Bowen had nine thousand men. But Grant had twenty-eight thousand troops in the field, and most of Sherman's XV Corps was marching down the Louisiana side of the river to the crossing site. Sherman left a reinforced division north of Vicksburg to maintain the diversion.

That afternoon, Loring and Tilghman showed up. The reinforcements were late and smaller than Bowen had hoped. Worse still, the Northerners were moving down the Jackson Road and were outflanking the Bayou Pierre line to the east. Bowen realized that the line would have to be abandoned or they would be trapped between the bayou and the Big Black River. He pointed this out to Tilghman and Loring who, as senior officer, was now in command. Loring agreed and abandoned the Bayou Pierre position that night.

Wade's Missouri Battery had guarded the suspension bridge across Bayou Pierre near Port Gibson on May 1, but no gunboats ever came. Now they were ordered to destroy it. It was made of steel and pillars of stone, and was extremely well constructed. "It was a hard job, and one of the most unpleasant I have ever engaged in," Private Truman recalled. It was also unnecessary. Grant crossed the bayou further upstream.

That afternoon, the U.S. engineers finished building an improvised pontoon bridge fifty yards long and fifteen yards wide across Bayou Pierre. Grant had about two thousand cavalry and they ran amok, stripping the countryside of everything moveable. They also confiscated all sorts of wagons, carriages, buggies and carts, and were robbing stores, plantations, homes and anything else of mules, oxen, chickens, cattle, hogs, food, and whiskey. Twenty-five hundred Negroes from the area went with them. Meanwhile, General Pemberton ordered Bowen to evacuate Grand Gulf. He did so that night. Everything that could be carried off was, including one hundred thousand pounds of bacon, several field pieces, and some of his munitions. Everything else was burned, blown up, or spiked.

Pemberton moved his headquarters to Vicksburg on May 2. He had already suspended private freight on the railroads and dictated that cars from one road would be permitted to pass to another road without delay or offloading. He ignored the protests. He now signaled Davis that he thought most of Grant's army was east of the river. He ordered all of his available forces from Grenada, Columbus, and Jackson to the Big Black, to protect Vicksburg's rear. He telegraphed Davis, stating (again) that he needed six thousand cavalry. He added ominously that Vicksburg and Port Hudson each had about thirty days' worth of provisions.

In the meantime, the Northerners occupied Port Gibson and plundered it. General Grant refused to allow them to set it on fire, however, declaring that the town was "too beautiful to burn." But they did loot the town, the homes and plantations. General McPherson headquartered at Mrs. Elizabeth Mary Meade Ingraham's plantation, "Ashwood," and, despite her pleas, did nothing to protect the place. He and his staff stole two five-gallon demijohns of whiskey. She recalled that the men who broke into her home were "as ravenous as wolves." They opened the dining room closet with a hatchet and stole all the silverware and table linen. They tore up and destroyed all of the papers in her husband's office, and took or broke every pan, pitcher, cup, bucket, etc. They brought up a wagon to carry off their plunder. The officers, she said, "wink at and authorize this plundering and thieving." They stole buggies, carts and wagons, and every horse and mule, except one who was about to foal and would not move. They also shot all the sheep and took all the cattle. They shot all but four of the hogs. They destroyed all the portraits of deceased family members and even stole her Bibles, although "What such rascals want with Bibles I can't tell," Mrs. Ingraham noted caustically. The thieves were joined by Negroes and some of the former slaves, who took dresses, sheets and every blanket they could find. ". . . the house was literally gutted, up stairs and down," she recalled. She asked the pillagers if they were fighting to free the slaves. Every one of them denied it. As if to prove their point, they proceeded to rob the blacks and the slave quarters. Kate, one of the slaves who had been robbed, walked over to U.S. General Hovey and told him how they stole her things, and told him to his face that the Yankees "came to rob the negroes, not protect them."[2]

That same day, in far off Virginia, Mrs. Ingraham's brother and General Pemberton's childhood playmate, Major General George G. Meade, was commanding the U.S. V Corps of the Army of the Potomac in the Battle of Chancellorsville against Robert E. Lee.[3] Two months later, he would command the Union forces in their decisive victory at Gettysburg.

The next day, May 3, Mrs. Ingraham's son Frank, a Confederate soldier, was killed in action at Mayre's Heights during the Battle of Chancellorsville. Another son and nephew of General Meade, Major Edward Ingraham of the 1st Confederate Regulars, had been captured at Farmington, Tennessee. He was shot three times after he surrendered. Picked up by his own troops, he was taken to a hospital in Corinth, Mississippi, but he succumbed to his wounds on May 10, 1862. His close personal friend, General Earl Van Dorn, held his hand as he died and cried like a baby.[4]

Although he was still unaware of what was going on south of Vicksburg, Johnston signaled Pemberton: "If Grant crosses, unite all your troops to beat him. Success will give back what was abandoned to win it." Pemberton noted later: "Up to the 2nd of May at best, Johnston gave me no intimation that under *any* circumstances I should abandon Vicksburg and its outposts to repel Grant."

Johnston also promised to send him fifteen hundred cavalrymen under the command of the celebrated Nathan Bedford Forrest, considered by Grant, Sherman, Beauregard, Robert E. Lee and many others to be the best cavalry general in the war. Pemberton must have been excited. But the promise was empty. Johnston did not send a single horseman.

Pemberton later wrote: "Without cavalry I was entirely unable to make a reconnaissance in force, and to prevent the enemy from obtaining from the adjacent country those supplies without which he could not have reached Jackson, fought the battle of Baker's Creek or sat down before Vicksburg."

Pemberton, meanwhile, decided to reconcentrate Loring's division. He ordered Featherston's brigade at Grenada to head south and rejoin the main body. It left on May 2.

On the morning of May 3, Admiral Porter occupied Grand Gulf, and Grant's quartermasters feverishly began converting it into a huge port and supply depot. The Federals immediately began pillaging and robbing. Mrs. Laura Gordon's three-year-old son was sitting on a gate post when a Union officer knocked him off for no apparent reason. Enraged, Mrs. Gordon grabbed her gun and tried to kill the bluecoat, but she missed. She was arrested and convicted of firing on a Federal officer and was confined in a Union prison until after the fall of Vicksburg. The child abuser was not punished.

That afternoon, the Confederates won the race to the flatboat bridge over the Big Black River at Hankinson's Ferry, twenty miles northeast of Grand Gulf. After the Southerners crossed, Bowen only left one company of Missouri infantry and a few engineers to destroy the bridge. Just after they cut it in half, a strong infantry force from McPherson's XVII Corps appeared and made a mad dash for the bridge. They ran off the Rebels and Grant had a half-destroyed bridge over the Big Black, posing a serious threat to Vicksburg from the south.

Earlier, General Halleck had ordered Grant to join with Nathaniel P. Banks to take Port Hudson. While Grant was establishing himself at Grand Gulf, news arrived that Banks, who was at Alexandria, Louisiana, could not reach Port Hudson when expected. General Grant—who did not want to work for Banks, anyway—had his pretext.[5] He decided to disobey orders and drive on to Vicksburg via Jackson.

From May 3 to 5, Grant established his base of supplies at Grand Gulf. His troops bivouacked in the Port Gibson area and near Willow Springs and Hankinson's Ferry, awaiting the arrival of Sherman's Corps. After Sherman came up, Grant had a field army of more than 50,000. Pemberton's movable army totaled only 18,500, but more troops were on their way from Vicksburg. Before long, Pemberton had three infantry divisions in the Big Black sector: Bowen's, Loring's, and Stevenson's.

Pemberton, meanwhile, had a fine defensive position in the rear of Vicksburg. The Big Black was deep and wide enough for steamboats. Its west side (the Confederate side) was lined with bluffs, and it arched around his fortifications about ten miles east of the city. Only on the north, between the Yazoo and the Big Black, was the position less than excellent. Pemberton was convinced that this was Grant's ultimate objective. But Grant did not attack the Big Black River line (with gunboat support) as Pemberton expected.

After he captured Hankinson's Ferry, seventeen miles south of Vicksburg, General McPherson sent out scouts who brought back disturbing news to General Grant. First, the terrain south of Vicksburg was similar to that around Port Gibson, where four Confederate brigades had held off four Union divisions all day. Defeating an entire Southern army in this kind of setting was problematic at best. Also, Pemberton was not retreating into Vicksburg as expected. His men were digging in around Redbone Church (nine miles south of the fortress) and behind the Big Black River, eleven miles east of the city. Grant also knew that the rough terrain ended at Rocky Springs, four miles east-southeast of Hankinson's Ferry. Most of the ground to the east was open, rolling countryside— where the Yankees would be able to deploy their superior artillery and make their numerical superiority felt. On the evening of May 5, instead of heading north for Vicksburg, Grant decided to drive to the northeast, for the Big Black River Bridge at Edwards Station. If successful, this maneuver would place him between Jackson and Vicksburg and allow him to cut the railroad and, with it, Pemberton's line of communications to the east.

Meanwhile, General McClernand arrived at Ashwood and asked Mrs. Ingraham's permission to make it his headquarters. She quickly agreed, because his protection was very much desired. She noted that he was "much more considerate and decent than McPherson."

Meanwhile, at 10:00 a.m. on May 4, for some unknown reason, a small Union tugboat towing two barges strayed to within range of the Confederate water batteries at Vicksburg. The Rebels opened fire and promptly blew up the tug. The barges were set on fire and sank. The Rebels captured about twenty-five prisoners, including three New York reporters from the *Tribune, Herald,* and *Times.*

The graves of Confederates killed at Port Gibson.

CHAPTER X

RAYMOND

On May 11, Grant left his camp at Rocky Springs and advanced in three corps abreast, on generally parallel roads, between five and ten miles apart. McClernand's XIII Corps (four divisions) advanced on the left, along two parallel roads, one along the Big Black, the others a few miles to the east. Sherman's XV Corps (two divisions) moved forward in the center, through Auburn and Dillon's Farm. McPherson's XVII Corps (three divisions) composed the east flank and marched through Utica toward Raymond, which was located about fifteen miles southwest of Jackson.

Pemberton believed Grant's vulnerability lay in his ever-lengthening line of supply. The U.S. Army was forty to fifty miles southeast of Vicksburg and its base of supply was up at Milliken's Bend on the Louisiana side of the river. His problem was that he had no cavalry, he had no authority to command Trans-Mississippi troops and he had no coordination with Kirby Smith. So, instead of severing Grant's supply line, as he had done at Holly Springs, Pemberton ordered Loring with sixty-five hundred men to front the Big Black River Bridge, while Stevenson came up on his left, north of the bridge, and Bowen deployed east and south of Loring. It was a strong position. The Big Black was deep and wide enough and was lined with bluffs. The Rebels dug in here.

Pemberton also had to hold Vicksburg. Here he posted Louis Hebert's Louisiana brigade between Snyder's Mill and Chickasaw Bayou; John C. Vaughn's Tennessee brigade, north of the city, where it could march to the aid of Hebert or Bowen; and Stephen Lee's brigade (including heavy artillery) in the city itself. He also had Forney's and Smith's divisions guarding Vicksburg; five thousand men defending Port Hudson, with two more brigades en route on May 7; Ruggles' brigade at Columbus, with a small force of mounted infantry and State Troops; and James R. Chalmers' brigade (eleven hundred men) at Oxford, which was about all he had to hold northern Mississippi. On May 8, Johnston acknowledged Pemberton's dispositions and called them "judicious."

General Pemberton intended to abandon Port Hudson and use the garrison to defend Vicksburg, but on May 7 President Davis signaled and ordered him to hold both Port Hudson and Vicksburg. Both must be held, he said, to keep communication with the Trans-Mississippi open. Pemberton ordered Gardner to return to Port Hudson with his troops.

Pemberton's lack of cavalry made it impossible for him to be sure of much, but he now correctly concluded that Grant was driving to the northeast. He hoped to be able to take Grant in the flank at Raymond. On May 10, he ordered John Gregg's Brigade and Wirt Adams' cavalry regiment to that town. He intended to have Adams scout for and support Gregg. The fact that he sent Gregg virtually all of his cavalry indicates how important he thought it was. Unfortunately, his order was poorly worded and was misinterpreted. Adams rode to Edwards Station instead of Raymond. The only cavalry force he had at Raymond was four enlisted men, commanded by Sergeant J. L. Miles.

Meanwhile, John Gregg and his infantry brigade marched from Port Hudson to Jackson.

John Gregg was born in Lawrence County on September 28, 1828, and spent his childhood in Alabama. He graduated from La Grange

College in 1847 and pursued his interest in law. He immigrated to Fairfield, Texas in 1852 and was elected district judge in 1856.

Gregg returned to Alabama in 1858 to marry Mary Frances Garth, the daughter of Jesse Winston Garth, one of the wealthiest plantation owners in the South. Garth was also a strong Unionist who offered to give up his slaves (hundreds of them!) if it meant preserving the Union. Here he split with his son-in-law, who was a member of the Texas Secession Convention and who was elected to the Confederate Congress in 1861. He resigned after the 1st Manassas in order to recruit the 7th Texas Infantry, which elected him colonel. He surrendered at Fort Donelson on February 16, 1862, and spent several months in Fort Warren, Massachusetts, in the middle of Boston harbor. Exchanged that fall, he was promoted to brigadier general on August 28.

Gregg's Brigade consisted of the 3rd Tennessee Infantry Regiment (Colonel C. H. Walker); the 10th/30th Tennessee Consolidated Infantry Regiment under Colonel Randal W. McGavock; the 41st Tennessee Infantry (Colonel Robert Farquharson); the 50th Tennessee Infantry (Lieutenant Colonel T. W. Beaumont); the 7th Texas Infantry, now commanded by Colonel Hiram B. Granbury; and 1st Tennessee Infantry Battalion (Major S. H. Colms). It was comfortably camped at Port Hudson on May 1, when General Gardner received an order from John Pemberton. "Send General Gregg's brigade at once to Jackson," it read. "On reaching Osyka, if transportation is not furnished, he must go up the road until he meets it. Direct him to move rapidly."

It was a difficult march. Initially, many of the inexperienced Confederates carried too much gear. "How many of us started with loads heavy enough to break down a mule . . ." one Rebel later wrote. "How we trudged along through hot, dusty lanes, panting with heat and thirst, breaking down under the unaccustomed loads, our feet blistered and legs swollen . . ."

They were outraged on the first day when a wealthy Louisiana woman refused to give them water, but let her slaves offer to sell it to them at $.25 per canteen. They preferred to drink from the dirty pools on the side of the road. As they struggled forward, they discarded surplus equipment, shoes, and clothing. When they reached Osyka, seventy-five miles from Port Hudson, they expected to find railroad cars, but learned that Grierson's raiders had destroyed most of the railroad as far as Brookhaven, Mississippi, so they continued marching. Their rations consisted of parched corn and peas, with a little rice. At Magnolia, they finally got excellent home-cooked meals, as the ladies competed with each other to see how much they could do for their Rebels. Here the troops finally boarded a train and got to ride for ten miles. Then they marched to Brookhaven (another twenty miles). Here they boarded another dilapidated train, which took them to Jackson, where they arrived on the night of Saturday, May 9. It had been an eight-day, 200-mile march. As the brigade camped along the banks of the Pearl River on Sunday, May 10, many of the boys plunged into the refreshing water. Meanwhile, General Gregg received another order from Pemberton: "Move your brigade promptly to Raymond, taking three days rations, and carrying only cooking utensils and ammunition; no baggage."

The bugle blew before sunrise on May 11 and, at 5:00 a.m., they marched off to the west. They were soon marching through the streets of Jackson, which were lined with well-wishing civilians while the band of the 3rd Tennessee played "The Girl I Left Behind Me." A private from the 3rd recalled that he glanced back "and could not restrain a feeling of pride in the splendid array of gallant men" that took the road to Raymond. They were ready for a fight.

When the boys in gray reached Raymond, they found what Sam Mitchell of the 3rd Tennessee described as "a small unpretending town, inhabited exclusively by women and children and old men. All the able-bodied men were in the army." They were greeted by virtually the entire population, and women and children threw bouquets of flowers to the dusty Confederates. But General Gregg was stunned when Sergeant Miles reported to him with four men, instead of an entire regiment. The 1st Mississippi Mounted Battalion, State Troops (Captain J. M. Hall), was nearby, but it only had forty men. The State Troops, however, reported that Gregg was only facing a single Yankee brigade, which

comported with what he expected.[1] He was confident he could destroy
the isolated enemy brigade.

John Gregg had accepted a false report. He was a lawyer by profession—not a soldier—and had probably never heard the military axiom:
"The first report is almost always wrong." As one Confederate soldier
derisively recalled, the State Troops who made the report did their washing at home. They were mostly local youths, undertrained and inexperienced. Instead of facing a brigade of 2,000 to 3,000 men, Gregg (who
had 3,000 men) was facing an entire corps of 23,749 Yankees.

In his scholarly monograph on this action, Warren E. Grabau wrote:
"The Battle of Raymond is a tale of confusion and cross-purposes from
beginning to end." John Gregg was badly outnumbered, but he fought the
battle as if he had a numerical advantage. General McPherson was advancing through woodland, so he could not see how many Southerners he was
facing. He had a great numerical supremacy, but he could not believe that
the Confederates would attack an entire corps with a single brigade. He
fought the battle as if he were outnumbered. That and the element of
surprise were all that saved Gregg's command from total annihilation.

Brigadier General John Gregg.

General Gregg ordered Colonel Granbury to take two companies of his Texas regiment and deploy them as skirmishers. He formed the rest of his brigade in line in the cemetery. When they were aligned, he raised his sword and gave the order "Charge!" It was almost exactly high noon.

The first Union line was just emerging from the woods when thousands of screaming Rebels fell upon them, smashing their first regiment. Lieutenant Colonel Davis, the commander of the 23rd Indiana Infantry, recalled that the Rebels advanced in four lines and "opened fire from each line in succession" and continued to advance "until they were within bayonet reach. Not having time to fix our bayonets, we attempted to beat them back with our muskets, but being overpowered . . . we were obliged to fall back." They scampered back to the second line, which was in a ravine in the trees. The Rebels routed this one as well.

U.S. Brigadier General John D. Stevenson reported that the 3rd (U.S.) Missouri was advancing to take a prominent hill when it was struck by "a most terrific fire" from three Confederate regiments and "retired in great disorder and with heavy loss." The "three regiments" was the 10th/30th Tennessee Consolidated Infantry Regiment, which totaled no more than three hundred men. They were led by Lieutenant Colonel James J. Turner, the regiment's second-in-command, who ordered his men to "cheer and yell and charge the enemy at the double-quick." At them they went, "yelling like savages." The Yankees delivered a single volley and "then broke in utter confusion."

The Tennesseans paused after an advance of six hundred yards when the Northerners brought up the 7th (U.S.) Missouri. The day was unseasonably hot and sultry, and there was no breeze in the thick Mississippi woods. In addition, there was a temperature inversion. The men were using black powder weapons. There was nowhere for the smoke to go. Visibility dropped to ten feet. The Rebel formations broke up as they plunged forward, and the entire brigade lost its organization.

Colonel Randal William McGavock, the commander of the 10th/30th Tennessee, was a tall, physically impressive man with a dominating personality. One soldier described him as "a clean, strong, brave man, a noble soldier, a loyal friend."

Colonel Robert W. McGavock, the commander of the 10th/30th Tennessee.

His regiment thought the world of him.[2] Unfortunately, he was fond of wearing a long gray coat with a scarlet lining, and he was at the head of his regiment, making him all too conspicuous. As he led them forward, Northern infantrymen fired a volley. Eight bullets penetrated his coat, and one went through his left breast, killing him almost instantly. Major Grace of the 10th/30th was also seriously wounded. The furious Confederates crushed the 7th (U.S.) Missouri but, as they pursued, found another Union line, which exchanged volleys with them. For a time, neither side could move the other, although the numerically superior Yankees seemed to get the best of it. Then the Federals outflanked the Confederates to the right. McGavock's successor, Lieutenant Colonel Turner, pulled back without bothering to tell anybody. (He had a bad habit of moving without telling his superiors.) The 50th Tennessee followed suit, and the Confederate left was turned. Fortunately, Gregg's reserve, Colonel Farquharson's 41st Tennessee, came up and stabilized the flank.

Meanwhile, on the right flank, the 7th Texas also wavered. Colonel Granbury recalled, "I held . . . until the men had exhausted their own ammunition and emptied the cartridge-boxes of the dead . . ." The Yankees, meanwhile, worked their way around Granbury's right. When the enemy poured a "murderous enfilading fire along my already shattered ranks, I then ordered a retreat," the colonel reported.

The 3rd Tennessee on Granbury's left was now exposed. Captain Flavel Barber recalled, "Our men by this time had shot away all their ammunition and a fresh column [of Yankees] was advancing directly upon us. No support appeared upon our rear or left and we had been so terribly cut up and scattered in the thick woods that the colonel [Calvin H. Walker] thought it best to order a retreat. We were barely in time . . . . All the way back we were severely galled by the enemy on both flanks. We had to leave many of our wounded in the woods, not being able to carry them away, in spite of their entreaties not to be abandoned." Among those wounded and captured was Private Billy Foote of the 10th/30th Tennessee, a native of Raymond and the son of former Mississippi governor and U.S. senator Henry Stuart Foote, who was now a Confederate congressman. Several men were too exhausted to go on and also were captured by the Yankees.

U.S. General Logan's Division, the Battle of Raymond.

General Gregg recognized that he had been checked and was nearly out of ammunition. He had also watched in consternation as regiment after regiment of bluecoats appeared at his front and on his flanks. His staff reported that their brigade had taken prisoners from eighteen different regiments. This was more than a single Yankee brigade! Gregg sadly gave the order to retreat before he could be destroyed and fell back in good order through the tree-lined streets of Raymond. The ladies of the town had prepared a fine picnic dinner for them, but the boys in gray had no time to stop and enjoy it. The Yankees got it.

Just as the battle was ending, six mounted companies of the 3rd (C.S.) Kentucky Infantry Regiment arrived. They covered the retreat.[3]

General Gregg reported 73 killed, 252 wounded and 190 missing. McPherson lost 68 killed, 341 wounded, and 37 missing.

McPherson still had no idea of the size of the force he had fought and pursued very slowly. One of his division commanders, Major General John A. Logan, personally interrogated one of the prisoners. When he was informed that they had only fought one brigade, he thought the man was lying and became furious. He declared loudly that the Confederates had driven his men from two lines, and no single brigade of Rebels could break his division like that. But it had.

In the town, six-year-old Estelle Trichell recalled, "The first wounded soldier I saw was a Yankee, a young officer. He was brought into town riding behind one of our soldiers. I remember the officer had red hair and he leaned his head on his left hand and held on to the captor with his right. I felt sincere pity for him even though he was a Yankee." They put the wounded Confederates in the courthouse, while the wounded and captured Yankees were placed in the Odd Fellows Hall and the Methodist, Episcopal, and Baptist Churches. Northern and Southern wounded were treated just alike. Several Yankees were kept in private homes. The owner of the local hotel even drove his carriage to the battlefield in a courageous effort to save as many of the wounded as he could.

"On our retreat through Raymond we saw ladies with quilts and bandages for the wounded, who were being cared for by their tender hands," one Confederate soldier recalled. "They would not be persuaded to leave the streets, even after the enemy's shells were flying and crashing through houses."

About 5:00 p.m., to the shock of the townspeople, the Yankees marched down the main street of Raymond, and immediately began to loot and pillage. Letitia Dabney, the eleven-year-old daughter of Judge Augustine Dabney,[4] recalled how they camped around their house, burned all the fences for their camp fires, emptied the hen house and smokehouse, and rode off with the family's cow and calf. Letitia's sister was very ill with typhoid fever and the cow's milk was all they had to feed her. Letitia's mother pleaded with them to leave the cow, but in vain.

While the women of Raymond tended their comrades' wounds, the healthy Yankees looted practically every house in town and stole everything in sight, especially jewelry. They shot cattle for the fun of it and threw the local newspaper's printing press down the town's well. Some of them even robbed graves. But Raymond was fortunate. There was no burning because so many injured Yankees were in private homes, being nursed by the brave and selfless women of Raymond.

Sanitation conditions were horrible in the "hospitals," which were, after all, really just churches, courthouses and meeting halls, and private homes. Flies were everywhere. No one in 1863 associated the contaminated local drinking water (drawn from open wells) with disease, and antiseptic surgery was unheard of in those days. Things got better when the Federal surgeons arrived, but not much. More than half of all Civil War surgeons on both sides had not practiced medicine before the war, so medical care even in hospitals was inadequate. Many men on both sides died unnecessarily.

On May 12, Private Frank Herron of the 3rd Tennessee was following Colonel Calvin Walker when a bullet struck him. After he realized that he was not dead, he hobbled to a tree, using his rifle as a crutch. When his command retreated, Herron was captured and taken to the home of Mr. McDonald, a planter and Southern gentleman. He and his family were allowed one room. The rest of the house was inhabited by Union officers and casualties, but all of the wounded were moved to town a few days later. Herron's wound was not dressed for six days and he was in great pain. Suddenly he saw a beautiful Southern girl with tears running down her face. Her name was Myra McDonald. She came and sat down by Herron, took his hand, and asked if he had a father and mother. She got a basin and some water and washed his face, combed his hair and got him something to eat. She tried to cleanse his wound, which was full of worms.

While Herron was at the field hospital, it was visited by Ulysses S. Grant. He gave the chief surgeon an order: "Give the wounded men every attention which is possible and make no distinction between Federals and Confederates." Herron remarked that he was not given this report. He was lying within twenty feet of Grant when he said it.

Later, Herron was moved to the Raymond Courthouse. There Myra visited him every day, occasionally bringing flowers or something good to eat. "Among the great mass of suffering humanity at the hospital could be seen the grand and noble daughters of the South, the majority of them raised in luxury, inexperienced in every sense for hospital work, with their sleeves rolled up to their elbows, hastening here and there, tenderly nursing the wounded and dying. Never was there more heroism and self-sacrifice . . ."

Myra McDonald saved Frank Herron's life. He was later exchanged and rejoined his command. After fighting at Chickamauga, he applied for a discharge, which was granted. He went home, joined the 48th Tennessee Cavalry of Nathan Bedford Forrest's command, and served with him until the end of the war. Myra and Frank eventually married other people, but corresponded for years after the war.

The next day, May 12, seventeen-year-old Private Patrick Griffin of the 10th/30th Tennessee, who had been taken prisoner in the battle, was given a brief parole to bury his friend, Colonel McGavock. He and some fellow POWs hastily nailed together a rough wooden coffin and hired a wagon. Escorted by a Union guard, a funeral procession of Confederate prisoners and a few townspeople, he was laid to rest in the Raymond Cemetery, where he had formed his regiment for the attack the day before.

General Pemberton thought that the Battle of Raymond never should have been fought. He wrote later: "General Gregg, gallant and noble gentleman that he was, did not conform to my repeated and positive orders, 'If the enemy advance upon you in too strong a force, fall back upon Jackson.'"

Following the Battle of Raymond, General Gregg did fall back in the direction of Jackson, where he was met on the road by the brigade of Brigadier General William H. T. Walker.

There was already panic in the Mississippi capital. Mary Ann Loughborough (pronounced Lof-bur-row) recalled,

> The depot was crowded with crushing and elbowing human beings, swaying to and fro—baggage being thrown hither and thither—horses wild with fright, and negroes with confusion; and so we found ourselves in a car, amid the living stream that flowed and surged along—seeking the Mobile cars— seeking the Vicksburg cars—seeking anything to bear them away from the threatened and fast depopulating town.[5]

On May 13, Lieutenant General James Longstreet was on his way back from North Carolina to rejoin Robert E. Lee's army at Fredericksburg. He stopped in Richmond to meet with Secretary of War James Seddon. The two began discussing the overall strategic situation and Seddon asked the general what he thought of the situation in the Vicksburg sector. Longstreet proposed taking two divisions to reinforce Bragg, who would send two divisions to Pemberton.

Seddon told Longstreet that the War Department favored sending new divisions to Mississippi, but General Lee thought the Union grip on Vicksburg could be loosened by invading Pennsylvania. At a cabinet meeting, the Confederate government had decided to go along with Lee.

It was one of the decisive mistakes of the war.

CHAPTER XI

FIRST BATTLE OF JACKSON

O n May 9, 1863, Jefferson Davis sent a telegraph from Richmond to General Joseph E. Johnston in Chattanooga, ordering him to start immediately for Jackson, Mississippi, to assume command of the Confederate forces assembling there. Secretary of War James A. Seddon also sent orders, instructing Johnston to go to Mississippi and take three thousand good troops with him, or have them follow as soon as possible. Significantly, instead of the customary salutation "With high esteem," Seddon ended his message with: "Acknowledge receipt." Johnston complained that he was sick and unfit for duty but would obey the order anyway. Because of multiple railroad cuts by the enemy, he had to travel the route Atlanta-Montgomery-Mobile-Meridian. He would not arrive in the Mississippi capital until May 13.

Giving Joe Johnston the task of assisting Pemberton and later saving Vicksburg was one of the worst mistakes President Davis ever made. Johnston had a deep aversion to attacking the enemy and, as Colonel Matthew F. Steele later wrote, he was intransigent and "neither acknowledged nor heeded authority above him. A devouring egotism caused him to reject and scorn all ideas and strategy not his own." He would be of no help to General Pemberton in the weeks ahead and *any* of Lee's corps commanders would have been a better choice. Several other Rebel generals would also have filled the bill, including Beauregard, Forrest, or Richard Taylor. Even Braxton Bragg would have been a superior choice. But Davis based his action on availability and seniority. He would come to lament this decision. So would a great many others.

James A. Seddon (1815-1880), the 4th Confederate Secretary of War.

Pemberton, who had no cavalry to speak of, spent May 12 improving his positions along the Big Black. He ordered Loring and Stevenson to bring their entire divisions to Edward's Depot, on the Southern Railroad of Mississippi (i.e., the road from Jackson to Vicksburg, hereafter referred to as the Southern Railroad). He signaled Davis that the enemy was apparently moving on Edward's Depot with heavy forces and he intended to meet him there, while leaving sufficient forces at Vicksburg to defend the place. He complained that he had received only fifteen hundred infantry reinforcements and urgently requested more, along with three thousand cavalry. He also issued a proclamation to his army, proving once again that he was a better communicator when using the written, rather than the spoken, word.

It read:

Soldiers of the Army, in and around Vicksburg:

The hour of trial has come! The enemy who has so long threatened Vicksburg in front, has, at last, effected a landing in this department; and his march into the interior of Mississippi has been marked by the devastation of one of the fairest portions of the State! He seeks to break the communications between the members of the Confederacy, and to control the navigation of the Mississippi River! The issue involves everything endeared to a free people! The enemy fights for the privilege of plunder and oppression! You fight for your country, homes, wives, children, and the birth-rights of freemen! Your commanding General, believing in the truth and sacredness of this cause, has cast his lot with you, and stands ready to peril his life and all he holds dear for this triumph of the right! God, who rules in the affairs of men and nations, loves justice and hates wickedness. He will not allow a cause so just to be trampled in the dust. In the day of conflict let each man, appealing to Him for strength, strike home for victory, and our triumph is at once assured. A grateful country will hail us as deliverers, and cherish the memory of those who may fall as martyrs in her defense.

Soldiers! Be vigilant, brave and active; let there be no cowards, nor laggards, nor stragglers from the ranks—and the God of battles will certainly crown our efforts with success.

J. C. PEMBERTON
Lieutenant-General Commanding

That night the general left Vicksburg for Bovina, to direct his field forces on the Big Black.

Pemberton already foresaw the possibility that Vicksburg might be cut off. He ordered all non-combatants out of the city. "Heretofore, I have merely requested that it should be done;" the general wrote, "now I demand it."

But the women did not obey. "We cannot leave here. Where can we go?" one lady asked Mary Ann Loughborough. "Here we are among friends. . .Let us at least share the fate of those we love so much."

On May 13, Pemberton was still unclear what the Yankees were up to, so he retained his positions along the Big Black River and awaited developments. He ordered Loring at Edward's Depot to make a reconnaissance-in-force to determine the location and strength of the main enemy body. Late that afternoon, Loring informed him that all sources, "both black and white," suggested that the Northerners were marching on Jackson.

General Pemberton knew that if he were to meet Grant on the Big Black River, he would not be able to keep him from taking Jackson if the Northern general decided to do so. But if he forced Grant to attack him across the Big Black, it was likely that he could defeat the Federal army, and if the Army of the Tennessee suffered a defeat here, isolated and between two Confederate armies, the repercussions would likely be disastrous for the entire Union cause. He therefore decided to run the risk of sacrificing the Mississippi capital for the greater good of saving Vicksburg.

That night, and early the next morning, Union gunboats shelled the Confederate fortifications at Warrenton. The sound of the battle could be clearly heard in Vicksburg, ten miles away. "How little we thought that was the commencement of music that would ring in our ears for weeks to come! —how little we thought it the beginning of our trouble!" one woman recalled. Shortly thereafter, the fort at Warrenton was quietly evacuated—or at least the guns were.

One of the great myths of the Civil War is that Grant cut himself loose from his supply line and simply lived off the land when he drove on Jackson. Grant himself perpetuated and deliberately promoted this myth after the war, but it is still false, as common sense would dictate.

It is true that Grant and his men robbed the towns and prosperous plantations along their route, leaving women and children, both black and white, to fend for themselves or starve, and this partially mitigated his need for rations. But the homes, villages, and plantations along the route had only minuscule amounts of medical supplies, bullets, and gunpowder. It is doubtful that they could have supplied even a brigade with these essential commodities, and they certainly did not have enough to supply an entire army. And the Mississippi civilians could provide nothing in the way of shot, shell, and cannon balls, even if they had been willing to, and they certainly wouldn't provide reinforcements or replacements for Grant's dead and wounded. Some of Grant's convoys from Grand Gulf to his army included more than two hundred wagons. Each wagon carried an average of three thousand pounds of supplies and some considerably more than that. (The maximum carrying capacity of a Civil War wagon was six thousand pounds.) This meant a convoy of two hundred wagons would carry more than three hundred tons of supplies to the Army of the Tennessee—so it was hardly an army "cut loose" from its supply lines.

Famous Civil War historian Edwin C. Bearss later wrote: "Contrary to Grant's claim that he abandoned his supply line when he marched inland, the Federal army did indeed have a long supply line of generously loaded wagons coming up from a well-stocked base at Grand Gulf." U.S. Senator William F. Vilas, then the lieutenant colonel of the 23rd Wisconsin, recalled, "[Our] route of supplies was so long as both to be inadequate and perilous."[1] If the Rebels had severed the supply line, Grant would have to reestablish it by fighting Pemberton at a place of the Rebels' choosing or break out of Mississippi any way he could. Under those circumstances, taking Vicksburg would be out of the question.

On May 13, Johnston arrived in Jackson. He found a total of six thousand men there, directed by Brigadier General John Gregg. Meanwhile, with sixteen thousand men, General McPherson cut the Jackson-Vicksburg Road. In spite of the fact that five thousand reinforcements were supposed to arrive the next day and more the day after that, and ignoring the fact that there was as yet no indication that the Yankees on the railroad were going to try to take the capital, Johnston quickly decided not to fight for the city. "Johnston seldom fought if retreat was possible," historian Michael Ballard wrote later. "I am too late," the cautious general signaled Secretary of War Seddon. Stranger still, Johnston ordered Pemberton to bring up his entire force and attack Grant in the rear at Clinton (twelve miles west of Jackson), although he was even then planning to retreat to the north—away from Pemberton.

From May 2 to 13, Pemberton and his army prepared their defenses on the Big Black River. Johnston failed to grasp Pemberton's concept of operations. Much of Pemberton's army had spent months engaged in garrison duties. They had never fought together as an army of maneuver and many of them were no longer in top physical condition. They were not ready for an offensive battle but could probably defeat Grant if they occupied naturally strong and well-prepared defensive positions, such as those on the Big Black River. In his telegram of May 8, Johnston had told Pemberton that his "Disposition of troops, so far as understood, [is] judicious." Yet now his orders interfered with Pemberton's plans and threw away the major Confederate advantage.

Johnston decided to abandon Jackson almost as soon as he arrived from Tennessee and perhaps before. He was still ignorant of the situation and had no information about the Yankees' strength or dispositions. He did not bother to consult with Pemberton or any of his staff officers, and showed no consideration for the fate of Vicksburg.

To make matters worse, Johnston sent his order to Pemberton by three different couriers. One of them was a Union spy. Grant knew what Pemberton's orders were before he did. Accordingly, he set up a large ambush in the vicinity of Clinton.

Meanwhile, Johnston ordered Gregg to take over the defense of the city and conduct a delaying action until the evacuation could be completed. He instructed Brigadier General John Adams, the commandant of the District of Jackson, to handle the evacuation.[2] Adams quickly and efficiently organized wagon trains and railroad trains full of military stores and munitions. On Pemberton's recommendation, Governor

Pettus had already moved the state records to safety earlier in the week. In the meantime, Johnston retired to his room in the Bowman House hotel.

May 13 saw torrential rain, and Sherman's men slogged through the mud as they approached Jackson from the southwest. Johnston, meanwhile, learned that significant reinforcements would arrive in Jackson within a few hours. He sent urgent dispatches, ordering them to halt, disembark, and move away from the capital in the opposite direction. Part of Brigadier General States Rights Gist's South Carolina brigade was already in Jackson; the rest was only ten miles from the city when it was intercepted by a courier and ordered to a place fifty miles from the capital. Brigadier General Samuel R. Maxey's Texas Brigade was stopped at a depot thirty miles south of Jackson. He was ordered to fall back on his wagons and head for Port Hudson. Brigadier Generals Evander McNair's Brigade and Matthew Ector's Brigade were halted at Meridian. Had Johnston not panicked, he would have had more than seventeen thousand men to defend the Mississippi capital.

Two of McPherson's divisions did, in fact, turn back on Jackson, advancing along the railroad. Gregg deployed the elements of Gist's brigade that were on hand on the Clinton Road, three miles west of Jackson. His own brigade (now under Colonel Peyton H. Colquitt) deployed on the right of Gist, while Walker's 1,000-man Georgia brigade supported Gist. Gregg sent the 3rd Kentucky Infantry Regiment to guard the Raymond Road on his left flank, along with a battalion of sharpshooters and a battery from Walker's brigade. At 9:00 a.m. on May 14, McPherson conducted a probing attack against the Confederate works from the west, while Sherman advanced from the southwest. The fighting became heavy at 11:00 a.m., but the Yankees were checked by Confederate canister. At 2:00 p.m., Adams sent word that the wagon trains were clear. Badly outnumbered, Gregg now began his retreat. Meanwhile, Sherman launched a flanking movement to the south and captured several guns and one hundred men. The Mississippi capital was in Federal hands by nightfall. So rapid was Johnston's withdrawal that the women employed at a clothing factory were still at their looms when Grant and

Sherman strolled into the place. The amused Yankee generals let the women leave with all the fabric they could carry; then they burned the factory to the ground.

Brigadier General William H. T. Walker, a fire-eating Georgian, was furious at having to retreat. "I know I couldn't hold the place," he told Colonel Fremantle, a visiting English observer, "but I did want to kill a few more of those rascals."

The Army of the Tennessee lost 295 men at Jackson (42 killed, 251 wounded, and two missing). Confederate losses were reported as 199 (17 killed, 64 wounded, and 118 missing), but this figure is almost certainly low. They also lost several guns.[3] Gregg joined Johnston at Canton, about twenty-five miles north of the city.

Pemberton received Johnston's orders to advance on Clinton between 9:00 a.m. and 10:00 a.m. on May 14. Even though Northern intentions were still unclear, he replied that he would move "with his whole available force," which he put at sixteen thousand men. (He had left seventy-five hundred at Vicksburg and three thousand more guarding various bridges and installations against Union cavalry raids, but this total is still low.) His main force was about twenty miles due west of McPherson's corps at Clinton and thirty-two miles from Jackson.

General Pemberton left Bovina that morning and arrived at Edward's Depot at noon. Here he learned that the Union "detachment" Johnston had referred to in his dispatch of May 13 was, in fact, an entire corps, which was almost as large as Pemberton's entire field force. The commander of the Army of Mississippi immediately called a council of war.

Pemberton opposed the idea of striking into Grant's rear, which he called "tactically suicidal." He wanted to remain in the good positions on the west side of the Big Black and await Grant's inevitable attack. He told his generals at length and "with great force" that he considered the foremost duty of the Army of Mississippi was to hold Vicksburg, even if it meant letting the Yankees ravage Mississippi. Although he didn't say so, this policy would also surrender the initiative to Grant. But if Pemberton was right and he could defeat Grant on the Big Black, the

Union Army was probably doomed. It would certainly not be in a position to execute a safe retreat.

Most of his generals disagreed. A majority wanted to fight and believed Johnston's orders should be obeyed, even though they did not understand his strategy. None of them wanted to march on Clinton, however, according to Major Jacob Thompson, who was present.[4] "There was not a voice in favor of moving on Clinton," he recalled. Stevenson and Loring wanted to advance southeast, to attack Grant's exposed supply lines. The rest of them wanted to strike across the Big Black, which they believed Grant had screened with a single division. They also believed it would take Grant some time to reduce Jackson. It did not occur to them that Johnston was already evacuating that city. John Pemberton, who still wanted to hold the Big Black and fight on favorable terrain of his own choosing, caved to majority opinion that the army had to take some offensive action. This tendency to compromise was perhaps his major weakness as a commander. But he at least rejected the Clinton idea. At 5:40, he sent a message to Johnston, outlining a plan to march on Dillon's Plantation and cut the Raymond-Port Gibson Road. If successful, he would isolate Grant's army in central Mississippi. Without a source of powder and ammunition, Grant would be in deep trouble. Since it was Loring's idea, Pemberton gave the task of cutting Grant's supply lines to him. The target was Dillon's Plantation on the Raymond Road, about seven miles southeast of Loring's right flank.[5] Pemberton sent Johnston a message, stating that his order of May 13 would not be obeyed. He suggested several ways Johnston could send him reinforcements. He still had no idea that Johnston had abandoned the field and taken these reinforcements with him.

Johnston received Pemberton's message on the morning of May 15. He immediately sent a message telling the general that his plan was "impracticable" and countermanded Pemberton's orders. Johnston instructed him to advance in the direction of Clinton, to link up with his "Army of Relief" as originally ordered—in spite of the fact that Johnston was marching *away* from Clinton. Remarkably, Johnston even admitted that he had no idea how strong the Union forces in the Clinton area were.

Given Johnston's defeat at Jackson and his failure to concentrate his forces, his own plan was even more impracticable. He even retreated in the wrong direction. He headed toward Canton, north-northeast of Jackson, whereas he should have fallen back to the northwest, placing his forces where they could threaten Grant's right rear when he turned towards Vicksburg and putting him (Johnston) in a position to conduct reinforcements to the Army of Mississippi.

That night, Johnston wrote what Ballard called a "rambling essay," suggesting that Pemberton cut Grant's supply line to the Mississippi River. (He later conveniently forgot he had made this suggestion.)

At the same time, a strategic conference convened in Richmond. It lasted from May 14 to 17. Present were Jefferson Davis, Robert E. Lee, and the entire cabinet. President Davis was troubled by the situation at Vicksburg. So was General Lee, who urged that Johnston be ordered to attack Grant quickly. But on the vital question of whether to send an entire corps to Mississippi or to invade Pennsylvania, Lee advised those present that he should march north, for provisions if for no other purpose. Virginia had been picked clean and he could no longer feed his army from there. He believed he had to retreat to Richmond and stand a siege or march north. A siege would ultimately end, he believed, in surrender. The president agreed with him, and Davis and the entire cabinet voted to invade the North, except for Postmaster-General John H. Reagan, who wanted to reinforce Pemberton.

Lieutenant General D. H. Hill was later very outspoken in his criticism of Lee for not sending a corps to Mississippi. He felt Pemberton could have crushed Grant with another corps. But Lee objected to even sending Pickett's Division to Mississippi.

Two weeks later, on May 31, Davis met with Lee again. The chief executive was not optimistic. "General Johnston did not, as you thought advisable, attack Grant promptly, and I fear the result is that which you anticipated if time was given," he said. Obviously, Lee believed that a siege of Vicksburg—if not broken quickly—could only end in defeat and surrender. Hope was fading in Richmond, along with a growing suspicion within Jefferson Davis that he had made a serious mistake in giving

Joseph E. Johnston command of the Army of Relief—but this is getting ahead of our story.

⚓

Meanwhile, Grant decided that Pemberton wasn't going to accommodate him by walking into an ambush at Clinton, so he turned towards Vicksburg. On May 15, McClernand's XIII Corps and McPherson's XVII Corps advanced west along the railroad. Sherman and his XV Corps stayed behind to burn Jackson. They did such a thorough job that the former capital of Mississippi became known as "Chimneyville." They destroyed the railroad, a carriage factory, hospitals, churches, private homes, and even the state penitentiary. Johnston's forces reoccupied what was left of Jackson after Sherman left.

May 15 was a debacle caused by poor Confederate staff work. The army was supposed to march at 8:00 a.m. with three days of cooked rations in their haversacks and five more in the hands of their supply units (commissaries). Things went wrong from the beginning. Food and ammunition from Vicksburg did not arrive in time, causing a six to seven-hour delay. The entire field force of the Army of Mississippi did a right face and marched south, toward Dillon's plantation. Their wagon train alone was two and a half miles long. But they did not march far. Baker's Creek lay between Loring's division and Dillon's Plantation. Because of the heavy rains of May 13 and 14, the creek could not be forded, and no one had thought to build a bridge or even to bring up an engineer unit. It was evening before an improvised bridge could be constructed. It was 10:00 p.m. before all of the troops had crossed. Instead of striking Grant's supply line in overwhelming force, as planned, the entire army managed an advance of only three miles. Loring's division bivouacked at Ellison Plantation, on the road which connected the two roads to Raymond. Wirt Adams' cavalry formed the advanced guard and camped about a mile forward of them.

Pemberton received Johnston's dispatch of May 15 at 7:00 a.m. on May 16. He immediately decided to obey it and ordered his army to do an about face, which meant that Grant dodged a bullet, metaphorically speaking. His supply line was now safe, for the time being. The head of the Confederate column now became the rear. This included about four hundred wagons, which now became the head of the column. The narrow country roads were in bad condition. Turning the wagons and the artillery around was a nightmare. One broken-down wagon could paralyze the whole field army. The entire march deteriorated into what James W. Raab described as "wholesale confusion."

Jack Pemberton had conflicting orders from Jefferson Davis and Joseph E. Johnston. He made a serious mistake by trying to obey both. Johnston wanted him to concentrate all of his forces against Grant. Davis insisted that Vicksburg be held. Pemberton obeyed Davis' orders, left two divisions (about ten thousand men) at Vicksburg, and moved to obey Johnston's orders, at least partially because he realized the move against Dillon's Plantation was going badly. Of course, Pemberton had no idea Johnston was not even going to attempt to join him. Had Johnston and Pemberton linked up, the Confederacy would have had almost forty thousand men at the decisive battle of Champion Hill (see below). As it turned out, Pemberton had only about twenty-one thousand men at the battle. Grant would have forty-four thousand in seven divisions.

At 6:30 on the morning of May 16, Pemberton received another order from Johnston, reiterating his directive to move north of the railroad so he could arrange a junction between the two armies. He was, in fact, heading for a meeting engagement of epic proportions.

CHAPTER XII

CHAMPION HILL

Pemberton was on the field at dawn and chose Champion Hill as his main defensive position. Even Grant later admitted that it was "well selected." A low ridgeline began at Champion Hill and extended to a point south of the Raymond Road. Champion Hill itself sloped down seventy-five feet, but the entire area was cut by steep ravines, tall trees, and thick underbrush.[1] It would be difficult terrain for an attacker to cross.

Grant would have to advance along three dirt roads that ran east to west, and Pemberton was blocking all three. The Rebel line ran north to south (or left to right) as follows: Stevenson's Division (seven thousand men), holding the vital position of Champion Hill and guarding the Clinton Road, which was also known as the Jackson Road; Bowen's Division (five thousand men), holding the Middle Road; and Loring's Division (sixty-six hundred men), covering the Raymond (also known as Ratcliff) Road. Adams' cavalry screened the front.[2] The line was two and a half miles long. Because it was a meeting engagement, it was without trenches or improved positions of any kind, except those dug on the morning of the sixteenth, and they didn't amount to much.

Jack Pemberton was uneasy in the beginning because the swollen Baker's Creek was in the rear of his army and the bridge was washed out. His first order was to Major Samuel H. Lockett. He instructed his chief engineer to take an engineer company and construct a bridge as quickly as possible. This move would save much of his army later in the day.

Pemberton's next order was to relieve Brigadier General Tilghman of his command. He had lost confidence in this brigade commander and former friend during the retreat from northern Mississippi, when Tilghman had destroyed some wet tents Pemberton thought should have been salvaged. For a reason that has not come down to us, the army commander chose May 16 to sack him. Unfortunately for Pemberton, Tilghman was in Loring's Division.

Brigadier General Lloyd Tilghman.

W. W. Loring was one of the most fractious generals in the Civil War—and that is saying something. This trait undermined his effectiveness as a commander and ruined his chances for promotion. He hated

John C. Pemberton, just as he had hated Robert E. Lee and Stonewall Jackson in Virginia before they got rid of him. Two staff officers in his division, Captain William R. Barksdale and Lieutenant William A. Drennan, agreed that Loring "would be willing for Pemberton to lose a battle provided that he would be displaced."[3] Distinguished historians Michael B. Ballard and James R. Arnold both have suggested that Loring knew he was in a position to cost Pemberton a battle and took advantage of the situation to do just that.

After Tilghman was fired, he, Loring, and Featherston were overheard saying, "harsh, ill-natured things" about Pemberton, and ridiculing his plans and orders. When Pemberton arrived to inspect Loring's lines, the foul-mouthed general demanded that Tilghman be restored to his command or Pemberton could dispense with his services as well. Pemberton did not want to lose a senior commander on the very day of the big battle—even an insubordinate one like Loring—so, writing on the pommel of his horse, Pemberton revoked the order firing Tilghman.

In hindsight, it is obvious that Pemberton made a serious mistake in not taking Loring up on his offer. Almost any general in the army would have performed better than Loring did on May 16.

The key position of Champion Hill was owned by Lieutenant Colonel Sid Champion of the 28th Mississippi Cavalry (State Troops), which was not present at the battle. It was seventy-five feet high, bald-crested, and sited about eight hundred yards southwest of the Champion House. It was the highest hill in the sector and commanded the surrounding area. Stephen Dill Lee, commanding Stevenson's lead brigade, recognized this fact at a glance and immediately occupied it with his Alabama brigade. Brigadier General Alfred Cumming's Georgia brigade took positions on Lee's right except for four companies, which covered the strategically important Jackson-Middle Road junction. They were backed by the six guns of Captain James F. Waddell's Alabama battery.

First contact occurred at 6:30 a.m., but it was unclear for hours where the main attack would come. Pemberton established his command post slightly to the left of center, at the Isaac Roberts' House, so he could have access to the entire line, but he spent little time there. He posted his cavalry in front and ordered Colonel Adams: "when forced to retire, fall back with your whole command in front of the strongest enemy."

Colonel Edward Goodwin's 35th Alabama took up blocking positions in front of Loring's Division. Shortly after 6:30 a.m., Wirt Adams reported that his pickets were skirmishing with Union troops on the Raymond Road, in front of Goodwin's position. He reported that there was a long line of U.S. infantry to the right. (This was McClernand's XIII Corps.) The cavalry fell back and Yankees launched a hasty attack against Loring's blocking force but were beaten back, in part by a racking fire from Bowen's artillery.

After a reconnaissance, Loring moved his line of battle back to the Coker House Ridge, named after a stately Greek-Revival manor house. Confederate surgeons immediately converted it into a hospital. Loring's division was now in a strong position. Artillery took positions on both sides of the Raymond Road, and Goodwin's 35th Alabama destroyed the bridge over Jackson's Creek as it retreated back to the main line of resistance. This checked any potential Yankee advances down the road. A. J. Smith's Division of McClernand's Corps did try, but was blocked by the stream. Union engineers tried to rebuild the demolished bridge but were stopped by Tilghman's cannons.

Grant's Army of the Tennessee came up and gradually made contact with the entire Confederate line between 8:30 and 10:30 a.m. Pemberton initially suspected that Grant was going to attack his right. It was soon obvious, however, that Grant was attempting to get around Stevenson and turn the Rebel left. Stevenson had to move his line, causing a gap between himself and Bowen. It was covered by Colonel J. T. McConnell's 39th Georgia. McConnell was wounded and replaced by Lieutenant Colonel Joseph F. B. Jackson, who blocked the Jackson Road.[4] A single regiment would certainly not be enough if Grant launched a determined attack here. Fortunately, he did not know this and struck elsewhere.

The main attack came against Stevenson's Division at 10:30 a.m., when two U.S. divisions hit his right flank like a tornado—"the attack broke upon us with great impetuosity and vehemence, in overwhelming force," General Cumming wrote later (see Map 12.1). The inexperienced

THE BATTLE of CHAMPION HILL May 16, 1863 (morning)

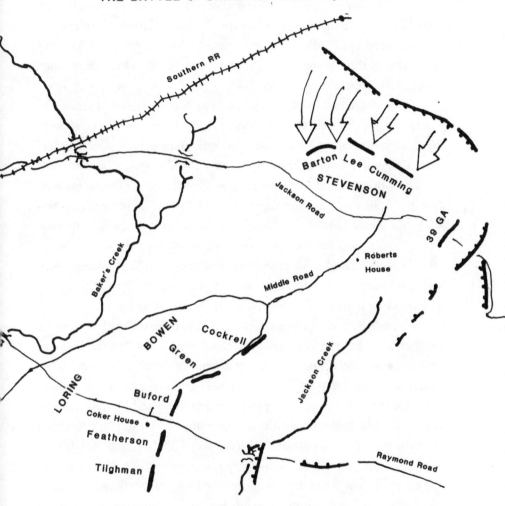

Map 12.1: The Battle of Champion Hill

34th and 39th Georgia Infantry Regiments had not even posted pickets, allowing the Yankees to get within seventy-five yards of the Rebel line without being detected. They unleashed a dreadful and demoralizing volley on the unsuspecting Rebels, and Southern losses were heavy.

While Cumming's brigade wavered, one of the Union brigades tried to outflank Lee to the left, where the Rebel flank was "in the air."

General Stevenson reacted quickly and sent Brigadier General Seth Barton's Georgia brigade, supported by the Cherokee Georgia Artillery and Captain Samuel J. Ridley's battery of the 1st Mississippi Light Artillery Regiment, to the threatened sector. They barely made it in time, but they checked the Federals, at least initially.

When the main Union attack was within three hundred yards, the Southern guns opened up with double canister, but the bluecoats kept coming. Stevenson's Alabama and Georgia units were in poor physical condition and did not fight as well as they could have.

Lee's Brigade and Cumming's Brigade checked the initial thrusts, but by 11:30 a.m. the fighting was hand-to-hand. General Lee was slightly wounded in the shoulder but ignored it. Cumming's Georgians finally broke, and Lee had no choice but to retreat as well. On the far left, Barton's Brigade also crumbled. The pursuing Northerners drove west and then south, capturing sixteen guns, overrunning Champion Hill and threatening to destroy the entire Southern army.

Barton's Brigade was in trouble.[5] It had been ordered to support Stephen Lee's left flank. It arrived at the double quick, but the Yankees had already turned Lee's left and were in the timber. The Georgians nevertheless pitched in and pushed the Northerners back, until their main force hit them. Barton's right promptly collapsed and then his left did the same. The brigade was almost surrounded and would have been destroyed except for the 40th Georgia and 42nd Georgia, which held formation and withdrew obliquely in good order. "We were handling the enemy in our immediate front in fine style, when all at once news came that our line was broken on our left, and orders came for us to fall back . . ." a disgusted Joseph Bogle of the 40th Georgia recalled.

General Lee rode up to the 40th and observed the disintegration of most of Barton's Brigade. With a sad smile, he turned to the men of the 40th Georgia, which was standing tall, and said, "Boys, there are not enough of you; if there were, we would redeem the day yet; as it is, you might as well go on with the rest."

Covered by the 40th and 42nd, Barton's Brigade retreated to the Big Black River bridge. Here General Barton rallied the remnants of his brigade and made a last stand. It was successful—but the brigade had been effectively pushed off the field of battle and had suffered 42 percent casualties.

Brigadier General Seth M. Barton.

"Had the Georgians and Alabamians stood up like men, like the Georgians and Alabamians at Manassas, Richmond, Sharpsburg and Fredericksburg, all would have gone well," Private Wesley O. Connor of the Cherokee Georgia Artillery Battery recalled bitterly.[6] But, as the Southern infantry moved smartly to the rear, the Yankees were soon almost on top of the Cherokee guns. They managed to fire one volley of double canister; then Captain Max van den Corput gave the order to abandon the field pieces, and his artillerymen joined the rout.

"Large numbers of Stevenson's men now met us, who were falling back in great disorder," Corporal Ephraim Anderson of the 2nd Missouri Infantry Regiment recalled. "These were the same men that afterwards ran out of the intrenchments at Missionary Ridge, and there caused the loss of the battle."

In the Confederate rear, Lieutenant Drennan (who was now in command of Loring's wagon trains) recalled, "I met bodies of men—some without hats—their guns thrown away—and looking as if they had just escaped from the Lunatic Asylum." His attempts to rally them were in vain.

Drennan rode closer to the front and ran into Colonel Theo Withers, who told them that the enemy was coming in his direction and that his Company A (1st Mississippi Light Artillery Regiment) had lost five of its eight guns. He also saw large numbers of wounded men, hobbling off the battlefield.

When the Yankee blow came, Pemberton was on the right, trying to get Bowen and Loring to attack. Neither was willing to obey orders, and Loring insisted that the enemy was too strong to attack. When Stevenson's men gave way and Champion Hill fell, the battle threatened to become a rout. Pemberton now took a desperate chance. He again ordered Bowen to turn left, charge, retake Waddell's guns, and roll up Grant's line. No doubt having second thoughts about his earlier insubordination, Bowen obeyed this order with dispatch.[7] Gambling that McClernand's Corps on Grant's left (southern) flank would remain inactive, Pemberton intended for Loring to cover the gap created by Bowen's departure with part of his division and join attack with the rest, but again Loring ignored his orders and did nothing.

The Battle of Champion Hill.

According to Corporal Anderson of the 2nd Missouri Infantry Regiment, the troops were "in fine spirits, animated, gay and buoyant." Their attack was superlative. Both sides later agreed that Bowen's charge was one of the most magnificent attacks of the entire war. Pemberton called it "splendid." Bowen was a tough disciplinarian and his thorough training methods had produced the best division on either side. The advance began at 2:30 p.m. It was led by Colonel Francis Marion Cockrell's Missouri brigade, followed fifteen minutes later by Brigadier General Martin Green's Arkansas brigade, which fell in on Cockrell's right. Cockrell charged on horseback, with a saber in one hand and a large magnolia blossom in the other. Meanwhile, Stephen D. Lee made what W. T. Moore called "a terrible appeal" to his men to rally. "As if by magic" the confused Rebels suddenly turned around, reformed, and joined the attack on the left of Cockrell. Advancing at the double quick, the Missouri troops passed General Pemberton (whom they cheered) and reached the Champion House area, where a group of ladies stood in the yard, cheering them on and singing "Dixie."

". . . the boys shouted zealously, and I could not refrain from hallooing just once, expressive of my admiration for the perfect 'abandon' with which these fair creatures gave their hearts to the cause," a Missourian recalled.

They continued forward. About two hundred yards further on, they ran into the Yankees. Bowen's men overran several Northern units, retook the lost positions and pushed Grant's left back more than a mile. They recaptured the lost Rebel guns, captured a Union battery, retook the Jackson-Middle Road Crossroads, and watched the Union teamsters flee in panic. The Army of the Mississippi had regained the initiative.

Grant and his lieutenants committed their reserves and the fighting soon became desperate. The Rebels drove them back three times, but each time they returned with fresh regiments. "Had they been supported by Loring's division, they could have cut [Grant's Army] to pieces," historian Spencer Tucker wrote later.

Green's brigade also experienced great success. Private A. H. Reynolds of the 19th Arkansas recalled his colonel, Tom Dockery, "as cool as an ice-berg," ordering them to load. "It was one of Colonel Dockery's hobbies to volunteer to take some battery or storm some difficult stronghold with his legion," Reynolds recalled. "My heart got right in my mouth and I believe every other fellow was in like condition . . ." but no one said a word except Dockery. "Forward, double-quick, march!" They advanced to Champion Hill, where Dockery was waiting for them. Mounted on his horse, as cool as ever, he ordered: "Halt on the right; by file into line, double-quick, march!" [8]

Thomas P. Dockery (left), shown after his promotion to brigadier general, and Francis Cockrell, seen after the war, when he was a United States senator. Both were excellent battlefield commanders.

This was a combat formation. The next command was "Fix bayonets!" Then came the order to charge.

They pushed the Yankees off the high ground, Private Reynolds recalled, but then were outflanked by Logan's U.S. division on its right. Reynolds and four of his friends went out to scout when a Federal regiment filed out of the road at trail arms. Each Rebel picked out a man and fired. Down they went, while the Southerners tried to scamper back to their main line. Reynolds was loading his rifle (a Springfield) and walking down the hill when he tripped over the root of a huckleberry bush and down he went. A split second later the Yankees fired a volley, which went over his head. The tumble had saved his life. An instant later the bluecoats were on them with their bayonets. One of them drew back to kill Reynolds. He had not had time to finish loading, but he fired anyway, and at point-blank range. The musket ball and his steel ramrod both flew into the Yankee's chest, killing him instantly. He fell on top of Reynolds, who was captured a moment later.[9]

While Reynolds was marched to the Union rear, Colonel Dockery retreated with the rest of his regiment. He had had two horses shot from under him and barely escaped himself. He was known thereafter as "the hero of Champion Hill."

Bowen's division was now outflanked and was fighting Yankees on its left, right and center. His men fell back out of the woods and into an open field, followed by the Northerners. Here the four guns of Lieutenant J. M. Landis' Missouri Battery opened up on them. The Yankees scattered and took to the woods. The terrain they had just taken was so broken that their artillery had not been able to keep up. Stalemate temporarily set in on the Rebel center.

Although Stevenson's division was now stabilized, everything was not well on the Confederate left. A section of Captain Samuel J. Ridley's battery (Company A of the 1st Mississippi Light Artillery) deployed near a farmhouse.[10] Suddenly, a strong enemy detachment sprang up from behind the garden and fired a devastating volley. All but one of the horses hauling the guns were shot down and two of the gunners were killed. Captain Ridley ordered his men: "Take care of yourselves!" A moment later, both he and his horse were shot dead, along with Major Joseph W. Anderson, General Stevenson's chief of artillery, and Hugh Mallary, the battery artificer. Another gunner was shot in the foot and ran away, limping. The survivors put him on the only horse that was still alive, and he managed to escape.

Now some of the Yankees surged forward and captured a driver. Private W. T. Moore tried to escape, despite the fact that a "nest" of Yankees was only fifty feet away. They shouted "Halt!" but the fleet-footed private kept running. The Northerners opened fire on him. One

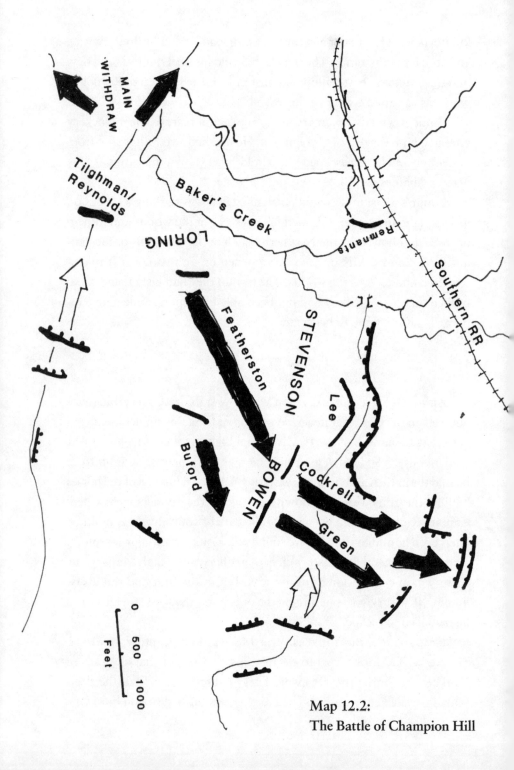

Map 12.2:
The Battle of Champion Hill

or more bullets ripped through his coat and another blew the hat off of his head, but he kept running—probably faster than before. He jumped two rail fences with bullets flying all about him and striking the rails, but he never looked back. The lucky and fast Rebel dashed across a cotton patch and into the woods, where he finally reached safety. He eventually made his way back to Vicksburg. All he had to eat for two days was some sugar. "We went there with 32 men and only came out with 8," he recalled. His gun (which the Northerners captured) did not fire a shot all day.[11]

Pemberton, meanwhile, sent "several staff officers in rapid succession" to Loring, ordering him to come to Stevenson's assistance. Pemberton knew that they would need Loring's men to sustain the momentum of the attack. But Loring ignored these orders as well. He also failed to close the gap between his division and Bowen's until after 3:00 p.m. Eventually he did send Featherston's brigade into the gap, leaving Tilghman's brigade on the Raymond Road on his right flank and Brigadier General Abraham Buford's brigade on the left. "I have received no explanation of the extraordinary failure of General Loring to comply with my reiterated orders to attack . . ." General Pemberton wrote later. "Perhaps Loring sensed that he was in a position to make sure that Pemberton did lose a battle," Ballard speculated later. He may have also cost the Confederacy much more than that. Famed historian Major General J. F. C. Fuller later wrote: "It is not too much to say that had Grant been decisively defeated [at Champion Hill] the South would have won the war." Grant, of course, was determined not to let this happen. He threw regiment after regiment into the fray. "Three times, as the foe was borne back, we were confronted by fresh lines of troops," Corporal Anderson recalled. "Their numbers seemed countless." The roar of musketry was deafening, but the Rebels were gradually forced back. Casualties in the forward units were very heavy. One company in the 1st Missouri Regiment was down to seventeen men. It had gone into the action with forty men and four officers. It was now commanded by the orderly-sergeant. Map 12.2 shows Bowen's attack and Pemberton's attempts to stabilize his lines and save his army.

By now, Grant was able to bring his superior numbers to bear in the Champion Hill sector, but Bowen threw them off again in fierce fighting; however, without reinforcements, he was unable to sustain the momentum. The combat was ferocious. About 3:00 p.m., Grant's men brought up sixteen cannons. The battlefield was so covered in gun smoke that the infantry fired without actually seeing their targets. They simply aimed at the muzzle flashes of their enemy.

Bowen was now running low on ammunition because General Stevenson had sent his wagons (including his ammunition wagons) back behind Baker's Creek when it appeared that his division was about to collapse. (Bowen never forgave him for this.) Meanwhile, Grant's right was reinforced by an entire division of fresh Yankee troops. Bowen fell back to the slopes of Champion Hill, where he met and repulsed several Federal attacks.

Around 4:00 p.m., two Georgia regiments of Cumming's brigade broke and fled in disorder for the second time that day. The surging Yankees surrounded most of Colonel Michael Woods' 46th Alabama. He surrendered with three hundred men.[12] Meanwhile, a good part of the routed Georgians were rallied by Pemberton and his staff. With the line temporarily stabilized, a furious Pemberton personally went in search of Loring. He had not gone far when he ran into Buford's brigade, which was finally coming up. Pemberton ordered Buford to send two regiments to support Bowen at the crossroads and to take the rest of the brigade to support Stevenson. The 12th Louisiana and the 35th Alabama temporarily stabilized Bowen's line, but the floodgates were clearly creaking. "You never saw hail fall faster than the Yankees' bullets flew," Private J. T. Kidd of the 20th Arkansas recalled.

Pemberton went to Loring's last known position, where he found only two regiments. He discovered that Loring had fallen back to the south—without orders and without bothering to tell his army commander. He had taken a little-known road and Pemberton was not able to find him. His 6,600-man division, as Pemberton stated in his official report, "took no active part in the battle" all day.

About 4:30 p.m., Stevenson's Division finally gave way. Half an hour later, General Bowen galloped up and personally informed Pemberton that his division could no longer hold its positions. His men were out of ammunition and were taking what they could from the dead. Just then Loring finally appeared, several hours too late. There was no time for recriminations. Pemberton gave him the task of covering the retreat to the south. Except for Stevenson's Division, the Rebels retired in good order, with Bowen's men forming the rearguard for the northern forces. About the time the retreat began, six companies of the 20th Mississippi Mounted Infantry Regiment arrived and were given the task of guarding the wagons, all of which escaped without loss.

Loring delegated the task of covering the southern portion of the retreat to General Tilghman and his brigade.

Lloyd Tilghman was in a good mood that day. Dressed in a new uniform, he posted his roughly fourteen hundred men and his artillery on Cotton Hill, west of the Coker house. A Yankee division attacked but was thrown back. Meanwhile the Yankees brought up a dozen guns. Now on foot, Tilghman walked up to the gunner of one of his 12-pounder Napoleons. "I think you are shooting rather too high," he said, and sighted the gun himself. He went to a small knoll to watch the effects of his work; then he suddenly collapsed. A three-inch piece of metal from an exploding Parrot shell had struck him in the upper part of his stomach and almost cut him in half. He lived about three hours but without regaining consciousness. He died in the arms of Captain Powhatan Ellis, his adjutant, under the shade of a peach tree. Meanwhile, Colonel Alexander E. Reynolds assumed command of the brigade. Tilghman's body was carried to Vicksburg by his son and aide, Lloyd Tilghman, Jr., who would be killed in the siege.

In the meantime, Bowen's and Stevenson's men crossed Baker's Creek, but the Federals were advancing south along the east bank of the creek to cut off Loring's retreat. Realizing that he could not cross on the

Raymond Road as originally planned, he turned south, looking for a ford.

A statue depicting the death of General Tilghman, Vicksburg National Military Park. Although not 100 percent accurate, it is nevertheless a fine piece of art.

He still had not found one when night fell. In the darkness and the mud, he abandoned all of his wagons and artillery, and gave up the idea of rejoining Pemberton. He did not see fit to send a courier to his army commander, to inform him of this fact. He headed southeast with about one-third of the Confederate field force and marched all night, around two Union divisions. At one point, he ran into a Union courier. He also spotted a Yankee picket on the road. Loring personally commanded the courier to order the picket to withdraw. He did, and the Rebels had a clear road. After marching forty-six miles with only a few rest stops, they reached Crystal Springs at nightfall on May 17. Here his men boarded trains and joined Johnston in Jackson on May 19. Without artillery, wagons, tents, equipment or baggage of any kind, Loring's Division had neutralized itself as a fighting force without having ever seriously engaged the enemy.

Colonel Wirt Adams and his cavalry regiment were covering the northernmost portion of the retreat toward Bridgeport, about three miles north of Edwards Station, when all of the infantry had crossed to the west bank. The engineers cut loose the pontoon bridge and the cavalry regiment was cut off. It was not captured only because darkness fell.

The 1st Mississippi Cavalry spent the night on the wrong side of the Big Black River. They slept under arms with their bridle reins in their hands. As soon as it was light enough to see, they headed cross country through fields and woods, because they knew they could not reach Edward's Depot via the main road. They found a crossing at a place known as Birdsong's Ferry. The men crossed by flat boat while the horses swam.

One report stated Pemberton sent an order to Adams to report to him in Vicksburg, but the colonel did not see how cavalry could be of any use to a besieged garrison, so he turned east and joined General Johnston instead. Another source stated that Pemberton ordered Adams not to enter Vicksburg but to join Johnston instead. In any case, the 1st Mississippi Cavalry eventually linked up with the Army of Relief and was not surrendered in Vicksburg.

Loring had 4,862 men on May 24. He had lost almost 2,000 at Champion Hill and on his forced march, and almost certainly he inflicted less than 200 casualties on the enemy. Parts of the 54th Alabama (of Buford's brigade) were cut off and, along with the City Guards (Captain E. B. Martin) and the Signal Corps (Captain C. A. King), they followed Captain J. J. Cowan of the 1st Mississippi Light Artillery into Vicksburg or went along with Lieutenant Drennan and the wagon train into the city. They amounted to 800 men. Many of Loring's stragglers were captured, and several hundred simply went home (i.e., they deserted).

Southern losses at Champion Hill were high, especially in Stevenson's Division. They were in poor shape and Grant's men ran down and captured a great many of them. Total Union losses were put at 2,457, including 410 killed, 1,844 wounded and 187 captured or missing. Pemberton's losses were variously reported as 3,069 (381 killed, 1,018 wounded and 1,607 captured or missing), and as 3,840 (381 killed, 1,018 wounded and 2,441 captured or missing). He also lost 27 guns. Stevenson's Division was especially hard hit. Cumming's brigade lost 995 men (121 killed, 269 wounded and 605 missing). Barton lost 901 (58 killed, 106 wounded and 737 missing). Stephen Lee lost 44 killed, 142 wounded and 604 missing. Among those taken prisoner was Captain Temple Franklin Cooper, the commander of Company K, 52nd Georgia Infantry Regiment, a great-great-grandson of Benjamin Franklin. He later died in a Union POW camp.[13] Other notable casualties included Colonel Alpheus Baker of the 54th Alabama, Loring's Division, wounded; Major Anderson, chief of Stevenson's artillery, killed; Colonel Skidmore Harris, 43rd Georgia, Stevenson's Division, killed; Colonel Woods, 46th Alabama, captured; Colonel McConnell, 39th Georgia, Stevenson's Division, wounded; Colonel E. P. Watkins, 56th Georgia, Stevenson's Division, wounded;[14] Lieutenant Colonel Findley S. Hubbell, 3rd Missouri, mortally wounded; Lieutenant Colonel William H. Dismukes, 19th Arkansas, killed; and Lieutenant Colonel H. G. Robertson, 20th Arkansas, killed.

Among the prisoners was Lieutenant Henry McLaughlin of the 35th Alabama Infantry, part of Buford's brigade. He was captured by his own brother, Lieutenant Colonel John McLaughlin of the 47th Indiana.[15]

In the Confederate rear, Father John B. Bannon of the 1st Missouri Brigade wanted to perform last rites on Private McGolfe, a gunner from Guibor's Battery. He refused because there was a wounded Yankee next to him. "Take away this Yankee boy, I can't lie quiet here with this Yankee by me!"

Bannon asked him to calm himself and confess his sins. McGolfe was blinded but he recognized the priest's voice. He knew the man beside him was a Yankee because he couldn't speak English and therefore had to be one of Lincoln's German mercenaries. McGolfe declared that his wounds weren't all that bad and that he would be all right in a day or two. Bannon said no, you are dying. "Your skull is split open, and your legs and arms are smashed; you cannot live out the day, and you must be prepared to meet God's judgment."

McGolfe insisted that the Yankee be removed. Father Bannon told him to forget the Yankee and attend to his own soul. Finally, the gunner agreed. Then Bannon attended to the Federal, who was indeed one of the German mercenaries. Although he did not speak English, the Yankee fervently kissed the crucifix when the priest held it out.

The following day, May 17, Father Bannon was following the retreating army into Vicksburg when he encountered some ambulances. One of them carried Private McGolfe who, remarkably enough, was still alive. "I can't help thinking of that poor Yankee," he declared. "I behaved like a brute to him. He died last night, but after you left him he never stopped saying his prayers, and he prayed like a good one. He made me think, I can tell you. I'm just sorry for the way I treated him, and if you can give me any more penance for it, do. Now if you'll stop by me, I'd like to make my confession again."

The priest said that he would give him no penance, because he had done enough. He gave him the last absolution. Private McGolfe died an hour later.

Although it is not widely recognized, Champion Hill—together with Gettysburg—turned out to be the decisive battle in the Civil War. The world-famous military historian Major General J. F. C. Fuller,[16] later wrote: "The drums of Champion's Hill sounded the doom of Richmond." He also declared that it was not going too far to state that, if the North had lost the Battle of Champion Hill, the South would have won the war.

Of the senior Confederate generals, only Pemberton and Bowen performed well. Loring refused to cooperate and was no help at all, while

Stevenson provided little leadership and was not able to control his men who, in general, did not fight well.

Pemberton has been criticized as a poor and hesitant field commander. But was he? Certainly he was not perfect on May 16, but neither was Grant. It is true that he lost, and contemporary historians judged him harshly precisely because he lost, but was he the hopeless bungler as he has so often been depicted? Personally, I don't think so, and neither did esteemed historian Bruce Catton, who wrote that "The Confederacy had few generals unluckier than John Pemberton." Unlucky and incompetent are vastly different things. The reader, of course, must draw his or her own conclusions. Had Pemberton's orders been obeyed, it is quite likely he would have won the decisive Battle of Champion Hill. Had he done so, Vicksburg would have held, Grant's army probably would not have escaped, the South might have won its independence, and John C. Pemberton today would be hailed as a hero of the extant Confederate States of America.

As things were, Pemberton did a creditable job on May 16. Major Jacob Thompson later wrote to Pemberton: "Being near your person throughout the several days of trial, I was struck with admiration at the prompt manner in which you discharged every duty devolved upon you in your responsible position."

As for Pemberton, he bitterly resented Johnston's interference, which forced him to fight at Champion Hill. He sent a dispatch to the commander of the Army of Relief, stating: "I greatly regret that I felt compelled to make the advance beyond Big Black, which has proved so disastrous in its result."

Later, General Pemberton would declare that, if he had to fight the campaign all over again, he would only do one thing differently: he would ignore the orders of Joseph E. Johnston.

CHAPTER XIII

THE BIG BLACK
RIVER

While Loring escaped, Pemberton retreated nine miles to the next natural defensive position: the Big Black River, which the army reached during the night of May 16–17. It was narrow but surprisingly deep. The river formed a naturally strong position, and it was here that Pemberton had originally planned to face Grant a week before. But now he had a different army; this one had been beaten, reduced by casualties and demoralized.

General Pemberton had shown foresight in both planning his retreat and in making contingency plans. Because he thought obeying Johnston's orders might be "suicidal," he sent Major Samuel Lockett, his chief engineer, to prepare makeshift bridges over the river even before Champion Hill. There was a railroad bridge over the river. Lockett built a floor over the rails, which would allow the passage of troops, artillery and wagons. Eight hundred yards south of the railroad bridge, he lashed together three steamers: the *Dot*, the *Charm* and the *Paul Jones*. The Confederates had brought them up the river from Grand Gulf, to prevent their capture. Now they formed the core of an improvised bridge, over which the Army of Mississippi could escape. But Pemberton also had another task in mind. He did not know Loring had marched southeast instead of west. For all the general knew, he was still at large and trying to reach the rest of the army. Pemberton had to keep an escape route open for him. For that reason, he stationed his best division—Bowen's—on the east side.

Major (later Colonel) Samuel H. Lockett.

Bowen's two depleted brigades were insufficient to hold the Confederate front, which was fifteen hundred yards long, so Pemberton gave him John C. Vaughn's brigade, fresh up from Vicksburg, in the center of the Rebel line.[1] But this was not a good brigade. Most of its troops were draftees from east Tennessee. They weren't particularly enthusiastic about the Cause and some of them were actually Unionists. They had never played a critical role in a major battle and did not want to do so now.[2]

Map 13.1: Big Black
River Bridge

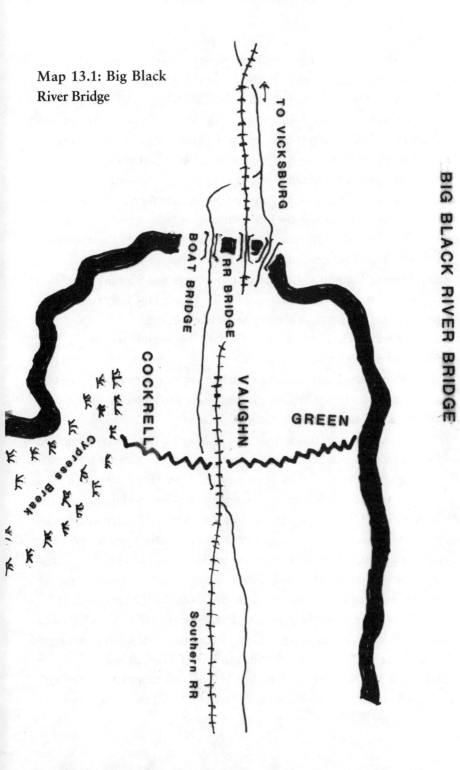

Bowen deployed his men along the main road to Vicksburg, with Green on the left, Vaughn in the center, and Cockrell on the right. Bowen's left flank rested on the Big Black and his right anchored on Gin Lake, which was essentially a cypress swamp, so Grant could not outflank it. A shallow bayou ran in front of the line, and the Rebels cut the trees along the banks, to give themselves a clear field of fire. They constructed a parapet along the west bank of the bayou, using cotton bales from a nearby plantation and throwing dirt over them. The ground in front of Bowen was mostly flat cottonfields, which were covered by eighteen guns. The infantry, meanwhile, dug rifle pits. It was a strong line which the Yankees could not go around, but which they could overrun, because Vaughn's brigade was not reliable and Bowen's other two brigades were not in good shape. Map 13.1 shows the Confederate dispositions for the Battle of the Big Black River Bridge.

Pemberton knew if Grant breached the Big Black River line, Haines' Bluff and Snyder's Bluff would have to be abandoned. Pemberton had about sixty days of provisions at Vicksburg and Snyder's Bluff, so he sent a warning order to Major General John Forney to be prepared to get the stores, troops and munitions back into the city.

About 9:00 a.m. on the morning of May 17, the Yankees emerged from a copse north of the railroad and attacked in a dense formation along a narrow front. Taken by surprise, the east Tennessee troops fired a single, ragged volley, jumped from their trenches, and dashed for the bridges, which were three-quarters of a mile away. Others simply surrendered. It was not Tennessee's finest hour. Bowen's center ceased to exist and his other two brigades were enfiladed. Colonel Elijah P. Gates' 1st Missouri Cavalry (Dismounted) of Green's Brigade held its front, but was surrounded flank and rear, and only about half of it escaped. Colonel Gates was among the prisoners, but he escaped three days later and made his way to Vicksburg, where he resumed command of his regiment.[3] Cockrell's brigade, according to Private Truman, was "blue with rage, at such cowardice" as Vaughn's brigade disintegrated, but Bowen's division now had only one chance of escaping, and that was to run.

So, they did. It was every man for himself.

"We made what resistance we could while running for the bridge. As we neared it, we were astonished to see it in flames . . . Just below it a steamboat had been turned across the river and bridged out at each end. I was among the last to cross upon it." His brother, Captain Johnnie Bachman, was too late. He had to swim the river, but he made it. A great many didn't and were either killed or captured.

Walsh's 1st Missouri Battery (aka Wade's Battery) was in a bad way. Its horses were on the other side of the river, about half a mile away. Walsh ordered all four guns spiked, and the artillerymen joined the rout. Company G of the 2nd Missouri Infantry was too late to cross the bridge. Its commander and several of his men were captured. Lieutenant Alford stripped to his shirt and drawers and swam to the opposite bank. He had to travel some distance without pants, boots or weapons, until he found a house near the road, where the residents gave him some clothes. Then he proceeded to Vicksburg.

Company G had gone into the Battle of Champion Hill with sixty-two men. When it reassembled in Vicksburg, only thirty-three men reported for duty.

Other units fared even worse. The 61st Tennessee lost 288 of its 400 men. Most of the 19th Arkansas was cut off and forced to surrender. Its commander, Lieutenant Colonel William H. Dismukes, was mortally wounded. Almost half of Green's brigade was lost.

The Battle of the Big Black River Bridge was the worst rout in Confederate history up to that date. About four thousand graycoats escaped. Cockrell's brigade now only numbered fifteen to sixteen hundred men, and Green had only twelve hundred men left.

Before Vaughn's brigade broke, Major Lockett noted "signs of unsteadiness in our men." He reported this fact to General Pemberton and prepared to burn the bridges.

After seeing that all of his retreating troops "still subject to command" had crossed to the west bank, Pemberton ordered the bridges burned. Major Lockett was ready. He had set turpentine barrels alongside each bridge for just such an emergency, and cotton soaked in turpentine burned quickly and effectively. As soon as the semi-organized units reached the west bank, the torches were lit. Within minutes the railroad bridge and all three boats were burning merrily. It would take Grant's engineers an entire day to construct new bridges. On the other hand, the slower Confederates were trapped east of the river and were easily rounded up by the Yankees. Grant lost 279 men. Pemberton put his losses at 1,024 and 18 guns. The entire battle had lasted thirty minutes.

Meanwhile, seven miles to the north, Sherman crossed the Big Black at Bridgeport, virtually without opposition, and headed for Haines' Bluff and Snyder's Mill. Even if Bowen had held, the Army of Mississippi was flanked.

A despondent John Pemberton ordered the army to retreat into the fortress of Vicksburg. At 10:00 a.m., he directed General Stevenson to conduct the retreat to the city. This was done in reasonably good order. He headed for the fortress himself, accompanied only by Major Lockett. "He was very much depressed," Lockett recalled. Mostly they rode in silence. Finally, the general said, "Just thirty years ago I began my military career by receiving my cadetship at the United States Military Academy, and today—the same date—that career is ended in disaster and disgrace." Lockett tried to cheer him up by pointing out that he had two good divisions in Vicksburg (Smith's and Forney's) and that he could hold Vicksburg until relieved.

Pemberton told Lockett that his youth and hopes were the parents to his judgment. The general did not believe his troops would stand the first shock of an attack.

That night, the evacuation of Snyder's Mill and the Chickasaw Bayou line began. But there were not enough wagons. A good part of Loring's wagons, which were still with the army, were sent there to carry off corn, but there was still not enough. Between twenty-five and thirty thousand bushels of corn had to be burned because they could not be transported into the fortress.

The ruins of the Big Black River Railroad Bridge.

CHAPTER XIV

INTO VICKSBURG

The fortification of Vicksburg had been going on for some time. It started under Earl Van Dorn in the summer of 1862, but picked up under Pemberton. According to his chief of staff, Major Robert Memminger, "the engineering skill of the commander and his fertility and expedients were conspicuously displayed." This is no doubt true, but John Pemberton had a huge amount of help. In fact, generally speaking, the skills of the military engineers on both sides exceeded those of their army commanders—often by a wide margin. In Vicksburg, Pemberton had Major Samuel Lockett, an engineering genius, and Martin Luther Smith, a decent division commander but a great military engineer.[1] Pemberton placed him in charge of developing a line of defense. It included a system of detached works (redans, lunettes, banquettes and redoubts) on the most prominent features and key locations. They were connected by rifle pits (now called trenches), and there were platforms for the artillery. Parts of it were protected by abatis of fallen trees with sharp stakes pointing toward the enemy. Trees were cut and houses burned to give the Rebel infantry a clear field of fire.

On Sunday, May 17, the ladies of Vicksburg were dressing for church when they heard the sounds of artillery. Startled, some of them sought an officer, who informed them that those were Confederate guns. They were firing at Yankees on the Louisiana side of the river, who were burning houses there. Thus reassured, Mrs. Loughborough, the wife of Major James M. Loughborough, a Confederate staff officer, and her friends, went to the Methodist Church.[2] Here she received another indication of the closeness of the war. Her pastor was not there. He had left to tend the wounded and dying on the battlefield. She received an uplifting sermon from a refugee, "a plain man, of simple, fervent words." When she and her friend emerged, they saw their first demoralized Confederates.

That Sunday, the defeated Army of Mississippi began pouring into Vicksburg. They were accompanied by hundreds of cattle, sheep, goats and hogs. Foreseeing a siege, Pemberton ordered his men to drive the local livestock into the city. He instructed his men to commandeer every available wagon, cart and buggy to collect corn, rice, and peas, and bring them into the fortress.

Many of the men entering Vicksburg were demoralized stragglers. One soldier found the streets "thronged with stragglers, and several hundred slightly wounded men seeking food and hospitalization. No sentries, no order . . . the army came drifting in, footsore, tired, hungry and dispirited." Emma Balfour recorded that "Nothing like order prevailed."

"I shall never forget the woeful sight of a beaten, demoralized army that came rushing back,—humanity in the last throes of endurance," Dora Miller recalled. "Worn, hollow-eyed, ragged, footsore, bloody, the men limped along unarmed, but followed by siege guns, ambulances, gun carriages, and wagons in aimless confusion."

"What can be the matter?" the ladies from the Methodist Church cried, as the streets were full of vanquished men.

The men passed them without saying a word. Finally one declared: "We are whipped, and the Federals are after us."

"Where are you going?" they asked another. No one answered, so they cried again.

"Where on earth are you going?"

Finally an embarrassed man answered: "We are running."

"From whom?"

"The Feds, to be sure," an awkward, weary-looking man replied.

"Oh, shame on you!" a woman cried. "And you running!"

"It's all Pem's fault," the awkward man replied.

"It is your own fault," a lady declared to his face. "Why don't you stand your ground?" A chorus of women derided the stragglers: "Shame on you all! We are disappointed in you! Who shall we look to now for protection?"

One of them said, "Oh, it's the first time I ever ran. We are Georgians, and we never ran before, but we saw them all breaking and running, and we could not bear up alone!" Further excuses followed, but the women of Vicksburg would have none of it. (The Southern infantry was tough, but the ladies of Vicksburg were tougher.) They told the soldiers to their faces that it was all their fault—they should have fought harder. Even so, they gave the defeated men water and fed them.

Even the Yankees expressed their admiration for the Vicksburg women. "Their sacrifices and privations are worthy of a better cause," one of them wrote, "and were they but on our side, how we would worship them."

Joseph D. Alison of Battery C, 2nd Alabama Artillery Battalion, wrote in his diary,

> The enemy attacked our forces beyond Big Black, for some reason our men would not fight and we were utterly routed. Report says we have lost two thirds of our army and the balance demoralized. I never saw men more dispirited. A rumor is circulated that General Pemberton has sold Vicksburg and many believe it. If an attack is made tomorrow, we are lost . . . I have never been low spirited before but things look too dark for even me to be hopeful.

Colonel Hall of the 26th Louisiana recalled,

> Mrs. Hall called my attention to scattered bodies of troops coming in, on the Jackson Road, which ran near my quarters; I saw at once it was our army in retreat, and in utter confusion—a long line of stragglers. There would be a squad of infantry, a horseman—a gun—a few more infantry, and so on; with no more order than travelers on a highway, seeking Vicksburg as a shelter. This stream of stragglers continued nearly all day. After breakfast, I went down town to hear the news. It was all one story, a fight, a repulse and a retreat. Every one I met had the gloomiest forebodings.

The demoralized and disorganized condition of the army challenged Pemberton's organizational skills. He had officers herd the stragglers into assembly areas and soon restored some semblance of organization. But only half of the army had been defeated. Other, fresh units were available for employment in Vicksburg. A good example is Colonel Jerome Bonaparte Gilmore's 3rd Louisiana and Winchester Hall's 26th Louisiana.

The 3rd Louisiana was formed in Camp Walker, New Orleans, on May 11, 1861, with 1,037 men. Sent to Missouri, it fought at Wilson's Creek, where it played a major role in winning the battle and captured five Federal guns. It also distinguished itself at Pea Ridge, where it suffered heavy casualties, and its first commander, Paul Hebert, was wounded and captured. Crossing the Mississippi River in April 1862, it fought at Corinth and Iuka, where it lost more than one hundred men.

On December 28, the 3rd Louisiana broke camp near Greenville and headed for Vicksburg, where the Battle of Chickasaw Bluffs was in progress. It marched across country until it reached Yazoo City, where it boarded boats, which took it to Snyder's Bluff. The regiment was without baggage, blankets, tents, and even knapsacks, and suffered severely in the cold. Ironically, it reached Snyder's Mill on January 2, 1863—too late to participate in the battle.

At Snyder's Mill, the 3rd had the job of reinforcing and protecting the 22nd Louisiana Infantry Regiment, which was really a heavy artillery unit. Snyder's Mill was where the bluffs touch the Yazoo. Just below it was "a solidly-constructed raft of huge logs completely blockading the stream." As it was perhaps the key position in the whole Vicksburg defensive network, both the 3rd and 22nd were posted there indefinitely.

The men of the largely Cajun 3rd Louisiana loved their new assignment. They had plenty of food, there was a friendly town nearby where they could go to on passes and buy liquor, and no one was trying to kill them. Sergeant Tunnard wrote: "The men were full of life, and passed their evenings in dancing, interspersed with music, both vocal and instrumental. Their new situation seemed to agree with them most wonderfully."

The 26th Louisiana, on the other hand, was organized at Camp Lovell, Berwick Bay, Louisiana,[3] in April 1862. It was sent to Jackson, Mississippi, in May, and was assigned to Martin Luther Smith's command in June. Here it faced a severe outbreak of measles. Today, measles is considered a relatively benign childhood disease, but it was a major killer of adults in 1862, and something Civil War soldiers on both sides took seriously. "We were ill-conditioned to offer resistance to the destroyer," Colonel Hall recalled. "It reigned in terror; we had no cots— many of the men were even without blankets; we had no hospital accommodations; we did not have, nor could we procure proper medicine and nutriment; nurses were out of the question. Soon the quarters were filled with the sick and the dying; and it seemed we were powerless to succor or to save." Several men died.

Colonel Hall went to Father Leray, a Catholic priest,[4] who secured aid for them from the Sisters of Mercy, who turned their home into a hospital. Every room was filled with patients, and the sisters saved many lives.

The 26th was sent to Camp Hall, eighteen miles from Vicksburg, in July 1862. It was in a beautiful grove of oak and hickory trees and was laid out military style, with streets between rows of tents. Cooking and horses were kept in the rear, giving the camp an attractive appearance.

The men spent most of their time preparing for drill and Hardee's *Tactics* became like a Bible to them.[5]

Reveille at Camp Hall was at 4:00 a.m. every day, followed by two hours of battalion drill. Surgeon's call was at 6:15 a.m., and 1st Sergeant's call was at 6:45. Breakfast was served at 7:00 a.m., and company drill and guard mounting began at 8:00 a.m. Dinner was served at 1:00 p.m.[6] The men were off duty from 2:00 p.m. to 6:00 p.m., during the heat of the day. Supper was from 6:00 p.m. to 8:00 p.m., when tattoo was sounded. Taps was ten minutes later.

The food lacked variety but the troops were amply supplied with cornmeal, fresh beef and small amounts of pork and bacon, rice, and molasses. White flour was only served to the sick. The men also found plenty of sweet potatoes in the local neighborhood, but they had no coffee or tea, and hadn't had any since they left Louisiana.

At the end of September 1862, the regiment struck tents and marched to Camp Lagarde, two miles to the rear of Vicksburg. The nights of October 25–27 were cold enough for ice to form, and two hundred of the south Louisianans were without shoes. Many of the men still had no blankets, and thirty-five soldiers came down with pneumonia. They were also without warm uniforms. Someone brought this to the attention of the ladies of Tensas Parish, Louisiana, who sent them boxes of clothing and cloth, including window curtains, which made very substantial shirts and "nether garments."

There were still no blankets, so Winchester Hall and a detachment of men went door to door in Vicksburg, begging for blankets. The first lady gave them several pieces of rag-carpet, which were perfectly suitable. Others gave them old blankets. Soon an African American woman approached them with several quilts, even though they had not solicited help from her. Charity, the colonel noted, "belongs to no creed and no race."

The "begging expeditions" continued for three or four days. One lady gave them a parlor carpet. Another had nothing for blankets, but she did offer them several socks, which they gratefully took. Soon the regiment was fully provisioned with blankets and had pretty much all it needed except for shoes and uniforms. Their uniforms were now old and in tatters.

In late fall, the 26th was sent to Camp Crow, near the Vicksburg Cemetery, next to Colonel Robert Richardson's 17th Louisiana. They made themselves quite comfortable by flooring the tents with boards and building chimneys. At that time, the men were armed with Enfield rifles, a good muzzle-loader for the period, courtesy of British manufacturers and Southern blockade runners. With these the men fought their first battle at Chickasaw Bluffs in December as members of Thomas' Provisional Brigade. Here the regiment distinguished itself and captured 300 Yankees. They remained in the area until February 1863, when the men were sent to Vicksburg proper, where they moved into vacant dwellings and warehouses. As of February 19, the 26th Louisiana had 674 men, most of whom spoke French as their native language.

About the first of March, new conscripts from Louisiana arrived in Vicksburg. They wore white woolen uniforms, which marked them as draftees. The men of 26th Louisiana, who were all volunteers, treated them with contempt. Then the quartermasters sent the rest of the regiment new uniforms—all of which were white! There was massive indignation and howls of protest from the veteran volunteers, but gradually they all yielded to the inevitable and put on the comfortable, warm uniforms.

The 26th was sent north in March 1863, where it opposed the Steele's Bayou Expedition and the Greenwood Expedition (April 2–14). It then returned to Vicksburg.

The men of the 3rd Louisiana were very excited on the morning of April 30, when a flotilla of Union naval vessels and transports ascended the Yazoo and attacked Snyder's Mill. The gunners of the 22nd Louisiana opened fire and hit the ironclad USS *Choctaw* fifty-three times in less than five hours. The 3rd Louisiana took positions on the levee and fired into the portholes whenever they opened. Meanwhile, six Union gunboats threw a heavy fire at the Confederate trenches, which remarkably resulted in no casualties in the 3rd. The 22nd Louisiana only suffered two men wounded and lost one gun when a 32-pounder cracked. Some Union infantry landed along the river bank but did not attack.

The U.S. forces continued to probe the Confederate defenses on May 1, but again did not launch an assault. At 3:30 p.m., a heavy bombardment began. It lasted four hours and several shells exploded inside Confederate lines and on the parapet, but again there were no casualties, and again there was no attack.

About 4:00 p.m., a Kentucky private (and a member of an Illinois regiment) deserted from an outpost on the river bank. He informed the Rebels that the Northerners were not strong enough to attack and never intended to. This whole operation was, in fact, a diversion in favor of General Grant, he said. The man was telling the dead-honest truth, but nobody believed him.

The next morning, May 2, the Confederates woke up and looked up and down the Yazoo. There wasn't a Union vessel anywhere.

The 3rd Louisiana was never more pleasantly situated than it was at Snyder's Mill. They had erected truly comfortable quarters and acquired some little conveniences which seemed like luxuries to soldiers, such as being able to bathe and to boil their clothes to kill the lice. They even received mail and daily newspapers. They also got their share of the "immense quantities" of supplies that were being transported down the Yazoo, including hams, eggs, chickens, hogs, beef, and other "luxuries."

The dawn of May 17 broke clear and warm as the 3rd Louisiana prepared to leave Snyder's Mill. They had no transport for extra clothing, stores, utensils, or most of their equipment. Each man selected what he could conveniently carry and filled his knapsack. Everything else was abandoned, including tents and extra blankets. The heavy siege guns were either spiked or loaded in such a manner that they would burst if fired. A detail was left behind to blow up the magazines and destroy the depot and commissary, which contained provisions that could not be carried off. Late that night, the infantry left. It was an intermingled line of foot soldiers, wagons and artillery. The night was dark, but the men were in excellent spirits. They considered Vicksburg impregnable and were proud to defend it.

That same afternoon, the 26th Louisiana was ordered to a point on the outer line of fortifications. That night, they slept on their guns in the trenches. The 27th Louisiana came up on their right. The next day, they were improving their positions, making rifle pits and deepening their trenches with picks and spades.

On the morning of May 18, the 3rd Louisiana was placed in the trenches, on the left of the Jackson Road, along with the Mississippi regiments of Brigadier General Louis Hebert's brigade. To the right of the road lay the 21st and Companies C and D of the 22nd Louisiana. General Hebert told them that they held the key to the city. "The regiment responded that they would sustain their blood-earned reputation, justify the confidence reposed in their bravery, and perish to a man ere they would relinquish their position to a million foes," Sergeant Tunnard recalled. Their position was exposed and there were no trenches on this part of the line, but they were given spades and pickaxes. They immediately went to work "with a desperate energy."

It was that way all up and down the line. In Stevenson's sector, for example, the battered 56th Georgia used their tents to construct sand bags, which were laid on the top of the outer banks of the ditches. Thirty paces forward of their main trench, they laid four-foot stakes, driven into the earth and sharpened, and facing the enemy at an angle of about 45 degrees.

But errors were made. For some unexplained reason, the 60th Tennessee made its regimental camp *east* of the trench line. The Yankees captured it the first day. The regiment lost everything except the clothes they were wearing, including their knapsacks and blankets. "I did not have a change of clothes for forty-seven days and nights," Private Backman recalled. He didn't have a single bath, either. Body lice were prevalent in both armies, but especially in the Confederate forces, and it was particularly bad in the 60th Tennessee. "Every few days, I would take my shirt and pick body-lice from it," he said later. One of his buddies swore he had found one louse which was so large that it was branded "C.S.A."

The 3rd and the 26th Louisiana were not the only fresh units available. Martin Luther Smith's entire division was rested and ready, as was John Forney's division. Their morale was certainly higher than that of Stevenson's and Bowen's divisions, which had only recently suffered major defeats. Many of the men returning from Champion Hill and the Big Black River thought surrender was inevitable. Rumors abounded, of course, as they always do in any army, including one that said Pemberton (a Northerner) intended to betray them and surrender to Grant. Quite a few called the general a coward and a traitor. Emma Balfour noted in her diary: "Gen. Pemberton has not the confidence of officers, people or men, judging from all I am compelled to see and hear." Union prisoners continued to wage psychological warfare, telling the Southerners that Grant and Pemberton already had an understanding, and that Pemberton was going to surrender the city on May 20. Even General Bowen took this rumor seriously. He told some of his officers that he would hang Pemberton "as high as Haman" if he made the first move to surrender and sent a dispatch to his army commander. "I find that the wildest and most absurd rumors are in existence, not only among the men, but the officers in command." He told Pemberton about the rumor that he was going to sell out the Confederacy and surrender Vicksburg without a fight.

The accusations struck a nerve. Pemberton shook off his depression and recovered his fighting spirit. He wrote a proclamation and had it read throughout the army: "You have heard that I was incompetent, and a traitor; and that it was my intention to sell Vicksburg," he wrote. "Follow me, and you will see the cost at which I will sell Vicksburg. When the last pound of beef, bacon, and flour, the last grain of corn, the last cow and hog and horse and dog shall have been consumed, and the last man shall have perished in the trenches; then, and only then, will I sell Vicksburg."

The dispatch had the desired effect. The Confederates recovered their morale quickly. They dug in even deeper. Many of the men worked hard and rapidly, shoring up the defenses weakened by the winter and spring rains. Others mounted guns. There were only five hundred shovels but many bayonets, which were used extensively. Unit bands assembled on the Courthouse hill, where they played patriotic tunes, including "Dixie" and "The Bonnie Blue Flag," to rally the troops. The newly energized general, meanwhile, went out to inspect his troops and try to further boost morale. It worked. The transformation was remarkable. The Army of Mississippi changed from a dejected rabble into a determined body of stalwart soldiers, almost in the blink of an eye.

Bowen's scattered division also quickly recovered. It assembled in the cemetery, about a mile northeast of the city. Here it reorganized, bivouacked, cooked one day's rations, and was ordered to be ready to move at 10:00 that night. Map 14.1 shows General Pemberton's dispositions for the Siege of Vicksburg. Map 14.2 shows his main positions.

Pemberton was inspecting his perimeter with several of his generals at noon on May 18, when he received a dispatch from General Johnston. "If you are invested in Vicksburg," he wrote, "you must ultimately surrender . . . If it is not too late, evacuate Vicksburg and its dependencies, and march to the northeast." He did not mention that he had no intention of trying to relieve the fortress, but the Philadelphian could read between the lines.

John C. Pemberton must have been appalled. He called a meeting of all his top generals. Then he wrote Johnston,

> On the receipt of your communication, I immediately assembled a council of war of the general officers of this command, and having laid your instructions before them, asked the free expression of their opinions as to the practicability of carrying them out. The opinion was unanimously expressed that it was impossible to withdraw the army from this position [Vicksburg] with such morale and material as to be of further service to the Confederacy. While the council of war was assembled, the guns of the enemy opened on the works, and it was at the same time reported that they were crossing the Yazoo River

at Brandon's Ferry, above Snyder's Mill. I have decided to hold
Vicksburg as long as is possible, with the firm hope that the
Government may yet be able to assist me in keeping this
obstruction to the enemy's free navigation of the Mississippi
River. I still conceive it to be the most important point in the
Confederacy.

Because Lockett had burned the bridges over the Big Black, it took
the Yankees the rest of May 17 and a good part of May 18 to cross the
river. They did not reach Vicksburg's outer defenses until late afternoon
on May 18. By then, Pemberton had organized his army and was prepared to defend the city. He also ordered all Yankee prisoners paroled,
so he wouldn't have to expend any of the garrison's rations on feeding
them. They were then shipped by tugboat to the fleet. The little tug made
trips all day long.

When the Federals closed in on the city, the veteran Northern soldiers
looked at the defenses and turned pale. One Union officer recalled seeing
"A long line of high, rugged, irregular bluffs, clearly cut against the sky,
crowned with cannon which peered ominously from embrasures to the
right and left as far as the eye could see. Lines of heavy rifle-pits, sur-
mounted with head logs, ran along the bluffs, connecting fort with fort,
and filled with veteran infantry..." Author Winston Groom noted that
the defenses looked like "the serrated walls of a medieval castle." The
approaches were all uphill. In most places, the Yankees would have to
advance across open fields. The Rebels had cut and burned the brush
and had given themselves clear fields of fire. "The approaches to this
position were frightful—enough to appall the stoutest heart," one Union
officer recalled.

Sherman's corps had crossed the Big Black upstream from the rest
of the army and headed for Chickasaw Bluffs, which the Rebels had
already abandoned. His XV Corps occupied the Federal northern (right)
flank, McPherson's XVII Corps took the center, and McClernand's XIII
Corps faced the Confederate right.

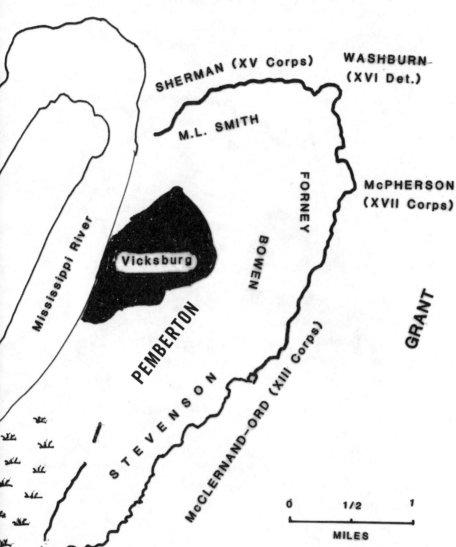

Map 14.1: Vicksburg: The Deployment

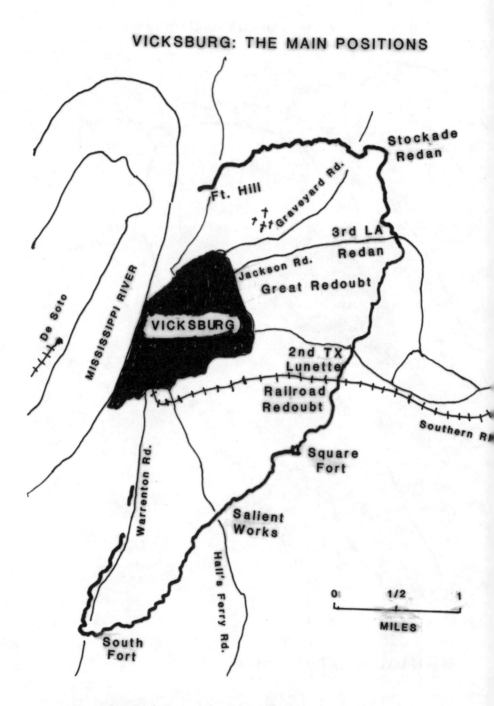

Map 14.2: Vicksburg: The Main Positions

Martin Luther Smith's division (three brigades, Mississippi State Troops, and a small part of Loring's division) faced Sherman. Their line extended from the Graveyard Road on the right to the river on the north, and compassed Fort Hill, a critical position.

Forney's division (two brigades) held the center. It extended two miles, from the Graveyard Road on the left to the railroad. Stevenson's four brigades extended from the railroad to the Warrenton Road and the river—about five miles. This was his poorest division and Pemberton positioned it on easily defended terrain, which was also the least likely place Grant would attack.

Stevenson's Division occupied the right (southern) Confederate flank with Barton's, Cumming's, and Lee's brigades. Behind it were fields which were not cultivated during the war. It was here the Army of Mississippi grazed its horses, mules, and cattle.

Pemberton placed Bowen's division (down to twenty-four hundred men) in reserve, with Cockrell's brigade behind Martin Luther Smith and Green's brigade behind Forney. Waul's Texas Legion (five hundred men under Colonel Thomas N. Waul) was in reserve behind Stevenson's division, in position to support John C. Moore's Brigade on the right or Stephen D. Lee's on the left.

Bowen objected to these dispositions. He wanted his division placed in the line. He thought that each of the four divisions should have its own reserve. Pemberton wisely overruled him and kept a centralized reserve. As a result, however, Bowen would lose command of much of his division as the siege progressed and individual regiments were committed to the threatened sectors of the other divisions.

Meanwhile, the Missouri division was reequipped with British-manufactured Enfield rifles, which were considered by some to be the best infantry weapon of the day.

The entire kidney-shaped fortified line was about eight and a quarter miles long and enclosed an area four miles long and two miles deep. In all, Pemberton had 18,500 muskets. Not counting reserves, he had a rifle strength of a little more than 15,500 men in the trenches. They were supported by 102 guns.

The first Yankees arrived about 3:00 p.m. and light skirmishing began between Sherman's men and Smith's in the Fort Hill sector about 5:20 p.m. The Siege of Vicksburg had begun.

Meanwhile, much of southwestern Mississippi was under Northern occupation or behind Union lines. The people of Port Gibson were suffering for lack of food but generally stayed at home. The African Americans also avoided the place and, as Mrs. Ingraham noted in her diary "do not consider Port Gibson safe for 'free people of color,'" as the former slaves now were. She also noted that the blacks had changed. "The negroes are as idle as darkies only can be," she wrote, "Nearly four weeks since 'their vacation began . . . and not a stroke of work [would they do]." She wrote this even though one of her former slaves brought her chickens, which kept her from hunger and perhaps starvation. Meanwhile, since Grant no longer needed to run supplies through the area, the Yankees pulled back to Grand Gulf. Undisciplined Union troops still "roam the country in small squads, robbing and setting fire to gins and houses at their pleasure." They woke people in the dead of night, demanding money and watches, and threatening to burn their homes and gins if they did not comply. Several gins were burned, and people were very worried about what the blacks might do.

Then, in early June, a new group arose. It was called the "Secesh"; it was an armed vigilante group of about twenty-five men. They whipped and threatened Negroes and hanged at least one, and ordered the rest to report for work in the morning "or else." At Ashwood, the frightened men showed up; the black women did not. Thus did the complicated history of American race relations turn another page, and we see the beginnings of the rise of the Southern night rider. Unfortunately, Mrs. Ingraham received word on June 11 that her last living son, Frank, had been killed in action at Chancellorsville on May 2, and she abruptly ended her diary, so we will leave it there.[7]

CHAPTER XV

THE ASSAULTS

On the Confederate northern flank, Martin Luther Smith placed his worst brigade (J. C. Vaughn's east Tennesseans) in and around Fort Hill, the northern anchor of the Rebel line and the most easily defendable position. Brigadier General William E. Baldwin's Mississippi brigade held his center, and Brigadier General Francis A. Shoup defended his right flank.

Shoup was a Northerner. He was born in Laurel, Indiana, in 1834, the oldest of nine children. He attended Indiana Asbury (now DePauw) University before being admitted to West Point, where he graduated fifteenth out of thirty-four in the class of 1855 and was commissioned second lieutenant in the artillery. He was stationed in Florida and South Carolina before his parents died in early 1860. Shoup resigned his commission and returned home to take care of his brothers and sisters. He studied law and was admitted to the bar later that year.

Francis Shoup was a Jefferson Democrat. "My whole nature rebelled against the Republican Party," he said later. As the war approached, he moved to St. Augustine, Florida, and was there when the South seceded. He petitioned Secretary of War Leroy P. Walker for a commission in the newly formed Confederate Army. Walker vetoed the application on the grounds that Shoup was a spy! Jefferson Davis overrode the veto and signed the commission with his own hand. "Say what you will," Shoup recalled, "Mr. Davis is a brick!"

Francis Shoup as a lieutenant, U.S. Army.

There was no reason for Shoup to join the Rebel army, other than his political principles and his admiration of the Southern people. He was sent to Fort Morgan, Alabama (on Mobile Bay), and then to Arkansas as an artillery officer. Promoted to major in November, he was General Hardee's chief of artillery. He commanded a 21-gun artillery battalion at Shiloh, prompting Beauregard to make him chief of artillery of the Army of Mississippi on April 10, 1862. On June 8, he was promoted to colonel and sent back to Arkansas, where he served on the staff of General Hindman and later General Holmes. Commissioned brigadier general on September 12, he commanded a brigade in the Battle of Prairie Grove, before returning to Mobile as chief of artillery of that department. On May 3, General

Pemberton named him commander of the Louisiana brigade, which was
then at Hankinson's Ferry.

By the morning of May 19, Pemberton had decided that the Yankees were massing along the Graveyard Road, which was one of the
natural approaches to Vicksburg. He posted Shoup on the left (north)
side of the road and Hebert on the right. The Stockade Redan on the
south side of the road was fourteen feet high with a seven foot ditch
in front of it, and it was packed with earth and logs.[1] The Redan was
defended by Colonel William W. Witherspoon's veteran 36th Mississippi,[2] which had only three hundred men, along with six companies
of the greatly reduced 5th Missouri on the east face and the consolidated 1st/4th Missouri on the north. The 3rd Missouri Infantry Regiment (now under Major James K. McDowell) and part of the 5th
Missouri were in reserve. Sergeant George Powell Clarke of the 36th
Mississippi recalled,

> At 10:00 a.m. the firing ceased and the Federals advanced in
> two lines of battle, halted about 300 yards from our position
> to reform their lines. Numbers of battle flags could be seen
> just behind the hill, waving in the morning breeze . . . and
> soon the long, glittering line of bayonets came in sight, as with
> martial tread this tremendous war machine marched to the
> attack. On reaching the top of the hill and coming into plain
> view, they gave a prolonged yell, and broke into a double
> quick towards our lines. At the proper time our batteries
> opened on them with grape, canister, and shrapnel shells,
> which told fearfully on their crowded ranks. When they had
> reached within fifty yards of our lines we opened upon them
> with musketry, using the 'buck and ball' cartridge with mur-
> derous effect. But they were brave men and did not falter,
> though hundreds were falling all around them, until within
> a few feet of us. They then wavered, rallied once, but finally
> gave way and retreated to their own position.

The Yankees were not finished, however. They rallied, committed fresh units, and charged again.

A withering fire of musketry, grape, canister, and shells greeted them as they came in sight, and men fell like grass before the reaper. Here, now, the eye witness could have seen war in all its awful sublimity and grandeur.

As we have seen, Smith deployed Shoup's Brigade on his right flank. The brigadier posted his regiments in the front line on the north side of the Graveyard Road. Shoup dispatched Colonel Leon D. Marks' 27th Louisiana and personally marched with it. He also brought up Colonel Winchester Hall's 26th Louisiana, to cover Marks' left flank. Major Thomas M. Carter's 2nd Missouri was held in reserve.

These were good moves. At 2:00 p.m., the Yankees attacked. The first assault was against the center of Shoup's brigade. It met a hail of musket and cannon fire from the two Louisiana regiments. The attackers broke and the survivors fled. Simultaneously, elements of U.S. General Steele's Division attacked the 17th Louisiana of Baldwin's brigade, on Shoup's left flank. It also was turned back.

On the afternoon of May 19, Grant launched a hasty assault against all three Confederate divisions. He was acting under the reasonable assumption that an army which had run away on May 17 would not offer serious resistance on May 19. Almost everyone in the Army of the Tennessee would have agreed, but they were all wrong. Also, Grant heretofore had seven advantages: 1) numerical superiority, 2) a navy, 3) a divided Confederate command, 4) Confederate uncertainty as to what he might do, 5) the element of surprise, 6) the threat of attacks and raids against the Southern rear, and 7) the threat of cutting them off from their supply base at Vicksburg. These factors had forced Pemberton to disperse his forces. Now, however, Grant had lost all of these advantages except the first two.

The day was warm. At 2:00 p.m., the XV and XVII Union corps made full charges, although the main attack was against Smith's division. The men in blue were in a cheerful mood as they advanced. Like their commander, they believed that the Confederate defenses would simply collapse and the fortress would be theirs by nightfall. But the first Rebel volley was devastating. Men fell in bunches all along a six-mile line. Sherman recalled that "the heads of [the] columns [were] swept away as chaff thrown from the hand on a windy day."

Against Smith's extreme right, Sherman attacked again with seven regiments. They were again met by the 26th and 27th Louisiana and 2nd Missouri, which had been reinforced with the 1st/4th Missouri.[3] The Southern fire was withering. After a second volley, some of the Yankees fled in confusion and disorder, leaving five sets of colors on the field. Others reached the base of the Confederate parapets and lay there trapped, unable to advance or retreat.

There was suffering on both sides. Colonel Winchester Hall of the 26th Louisiana had been walking slowly up to the right of his line when he felt something strike the calf of his right leg. He initially thought a clod of dirt had been thrown up against it, but he soon felt dizzy and then faint from a loss of blood. A medical orderly, unable to evacuate him to a hospital, gave him a drink of whiskey, which revived him, performed first aid, and left him in a wagon rut, which offered at least a little protection. The former Chicago hardware dealer lay there until nightfall. He was hit in the side by another musket ball, but fortunately it was spent. After sunset, he was removed to a field hospital, where he listened to doctors debate whether or not to cut off the leg. They decided it could be saved and it was, although the operation left the colonel with a limp for the rest of his life. He later joined his wife and children in Vicksburg, where he began his recovery.[4]

Meanwhile, Sherman's men attacked Fort Hill. As we have seen, Pemberton and Smith placed the remnants of Vaughn's brigade here because it was nearly impregnable but, because they considered this a key position, they stacked it with a truly impressive array of heavy artillery from the 1st Louisiana Heavy Artillery Regiment, Colonel Andrew Jackson, III's 1st Tennessee Heavy Artillery Regiment,[5] the 8th Louisiana Heavy Artillery Battalion, and two companies of the 22nd Louisiana Infantry Regiment.[6] They were also backed by the 350 Louisianans of Colonel Thomas' 28th/29th Infantry Regiment, which were posted there in case the east Tennesseans bolted again.[7] Charles B. Lewis of Smith's division recalled,

> Illinois, Indiana and the 13th Regulars took the lead. Within four hundred feet of their starting point regiments lost their alignment, from the broken nature of the ground. Chasms had to be crossed, hollows descended and slopes climbed, and directly they encountered the felled trees, and then it looked to the Confederates behind the works as if a great mob in blue was pushing ahead.
>
> Now they came under fire and the fight opens. The monster guns in the forts, aided by the [13] field pieces, put in position, sweep the crests of the ridges as with brooms of fire, and men demoralized for the instant crowd into ravines for cover, only to find that there is no hiding place safe from shot and shell. Two or three times the blue mass pauses and wavers, and seems to circle round, but each time it gathers strength for a rush that carries it nearer [to] the belching cannon and flaming muskets.

One officer recalled,

> I could look over the smoke and see the ground blue with Federal dead . . . .Slowly, steadily, and with a determination which commanded the admiration of friend and foe, the advance finally gained the ditch in front of Fort Hill. Here the broken Twenty-seventh Illinois halted on the open ground, within half-pistol shot of five thousand muskets, formed their lines anew, and with the first cheer of the assault, dashed at the ditch and over it. The Eighty-third Indiana followed, and the Thirteenth Regulars came up on the flank. The ditch was passed, and the slope was gained, and they could go no further. The slope was too steep . . . Lighted shells were rolled down the slope to play terrible havoc, and the Federal flags

planted in the earth were shot to shreds in less than ten minutes.

Confederate positions on the other side of the highway were also attacked, Lewis recalled, "but Pemberton did not allow these feints to distract his attention from Fort Hill. That was the point aimed at, and that was the point to be defended."

The Regulars lost one third of their number. Confederate losses were negligible.

The Yankees attacked in four lines. They got close enough to plant several flags on Confederate works. In places, the Rebels fired grape and canister instead of shells. Sherman admitted later that "the enemy fought hard and well." A proud General Smith later reported, ". . . my troops and artillery were all withdrawn within the mainlines and placed in position [on the night of May 18], from which they were not for an instant dislodged during the entire siege."

Major General Martin Luther Smith, commander of Pemberton's northern flank.

The center of the line was held by Major General John H. Forney's (formerly Maury's) division.[8] He had about forty-seven hundred men and twenty-seven guns. Forney was a tall man of impressive physique. One lady recalled that "He looked to belong to those daring, daunt-less steel-clad cavaliers of the Cross, than his unheroic age." He had previously commanded troops at Chickasaw Bluffs, while Smith directed those in Vicksburg. Born into a Huguenot family in North Carolina in 1829, John Forney was the younger brother of Brigadier General William H. Forney, first cousin of Brigadier General Robert Daniel Johnston, and second cousin of Major Generals Robert F. Hoke and Stephen D. Ramseur. His family moved to Jacksonville, Alabama, in 1835.

Forney entered West Point in 1848. Two years later, he was on cadet leave and went to Talladega, to attend a girls' school commence-ment. Here he saw a "comely and gracious" girl named Septima Sexta Middleton Rutledge. "That's the girl for me," he decided. But he had a difficult time courting her. "Her father [Colonel Henry A. Rutledge of Talladega] had always annoyed me," he recalled, "seeming to think that as an army officer, I always came to see him."

Lieutenant Forney's military career put his courtship on hold. He was commissioned in the infantry and commanded a pioneer detach-ment in Albert Sidney Johnston's Utah campaign. He was an instruc-tor of infantry tactics at West Point when Alabama seceded. He resigned his commission and, in the space of three months, was named colonel of Alabama State Troops and aide-de-camp to the governor; Confederate colonel and inspector general on Braxton Bragg's staff; and was elected colonel of the 10th Alabama Infantry.

Forney was assigned to the Army of Shenandoah, where he was promoted to brigade commander. He fought at Bull Run and was severely wounded in the arm during the Battle of Dranesville, Vir-ginia, that winter. This injury bothered him for the rest of his life. Promoted to brigadier general in March 1862, he was apparently not yet able to return to field duty, so the War Department stationed him at Mobile. Here he was promoted to major general on October 27. He commanded the Department of Alabama and West Florida before becoming commander of one of Pemberton's districts in 1863.

That same year, he married Septima after a thirteen-year courtship.[9] "I met this young woman on cadet furlough in 1850," he recalled, "and kept up the approaches for 13 years, when the citadel finally yielded to a wounded Confederate soldier."

John Forney was a tough disciplinarian and was therefore not particularly popular with his men. Several historians have stated that Forney had done nothing to justify his rapid advancement and have implied that he was not the best choice to command a division. That may be so, but I have found much to praise and little to criticize in his performance at Vicksburg. On May 19, the Union regiments attacking his division were checked and basically stopped cold.

To the south, McClernand was slow getting into position and only launched a few probes against Stevenson's line, but they were weak and half-hearted. The Northerners here suffered few casualties but accomplished nothing. All told, Grant lost about one thousand men, against about one hundred Confederate casualties.

Pemberton was very much encouraged by the events of May 19. By their actions in combat, his men had made it clear to all that they had shaken off the depression engendered by the defeats at Champion Hill and Big Black River. The commander of the Army of Mississippi was no fool. He knew that the Yankees could eventually concentrate enough men at Vicksburg to overwhelm his defenses, but that would take weeks. He also knew that it was common knowledge that this was the decisive point of the entire war. He took it for granted that the Confederacy and Joseph Johnston would move heaven and earth to relieve him, because the loss of Vicksburg would very likely mean the loss of the war. His men felt the same way, and their morale soared as a result of their victories on the nineteenth. Only gradually did it dawn on them that they might be wrong.

Major General John H. Forney.

That night, fearing a rumored attack by gunboats, the women of
Vicksburg slept fully dressed. There were already plenty of caves in
the Mississippi hills for them to take shelter in if there were a bombardment. But, on this particular night, there wasn't one. Meanwhile,
Grant met with his generals. They decided that the attack had failed
because it had concentrated against Pemberton's strongest positions.
Because of the terrain (steep ravines, deep gullies and dense vegetation), they had followed the roads leading into the city, which in effect
channeled their advance. Pemberton had anticipated this, and his men
were ready for it. Grant now decided to launch a prepared attack. He
set the time for 10:00 a.m. on May 22.

At dawn on May 20, Grant started the bombardment of Vicksburg with 200 guns, including sixty he had captured in the three
weeks prior. "The place was a perfect pandemonium," a Rebel sergeant recalled. Confederate military positions were also pulverized.

Admiral Porter joined in by blasting the town with his mortars, which fired 13-inch (200-pound) shells up to three miles. They blew up entire buildings. Major Lockett measured a crater left by a naval mortar round; it was eleven feet deep. The ironclads also opened up on the city. Confederate gunners did not respond very much because they were conserving ammunition.

Everyone knew that if a mortar shell struck the top of a cave, it could cause the cave to collapse, burying alive everyone inside. "I shall never forget my extreme fear during the night," Mary Ann Loughborough recalled, "and my utter hopelessness of ever seeing the morning light. Terror stricken, we remained crouched in the cave, while shell after shell followed each other in quick succession. I endeavored by constant prayer to prepare myself for the sudden death I was almost certain awaited me. My heart stood still as we would hear the reports from the guns, and the rushing and fearful sound of the shell as it came toward us."

Union snipers were also very active. The 3rd Louisiana alone lost nine men killed or wounded to snipers that day. The 17th Louisiana lost its lieutenant colonel, Madison Rogers of Ouachita Parish, who was killed.

Isaac W. Patton, who assumed command of the 22nd Louisiana only five days before, was severely wounded in the hip. He was one of four Virginia brothers who became colonels in the Confederate Army: John, Waller, and George S. were the other three. The original George S. Patton was the grandfather of the famous World War II general. He was mortally wounded near Winchester, Virginia, in September 1864. Waller was mortally wounded during Pickett's Charge and died on July 21, 1863. Isaac survived the war.[10]

General Pemberton wrote Johnston and estimated that Grant had at least sixty thousand men. He again called for rapid relief, but Johnston had already convinced himself that all was lost because his orders of May 13 and 15 had not been obeyed. He already had a scapegoat (Pemberton), so he did not have to risk a battle.

A 13-inch mortar, which could throw a 200-pound shell three miles.

Meanwhile, on the morning of the twentieth, patrols from various infantry regiments went out and probed the Union lines. They returned and reported back to Pemberton that the Yankees were not digging in— i.e., they were not preparing for a siege. This could only mean one thing: they were planning another major assault. Pemberton, however, already had most of the pieces in place to defeat it.

The mortar bombardment continued on May 21. The ironclads joined the battle that afternoon, while Grant's artillerymen spent much of their time erecting new batteries. Pemberton sent four messages to Johnston that day, calling for help. He also ordered that all soldiers being held for trivial offenses be returned to their commands. Chewing tobacco was confiscated, and skirmishing without any specific objective was forbidden.

General Pemberton ordered that "ammunition should be hoarded with the most zealous care." He placed Stevenson in charge of supplies. This general feared for the safety of the powder magazines, so he organized a detachment of the city's most reliable citizens to guard them.

Scouting reports on May 21 indicated that there was a lot of enemy activity opposite the 2nd Texas Lunette in John C. Moore's sector (on Forney's far right flank) and against the Railroad Redan, which was defended by Stephen D. Lee's brigade on Stevenson's left flank. That afternoon, Pemberton posted Green's brigade in reserve near the lunette and Waul's Legion behind the Railroad Redan.

Heavy and rapid Union firing continued all day. Mortar shells tore houses to pieces and several citizens were injured. Union snipers and artillery batteries concentrated their fire on Confederate gun crews. Anyone who exposed himself was in serious danger. In one sector, five cannoneers tried to apply a lighted fuse to the vent of a gun. All five were shot by snipers.

After the shelling slackened, the Yankees opposite the 3rd Louisiana engaged in a shouted conversation with an acquaintance of theirs, Private "Shanghai" Masterton of E Company. They invited him to visit them in their lines with a promise that he would be allowed to return. Masterton accepted and was cordially welcomed. The Yankees showered him with "delicacies and substantials," which they had in abundance. After the feast, they broke out a bottle, and enjoyed a sociable chat over several drinks. A tipsy Masterton then returned to his own lines.

There was no socializing on May 22, which was the day of Grant's big attack. It was a bright, clear day with blistering sunshine. The artillery bombardment began in the morning, featuring heavy guns and naval artillery, supported by a great many snipers. Major Maurice K. Simons of General Moore's staff recalled, "At daylight this morning, the cannon opened their fire with unusual fierceness . . . roaring all round us. I have just been counting the number per minute & find it to average ten to forty per minute . . . There has been hundreds of shot & shell fallen all round us."

The Yankees were well prepared and one historian noted that "it was one of the most carefully planned assaults in modern warfare." U.S. General Francis P. Blair, Jr., had mounted twenty-seven guns in emplacements on either side of the Graveyard Road. They blasted the 27th

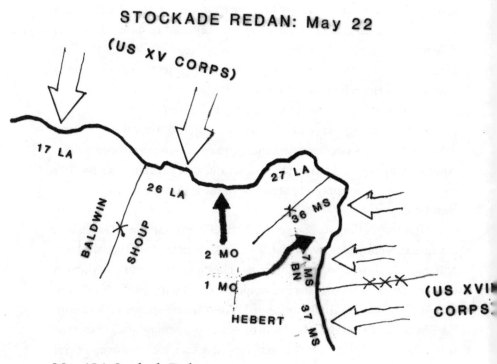

Map 15.1: Stockade Redan

Louisiana and pulverized General Shoup's positions until they ran out of ammunition.

Sherman opened the dance by launching another attack on Fort Hill. Charles B. Lewis of Smith's Division recalled, "The van of Sherman's assault was composed of a thin line of skirmishers, followed by the men detailed to carry planks and ladders and pick-axes and shovels." Then came the solid lines of blue. "The Confederates who were watching every movement say that a grander sight was never seen during the war," Lewis recorded later.

Sherman concentrated the fire of twenty-eight guns on Fort Hill alone. When the Northerners attacked, the Confederate sharpshooters ran back to their main line of resistance as fast as they could, leading the

Yankees to hope that they were running away and would meet little or no resistance. "Sherman's first brigades had reached within a stone's throw of Fort Hill before a bullet fell among them," Lewis recalled. "Then death came with the rush of an avalanche. At a word, a thousand Confederates sprang upon the crest of the parapet, and a thousand muskets flamed and cracked and sent their bullets right down into the crowded ranks."

Elsewhere the story was similar. Many of the Rebel infantrymen were armed with British manufactured Enfields, which had a maximum effective range of about 300 yards; they were, contrary to myth, much better armed than many of their Northern counterparts, as Grant pointed out in his memoirs. The Southern infantry commanders let the attackers get within 150 yards before they opened fire; then they ripped huge gaps in the Union formations.

One focus of the Union attack was against Shoup's and Hebert's brigades of Forney's division, which had been reinforced by Cockrell's 1st Missouri Infantry Brigade. They concentrated against the Stockade Redan. Sherman sent 150 men forward with a portable bridge, to cross the deep ditch the Rebels had dug below their works. They advanced down the Graveyard Road toward the Redan and were well supported by their cannons and howitzers. Most of Shoup's artillery had been dismounted and the Confederates let them pass through a steep cut in the road embankment. When they got close, the Rebels fired a devastating volley. But on they came, supported by Missouri and Ohio regiments. Some of the survivors reached the top of the slope and one man planted a regimental flag there. The rest huddled at the base of the Redan. The Rebels devastated them by igniting five-second fuses on artillery shells, which they rolled down upon the Northerners.

General Sherman's artillery concentrated on Fort Hill, keeping many of its guns silent and clearing the parapet for the infantry. The bluecoats made a dash for the parapet, but the Rebel infantry from east Tennessee rose up and fired a shattering volley. They were so close that many Yankees suffered powder burns to their faces. "It was butchery," Lewis declared.

Sherman reported that the Confederates "rose behind their parapet and poured a furious fire upon our lines; and, for the next two hours, we had a severe and bloody battle, but at every point we were repulsed." Martin Luther Smith reported that the Union attack was "dispersed without great effort and with considerable loss." In places, the ground was literally blue with Union dead and wounded.

The story was the same in the zone of the 27th Louisiana, which had been reinforced by Major Thomas M. Carter's 2nd Missouri (see Map 15.1). "The attacking lines, after making a very determined stand, and altogether a desperate struggle, were repulsed with great slaughter," Corporal Anderson recalled. "Three times they rallied, or brought up fresh troops, and renewed the attack, but were thrice driven back under the cover of the woods and out of range."

The 27th Louisiana (of Shoup's brigade) defended the left flank of the Stockade Redan on May 22, while the 36th Mississippi of Hebert's brigade held the Redan itself, supported by six companies of the 1st/4th Missouri on the east face and 3rd Missouri on the north face. The 36th Mississippi both suffered and inflicted heavy casualties. Its losses that day were not reported separately, but it lost one hundred men (twenty-eight of them killed) during the siege. That amounted to one-third of its total strength. The Missouri units (Cockrell's brigade) lost twenty-eight killed and ninety-five wounded on May 22. Major Alexander Yates of the 36th Mississippi was among the dead.

General Forney experienced success all up and down the line. The Yankees formed three lines in front of his division and advanced in nearly perfect order.

When they were about one hundred yards from the Confederate trenches, the Rebels opened up with rifle and artillery fire. A few brave Union soldiers actually reached the breastworks and tried to scale them, but they were promptly shot down. An Irish regiment planted its flag on the Great Redoubt, but they could not climb to the top because of a miscalculation. They needed eighteen-foot ladders but only brought twelve-foot ladders. They ended up huddling at the base of the redoubt, where the Rebels dropped short-fused artillery shells on them.

Meanwhile, the right side of Forney's line was held by Brigadier General John C. Moore's Brigade of Alabama and Mississippi regiment, along with Moore's own former command, the 2nd Texas.

The red-headed, red-bearded and red-faced Moore was born in Tennessee in 1824 and graduated from West Point in 1849. After fighting the Seminoles, he resigned from the army and was a professor at Shelby College in Kentucky when the war broke out. He fought at Shiloh and was promoted to brigadier general on May 26, 1862, despite the objections of Lieutenant General Hardee, who despised him. Prior to his promotion, one of Moore's soldiers described him as a "brave and gallant officer, but not a Christian." Moore was noted for being hot tempered and, "It was only a short time until I had strong suspicions that I had joined a regiment of devils."

On May 22, five regiments from Illinois and Ohio struck the 2nd Texas Lunette,[11] which was now under the command of Colonel Ashbel Smith. The Texans were alert and well prepared. In addition to their Springfield rifles, each man was armed with five smoothbore muskets, loaded with buck and ball. These muskets were obsolete by 1863 standards but were still good enough for close combat. They were loaded with a large rifle ball designed to kill a bear and three to ten buckshot on top of it.

The position was of a half-moon shape, which is why it was called a "lunette." It was protected by a parapet four and a half feet high with two embrasures for cannons. Its walls were fourteen feet thick and its revetments were constructed from cotton bales. It was also protected by a ditch, which was six feet deep. The lunette itself only held four companies, but Smith stationed two companies in the trenches on the right. Lieutenant Colonel Nobel L. McGinnis covered the left flank with the equivalent of a battalion, but there was one hundred yards of open space between McGinnis and the lunette. All brush and trees on the Confederate front had been cut and burned, so the Rebels had clear fields of fire. Behind the main positions, Smith's men dug a second line of trenches.

At 10:00 a.m., when the Yankees neared their positions, the Texans opened up at close range, and the Federals piled up in the ditch. General

Forney reported that, "The road in front of this position was left covered with the dead bodies of the enemy." More Yankees pushed forward, however, shouting "Vicksburg or Hell." They scaled the parapet and took a cannon after killing all of the gunners. "Old Jingle" Smith called for volunteers to retake the lunette. The Texans responded immediately and threw the Yankees back into the ditch. Two hundred bluecoats who could not escape were taken prisoner.

Thomas J. Higgins, the color-bearer of the 99th Illinois Infantry Regiment, was an extremely courageous man. As his comrades fell about him, he stumbled over their bodies but kept charging forward until he was all alone. "Suddenly, as if with one impulse, every Confederate soldier within sight of the Union color bearer seemed to be seized with the idea that the man ought not to be shot down like a dog," Private Charles I. Evans recalled. "A hundred men dropped their guns at the same time; each of them seized his nearest neighbor by the arm and yelled to him, 'Don't shoot at that brave man again. He is too brave to be killed that way.'" Many of the Texans threw their hats into the air and cheered him, crying, "Come on, Yank! Come on."

Higgins did come on. He scaled the breastworks and planted his flag. Then Corporal Charles I. Evans of Company G simply reached up, grabbed him, and pulled him into the Southern trench. He remained a POW until the end of the siege.[12]

Meanwhile, casualties in the lunette were mounting. One of the two cannons burst, killing two Texans and wounding several. The second cannon could not be fired because its gunners had been shot by surging Unionists. In addition, the cotton bales used to support the lunette began to burn and filled the fortification with smoke. The Yankees actually succeeded in scaling the parapet and capturing one of the embrasures, but Sergeant William T. Spence rallied the troops and threw them off again. Spence himself was shot and died a few days later, but the Texans were now in full control of the lunette. They now used the cannon balls as hand grenades and rolled them down on the Yankees, killing the men in the moat. By 3:00 p.m., the ditch had been cleared of living Northern troops who were not seriously wounded, and a lull fell over the 2nd Texas Lunette.

Another major thrust fell on the 40th, 42nd, and 37th Alabama Regiments of Moore's Brigade. Private S. L. Burney of Company G, 37th Alabama, recalled,

> . . . their line was only 150 yards distant. At a given signal they bounded at our men in a dead run, but their ranks were literally cut to pieces by our infantry and artillery. The field guns were double charged with canister put up in tin cans containing about 75 balls to the can. As they leave the gun the box is ripped and the mortally is fearful at so short a range . . .
>
> Notwithstanding this fearful slaughter, some of them reached our trenches, only to be knocked in the heads with the butts of guns or run through with bayonets. These charges are repeated several times.

The Yankees managed to secure one foothold and it did not last long. Colonel John Wesley Portis of the 42nd Alabama led another counterattack and killed or captured every man who broke through.[13]

Rebel losses were relatively light. Forney's division was attacked seven times: three on his extreme left, twice on the Jackson Road and twice on the Baldwin's Ferry Road. His entire division only lost forty-two killed and ninety-five wounded all day. Among the dead, however, was Colonel Charles H. Herrick, the commander of the 22nd Louisiana Infantry.

McClernand's corps advanced along the Vicksburg-Jackson Railroad and along the Baldwin Road at 10:00 a.m. The terrain here was less difficult to cross than that which Sherman faced, and the men of the XIII Corps moved forward quickly. It appeared for a moment that the Rebels had given up and vanguards were going to walk right into the forts. But just as the troops in the rear were raising cheers of victory, the Southern infantry rose up and delivered a "terrible" volley at close range. They fired volley after volley. Every third man in the forward ranks was killed or wounded.

The Union artillery breached the Railroad Redoubt, south of the 2nd Texas Lunette. McClernand asked for one hundred volunteers to storm it. Apparently, there were no takers, so he offered $300 and an honorable discharge for every man who stepped forward. He got his volunteers in no time. Sixty of these brave men actually reached the redoubt and planted two colors on the parapet. But Colonel Isham Garrott's 20th Alabama Infantry Regiment launched an immediate counterattack and it was joined by two companies of Waul's Texas Legion from Pemberton's reserve. General Stevenson later reported that no more gallant attack was launched during the war. The Yankees' bridgehead was quickly wiped out.

All along the line, Ohio, Illinois, and Indiana regiments surged forward and planted their flags on the Confederate works, but could not scale the parapet. Small detachments did penetrate the forts, but here they were cut down or taken prisoner.

One brigade attacked George W. Mathieson's 31st Alabama. "It was a tornado of iron on our left, a hurricane of shot on our right . . ." one Iowa soldier recalled. "We passed through the mouth of hell."

"No Abolitionist could show his head without danger from ball or buckshot," an Alabamian recalled. Major Mathieson estimated his men killed 150 Yankees. The 31st Alabama lost only one man.

Meanwhile, the Union artillery created a breach in Stevenson's line, and this time the Yankee spearhead scrambled through it, followed by two Ohio and Illinois regiments. They then discovered that the Rebels had fallen back to a second defensive line, where they were reinforced by Waul's Texas Legion. This line the Northerners could not break.

By now, McClernand was sure that he was about to win the battle. His front was all up, his advanced brigades were lying right under the Rebel works, and he had silenced many of the guns above them. He believed that reinforcements and one more push would break the Confederate lines. He also thought Porter's tremendous naval bombardment would help, but the sailors could not see their targets. The bombardment did not silence a single Southern gun.

About noon, McClernand sent Grant a message, stating that he was in partial possession of two forts and a "vigorous push ought to be made all along the line." Grant received the dispatch at 2:00 p.m. The message was true, but Grant turned to Sherman and said, "I don't believe a word of it." Sherman, however, convinced his friend that the note had to be accepted at face value.

Grant sent a fresh division to support McClernand. Instead of launching a concentrated attack, however, he broke the division up and sent it to various elements of his corps, which were now pinned down in front of Rebel lines. Meanwhile, Sherman and McPherson attacked again, using their reserves. Their objective was to prevent Pemberton from concentrating against McClernand's corps. McPherson's attacks amounted to little more than probes. Sherman, however, sent in two fresh brigades. They were promptly cut to pieces. "This is murder!" Sherman cried, and withdrew his troops.

To the south, in Stevenson's sector, the Yankees overran the Railroad Redan, which was defended by a detachment of the 30th Alabama and supported by Major Steele's battalion of Waul's Legion. Suddenly, at about 3:00 p.m., there was an extremely loud Rebel yell. Southern forces, led by the indomitable Colonel Pettus, counterattacked and overran the Yankee defenders, routed the forward units, recaptured the Redan, and pushed the Northerners back to their starting line.[14]

The Yankees were nothing if not persistent. At 5:00 p.m., they launched yet another massive assault against the 2nd Texas. They breached the Rebel line to the left of the lunette and pushed an artillery battery forward, threatening the defenders with annihilation. Colonel Smith quickly counterattacked but was unable to eject the Northerners. The enemy was now within the Vicksburg defenses and Smith was out of reserves, so he desperately called for help. Fortunately for the Rebels, help was not far off. Brigadier General Martin Green quickly shifted his brigade to the south, attacked, and drove the Lincolnites back in confusion.

Colonel Smith reported,

The loss of the enemy was enormous. The ground in our front
and along the [Baldwin Ferry] road . . . was thickly strewn
with their dead. In numbers of instances two and three dead
bodies were piled on each other. Along the road for more than
200 yards the bodies lay so thick that one might have walked
the whole distance on them without touching the ground.

The Yankees lost 3,199 men on May 22 (502 killed, 2,550 wounded
and 147 missing), against less than 500 for Pemberton's men. In terms
of losses, it was the fourth worst Union attack of the war, after Fredericksburg (13,500 casualties), Cold Harbor (7,000 lost) and the Crater at
Petersburg (3,800 casualties). Because of the failed attacks of May 19
and 22, Grant decided to let the snowball "melt by the force of nature—
with the gentle assistance of harassing fire and mines." In other words,
he decided to starve the garrison into surrender.

The Union killed and wounded lay in no-man's land between the
armies during the night of May 22. They suffered and screamed, and
some of them died, but there was no truce. A few Rebel soldiers went out
to help the wounded after night fell, but the vast majority received no
medical attention.

One Rebel recalled,

It is truly horrible to relate that some of the enemy's wounded
lay in sight and died for want of attention: one poor fellow,
in full view of our regiment, about seventy-five yards from
the works, although never heard to call out, yet was seen
repeatedly raising both his arms and legs for nearly two days,
when he became still—was dead, most probably from want
of timely and proper attention.

Several of the Confederate division and brigade commanders—distressed over the suffering and cries for help—sent notes to their counterparts on the other side, suggesting a truce so that they could tend to their wounded and bury their dead, but to no avail. Grant would not consent to a ceasefire.

It was customary for the loser of a battle to ask for a truce, but this Ulysses S. Grant would not do. General Pemberton finally took matters into his own hands and, in a gesture of humanity, sent a message to Grant, asking for a ceasefire. He added that if the Yankees did not want to bury their dead, his men would do it for them. Still Grant refused.

Meanwhile, most of the wounded who could not make it back to Union lines perished. Those who were killed on May 19 began to rot and stink under the hot Mississippi sun.

On May 25, Grant's soldiers began to complain about the smell. The medical officers warned him about the health issues associated with decaying bodies—especially the danger of cholera. Grant finally agreed to a truce, beginning at 6:00 p.m. on May 25.

CHAPTER XVI

SIEGE

Grant's losses in the assaults of May 19 and 22 were made good immediately. Brigadier General Lauman's Division arrived on May 20. It included twelve regiments and five batteries, mainly from Illinois, but also with units from Indiana and Wisconsin. It was assigned to the XVI Corps Detachment under Cadwallader C. Washburn.[1]

From May 23, ten or more U.S. divisions occupied twelve miles of frontage. Most of their positions were about six hundred yards from the Confederate line. They soon began working on "mining approaches" or "parallels" aimed at reaching Southern positions. Their battle plan involved more or less constant artillery fire and/or naval gunfire, to wear down the defenders. Union sharpshooters were also extremely active. They rotated fresh men every day and sent them out before dawn with two hundred rounds of ammunition. They were instructed not to change positions all day for any reason, including biological necessity. They carried two canteens with them—one full of water and one of whiskey—and were instructed to fire all two hundred rounds by sundown.

Grant, meanwhile, signaled Halleck for reinforcements and called ten thousand more men down from Memphis. He also asked Banks to bring twelve thousand men up from Port Hudson, but Banks did not comply. Halleck, on the other hand, sent everything he could, even after Robert E. Lee began moving northward.

The opening of regular supply lines to the North did not stop Yankee plundering. Mrs. Eliza Ann Lanier, who lived near Vicksburg, recalled, "It seemed to me the whole army was in our yard. They stripped our smokehouse and storeroom of all provisions . . . We had had the year's supply for our family and our eighty slaves . . ." They left a little sugar in one hogshead, as well as some spilled on the floor. That was all Mrs. Lanier and her children had to eat for three days, until one of her neighbors baked a pan of cornbread and sent it to them. The bluecoats took forty mules and horses, twenty milk cows, seventy other cattle, more than one hundred hogs, 165 sheep and "lots" of poultry. They also took Mr. Lanier and several other civilians and threw them in prison without any charges for two weeks. During that time, the family's plantation was raided and robbed of what little they had left by Federals and bands of hungry Negroes. After Mr. Lanier was released, the family abandoned their home and became refugees.

May 23, 1863, the sixth day of the siege, was a cloudy day, featuring light rain and summer showers. The Rebels repaired their breastworks and brought up cotton bales and heavy timbers. The Yankee artillery was unusually quiet until late afternoon, but the mortar fleet kept up a heavy fire all day and the sharpshooters were very active. The 3rd Louisiana alone lost thirteen men, killed or wounded.

John C. Pemberton received his first report of forage shortages on the twenty-third. He gave first priority to artillery horses and horses pulling ambulances. Food for the horses of staff officers was dropped as a costly luxury. From then on, they would have to subsist on the tree leaves, especially mulberry leaves. The soldiers were already on half rations: two-thirds of the usual issue of cornmeal and one-third the usual amount of meat. The commissaries now began to issue peas. "Cow peas," as Southerners called them, were small, rather hard beans, cultivated throughout the South as a cattle feed. Because there was a sizable supply of them in Vicksburg, they now became the principal vegetable staple of the army. The men were also occasionally issued a ration of rice or sweet potatoes.

After dark, because of an ammunition shortage, Pemberton ordered General Stevenson to collect all ammunition from the cartridge boxes of the abundant Union dead. In the trenches, the men were optimistic and hopeful that Johnston was on his way to relieve them.

To the east, the "Army of Relief" was rapidly gaining strength. Gregg's brigade and W. H. T. Walker's brigade totaled six thousand men,[2] and Johnston was joined on May 20 and 21 by the rest of Brigadier General States Rights Gist's South Carolina brigade from Beauregard and Brigadier Generals Matthew D. Ector's and Evander McNair's brigades from Bragg. Johnston had already been reinforced with Loring's division from the Army of Mississippi and Samuel B. Maxey's brigade from Port Hudson, giving him more than eighteen thousand men. At this point, Grant would have had difficulty defeating both Pemberton and Johnston simultaneously, but the Army of Relief made no move toward Vicksburg.

Meanwhile, Pemberton's proclamation and prompt actions had partially restored the men's faith in him. One Missouri soldier wrote that his critics had misjudged him. "He was incapable of harboring a thought of treason; he may not have been an able commander, but he was brave and true, and they soon found that he would surrender to nothing but starvation."

"I have been thinking of Genl. Pemberton's course in the defense of this place for several days past and I have come to the conclusion that he has done as well as anyone else could have done," Lieutenant Drennan wrote to his wife. He added that he intended to say so publicly as soon as he could.

While the soldiers were digging in, the civilian population constructed caves in the sides of the steep hills. By the end of the second week of the siege, there were an estimated five hundred caves in and around Vicksburg. ". . . the earthy, suffocating feeling, as of a living tomb, was dreadful to me," Dora Richards Miller wrote in her diary. There were so many caves that the Yankee soldiers jokingly called it "Prairie Dog Town." The good loess soil of the region was very solid and perfect for digging caves, without the need for supporting timbers. They made excellent shelters and bunkers, and cave-ins only occurred when solid shot from heavy Union guns scored a direct hit on them. General Pemberton himself was known to dive into a cave during bombardments. Some of the wealthier citizens converted their caves into elegant dwellings, complete with carpets, works of art, and even pianos. Closets and shelves were built inside the caves, and the floors of some of them were covered with planks. Some entrances were covered with tent flaps. Some enterprising African Americans (apparently free Negroes) saw an opportunity here, and they offered to build caves for $30 to $50 per cave. They soon had all the business they could handle.

Despite the efforts put into making caves comfortable, they were still caves. They were dark, damp, and flooded when it rained. They also attracted snakes. One woman found a serpent six feet long. She fled in terror and fetched an officer, who pinned it with a sword and cut its head off. Another lady discovered a rattlesnake under the mattress she had slept on all night. There were also too many people living in some of the caves. Eleven-year-old Willie Lord got tired of "squalling infants, family quarrels and the noise of general discord." Fortunately for him, his mother convinced his father, Dr. Lord, to have his own cave dug.[3]

Some people could not be persuaded to leave their homes, no matter what. Mr. McRae, a prominent merchant, was one such person. As he was sitting in his home one night, a minie ball passed through his bread. He would still not leave, but his wife did, along with their children and slaves.

Some of the caves held up to two hundred people, including recuperating soldiers, upper crust ladies, poor whites, plantation owners, slaves and free people of color. There was no class distinction here. Blacks and whites and rich and poor all slept side by side.

In addition to caves, the citizens constructed "dugouts" or "rat holes." If someone was in a store, shop, or business, or was in his or her home when Union artillery suddenly opened up, they might not have time to reach their caves. Instead, they would dive into a "rat hole." As they rushed out, they frequently shouted to each other, "Every rat to his hole!"

Soldiers and civilians alike soon learned to walk down the middle of the streets, so that they would better be able to see incoming shells. Once a shell passed over their heads, they felt safe. When a shell exploded, its fragments generally flew forward, so there was little danger to those behind it. Many considered the streets as safe as the caves, because there was no danger of cave-ins.

During lulls in the firing, Vicksburg came to life. The civilians acted as if the siege did not exist. They went shopping, and many collected spent shell fragments, spent bullets, etc. When the shelling resumed, Vicksburg became a ghost town again.

May 24 was a clear and beautiful Sunday, but the houses of worship were mostly deserted. The Union fleet kept up its bombardment all day. The Southern men were in the trenches or at their stations, and the women and children hid in the caves. At the front, the Yankees launched a sortie and established themselves directly beneath one of the 3rd Louisiana's parapets. They immediately began to undermine the position, with the intent of blowing it up. The Louisiana boys countered by dropping 12-pounder shells with five-second fuses and kegs filled with powder, shells, nails, and scraps of iron. The sortie failed.

Rumors filled Union lines about Johnston's growing strength, and this time they were true. Grant positioned his troops and artillery so that they could be used against either Johnston or Pemberton. Nowhere were Union lines more than six hundred yards from Confederate lines, and Grant's men had an inexhaustible supply of ammunition, so his sharpshooters and snipers fired more or less constantly. Pemberton's men, on the other hand, were more limited. They were especially short of musket caps. They had a million more cartridges than caps.

On May 25, Grant issued orders for the beginning of a siege, which had actually already begun. His men constructed twelve miles of trenches (mostly at night), backed by artillery. He would eventually have

eighty-nine batteries and more than three hundred guns. With Chickasaw Bluffs firmly in Union hands, he no longer had to depend on Grand
Gulf, which he abandoned. His supplies came straight down the river
from Memphis and were off-loaded within a few miles of the front.

The twenty-fifth was another clear, hot day. "The effluvia from the
putrefying bodies had become almost unbearable to friend and foe
[alike]," Sergeant Tunnard recorded. Finally, the Yankees raised a flag
of truce, so they could bury their dead. During the ceasefire, hundreds
of troops from both sides climbed over the breastworks and freely social-
ized. Numerous Rebels accepted Union offers to visit their lines. They
were "hospitably entertained and warmly welcomed," Tunnard recalled,
and were given abundant amounts of food and alcoholic beverages. "It
was a strange sight," Lieutenant Drennan said in a letter to his wife, "to
see men who an hour before were engaged in deadly conflict—laughing
and talking . . ."

The banter wasn't always friendly. One Southerner said something
that offended a Northerner. "Go to hell!" the Yankee snapped.

The Rebel replied that he couldn't because "hell was so full of blue-
bellies, there was no room for a white man." Generally speaking, however, the meetings were cordial. Ephraim Anderson of the 2nd Missouri
watched two brothers—one Confederate and one Federal—sit on a log
together and talk throughout the entire armistice. Elsewhere, men traded
tobacco for real coffee.

Seventeen-year-old Corporal Robert H. Bunn of the 42nd Alabama
recalled that "we [were] allowed to mingle with the survivors of the
regiment and it was sad to see brothers and friends searching for their
own among heaps of fallen heroes."

Captain Gallagher, the commissary of the 3rd Louisiana, befriended
a Yankee officer, who gave him excellent food and fine liquor. When the
truce expired, the Federal wished him good day and added, "I trust we
shall meet soon again in the Union of old."

"I cannot return your sentiment," Gallagher retorted. "The only
union which you and I will enjoy, I hope, will be in the kingdom come.

Good-bye, sir." It was that way all along the line. The Yankees were in good spirits and confident, the Rebels defiant and undaunted.

It seemed strange to the Confederates that, as soon as the truce was over, the people with whom they had just been so friendly were again trying to kill them.

Despite the tightness of the siege, it was still possible for couriers to carry dispatches back and forth. Pemberton sent a message to Johnston on May 20, saying, "An army will be necessary to save Vicksburg, and that quickly. Will it be sent?" On May 25, he got an answer. "Bragg is sending a division. When it comes, I will move to you. Which do you think is the best route?" Pemberton replied that the best place to come to was Haines' Bluff.

May 26, the ninth day of the siege, was a beautiful spring day. It was characterized by fighting all day. Several ladies in Vicksburg were killed or wounded by mortar shells. "The prospects of our success and deliverance seems to darken every day," Private Rollie Clack of the 43rd Tennessee Infantry wrote in his diary.[4] "Oh! May the God of heaven aid and deliver us from this unhappy state is the constant prayer of the writer."

Already there were shortages of good water. In the zone of the 2nd Texas, soldiers dug shallow wells in the hollows behind the lunette. The water was poor and of little quantity, so it was only used for drinking and cooking. Colonel Smith had it guarded day and night so the water could be rationed.

The Vicksburg hills were already crowded with caves. That day, Major Simone wrote,

> After breakfast the Ball was again opened and now cannon and small arms are booming away . . . I have some men at work digging me out a cave in which to sleep & sit when the shells are falling, these have become so common that there's not a hill, that has not [a] number of inmates; the fact is, the inhabitants of Vicksburg are now all living underground 'in these dens.' I will try mine tonight . . .

The Union artillery and heavy naval guns concentrated on trying to knock out Pemberton's upper batteries in and around Fort Hill. They tried again on May 27 and thought the Confederate heavy guns had moved, but they had not. Admiral Porter did not want to attack, but Grant and Sherman had both assured him that the Rebels had moved their heavy artillery and that Sherman's sharpshooters could keep the remaining gun crews pinned down. They were wrong on both counts, but Porter gave the order to advance, despite his misgivings.

Confederate Army Captain William P. Parks, who commanded eleven heavy guns on top of the bluff, had obtained the Union signal code and learned their plans. (A Rebel soldier had found a copy of the Union codebook—floating in the Mississippi! It had been passed on to Parks.) To deceive the Yankees, he moved his guns off the bluff on May 26, but brought them back that night and camouflaged them in the bushes or lowered them below the level of the parapet where they could not be seen, and waited in ambush.

About 11:00 a.m., four Union gunboats and the ironclad *Cincinnati*— a large stern-wheeled ship with thirteen heavy guns—rounded the penin-sula.[5] Their goal was to destroy the two heavy guns on the Mississippi, which were causing difficulties for Sherman's right flank. As soon as the ironclad was in easy range, Parks and his Arkansas gunners opened up, much to the surprise of the Northerners. The very first shell was a direct hit, passing through the front of the *Cincinnati* and exiting out the bottom of the ship. Another shell smashed its steering mechanism. Parks and his men scored hit after hit. The bluff was so high the *Cincinnati's* guns could not be elevated sufficiently to reach the Rebels. It also could not hold its course and the current swung her around, so that her stern (the most vulnerable part of the ship) was facing the bluff. Parks' men promptly smashed it. In forty-five minutes, the *Cincinnati* was a complete wreck and was rapidly taking on water. Another shell penetrated her hull below the water line and went through the bottom. The captain gave the order: Abandon Ship! Those who could swim did so. The captain tried to run his ship aground, but it slipped back into the river.

In spite of Southern artillery fire, six courageous Yankee sailors swam to the *Cincinnati* and returned in a damaged lifeboat. They rescued several badly wounded men and those who could not swim, one of whom was the captain. They were all awarded the Congressional Medal of Honor. The huge ironclad went down in shallow water near a sandbar, with part of it remaining above the surface. Twenty members of the crew were killed or drowned.

The USS Cincinnati.

Other Union gunboats threatened to attack the batteries, but turned around before they came within range of the Southern guns. "Gunboats are now as much afraid of our batteries as we were once of them," Lieutenant Alison of the 2nd Alabama Artillery noted.

Hundreds of Vicksburg women watched the battle from Sky Parlor Hill, the most prominent hill in the city. Getting there was not easy, for the fashionable ladies had to climb the steep hill, wearing tight corsets and high-button shoes and carrying silk parasols. This was especially difficult on a day like this, with cold temperatures and a strong wind, but on they came. Throughout the siege, they consistently thought nothing of exposing themselves to enemy artillery fire to watch combat. Today they returned home happy.

The loss of the *Cincinnati* seemed to satisfy the Union ground forces' taste for combat on May 27. There was little firing the rest of the day. But there was an ominous development. A soldier in Moore's Brigade recorded, ". . . rations began to fail. The corn was exhausted and peas were ground up for meal. The meat also was exhausted and mules were killed and eaten."

A standard staple in both armies (at least early in the siege) was hardtack, an unleavened rectangular cracker about three inches long, two inches wide and a quarter of an inch thick. (Some were 3 x 3 inches square.) They were of some nutritional value but not very tasty and were often so hard that they had to be boiled, because unless they were moistened, they were difficult for a man of ordinary strength to break. Sometimes they had to be broken with rifle butts.

The 17th Louisiana preserved their morale throughout the siege. One way they did it was to brew a huge pot of sassafras tea, which was available to all. Sassafras tea is made from the roots of a deciduous tree of the same name. When broken, this root smells like root beer. When boiled, the water tastes like root beer. The 17th kept the pot at a slow boil throughout most of the siege and merely added water when necessary, although the flavor no doubt diminished over time.

May 28, the eleventh day of the siege, was clear and hot. "We are utterly cut off from the world, surrounded by a circle of fire," Dora Miller wrote in her diary. "The fiery shower of shells goes on day and night . . . People do nothing but eat what they can get, sleep when they can, and dodge the shells." She noted there were three daily lulls: about 8:00 a.m. and 8:00 p.m. (when the Federals let their guns cool) and at noon, when they ate lunch.

The 3rd Louisiana had suffered heavily from Union sharpshooters. They were equipped with M1841 "Mississippi Rifles," which were considered excellent during the Mexican War but were now totally obsolete. They sometimes exploded when fired and were so inefficient that the enemy boldly exposed themselves and taunted the Louisiana men over their poor shooting. But today the Southerners received Enfield rifles with Ely's cartridges, which contained a peculiarly-shaped elongated ball, and the very finest English powder. These guns had been run through the blockade at Charleston and had been smuggled into Vicksburg by some undisclosed means. The boys in gray could not wait to test them and gunned down several sharpshooters before the Yankees realized that the tables had turned. They quickly retreated to the safety of their rifle pits and earthworks.

During the unofficial evening truce, the Northerners wanted to know where the Rebels had procured such fine weapons. When told, they had some colorful expressions for the British and their manufacturers. The 3rd Louisiana lost only two men wounded that day.

Meanwhile, the Federal earthworks were getting closer so, along with the Enfields, each Louisiana soldier was issued a musket, loaded with buckshot. They were useless against snipers but deadly at close quarters, if the Yankees attacked.

There was a large poplar tree, more than four feet in diameter, about three hundred yards north of Jackson Road. Union shells and bullets stripped it of its foliage and, after being hit by more than two hundred cannon balls, it finally toppled into a hollow behind the 27th Louisiana's parapet.

Several Louisianans built a fire against the tree one morning and were frying meat for breakfast when the flames reached a shell buried in the tree. The shell exploded and knocked a sizable number of soldiers to the ground. Ephraim Anderson thought for a moment they had all been killed, for about a dozen of them were within three feet of the explosion. Remarkably, no one died, although one man was stunned and senseless for some time. Only one man was injured enough to require hospitalization, although the beards and hair of several were severely singed.

General Pemberton was unhappy that evening. A courier arrived from Johnston—the first in ten days. He carried with him eighteen thousand cartridge caps but, to Pemberton's amazement, no dispatches.

John C. Pemberton was understandably growing depressed. His next-door neighbor, Emma Balfour, was of an optimistic nature, and she made it her business to keep him positive. With Pattie (Mrs. Pemberton) and the rest of his family gone, she helped fill a void in his life. She and her husband invited him over frequently, and she and her lady friends made every effort to cheer him up. They told him not to be depressed. They even threw a party, celebrating Johnston's coming—which turned out to be a false rumor.

"I think he is inclined to be despondent," Emma wrote in her diary, "and very persistent hopefulness cheers him. I hear I am a great favorite with him."

Emma Balfour.

Even so, Pemberton's faith "progressively crumbled," according to his grandson. The attrition, the bombardments day and night, the weariness of his men, and the dwindling food supply concerned him greatly and wore on his nerves.

May 29, the twelfth day of the siege, broke clear and hot. It was the day a message finally arrived from Johnston; dated May 25, it read, "I am too weak to save Vicksburg; can do no more than attempt to save you and your garrison. It will be impossible to extricate you unless you co-operate and we make mutually supporting movements." He again asked Pemberton what he thought the best route might be. Johnston also announced that he had sent two hundred thousand caps, although only thirty-eight thousand actually arrived.

Pemberton replied that he had eighteen thousand men at the front with no reserves. He again advised Johnston to move against Snyder's Mill, but not until he had thirty to thirty-five thousand men. Major General John C. Breckinridge's veteran division (fifty-two hundred men) arrived on June 1, bringing Johnston's strength to more than thirty-one thousand. But still he did not move.

In the meantime, the Yankees subjected Vicksburg to four hours of unremitting hell. Several citizens and soldiers were killed or wounded, and many buildings were destroyed. Pemberton ordered Major H. M. Matthews, the ordnance officer, to collect unexploded Parrot shells (of which there were many) and send them back to Paxton's Foundry in town, where they were recycled and recapped.[6]

May 30 was clear and unusually hot. "The constant daily fighting, night work, and disturbed rest began to exhibit their effects on the men," Sergeant Tunnard noted. "They were physically worn out and much reduced in flesh." That day, the meat ration was cut in half. It was also on that day that a mixture of ground peas and cornmeal was first issued. It was almost impossible to thoroughly bake a mixture of pea flour and meal that was fit for human consumption, and the new dish was universally hated. The longer the mixture was cooked, the harder the outside became—but it grew relatively softer on the inside, and there was always raw pea-meal in the center. Even after cooking it for two hours, the inside was still raw, "yet, on the outside it was so hard, that one might have knocked down a full-grown steer with a chunk of it," one soldier recounted.

After three days, the 1st Missouri Brigade declared the experiment a failure and pea-bread was abandoned, although peas were still issued and soon constituted half of their rations. Elsewhere, other regiments were still fed pea-bread.

To soften the blow of decreasing rations and to improve morale, Pemberton issued some chewing tobacco.

General Pemberton received complaints that several privileged gentlemen were drawing more than their allowances of food, soap, and other items. He summoned his commissary, Major G. L. Gillespie, and ordered him to make sure each officer received only one ration per day and only one ration per servant. Gillespie did as he was told. He was very efficient and was soon very unpopular in certain quarters.[7]

From May 31 to June 6, the Army of Mississippi suffered day and night bombardments. It was beginning to suffer from attrition. The 3rd Louisiana lost two men wounded, bringing its casualty total to fifty. Pemberton's faith in Johnston, meanwhile, continued to diminish, and the exhaustion of the men in the trenches greatly concerned him.

The local newspapers and men in the rifle pits, on the other hand, retained their confidence in Johnston much longer than did Pemberton. As late as June 13, one editorial declared, "The utmost confidence is felt that we can maintain our position until succor comes from outside. The undaunted Johnston is at hand." But he wasn't.

May 31 was characterized by a beautiful clear blue sky and budding flowers. The Union mortar fleet concentrated its fire on the courthouse and finally hit it. It was occupied at the time by a company of 5th Mississippi Cavalry (State Troops), which quickly "skedaddled," leaving behind five dead and eleven wounded.

To assure that their grand courthouse was not destroyed, the Confederates sent word to the Yankees that they were housing captured Union officers there. When word of this development reached Admiral Porter, he ordered his boats not to fire on it. Occupying it now became the ultimate symbolic objective of the Union army. It is still extant, and today houses an excellent museum.

Incidentally, the report was untrue—Union officer prisoners were held in the jailhouse across the street from the courthouse, not in the courthouse itself. But Admiral Porter did not know that. It probably would not have mattered in any case. A mortar shell aimed at the courthouse was as likely to hit the jail as its target.

That night, Lieutenant Wilkerson of Company B, 1st/4th Missouri, and fifty men sneaked out to the wreck of the *Cincinnati*. They burned it under the noses of the Yankees and escaped without losing a man.

"Each day now presented a succession of fighting; the ringing of rifles, the thunder of artillery, the incessant explosion of shells, saluted the ear as a morning reveille, and lulled us in the hours of sleep," Corporal Anderson recalled.

Union shelling was fiercest at dawn. No place in the encircled area was safe. "Women, children and the wounded were exposed more than the soldiers in the trenches," Colonel Hall recalled. Every night, Confederate engineers worked to repair the damage done the day before by Grant's heavy guns. The hard work, inadequate rations and lack of rest was beginning to tell on them, but they persevered. "During the whole siege we stayed in the ditches under the following orders: No one allowed to take off his cartridge-box, shoes or any article of clothing, day or night; one-third of the men to be on guard at all time," Lieutenant Cantrell of the 56th Georgia recalled.

June 1 and 2 were clear, unusually hot days. The Rebels created shade with outstretched blankets and small excavations. The bombardments continued. One of the shells exploded in the trench occupied by Company F, 3rd Louisiana. One man was killed and four were wounded on June 1. Two more were killed and one was wounded on June 2. Attrition was slowly beginning to set in on the Confederate infantry.

On the evening of June 1, a mortar shell set a city block on fire. Three stores burned down, along with a considerable quantity of sugar, flour, and other foodstuffs.

Elsewhere, where heavy shells scored direct hits on caves, there were cave-ins. One night, a large shell buried itself six feet deep in the top of a hill and exploded. Dirt poured in from the ceiling of a cave constructed in the side of this hill. Ten-year-old Lucy McRae was buried alive.

Fortunately, Dr. Lord saw her disappear. He and her frantic mother dug the terrified little girl out, although she was bleeding from the nose and mouth. Then another explosion rocked the cave. Thinking it was about to collapse, screaming people rushed into the street. Then a shell burst near them, so they rushed back into the cave again. While all of this was going on, a child was born in the same cave. He was perfectly healthy. The mother named him William Siege Green.

There were plenty of other close calls. Mrs. Loughborough recalled how a live shell rolled into her cave. Fortunately, George, one of her slaves, was both quick-witted and brave. He grabbed the shell, ran outside and threw it away. After that her husband, Major Loughborough, found his family and servants a cave closer to the front, where it was safer. The Union gunboats didn't want to take the chance of overshooting and lobbing a shell into Federal lines.

Some people did not have caves or would not stay in them. Quite a few of these slept in churches, where there were plenty of good, commodious pews. They brought their own blankets and pillows, and used old newspapers for mattresses.

Private John Hanger and several other soldiers were in Vicksburg, where they purchased a considerable amount of rice for a high price. A pot of it had been boiled, and the men were sitting around eating it, when a shell exploded nearby. A small piece of shrapnel struck Hanger's spoon, just as he was putting it in his mouth. It tore a hole in the spoon and splattered rice all over Hanger. "That was cool," he calmly declared, and continued eating his meal.

On June 3, Grant received further reinforcements in the form of Brigadier General Kimball's division, which came down from Memphis. It included twelve new regiments from Illinois, Michigan, Ohio, Minnesota, Iowa, and Wisconsin. It was assigned to Washburn's XVI Corps Detachment.

Johnston was also receiving reinforcements. By June 1, Evans' brigade had arrived from South Carolina, and on June 3 Brigadier General William H. "Red" Jackson's cavalry division (three thousand horses) arrived in Canton from Spring Hill, Tennessee, after a ride of 350 miles.

The Army of Relief, in fact, was growing faster than Johnston could handle. Because it did not exist a month before, it had little infrastructure. It was deficient in supplies, guns, wagons, horses, mules, food, tents, and other equipment. But it now had five divisions—Loring, Breckinridge, Walker, Samuel G. French, and "Red" Jackson—and was capable of assuming the offensive with thirty thousand men. Grant himself later admitted that he was very concerned about the possibility of Johnston attacking his exterior lines, followed by a Pemberton offensive. Such a thrust could have easily cut the Army of the Tennessee in half, but it was weeks before Johnston even attempted to cross the Big Black River in force. In a rare moment when he let his emotions show, Pemberton said, "General Johnston may have seemed to have written orders enough; but unfortunately he did not cause them to be executed . . . Like his proposals to attack the enemy, they all perished just as he was on the verge of executing them."

Johnston's subordinates showed much more initiative than he did. Walker offered thirty days furlough and a good saddle horse to ride for the rest of the war to any man who would carry a dispatch to Pemberton. He got several. Loring called for volunteers to carry percussion caps to Vicksburg. Thirty men stepped forward. Only two reached Rebel lines. Almost all of the rest were killed or captured. One who was not was Captain W. L. Gay of the 22nd Mississippi. He spent ten days inside Union lines, subsisting on blackberries. Then he returned to Loring. He never reached the city. "When the real investment began, a cat could not have crept out of Vicksburg without being discovered," Colonel Hall lamented.

This was not exactly true. Couriers still made it out of Vicksburg. They would normally swim or row across the Mississippi River to the De Soto peninsula, then proceed south down the west (Louisiana) bank, where they would again cross the great river back into Mississippi. There were still Yankees in the area south of Vicksburg but, with Grand Gulf abandoned and most of the Union army besieging Vicksburg, the couriers now had a reasonable chance of reaching Jackson and friendly lines.

Joseph E. Johnston hated Jefferson Davis, with whom he was barely on speaking terms. On June 4, he signaled Secretary of War Seddon instead of the president, and informed him that his army was still too weak to relieve Vicksburg. He deliberately underreported his numbers, so Secretary Seddon called him on it. At that moment, Grant's forces outnumbered the two Rebel armies, but not overwhelmingly so; however, the odds were steadily shifting more and more in favor of the Union. Seddon urged Johnston to attack, but the general did nothing.

Meanwhile, Vicksburg continued to bleed. The ranks were thinning because of casualties, sickness, and now the heat. June 4 was a clear, hot day, characterized by heavy firing. In the city, the army seized all surplus provisions and began issuing food to soldiers and civilians alike. Rations for the troops were reduced again to 1/3 of a pound of peas, 5/9 of a pound of meal (or almost nine ounces) and half a pound of beef (including bones and shanks), with small amounts of lard, soup, and salt, but plenty of sugar. "It seemed wonderful that human endurance could withstand the accumulated horrors of the situation," W. H. Tunnard recalled. "Living on this slender allowance, fighting all day in the hot summer sun, and at night, with pick-axe and spade, repairing the destroyed portions of the line, it passed all comprehension how the men endured the trying ordeal."

June 5 was another hot day. The bombardment continued, but the gunboats took a day off. A little girl and a citizen (possibly her mother) were killed by a Parrot shell.

The next day was one of the hottest of the year. The city was rife with rumors about Johnston drawing near. Then the defenders heard the report from a cannon in the direction of the Big Black River. The Rebels thought it heralded Johnston's approach, and there were shouts and cheers all down the line. But the rumors were false.

"The sharp shooters opened fire at daylight this morning but in a milder manner than common—continued all day," Private Clack of the 43rd Tennessee recorded in his diary. "Night has come on and the firmament is again decked with beautiful stars, while we lay us down again to sleep upon the rough ground of Vicksburg. I pray heaven's blessings to rest upon us."

The Federals set up long range rifles and several Parrot guns on the west bank of the Mississippi. They fired into the town, making it even more dangerous for pedestrians to walk down the streets. Grant's artillery on the east side of the river also opened fire. The bombardment lasted all night.

The next day, Sunday, June 7, was another hot day. For the first time in the siege, they heard the sound of guns from another Confederate force. On the west bank, Major General Richard Taylor advanced on Milliken's Bend (twenty-five miles upstream from Vicksburg) with four thousand men of Major General John G. Walker's Texas "Greyhound" Division. On June 6, Walker sent Brigadier General James M. Hawes' brigade to attack Young's Point and kept Colonel Horace Randal's brigade in reserve six miles north of Richmond, Louisiana. The attack on Milliken's Bend was entrusted to Brigadier General Henry McCulloch's 1,400-man Texas brigade. They struck an African American brigade and a white regiment from Iowa.

Incredibly, many of the blacks had not been given firearms until the day before, when Union scouts from the 10th Illinois Cavalry reported Walker's advance. The Northern cavaliers were quickly defeated when Major Harrison launched a sudden charge with his 15th Louisiana Cavalry Battalion. Eight Yankees were killed and twenty-five captured.

The African Americans were armed with obsolete Austrian muskets, which were notoriously unreliable. The Rebel strike force included the 16th, 17th, and 19th Texas Infantry Regiments and the 16th Texas Cavalry (Dismounted). The Union commander, Colonel Herman Lieb, reported that they charged "with yells that would make faint hearts quail." Nevertheless, the blacks fought well. General McCulloch reported, "The charge was resisted by the negro portion of the enemy's force with considerable obstinacy, while the white or true Yankee portion ran like whipped curs almost as soon as the charge was ordered."

Brigadier General E. S. Dennis, who commanded the Union forces on the west side of the river, agreed. It was "impossible for men to show greater gallantry than the negro troops in that fight," he told Charles Dana, who would soon be an assistant secretary of war.

"No quarter to the officers!" the charging Rebels yelled. "Kill the damn abolitionists! Spare the niggers!" The black regiments had only white officers and many of them fled immediately and took cover behind the levee. One of the colonels was later cashiered for cowardice.

The Battle of Milliken's Bend, June 7, 1863. From Harper's Magazine.

Because of poor leadership, antiquated muskets, and their unfamiliarity with their weapons, the black Yankees put up a good fight, but they only got off one or two shots before the Texans were on top of them. Hand-to-hand combat with bayonets and musket butts ensued before the Yankees gave way. The Southerners poured over the first levee "like a tidal wave" and the blacks "stampeded pell-mell over the levee, in great terror and confusion," Private Blessington of the 16th Texas wrote later. "We clubbed [with] guns, bayoneted, cut with sword, until the enemy fled helter skelter," Peter Gravis of the 17th Texas recalled. The Yankees were soon pushed back behind the last levee, where they were saved by the Union gunboat *Choctaw*, which had a huge 100-pounder Parrot, as well as three 9-inch smoothbores, and two 30-pounders. Confederate infantry was generally afraid of gunboats, so it stayed on the western side of the levee. By 10:00 a.m., the fighting died out. The temperature by then was ninety-five degrees Fahrenheit in the shade.

The ironclad USS Choctaw, *a 1,020-ton side-wheel steamer, which saved the Union ground forces at Milliken's Bend.*

Union losses on June 7 were 131 killed, 285 wounded, and 266 missing (mostly captured), a total of 682.[8] The Texans lost 44 killed, 131 wounded and 11 missing, 186 total. General Taylor thought that McCulloch should have pushed across the levee and destroyed the entire brigade. "Had common vigor and judgment been displayed, the work would all have been completed by 8 a.m.," Taylor reported. "I discovered too late that the officers and men of this division were possessed of a dread of gunboats." Taylor held General McCulloch responsible and relieved him of his command.[9]

In retaliation for their drubbing at Milliken's Bend, the Yankees burned the town of Richmond to the ground.

The Texans actually seemed proud of the black Yankees, who were, after all, Southerners too. They treated their black prisoners with kindness and respect. (This was certainly not always the case in the Civil War.) Their white officers were another matter. At least two were sent to Monroe, Louisiana, where they disappeared and were never seen again.

The attack came too late to do any good. If it had been launched five weeks before, it would have cut the main U.S. supply line and placed Grant's entire army in jeopardy of total destruction. Now, however, his main supply route was entirely north of Vicksburg. He no longer depended on the Milliken's Bend-Grand Gulf route.

Back in Vicksburg, the 3rd Louisiana was disappointed over Johnston's no-show. It took its frustration out on the Yankees, fighting with vigor and killing several Federals. It lost one man wounded. At headquarters, General Pemberton sent Johnston a dispatch, stating that the men were constantly in the trenches but were still in good spirits. He asked again when he might expect relief. He added ominously that his subsistence was down to twenty days.

June 8, the twenty-second day of the siege, was clear and hot. The Yankees were getting closer. The struggle "was daily becoming more fierce and more deadly," one sergeant recorded. In the zone of the 3rd Louisiana, the Northerners procured a railroad car frame, which they placed on wheels and loaded with cotton bales. They could now safely dig their approach trench behind it. The Louisianans fought all night, but to no avail. By the afternoon of June 9, the car was getting dangerously close.

Meanwhile, Lieutenant W. M. Washburn of Company B came up with an idea to destroy the moveable breastwork: fill the cavity in the butt of an Enfield rifle ball with some flammable material which would ignite when the rifle was fired. They chose to use cotton soaked in turpentine. Lieutenant Colonel Samuel I. Russell ordered that the "fire bullets" be employed immediately and fired the first round himself. The Rebels fired at least three such rounds without results. Everyone was disappointed and most of the tired soldiers lay down and went to sleep.

Early that morning, well before dawn, a guard suddenly shouted, "I'll be damned if that thing isn't on fire!" The entire regiment was soon up and "like a hive of disturbed bees" grabbed their rifles. Five companies kept up a constant and rapid fire, to prevent the Yankees from extinguishing the flames. Several brave bluecoats tried but, without cover and silhouetted by the fire, all were promptly shot dead. The railroad car frame was totally consumed. The 3rd Louisiana lost three men that day— all killed.

That same day, the enemy pushed to within seventy-five yards of General Shoup's left flank. At night, the Rebels constructed a rough stockade there.

It began to rain before dawn on June 10, the twenty-fourth day of the siege. After a gray dawn, rain fell in torrents. Rain fell all day, but did not slow the fighting. The trenches filled with water and drenched the exposed, unsheltered men. They nevertheless soldiered on, despite the mud and water, and made sport of their own and each other's suffering.

Joseph Alison of the 2nd Alabama Artillery wrote in his diary,

> Surely Johnston could have reached here in this time. Our situation is now becoming desperate. No place of safety. If you stand still there is danger from the pieces of shell that fill the air, and if you move the danger becomes greater. The whole town is enfiladed . . . Our hospitals are crowded with wounded. Some poor fellows are compelled to lay out in the open air and get attention from any Dr. who happens to pass that way. . . They can't stand up without having a dozen bullets whistling around their heads, and to attempt to walk around is certain death.

On the west bank, the wet Yankees were busy. They set up seven heavy mortars, with which they blasted Vicksburg day and night.

The Yankees were now within sixty to seventy yards of the Confederate front line in the zone of the 26th Louisiana. The regiment set up brush entanglements, to prevent the Yankees from trying to rush them.

The Rebs and Yanks were now close enough to each other to talk and engage in taunting. Confederates would poke fun at the bluecoats for their lack of success and ask when they were coming over for a visit. Soon, the Yankees would reply. One Northerner declared that he would come over when the Southerners showed better manners.

In his dry headquarters, Pemberton again wrote to Johnston and complained that he had heard nothing from him since May 25. "I should endeavor to hold out as long as we have anything to eat," he wrote.

It continued to rain heavily on the morning of June 11, but the day broke off cloudy, cool, and pleasant. General Shoup reported, "Enemy is running a regular zig-zag and sap-roller in front of the redan." A sap roller was a large roller made of saplings. It was about six feet long and four feet high, and was pushed along in front of soldiers digging an approach trench. It was used by the Yankees to avoid being hit by Confederate small arms fire. But the Rebels had an answer for it, too. Word of Lieutenant Washburn's innovation spread up and down Southern lines like wildfire. Before long, Lieutenant William Allen of the 2nd Texas used "turpentine fireballs" to destroy a sap roller on the Baldwin Road, and Lieutenant Burt of the 1st Mississippi Light Artillery destroyed another in the same area. In the 38th Mississippi's sector, near the Jackson Road, Captain L. B. Taylor of General Hebert's staff destroyed another in the same manner.

Now, in General Hebert's sector, the enemy was able to place two 10-inch Columbiads barely one hundred yards from the Southern line. The guns featured heavy screams and fierce explosions. They smashed the 3rd Louisiana's breastworks to pieces. The Northerners became good at rolling their cannon balls down behind the hill where the Rebels had their trenches, endangering the shelters on the back side. In one such shelter, Lieutenant Colonel Samuel D. Russell was having a conference with some of his men when a cannon ball exploded. Only one man was killed, but Russell, Lieutenant Washburn, and two other officers were wounded. Otherwise, the regimental losses were surprisingly small: two killed and six wounded. The 3rd Louisiana had suffered seventy-five casualties since the siege began.

Grant received further reinforcements on June 11 when Major General Herron's division arrived from Missouri. It included eight fresh regiments and three batteries from Indiana, Illinois, Iowa, and Wisconsin. It was assigned to McPherson's XVII Corps, opposite Forney. In this sector, enemy sappers pushed to within sixty-five yards of the outer works on the Graveyard Road and to about one hundred yards in Forney's sector on the Jackson Road. An hour before sunset, they attacked and breached the Confederate works. General Pemberton rushed a 9-inch Dahlgren and his only 9-inch mortar to the threatened sector. Forney healed the breach with his reserves, although the fighting continued until midnight.

On June 12, Grant received further reinforcements, when Brigadier General W. Sooy Smith's division arrived from La Grange, Tennessee. It controlled fourteen regiments and four batteries, and was assigned to Washburn's XVI Corps Detachment.[10]

On the Rebel side, a courier arrived from Johnston with twenty thousand caps, but he carried no message.

The day was clear and pleasant. The Yankees took advantage of the weather to fire muskets and heavy mortars in considerable volume. Their siege guns smashed the right flank of the 3rd Louisiana, wounding four men. "No prospect of assistance, and provisions were becoming very scarce," Sergeant Tunnard wrote. The fresh beef was long since gone, and sheep (of which there had been many) were now eaten. They still had the horrible "blue" bacon. The soldiers joked about how bad it was, declaring "Our bacon outranks General Lee." Pemberton now ordered Stevenson to impress all of the cattle in the city.

One of the objectives of the Union sharpshooters was to silence the big Confederate guns. They did this by picking off artillerists and, in a few instances, were quite successful. Some of the Southern cannons were struck by as many as sixty bullets. One wooden shield used to protect the gunners was struck forty-four times in eight hours. "On the other hand," Charles B. Lewis declared, "the Federals suffered even more than the Confederate sharpshooters, because [they were] less sheltered." Perhaps so, but not by much. The large number of Union snipers with their unlimited supply of ammunition were killing or wounding ten to one hundred Rebels per day. But, as General Grant pointed out in his memoirs, the Confederate infantrymen had an advantage they should not have had—superior weaponry. Many Rebels had Enfield rifles, which were vastly superior to the U.S. flint-lock muskets which had been converted into percussion weapons, or the Belgium muskets Uncle Sam imported early in the war. The Union Army partially replaced them with such a variety of weapons of so many different calibers that it had trouble distributing ammunition.

By now, the works in front of General Hebert's Louisiana brigade were nearly demolished. Smith's and Forney's fronts were smashed. As night fell, the Union sappers pushed their works to within fifty feet of the Confederate front. They tried to eliminate the Rebels using hand grenades, but this weapon was generally ineffective.

(It should be noted that the Civil War hand grenade was not the reliable weapon today's American soldier knows. Today one simply pulls the pin, flicks the lever, and the grenade explodes five seconds later. In 1863, most grenades were Ketchum grenades. They were about the size of a goose egg and filled with buckshot-like projectiles. There was no timer, but there was a plunger on top. If you threw a grenade and the plunger did not strike the ground properly, or if the surface it struck was too soft, the grenade did not explode. Now the enemy had a grenade to throw back at you.)

According to Yankee survivors, hand delivered Confederate artillery shells made much more effective "grenades" than Union hand grenades. The Rebels waited until the Northerners were just below their parapets, then lit the fuses and rolled the artillery shells down on top of the Federals. They weighed six to ninety pounds and caused serious casualties. Even U.S. Major General John Logan narrowly escaped one of their explosions.

As the siege wore on, the Confederates designed a somewhat better grenade. It weighed about a pound, was shaped like a hen's egg, and was filled with powder. On the rear end, they constructed a rudder of feathers, which kept the nose pointing forward, so that the percussion rod on the front would strike first and was more likely to cause a detonation when it reached its target.

Just before daylight on June 13, Captain Sanders arrived from Jackson with a message from Johnston. It had taken him two weeks to get through with a dispatch, which basically said nothing new. Johnston repeated that he was too weak to save Vicksburg but could attempt to save the garrison. He wanted Pemberton to communicate his plans to him if possible, but did not reveal any of his own plans, troop dispositions or ideas. On the helpful side, the captain did bring two hundred thousand percussion caps.

The rations were reduced again on June 13 from 13 ounces to 5/9 of 5/6 pound (7.4 ounces) of meal and six ounces of peas per day.

Inside the Confederate perimeter, the livestock consumed all of the hay, grass, and forage. Every day some of the cattle starved to death. Beef from starved or starving cattle is repulsive and bluish in color. For weeks, the quartermaster of the 26th Louisiana lay quarters of blue beef on benches in front of the commissary for anyone to take, but there were few takers, even among hungry soldiers.

Shells continued to burst over the city. On June 13, Dora Miller wrote in her diary, "Shell burst just over the roof this morning. Pieces tore through both floors down into the dining room. The entire ceiling of that room fell in a mass. We had just left it. Every piece of crockery on the table was smashed."

This siege, like most others, had now developed a certain monotony. Every day was characterized by heat, sniper fire, and bombardments of greater or lesser intensity. The climate gave the Rebels one advantage, however. In the heat of the day, the Northern gunners and some of their sharpshooters abandoned their bombardment and headed for the shade of trees. The Rebels stayed in their trenches and suffered, but at least they weren't being bombarded. Adding to their discomfort was the annoying problem of lice, which infested their bedding and clothes. Practically the entire Confederate Army had it.

One insect which tormented both sides was the mosquito. A nineteenth-century joke ran, "In Mississippi, the only crop which never fails is mosquitoes." They seem to have been especially bad in 1863 and neither side was able to do anything to escape them. "When on picket I dreaded the mosquitoes more than the Yankees," Private Bachman of the 60th Tennessee recalled. At night, the pickets seldom fired upon each other and would often call an unofficial truce and visit with one another. Mosquitoes tortured both sides all the time, but especially at night. "I would press my old hat tightly over my face, wrap my blanket around my head, stick my hands under my semblance of a coat, yet the mosquitos would so bite me as to make me look in the morning as if I had chicken pox," Bachman wrote later.

In town, there were plenty of close calls. Mr. Aquila Bowie abandoned his home and lived in a sophisticated tent, which was so near the fortifications that he could step from his front gallery to the embankment. One day he was resting on the couch while his daughter Hester played the piano and Elizabeth, a younger daughter, sat in a chair. Suddenly a Federal shell burst through the tent, struck the arm of the chair and went through the floor, but did not explode. Elizabeth screamed and shook uncontrollably.

"Elizabeth, you look like one dead," Hester said, "you are trembling like an aspen leaf."

"If you had come so nearly being killed as I have three times during the siege, you would tremble too!" Elizabeth retorted.

The next day, June 14, was the twenty-eighth day of the siege. It was clear and warm. Cannonading and musket fire continued. The Yankees were now very close to the 3rd Louisiana Redan. Three of the regiment's men were wounded, including one who lost his right eye to a sniper. Elsewhere, the enemy zig-zag trenches pushed to within twenty-five yards of the Southern front on the Graveyard Road. General Shoup reported, "Enemy disabled our 12-pounder gun . . . Have organized my artillerists into a hand-grenade and thunder barrel corps, since our guns [because of Union snipers] are of no service."

"Another Sabbath has passed and we are still confined to this same unhappy place and almost without any ray of hope of deliverance," a Tennessee private wrote. "Oh! Lord how long shall we remain in this state? Deliver us at once Oh! Lord."

From June 14 to 17, Grant received further reinforcements in the form of Major General John Parke's IX Corps, which came from the Department of the Ohio. It included Brigadier General Welsh's division (nine regiments) and Brigadier General Potter's division (ten regiments). Grant kept the entire corps in reserve, in the unlikely event he had to deal with Johnston. The only reinforcements Pemberton received were two couriers from the Army of Relief. Between them they carried two hundred thousand percussion caps.

Inside Vicksburg, the ration was reduced to eight ounces of bread per day. It was half rice, half flour. There was almost no meat available. When the rice and flour ran out, the bread was made with equal parts of peas ground into meal and cornmeal. Mrs. Dorsey described it as a "nauseous composition," which "had the properties of india-rubber, and was worse than leather to digest."

On June 15, the twenty-ninth day of the siege, Pemberton wrote to Johnston,

> The enemy has placed several very heavy guns in position against our works, and is approaching them very nearly by sap [i.e., trench]. His fire is almost continuous. Our men have no relief, are becoming much fatigued, but are still in pretty good spirits. I think your movement should be made as soon as possible. The enemy is receiving reinforcements. We are living on greatly reduced rations . . .

At least this day was cloudy and somewhat cooler, with a threat of rain. In Shoup's sector, the Union sap pushed ever closer. They were now within ten feet of the ditch in front of the Stockade Redan. That day, the Yankees charged the breastworks of Colonel Marks' 27th Louisiana. The 3rd Louisiana, which was on the 27th's right, enfiladed the attacking columns and, using a small rifled gun, plowed cannon balls through the Northern ranks, leaving huge gaps. This skirmish cost the 3rd two men killed, but the Northerners soon returned to their own lines.

Elsewhere, the situation was even bleaker. Johnston telegraphed Secretary of War Seddon, "I consider saving Vicksburg hopeless."

The next day, Seddon signaled back, "Your telegram grieves and alarms us. Vicksburg cannot be lost, at least [not] without a desperate struggle. The interest and honor of the Confederacy forbid it."

Johnston was unmoved. He signaled back, "I think you do not appreciate the difficulties in the course you direct."

Seddon replied that ". . . the eyes and hopes of the whole Confederacy are upon you, with the sentiment that it were better to fail nobly daring than, through prudence even, to be inactive. . . . I rely on you for all possible [efforts] to save Vicksburg."

Johnston remained unresponsive, because he preferred not to fight a battle, rather than run the risk of losing one. "Nobly daring" was simply not in his nature.

On June 11, Johnston had actually told General Walker that preparations for a forward movement were nearly complete, but he did not move until June 18. By now he had thirty-two thousand men, seventy-eight guns, and hundreds of supply wagons. The Army of Relief moved forward into its staging areas, but here Johnston dallied. It was probably just as well. Pemberton's army had been reduced to eighteen thousand combat effectives. Adding this to Johnston's thirty-two thousand, the total available Confederate forces numbered approximately fifty thousand men. By this point, Grant had eighty-five thousand men—enough to hold Pemberton's weakened regiments in check and simultaneously defeat Johnston. It was now too late. The opportunity had passed.

June 16, the thirtieth day of the siege, was pleasant with light summer clouds. Rapid and heavy musket fire continued. "The crack of the rifles of the sharpshooters was never hushed, even at night, and scarcely a day was passed that some demonstration was not made to create apprehension." That day, a Confederate river battery shelled—and for a time silenced—two large U.S. guns on the peninsula opposite Vicksburg. These guns had already killed and wounded many civilians, including women and children, but had accomplished little militarily.

Meanwhile, part of the 43rd Mississippi Infantry Regiment enjoyed a rare and unusual feast.

In the 1850s, U.S. Secretary of War Jefferson Davis brought camels from overseas to America, for use by the army. The experiment failed because of the American love for horses; most soldiers were put off by the idea of replacing horses with camels. The humpbacks were released into the wild, and there were camel sightings in the American West as late as the mid-1870s. Somehow, Company A of the 43rd Mississippi Infantry acquired one as its mascot. At first he frightened the horses, but before long he became everyone's favorite. The beast, now named Old Douglas, was a friendly, quiet animal but, for some reason, a Yankee sniper killed him. Furious, the men of "the Camel Regiment" hunted down this sniper and did him in. The Rebels carved the camel's carcass up into steaks and ate it. Apparently, it was quite good. Old Douglas now has a marker in the Old Vicksburg Cemetery.

The Missouri brigade occupied a regimental-sized sector to the left of the Jackson Road. It now controlled four regiments: the 2nd, 3rd, 5th, and 6th Missouri Infantry. One regiment would occupy a part of the front line and would rotate out every six hours. Fresh Missourians thus continually occupied a portion of the front line twenty-four hours a day, while three top-notch regiments lay in reserve near one of the most threatened parts of the Confederate line at all times.

June 17 was cloudy and unusually sultry. On the firing line, Colonel Isham W. Garrott, the commander of the 20th Alabama, borrowed a rifle and was trading shots with Union sharpshooters. As he rose up to fire, one of them put a bullet through his heart. He never knew that he had been promoted to brigadier general three weeks before. He was replaced by Lieutenant Colonel Edmund Pettus,[11] an officer noted for his fearlessness and his ferocity in combat.

Isham W. Garrott, commander of the 20th Alabama, and his successor, Lieutenant Colonel (later Brigadier General) Edmund W. Pettus, shown here when he was a United States senator. A famous bridge in Selma, Alabama, is named after him.

In the zone of the 3rd Louisiana, another Columbiad opened up at close range. The Yankees were so near that the men threw scraps of paper back and forth. One Northerner tossed a hardtack biscuit into the 3rd Louisiana trenches with the word "starvation" written on it. The Rebels immediately wrote on it, "Forty days rations, and no thanks to you," and threw it back.

But this was not true. The garrison was now on one-quarter rations—enough to prevent starvation but not enough to satisfy hunger. Their meals now consisted of two pea-meal (also known as peabread) biscuits, and two pieces of bacon per day. Some soldiers ate two meals all at once and went hungry the next day, preferring to have at least one good meal every two days. They also learned that sugar cane shoots taste good; like Chinese bamboo shoots, they can be eaten if boiled.

The town and the army were now running out of everything to eat. Mary Loughborough recalled, "Fruits and vegetables were not to be procured at any price. Everyone felt . . . the fear of starvation." Flour now sold for $5 a pound ($113 in 2016 dollars); oxen, horses, and milk cow meat was $2.50 a pound ($56 in today's money); and molasses sold for $10 a gallon ($225 today). Only the wealthy could afford it. Dogs and cats disappeared; some starved to death and some were killed or eaten. Owners could no longer feed their pets anyway.

The troops also ate horses and cattle killed during the bombardment. Finally, Pemberton ordered that the mules be killed for food. An animal lover himself, the general could not bring himself to eat mule. Every time he tried, he saw the face of a loyal mule. But he did learn to eat alligator tongue.

The men were always hungry, but they never complained, even though scurvy had broken out by mid-June. It is remarkable, but Confederate morale remained high, although faith in Johnston was beginning to sag.

By June 17, there were nine "parallels" crawling toward Vicksburg. Each was big enough to conceal large numbers of soldiers, artillery pieces, and wagons loaded with black powder kegs. General Shoup noted,

"We are on speaking terms with the enemy at the redan." At night, the pickets established unofficial truces and traded tobacco for coffee.

Because they were too close to the Rebel lines, it was difficult to employ standard artillery against them, so the Yankees began using light mortars, called coehorns. They were short bronze or iron tubes set in a wooden bed. Some of the coehorns were wooden. Made by both sides, they were built by boring into hardwood logs that were reinforced with iron bands. The short-barreled mortars fired 12-pound shells high into the air, used a small powder charge, and its crews were not as exposed as regular gun crews.

June 18 was cloudy and hot. There was nothing special to report, except that the enemy's approach works were getting even closer. "Our men are nearly worn out . . ." Major Simons of Moore's Brigade wrote in his diary. "Never have a set of men exhibited more fortitude & endurance than has those that now defend the City of Vicksburg." The Yankees were now within twenty-five feet of the Stockade Redan, guarding the Graveyard Road. In the center, they were close to the 3rd Louisiana Redan and the Great Redoubt, positions which blocked the Jackson Road. The Rebel works blocking the Baldwin Ferry Road were also threatened. Pemberton begged Johnston to come—but it is obvious that he never intended to even try. Later he claimed that his assignment in Mississippi tied his hands, because he no longer had authority over Bragg and therefore could not draw on the Army of Tennessee for reinforcements. This was a fabrication and President Davis later heatedly denounced this thin excuse.

The Vicksburg *Daily Whig* published a rare special edition on June 18, but it apparently used someone else's printing press, since its office was destroyed by a direct hit from a U.S. Navy shell on May 9. For most of the siege, the *Daily Citizen* was the only functioning newspaper, although it was no longer printed daily. Its editor, J. M. Swords, tried to keep up the morale of both citizens and soldiers by printing encouraging stories and editorials. When he ran out of newsprint, Swords also used wallpaper, of which he had a goodly supply. His office was hit by a mortar bomb on June 16. It went through the roof and the floor and ended up in the basement. Although it caused consternation and made a mess, it missed the printing press. When the civilians finished reading the newspaper, some of them used it for its designed purpose (i.e., as wallpaper). Its pink and green flowered design was apparently quite attractive. The newspaper continued to operate until July 2. Swords could not bring himself to print another edition after he learned that surrender negotiations had begun.

In the meantime, the Union Navy and Army blasted the city with incendiary shells. Tunnard noted that "the enemy became imbued with the mania for setting fire to the city, and, as the shells exploded, a stream of liquid fire descended from them. At night they presented a beautiful spectacle, notwithstanding their destructive mission." They destroyed several homes and buildings, but did no serious military damage.

Mortar bombs continued to fall on Vicksburg with monotonous regularity and tragedies continued to mount. Mary Ann Loughborough told the tale of a little black child who was playing in the yard and found a shell and, apparently thinking it a toy, played with it, and accidentally pounded the fuse. ". . . [T]he terrible explosion followed, showing, as the white cloud of smoke floated away, the mangled remains of a life that to the mother's heart had possessed all of beauty and joy."

During a lull in the bombardments, a young girl went out to play. As she came back to the cave, the bombardments started again. She screamed and ran to her mother, "sinking like a wounded dove, the life blood flowing over the light summer dress in crimson ripples from a death-wound in her side, caused by a shell fragment."

A little boy was playing near the mouth of his mother's cave when a shell landed nearby. One of the fragments broke his arm.

All three of these incidents occurred in one day.

The firing was on June 19, which was clear and hot. Summer had arrived in Mississippi and even light physical activity produced perspiration. The Southerners in the trenches continued to suffer without complaint. "It is the noble men in the rifle pits [trenches] that Vicksburg will owe aught of honor she may gain in this siege," one staff officer said. "I revere them, as I see them undergoing every privation with courage and patience, anxious only for the high reputation of the city."

During World War I, it was axiomatic that soldiers who stayed in the forward trenches more than forty-eight hours lost their combat effectiveness and were no longer fit for duty. The stoic Rebels stayed there for weeks. The terms "combat fatigue" and "post-traumatic stress disorder" had not been invented yet, but the Civil War physicians did have the word "neurasthenia," which was the same thing. It was not yet common in Southern ranks, although some of the men were beginning to crack. They spent day after day in the trenches under the hot Mississippi sun, with inadequate food or water, unable to bathe, change clothes or exercise, and hardly able to move. Their limbs began to swell, they were covered in lice, and their bodies stank. The unrelenting daily pressure began to prey on their minds. "Should the siege last a month longer there will have to be built a building or either a building will have to be arranged for the accommodations of maniacs," one man wrote. "I notice men . . . every day that I am satisfied are more or less becoming deranged."

Sometimes the soldiers amused themselves by whittling. Lying in their trenches, where raising their heads above the parapet would result in almost certain death, they became extremely good at it. Major Fry of Texas fashioned an arm chair out of a minie ball. It was very small, but perfectly symmetrical in every way. Other times, the men used parapet wood.

Fry was not the only excellent whittler. There were many. Once, a little girl was hit by a bullet. She was taken to a hospital, where a physician removed it. A recuperating soldier asked for the bullet and carved it into a miniature set of knives and forks, to the great delight of the young lady.

Another popular game in the trenches was marbles. The marbles were iron balls taken from Union shells which did not explode. Soldiers also played cards, checkers, and other games which did not require them to raise their heads above the top of the trench.

Inside Vicksburg, the town had become a giant medical ward. At any time from May to July there were about five thousand men in the hospital, suffering from wounds or illness. This amounted to a sixth of the army. As soon as the army retreated from the Big Black, the sick and wounded overwhelmed the existing hospitals. According to Captain Charles A. Brusle of Hebert's staff, there were two types of hospitals in Vicksburg: those for the sick and those for the wounded. A week before the siege, Washington Hospital had three hundred sick and averaged five to eight deaths per day. During the siege, it averaged eight hundred patients per day, with eighteen to twenty deaths every twenty-four hours.

In terms of location, there were a variety of hospitals in the city. A few were in public buildings, many were in private homes, and others were in tents.

Many of the hospitals were scarcely that. "I visited the infirmary," Lieutenant Cantrell recalled, "and there I saw a scene of suffering which can scarcely be described; around me lay the sick, the wounded, the dying; the wounded were in great numbers; some with arms torn off, some with eyes out, and some with legs broken; my sympathies were touched, but mere sympathizing with the suffering soldiers added nothing to their comfort."

At one point in June, one of Porter's gunboats fired on a hospital, despite the fact that it was in a prominent location and flying a yellow (hospital) flag. Several shells penetrated the building, killing eight and wounding fourteen, several of whom were already wounded. One huge shell exploded near the Surgeons' Room, destroying a scanty supply of medicines and wounding the chief surgeon, who was buried under the rubble. He realized that an artery had been severed, so he tied it off, effectively operating on himself. This saved his life, but he lost the leg. Another hospital on the south side of Vicksburg was also attacked in a similar fashion.

Despite their ordeals, the morale of the Rebel soldiers remained remarkably high and they were in good humor. On June 19, their daily rations consisted of a quarter of a pound of flour, a quarter pound of rice flour, and a quarter pound of peas. They also received small portions of rice, sugar, and salt.

After midnight on June 20, there was a lot of Union activity around Snyder's Mill, prompting the Rebels to hope Johnston was near. He wasn't. The Yankees were preparing a huge bombardment. At 3:00 a.m., over two hundred Union guns opened up and continued to fire for six hours. Porter's gunboats and mortars also joined the chorus. It was the most severe bombardment to date. "The earth trembled," Sergeant Tunnard recalled. Pemberton had ordered that shot and shell be saved for the next big assault, so the Rebels did not return fire. The bombardment did heavy damage to the Confederates' works but, because of the smoke and the dust they kicked up, the Yankees couldn't see and didn't realize it. They continued a less intensive bombardment for the rest of the day. That night, Southern engineers repaired some of the damage, as they did every night. But they, too, were experiencing exhaustion. Captain M. R. Banner, the engineer company commander of Cumming's brigade, noted, "My work is very hard and most of the time have had to work from dark until day light, since we got here."

This day the army's supply of corn meal was exhausted. Instead, the men received four ounces of flour, four ounces of rice meal, four ounces of peas, four ounces of bacon, and a small ration of sugar.

By now, the Rebels could tell the different sounds the artillery made. Rifled Parrots went "bang," Whitworth guns went "crack," 6-pounders and 12-pounders made a "boom" sound, and the big guns went "whirr."

The gunboats also continued to shell Vicksburg. One of them struck the Willis-Cowan house, where Jack Pemberton lived. The shell did not explode, but the general and his staff decided it was too dangerous to try to remove it. It never was defused and is still there, clearly visible, for anyone who wants to see it.

Union mining continued. To the left of Hall's Ferry Road they were now within two hundred yards of the Confederate works.

In contrast to the day before, June 21 was quiet, with little firing all day. But there was one serious loss. A sharpshooter's bullet struck Major W. W. Martin of the 26th Louisiana, killing him instantly. He was twenty-two years of age and was looked upon as one of the most promising young men in the whole Confederacy. Lieutenant Colonel L. L. McLaurin of the 27th Louisiana was also killed that day.

In mid-afternoon, two couriers arrived with duplicate messages from Johnston, advising Pemberton that all he could do was save the

garrison—i.e., Vicksburg could not be saved. He demanded exact cooperation. He again demanded to know the point to which he should try
to advance.

Once again, Pemberton responded immediately.

> If it is absolutely impossible, in your opinion, to raise the siege
> with our combined forces, and that nothing more can be done
> than to extricate this garrison, I suggest that, giving me full
> information in time to act, you move by the north of the
> railroad . . . [and] on that night I move by the Warrenton road
> by Hankinson's Ferry, to which point you should previously
> send a brigade of cavalry, with two field batteries, to build a
> bridge there and hold that ferry; also Hall's and Baldwin's
> [Roads], to cover my crossing at Hankinson's. I shall not be
> able to move with my artillery or wagons . . . all other roads
> are too strongly intrenched [sic] and the enemy in too heavy
> force for a reasonable prospect of success, unless you move in
> sufficient force to compel him to abandon his communication
> with Snyder's, which I still hope we may be able to do.

June 22—the thirty-sixth day—was another clear, hot day. There
was a lot of sniper fire, but the Union artillery remained relatively quiet.
Two Texas regiments (on the right of the 3rd Louisiana) suddenly charged
Union lines. They took the Yankees totally by surprise, killed or wounded
forty of them, and captured a colonel, a lieutenant colonel, a captain,
and eight privates. Apparently, they suffered no losses. The raid caused
enthusiasm all along the Rebel line.

In town, an ordinary sized pone of corn bread cost $2.50 and meal
cost $35 per bushel. Confederate privates theoretically received $11 a
month pay and were paid every two months. They were now unable to
supplement their rations by purchasing food in town.

That night, Cumming's Georgia brigade of Stevenson's Division
made a midnight sortie. During the Siege of Vicksburg, this brigade was
the most aggressive of the Confederate commands. Perhaps its men were

embarrassed by their poor performance at Champion Hill. In any case, they captured twelve men, assorted entrenching tools, and several canteens full of alcoholic beverages. They even tossed some dead Yankees into their sap trench and filled it in before they left. But one of the dead Yankees—a lieutenant colonel—was not dead. After a few spades full of dirt had been tossed on top of him, he came straight up out of the grave and declared that he was not ready to be buried alive. The burial detail took him prisoner—after they got over the shock.

That same day, Sergeant Andrew R. Denton of the 43rd Tennessee was cut down. He died of his wounds on June 26. He never got to see his only child, a son, who would be born on November 8.[12]

Shells continued to fall in the city at irregular intervals. One mother and her four-year-old daughter were caught when two shells exploded near them. Neither were hurt, but the little girl began to cry. The mother comforted her, saying, "Don't cry, my darling. God will protect us."

The little girl replied that she was afraid God had already been killed.

June 23, the thirty-seventh day of the siege, was cool, clear and pleasant. A dispatch arrived from Johnston, stating that "I will have the means of moving in toward the enemy in a day or two . . ." He went on to tell Pemberton that, if he could not relieve him, he should try to cross the river, rather than surrender, if he could communicate with General Taylor. This suggestion was completely unrealistic, because the Yankees had two fleets around Vicksburg and Pemberton hardly had a rowboat.

Sensing that help was never coming, Pemberton countered with an equally unrealistic suggestion. He suggested that Johnston approach Grant and convince him that the city could hold out for a long time. Grant might be willing to let the army march out in exchange for Vicksburg. This was a desperate, impractical idea, but Pemberton apparently hoped that maybe it would get Johnston to do *something*. It didn't.

In the zone of Stevenson's division, six companies of the 43rd Tennessee attacked a forward Union position and filled in a sap trench but suffered heavy losses in the process: twenty-one killed or wounded. The Yankees were soon digging again.

Lieutenant Alison noted that "the mortars have ceased firing. I think they must have worn out, as the last shots fired all fell short."

Elsewhere, the day was relatively quiet. The troops from the two sides exchanged banter and the Federals exchanged hard bread for Confederate tobacco. Rations for the day were four ounces of flour, three ounces of rice meal, four ounces of peas, four ounces of sugar, four ounces of beans, and four grams of bacon. Some mail also arrived for General Bowen. Pemberton's recommendation had been approved and he had been promoted to major general on May 22.

The thirty-eighth day of the siege was June 24. The troops were now on one-quarter rations. It rained during the night, but heavy skirmishing began long before dawn. After being silent for three days, Porter's fleet opened up again and kept firing until well after dark. Mortars and four batteries of rifled guns kept a continuous fire on the town from the east. Long range rifled heavy guns plastered Vicksburg from across the river. One man walking on Washington Street was killed and two others were wounded. One hundred and seventy-seven shells fell on Vicksburg that day. One of them hit Paxton's Machine Shop and damaged some of the machinery.

Earlier that day, an old slave approached his owner. He had been with the family so long he was considered a family member. "Mistess, I feel like I ain't gwin' to live much longer," he declared. "Tell young master, when you see him, that I've been praying for him dis day; tell him it smites my heart mightily to think I won't see his young face dis day with the children. Please tell the young folks, mistess, to come, and let me pray with them."

"Oh, uncle" the lady answered, "don't talk that way; you will live many years yet, I hope." But she gathered all the young white ladies to his side. They all knelt and prayed. Then he shook hands with each one of them, and spoke with each one separately as they left.

That night, as he was smoking his pipe next to the entrance to his cave, a Yankee shell ripped his hip from his body. The women carried him into the cave, but he only lived a few moments. His last words were, "Don't stay here, mistess. I said the Lord wanted me."

The family was so stricken with grief and horror at the death of their loved one they panicked and rushed outside, where Union shells were still falling. A gentleman heard their cries of anguish and took them to a place of safety.

Meanwhile, General Pemberton ordered all men to sleep with their weapons during the night of June 24–25, because he expected a major attack.

He was right.

June 25 was the day of the Battle of the 3rd Louisiana Redan.

The Redan was near the center of the Confederate line on the north side of the Jackson Road and bulged out. U.S. engineers began digging operations at the Shirley House, a quarter of a mile away, near the beginning of the siege, and three hundred men continued digging day and night. They also dug a 400-yard trench (called Logan's Approach) from the Union line to the Redan. It was eight feet wide, seven feet deep, and their sap featured timber loop-holes for sharpshooters. They reached the ditch beneath the Redan on June 22. That night, thirty men with pics, shovels, and drills, began to dig a mine shaft five feet deep and four feet wide beneath the Southern position. When they had pushed forward forty-five feet, they branched out and began placing eighty-eight 25-pound bags of gunpowder, a total of twenty-two hundred pounds, beneath the Redan.

Artist's conception of the explosion under the 3rd Louisiana Redan,
June 25, 1863.

The Confederates heard the tunneling and Major Lockett began countermining. He intended to drive a vertical shaft fifty feet deep. Then he would detonate an explosion and destroy the Union mine. But the Yankees struck first.

The mine exploded at 3:30 a.m. In a split second, the 3rd Louisiana Redan ceased to exist. Men, artillery pieces, mules, and wagons were thrown toward the sky. Nothing was left but a huge crater. Before the dust settled, Union soldiers charged down the Jackson Road, four abreast. They poured into the crater and, for a moment, the excited Yankees thought they had broken Pemberton's line and would soon be in Vicksburg. Then they ran into a hail of lead.

Brigadier General Louis Hebert.

Before the explosion, Brigadier General Louis Hebert, the brigade commander, figured out what the Yankees were up to. He moved most of the 3rd Louisiana out of the Redan and into a second line of trenches behind it. He also brought up Colonel Eugene Erwin's 6th Missouri (nicknamed "The Bloody Sixth") for a possible counterattack. The Northerners had not counted on this contingency and found themselves trapped. They were in a crater which was twelve feet deep, and they could not scale it without exposing themselves. On top, the Rebels were tossing in lit artillery shells. They also brought up a cannon and fired into the crater, with great success.

Other Union regiments charged forward and there was fierce, hand-to-hand fighting. The men of the 6th Missouri immediately rushed to the aid of their comrades and beat back the attackers. Among those killed, however, was Colonel Erwin, a grandson of Henry Clay, Lincoln's political icon. Noted for his extreme bravery, Erwin was "universally loved" by his men.[13] He left behind a wife and three little girls.

Grant threw in regiment after regiment, but the Southern line refused to budge. Both sides freely used hand grenades. Just after noon, the Yankees blew another mine on the left of the Jackson Road, also in Forney's sector, possibly in hopes of diverting the Rebels. It did little damage. During the battle, the 3rd Louisiana lost thirty men, eight of whom were killed. Forney's entire division lost only eighty-eight men killed and wounded that day. The losses of Bowen's division were not reported separately. General Green was slightly wounded.

June 26 was a clear and hot day. During the night, the Rebels partially repaired the 3rd Louisiana Redan. The 5th and 6th Missouri remained near at hand, in case the Yankees attacked again, but they did not. More damage was done to the town than the Confederate lines that day. The U.S. Navy continued its terrorist attacks on the town and killed or wounded several civilians.

Mrs. McRae was in a tent outside of her cave, brushing her ten-year-old daughter's hair when they heard the sound of a shell coming their way. The civilians now had had enough experience that they could tell from the sound of a shell where it was going to land. "Get into the cave!" the mother screamed. But there wasn't enough time for both of them to make it, so the little girl jumped into a small "rat hole" in the side of the hill, which the children had dug for just such an emergency. Young Lucy felt the heat of the blast and was stunned but otherwise unhurt. Her mother reached the cave just in time and was fine, but the washstand they had been standing beside moments before was a total write-off.

In his diary, Major Simons calculated that 3,984,000 pounds of iron had been thrown in Confederate lines by the mortars alone, and that wasn't half of the total volume of shelling. It would require 4,980,000 pounds of powder to accomplish this.

The bacon was now exhausted and the Confederates were using mule meat as a substitute. General Pemberton was pleased that the officers and men found it "not only nutritious, but very palatable, and in every way preferable to poor beef."

Of the general at this time, Douglas Southall Freeman wrote, "To those closest around him, Pemberton appeared still as cool as arctic ice, and as solid. Holding to his contracting ground he refused to believe he was forsaken by his comrades in arms."

But optimistic thinking was not enough. On June 27, Sergeant Tunnard visited Vicksburg and declared that it presented a "fearful spectacle." He recalled,

> . . . [H]ouses dilapidated and in ruins, rent and torn by shot and shell; the streets barricaded with earth works, and defended by artillery, over which lonely sentinels kept guard. The avenues were almost deserted, save by hunger-pinched, starving and wounded soldiers . . . The stores, the few that were open, looked like the ghosts of more prosperous times, with their empty shelves and scant stock of goods, held at ruinous prices . . . Palatial residences were crumbling into ruins, the walls torn up by mortar-shells . . . Fences were torn down, and houses pulled to pieces for firewood . . . Dogs howled through the streets at night; cats screamed for their food, would scamper around your feet . . . lice and filth covered the bodies of the soldiers . . . Added to all these horrors . . . the deep-toned thunder of mortars and heavy guns, the shrill whistle of the rifle shot, or the duller sound of flying mortar-shells; the crash of buildings torn into fragments; the fearful detonations of the

explosions shaking heaven and earth; the hurtling masses of iron continually descending . . .The Spartan band of Southern heroes held their position, utterly regardless of the furious storm of grape, canister, shell and shot poured upon them by overwhelming forces.

Brigadier General Martin Green was one of the most popular men in the army and the commander of the 2nd Brigade of Bowen's division (a mixed Arkansas/Missouri unit). On June 27, he was observing the enemy through a pair of binoculars when a Union sniper's bullet struck him in the head and killed him instantly. He was replaced by Colonel Dockery, the commander of the 19th Arkansas. Officer losses continued to mount that evening. In Martin Luther Smith's sector, Lieutenant Colonel Sydney H. Griffin of the 31st Louisiana was killed instantly when a minié ball struck him in the head.

Brigadier General Martin Green. The exact location of his grave has been lost.

Sunday, June 28, was another hot day. In town, the Catholics held services in their cathedral, despite the dangers involved. As they were leaving, they were spotted by the enemy across the river, and Union heavy guns opened up on them. Several were wounded, but none were killed. The Rebels were outraged at this "unheard of ruthless and barbarous method of warfare"—firing on civilians, and mainly women and children at that—who were coming out of church.

The river batteries, including elements of the 1st Tennessee Heavy Artillery Regiment, commanded by Colonel Andrew Jackson, III, and Lieutenant Colonel Beltzhoover's 1st Louisiana Heavy Artillery, began counter-battery fire immediately and succeeded in silencing the guns across the river.

Some of the churches remained open throughout the siege. Dr. Lord put on his priestly garb and opened the Christ Episcopal Church every day, and had a talent for calming people, even though organ music had been replaced by the boom of cannons. Emma Balfour recalled, "The church has been considerably damaged and was so filled with bricks, mortar and glass that it was difficult to find a place to sit."

In the trenches, the men were issued mule meat at a half pound per man per day. Several Spaniards from the Texas regiments converted the rest into jerky. Some of them sold it to the citizens at $.50 per pound. "Mule-flesh, if the animal is in good condition, is coarse-grained and darker than beef, but really delicious, sweet and juicy . . ." one Louisiana soldier remarked. He added that hunger changes the most fastidious tastes, and the quantity of the food, not the quality, becomes the great consideration.

By now, scurvy was widespread in the garrison. In town, speculators and black marketers sold flour for $400 a barrel and coffee for $10 a pound. Only the very rich could afford it.

Rats were another source of food. In Vicksburg, they were offered for sale in butcher shops and hung up next to the mule meat. "Wharf rats were considered a delicacy by many of the soldiers," a Tennessee infantryman recalled. In the trenches, the men made traps for them. The soldiers remarked that they tasted like squirrel and, before the siege ended, they were consumed in such numbers that they actually became scarce.

Because of Union sharpshooters, such rations as were issued were distributed at night. Colonel Hall noted that they had been periodically reduced "until it was insufficient to sustain life." Desperate men were now gathering and cooking weeds, grasses, tree buds, and cane root.

Phil Robertson of *Duck Dynasty* fame told me a story about how his great-great grandfather, who was serving in a Louisiana regiment, survived. He and his comrades found a dog which had just had a litter of puppies. Mr. Ivans let his comrades kill and eat the puppies, but he kept the mother alive for himself. He suckled off the animal. Ivans later gave that dog credit for saving his life. Even so, when he returned home after the siege, he looked like a walking skeleton.

Within the garrison, hope was fading. "The expectation of being relieved by Johnston merged into hope, and hope had vanished, as the cloud of a burst shell in mid-air," one Louisianan recalled. And yet the men in the trenches held on. Why? In part because of stubborn optimism, in part out of habit, in part out of patriotism, and in part because of loyalty to their unit and to their comrades. War sometimes bonds men together with ties that are often stronger than those which connect brothers.

The most noteworthy casualty on June 28 was Colonel Leon D. Marks, the commander of the 27th Louisiana, who was badly wounded by an exploding shell. A prominent Shreveport attorney, newspaper editor, and highly capable military commander, he was one of six Confederate colonels of Jewish descent and was well-liked by his men.[14] His lieutenant colonel, L. L. McLaurin, had already been killed and Major Alexander Norwood was wounded, so command devolved on Joseph T. Hatch, the senior captain.

Colonel Marks never recovered from his wounds. After his parole, he returned to Shreveport, where he died on September 23, 1863.

Meanwhile, both citizens and soldiers smelled. There was enough water for cooking and drinking, but not for bathing or washing clothes. "Our dirty hands and faces were strangers to water for many days," Robert Bachman lamented. Also, many soldiers and people who had lost their homes had only the clothes on their backs. They went weeks without washing, bathing, or changing clothes—in Mississippi, in June. They were dirty and grimy with gunpowder and dirt from the caves. Even so, there was little complaining. A few people drew up a petition, asking General Pemberton to ask Grant for a truce, so the women and children could be evacuated.

Pemberton never saw the petition. Except for those who drafted it, no one would sign it.

June 29 was a hot day with floating clouds. Sergeant Tunnard breakfasted on fried rats, which he found fully as good as squirrels. The firing was not as brisk as usual, but mining and countermining continued apace. The Yankees had been mining in the zone of the 2ⁿᵈ Texas for some time. Here Colonel Smith organized a countermining operation, and the two shafts actually met. The Texans captured the surprised Northern miners. But the Rebels were not this lucky everywhere.

A local attack against the 43ʳᵈ Tennessee was repulsed. There was no despair in Southern ranks.

On the western side of the river, the Trans-Mississippi forces launched another probe against Grant's western screen. Two Confederate cavalry regiments under the command of Colonel William H. Parsons attacked two companies of the U.S. 1ˢᵗ Arkansas Infantry Regiment, African Descent, at Mound Plantation. The outnumbered black troops held their positions, if only barely, until a Confederate infantry brigade under Brigadier General James C. Tappan arrived. The white Union commanders then surrendered, on the condition that the white officers be treated as regular prisoners of war. The Negroes were surrendered unconditionally. Tappan took 113 prisoners. Parsons' men then rode on toward Lake Providence, burning cotton and leasing plantations as they went. They captured two thousand contrabands.

Northern newspapers reported that the ex-slaves were tortured, burned alive, and even crucified. General Grant read the stories and ordered an investigation. He later reported to General Halleck that the stories were "entirely sensational . . . I have no evidence of ill-treatment to any prisoners captured from us . . ."

Back in Vicksburg, bright sunshine continued the next day, June 30. Sharpshooting was slow but constant. The gunboats fired on Confederate trenches, but did little damage. In the city, rats were now being sold at $3 per rodent.

Charles B. Lewis of Smith's division recalled, "In the last days of June, Pemberton fully realized his position. He might repulse another assault upon his lines, and the river batteries might now and then disable a gun-boat, but the end must come."

CHAPTER XVII

THE SURRENDER

The first day of July was one of intense, suffocating heat. There were rumors of an attempted breakout. Major Simons of Moore's staff wrote, "The men have been in the trenches for so long a time on short rations & having taken no exercise all the time that I do not think they could now march five miles. And I think it would [be] worse than folly for us [to] attempt it . . . Yet I would be more than willing to make the effort for there is nothing pleasant in the thought of being a prisoner . . . All have long faces & all despair of our holding this place beyond a few days . . . All looks dark & gloomy ahead."

The enemy had constructed a second gallery off Logan's Approach (under the 3rd Louisiana Parapet) and loaded eighteen hundred pounds of powder under it. They detonated it at 2:00 p.m. "A huge mass of earth suddenly, and with tremendous force and a terrible explosion, flew upwards, and descended with mighty power upon the gallant defenders, burying numbers beneath its falling fragments, bruising and mangling them most horribly," one survivor recalled. "It seemed as if all hell had

suddenly yawned upon the devoted band, and vomited forth its sulphu-
rous fire and smoke upon them."

"We seemed to stand upon the brink of a volcanic crater," Corporal
Anderson of the 2nd Missouri Infantry Regiment recalled, "ready to
engulph [sic] us in its fiery flood." Then more than fifty Union guns
opened up on the parapet.

Since June 25, Francis M. Cockrell's 1st Missouri Brigade was intermixed with the Louisianans. The mine blew up in their part of the line.
Dozens of Missourians were killed or wounded. Others were shocked
and bruised. Colonel Cockrell himself was tossed high into the air. Like
many Missourians he was stunned, but only for a few moments. The
survivors did not look for their comrades but immediately rushed into
the gap to check the Yankees. This they succeeded in doing in record
time. When the line stabilized, more than one hundred Missourians were
dead or wounded. The 3rd Louisiana lost five men killed and twenty
wounded.

Although only a short distance in the rear, the Northern attack had
been beaten back by the time the 2nd Missouri reached the crater. One
Missourian called the sight "frightful." As they tried to rescue men who
were buried alive, the Yankees shelled the crater with mortars and heavier
guns. The shelling lasted for two hours. Among the dead was Lieutenant
Colonel Pembroke S. Senteny of the 2nd Missouri, who was struck in the
head by a minié ball about nightfall.

Two whites and eight blacks had been working on a countermine for
the Confederates and were about forty feet deep when the Union mine
exploded. One of them, a black man named Abraham, was thrown so
high into the air that he landed behind Union lines. Incredibly, he was
not only alive, but not even seriously injured, although he was understandably in a state of shock. When he was able to talk, the Yankees
asked him how high he had been thrown. Abraham estimated about
three miles.

It was a miracle that Abraham survived and his story spread quickly
through Union ranks. Some enterprising Northerners put him in a tent
and charged their comrades $.50 each to see him. When General Logan

heard about this, he put an end to it. Abraham became a servant at Logan's headquarters until shortly after the surrender, when he was released.

The Confederates repaired the parapet that night, although Union snipers fired on the work parties and killed at least one man. Among those who visited the site of the explosion was General Pemberton, who was accompanied by General Bowen.

Corporal Anderson wrote in 1868,

> I have heard General Pemberton accused of being a traitor and of selling Vicksburg: it is scarcely possible. Looking upon that care-worn and deeply-concerned countenance, and beholding the expression of anxious solicitude upon his face, as he surveyed the work that was going on around him by the dim light, his loyalty to his pledges and honor cannot for a moment be doubted. If look and manner can speak at all, they plainly declared that he was true and faithful to his positions.

While visiting the trenches, Pemberton praised the Missouri brigade, and said that if he had ten thousand more Missourians, he would cut his way out of Vicksburg.

The 56th Georgia was also threatened with a Union approach. Lieutenant Cantrell recalled,

> . . . [A]t one place the enemy mined our breastworks, and blew them up with powder; our men, being aware of what was going to take place, erected new breastworks and dug new ditches [trenches] in the rear of the original ones, and fell back to them before the enemy had the tunnel completed; when the explosion took place, the enemy made a charge, thinking that they would bayonet what few of our men were

not killed by being blown up, and then march inside the fortifications; but a volley from our men in the new ditches,
killing about half of them, warned the survivors of the trick,
and they fled in wild confusion.

General Pemberton was now working out of a "rust-encrusted dug-
out" in a hillside. He sent a letter to his division commanders, asking
them to assess the condition of their troops and to report back as soon
as possible. Could they evacuate, he wanted to know. He hinted at a
possible surrender.

Pemberton met with his divisional commanders later that evening.
He hoped aloud that Grant would simply allow the army to march out
with its flags flying. This piece of wishful thinking was totally unrealistic. Carter Stevenson believed that, rather than capitulate, his men would
prefer to try to break out. John Forney said his men would prefer to
withstand the siege, rather than give up. Martin Smith thought it best to
propose surrender terms before they were forced to capitulate because
of a lack of provisions. Only Bowen said it was time to surrender.

July 2 was clear and hot. The day began with a Union bombardment
by mortars, Columbiads, and Parrot guns, and they kept it up for some
time. "It was the hour that tried the souls of men," Sergeant Tunnard
recalled. About sunset, the 100-pounder Parrots opened up on the city.
Confederate guns remained silent.

Pemberton held a second council of surrender that day and this time
invited the brigade commanders and some of the regimental commanders. Most of the officers present thought that surrender was the only
practical option. The army commander asked each of the divisional
commanders to submit a written report, expressing their views. With a
heavy heart, Pemberton wrote to General Grant, suggesting both of them
appoint three commissioners to negotiate surrender terms.

Later that day, each division commander submitted his report. John
Forney wrote, "I concur in the unanimous opinion of the brigade and
regimental commanders that the physical condition and health of our
men are not sufficiently good to enable them to accomplish successfully

the evacuation. The spirit of the men is still, however, unshaken, and I am satisfied they will cheerfully continue to bear the fatigue and privations of the siege."

Bowen, Stevenson, and Smith forwarded similar reports. General Smith declared that he had about three thousand men in a condition to march eight to ten miles a day "in this weather," but he considered only two thousand to be reliable in an encounter against strong opposition. Even now, Smith expressed faith that General Johnston would rescue them.

Unlike Smith, Bowen expressed a lack of confidence in Johnston and stated that, if a breakout were attempted, only a handful of men would reach the Army of Relief. "I see no alternative but to endeavor to rescue the command by making terms with the enemy."

Stevenson declared that his men were cheerful but "much enfeebled and a considerable number would be unable to make the marches and undergo the fatigues" necessary for a successful breakout.

Pemberton later stated that, as far as he knew, not a single brigade or regimental commander favored breaking out. Only two believed more than half of their commands would be available for that purpose.

The soldiers also realized the end was near. There was another rumor that Johnston was fighting on the Big Black River. "This was not readily credited, as the army had almost ceased to look or hope for relief from that quarter," Corporal Anderson recalled. Members of the 2nd Texas joked nervously after whether they would prefer imprisonment at Camp Chase, Camp Douglas, or Johnson Island.

Exhausted men were now becoming careless and even reckless, resulting in needless deaths. To make matters worse, bacon was no longer issued to the troops. The small amount available was reserved for the wounded.

About nightfall, a storm came, with a great deal of lightning. The storm blew over during the night and the morning of July 3—the forty-seventh day of the siege—was clear. Heavy storm clouds gathered over the city, but the night was clear and quiet. There was some Union cannon fire. Pemberton held a conference of generals that morning. Also present was Colonel Allen Thomas, the commander of the 28th/29th Louisiana.[1] It was ascertained that the entire combat effective force of the army was a little over eleven thousand men; that the men had been subsisting on a diet barely able to sustain life for weeks; that they would be out of ammunition in a few days; that most of the men were physically unable to undergo moderate exertion; and they had no horses left to haul the artillery.

The initial surrender negotiation delegation consisted of Major General John S. Bowen and Lieutenant Colonel Louis M. Montgomery, Pemberton's adjutant. They left Pemberton's headquarters on Crawford Street at 10:00 a.m. and rode down the dusty Baldwin's Ferry Road to the 2nd Texas Lunette. Bowen was chosen because he and Grant had been neighbors and on good terms before the war, when Grant was going through hard times and Bowen bought fire wood from him. Despite the fact that he was seriously ill with dysentery, Bowen put on his dress uniform and rode toward Union lines under a white flag—or so Bowen thought. He was met by a hail of bullets. Colonel Montgomery had forgotten to unfurl the white flag! He and Bowen scampered back to safety. They were just plain lucky that no one was hit.

Bowen tried again. This time there was a white flag and he and Montgomery were allowed to cross Union lines. About seventy-five yards east of Confederate lines, they were stopped by Ohio infantrymen, who blindfolded them and took them to the headquarters of U.S. Brigadier General Stephen G. Burbridge. Burbridge was too ill to receive Bowen, so he was taken to the tent of Colonel William Jennings Landrum, another brigade commander.

To Bowen's annoyance, he was forced to wait and was not taken to Grant. Landrum took the letter from General Pemberton to Grant asking him to speak to Bowen, and sent it to his divisional commander, General A. J. Smith. Smith took it to Grant.

While they waited, Bowen and Colonel Landrum had a relaxed, amiable conversation. They talked about Port Gibson, Champion

Hill, and other battles. Bowen remarked that there had been enough iron thrown into Vicksburg to stock immense foundries.

After about an hour, A. J. Smith returned to Landrum's tent and announced that Grant refused to meet with Bowen, and the only terms he would accept were unconditional surrender. The Rebel commander then asked if Grant would speak to Pemberton. He agreed and the meeting was set for 3:00 p.m., in front of McPherson's corps.

Pemberton was furious when he learned that Grant demanded unconditional surrender. He nevertheless put on his best uniform and rode to the appointed place. Bowen did not tell Pemberton that the idea for them to meet was his, not Grant's. Had he done so, Pemberton would probably not have come.

At 3:00 p.m., Pemberton, Bowen, and Montgomery met with Grant, McPherson, Major General E. O. C. Ord, John Logan, and A. J. Smith. (Grant had sacked McClernand and given command of the XIII Corps to Ord.) It did not go well. Bowen made introductions in a warm and engaging manner, to ease tensions, and Grant was friendly to Pemberton, but the meeting quickly deteriorated. When Pemberton asked for terms, Grant replied that the terms would be the same as mentioned in his letter—i.e., unconditional surrender. "The conference might as well end," Pemberton said; "rather snappishly," Grant recalled.

The Union commander tried to persuade Pemberton to surrender unconditionally, which meant that his men might end up in Northern prison camps, and his officers certainly would. Pemberton, who was in a bad mood anyway, rejected the idea out of hand. He had only one negotiating chip left, and now he played it. "I can assure you, sir, you will bury many more of your men before you will enter Vicksburg!" he snarled at the Federal general.

In saying this, John C. Pemberton performed a last, great service for his men. Grant was startled by the remark. He suggested that he and Pemberton step aside and let McPherson, A. J. Smith, Bowen, and Montgomery work something out. Pemberton was surprised.

Grant was, in effect, acquiescing to Pemberton's original peace commission proposal and backing off from "unconditional surrender."

Formal portrait of Lieutenant General Pemberton, U.S. National Military Park, Vicksburg. His sword is in the foreground.

Grant and Pemberton retreated to the shade of a large oak tree, where Grant chewed on an unlit cigar and Pemberton chewed on a piece of straw. Neither spoke very much.

John Bowen naturally tried to obtain the best terms possible. He proposed that the Army of Mississippi be allowed to march out with its arms but not its artillery. It would leave behind all public property except the food it needed to sustain itself. The idea was brought to Grant, who rejected it. Fine, Pemberton said, if you don't like Bowen's proposal, you must come up with another one. Grant agreed and said he would submit one to Pemberton by 10:00 p.m. that night. He called for a ceasefire until that time. Pemberton consented.

Meanwhile, the soldiers on both sides wandered into no-man's land and traded tobacco for coffee and food.

Grant's letter reached Pemberton's headquarters at 10:00 p.m. If he surrendered, it read, his men would be paroled, fed, and allowed to go home. Thus, the soldiers of the Army of Mississippi escaped Yankee prisons, where the mortality rate was 12 percent. But given the depleted physical condition of the defenders of Vicksburg, their death rate would certainly have been higher.

Pemberton immediately called for a conference of his generals. All of them voted to accept the surrender terms except William E. Baldwin and Stephen Dill Lee, who wanted to keep fighting.

General Pemberton then told his officers that he knew opprobrium would be poured on him for surrendering, especially on the Fourth of July. He remarked that he would prefer to try to fight his way out at the head of his army, rather than face "the shame and disgrace" that would be heaped upon him. However, "It is my duty to sacrifice myself to save the army, and I therefore shall offer to surrender this army on the 4th of July."

Several of the officers objected to this date because it would be a double humiliation. Pemberton, however, disclosed his reasoning. "I am a Northern man," he declared, "and I know my people. I know their peculiar weaknesses and their national vanity. I know we can get better terms from them on the 4th of July than any other day of the year. We must sacrifice our pride to these considerations."

Colonel William H. McCardle of Pemberton's staff was present at the meeting. He recalled Pemberton saying, "Those fellows will be so elated to get in here on July 4th, that they will give us better terms."

Pemberton responded to Grant's terms, asking for a rather complicated face-saving gesture. His message arrived at Grant's headquarters shortly after midnight on July 4. Pemberton's soldiers would be allowed to march out of the fortifications bearing their arms and flags before the Yankees marched in. After the army had gone a considerable distance, it would stack its arms and colors. Meanwhile, the Northerners would occupy Vicksburg. Officers could keep their sabers, sidearms, and personal property, including such horses as had not been eaten. Grant agreed to all of this. Once the Rebels had stacked arms, however, they would have to march back into town to be paroled, Grant declared. Pemberton agreed to this.

Pemberton was probably right when he declared the garrison would get better terms if it surrendered on the Fourth of July than on any other day. He was certainly right when he predicted he would be the target of anger when he did so. The 3rd Louisiana, for example, received the news with "indignant rage." They smashed their trusty rifles and scattered their remaining ammunition on the ground so that the Yankees could not use it. Some units tore up their beloved battle flags and distributed the pieces to the men, rather than surrender them to the Northerners.

About 9:00 a.m. on July 4, the Army of Mississippi stacked arms. The Union soldiers did the same. "Then in broken ranks they came up the hills we had held so long, calling to us in a jocose way, and extending their hands in friendly greetings," Robert Bachman of the 60th Tennessee recalled. "Soon there was a general mingling of gray coats and blue coats, as if there were no differences between them and never had been."

The Confederate army marched out of their trenches at 10:00 a.m., in accordance with the surrender terms. There was no talking. Only eleven thousand men were healthy enough to take part in the ceremony. All of them were depressed, and some of them were crying. The Union soldiers stood by silently, some with their hats off. It was like a funeral. One Northern division even cheered the tattered Rebels. One Confederate officer said the Yankees behaved "splendidly."

When the Northerners marched into Vicksburg, every house was closed. Inside, most of the civilians wept.

General Steele's division was given the honor of being the first to enter Vicksburg. They took possession of the courthouse, the post office, and what was left of the city. General Grant rode in with the troops and went to the river, to congratulate the sailors. ". . . [T]he fate of the Confederacy was sealed when Vicksburg fell . . ." he wrote later. "Really, I believe there was a feeling of sadness just then in the breasts of most of the Union soldiers at seeing the dejection of their late antagonists."

After the ceremony, Grant paid an unannounced visit to General Pemberton at General Forney's Headquarters.[2] Pemberton was sitting in a damask-cushioned, armed rocking-chair, and one witness said he was "the most discontented looking man I ever saw." Grant was clearly unwelcome. There was no seat available and neither Pemberton nor any of his officers offered the Federal his chair. Grant had no official business to discuss and tried to make small talk, but Pemberton would have none of it. After about five minutes, the conqueror left.

Black Confederates and now-liberated slaves were given a choice by the Yankees: they could be granted freedom and remain in Union-held territory or ask for a pass and return to Rebel lines with their masters. General McPherson was given the duty of issuing these passes. To his shock, so many African Americans requested passes that he had to discontinue the practice. Blacks without a pass were kept behind Union lines. Some of those asking for passes were not servants at all, but laborers brought in to work on the fortifications.[3]

"The Federals have issued an order prohibiting any negro passing their lines," Captain W. L. Faulk of the 38th Mississippi recounted. "It looks very hard [,] for many of them are anxious to return to their homes."[4]

According to William Pitt Chambers' diary, one black Confederate asked the Yankees for a parole each day, "but was put off on one pretext or another." On the day the soldiers marched out of the city, they tried to shield their black comrade by placing him in the center of the group. "But one of the enemy saw him and elbowing his way among us seized the negro by the collar and led him out of the ranks." Another black Rebel was smuggled out in the wagon, hidden by a box of crackers.

The South lost 9,091 killed and wounded in the Vicksburg campaign, including 2,872 in the siege itself. Some 16,822 Union soldiers died in and around Vicksburg, 12,719 of whom are in unknown graves. They lost 4,910 killed and wounded in the siege itself. Twenty-nine thousand, four hundred and ninety-five Confederates surrendered, along with 102 guns. Less than 100 civilians were killed in the battles,[5] a testimony to the effectiveness of the caves as protective positions. Almost every building in the town had suffered at least some damage. One Northern newspaper reported that there was not "a whole pane of glass to be found anywhere."

Some units naturally suffered more than others. General Forney's Division (Hebert's and Moore's Brigades) started the siege with 4,700 men. It lost 275 killed and 1,365 wounded, or 1,640 total. This amounted to 38 percent of the division. The 43rd Tennessee, for example, entered the campaign with more than 900 men. Less than half of them were still in the line when they surrendered. Their silk battle flag, given to them by the ladies of Mount Sterling, Tennessee, reportedly had 972 bullet holes in it. The 42nd Alabama, on the other hand, had only lost 8 men killed and 19 wounded, for a total of 27. Parole certificates were issued for 556 men. Private Joseph T. Harris of the 42nd recalled, "We fought like lions, but surrendered like lambs." But not all of them. About 700 Confederate soldiers refused to accept parole. They were sent to prisons in the North. Among them was Major Loughborough, Mary's husband.

The shock of the fall of Vicksburg, coupled with the news from Gettysburg, shook the South to its core. Jefferson Davis was so sick about it all that he had to be confined to his bed. Lieutenant General James Longstreet wrote, "For myself, I felt that our last hope was gone, and that now it was only a question of time for us."

In the Vicksburg trenches, Private Clack recalled, "The Yankees visited us today and we conversed freely and friendly together. We are treated with great hospitality by them."

Almost every Yankee came into the town with a haversack full of provisions, which he gave to some famished Southerner. "Here, Reb," one of them remarked, "I know you are starved nearly to death." Their officers expressed amazement that the fortress could have held on as long as it did. The former enemies mingled freely and the bluecoats expressed their sympathy for the Rebels in every way possible.

The Yankees were less charitable to the civilians. They began looting stores and private residences almost immediately. The officers exercised very little control over them.

Meanwhile, Joseph E. Johnston began probing Union lines on the Big Black on July 1, and actually drew closer to Vicksburg, but of course without becoming seriously engaged. He spent the next three days in reconnaissance but did not cross the Big Black River in strength.

Grant had given Sherman six divisions (in addition to the seven he already had), to block Johnston in the event that he tried anything. On July 4, the vanguards of the Army of Relief noticed that there was an ominous silence from the direction of Vicksburg. They knew what that meant. Johnston retreated rapidly in the direction of Jackson. By July 7, after a retreat of twenty-five miles, the army (now thirty-six thousand strong) was back in the Mississippi capital. Its defensive position was good: an irregular crescent-shaped line, two miles long, with both flanks anchored on the Pearl River. Johnston placed Loring's division on the right, Walker and French in the center, and Breckinridge's division on the left, with cavalry on both flanks.

William T. Sherman directed the pursuit, and his vanguards reached Jackson on the afternoon of July 10. His main body caught up with Johnston on July 12 and his artillery fired three thousand rounds into the city that day but, oddly enough, Sherman did not attack. He believed that the Confederate position was too strong to take by storm. It is also quite likely he also he felt that Johnston would retreat on his own accord, without a battle. If so, he was right. The bombardment continued until the night of July 16, when Johnston stealthily evacuated the city. From July 17 to 22, his men marched about sixty miles away from the enemy.

When he realized that he was not going to catch Johnston, Sherman burned Jackson (again) and returned to the Big Black.

The Army of Relief was partially disbanded in August 1863. Breckinridge's division was sent to Chattanooga, Walker went to Atlanta, and other units were sent wherever there was a threat—and there were a great many. By the end of August, only six thousand men under Loring and Red Jackson defended eastern Mississippi. It was not until December 16, 1863, however, that Jefferson Davis formally relieved Johnston and gave him command of the Army of Tennessee.

On July 5, 1863, the Northerners gave the Rebels five days' rations, including real bacon, hominy, peas, coffee, sugar, salt, bread, candles, and soap. This amounted to almost a month's Confederate rations. Moore's Brigade received 1,350 pounds of coffee—the first coffee they had seen in a year. "The Yankees came freely among them, and were unusually kind," Tunnard recorded. After a day's rest, the paroling began on July 7. The paroles read:

> Know ye, that I, _____, a private, Company ___, _____ Regiment, _____ Volunteers, C.S.A., being a prisoner of war in the hands of the United States forces, by virtue of the capitulation of the City of Vicksburg and its garrison by Lieutenant General John C. Pemberton, C.S.A., commanding on the 4th day of July, 1863, do in pursuance of the terms of said capitulation, give this my solemn parole, under oath:
>
> That I will not take up arms against the United States, nor serve in any military, police or constabulary force in any fort, garrison or field-work held by the Confederate States of America, against the United States of America, nor a guard of prisons, depots, or stores, nor discharge any duties usually performed by officers or soldiers, against the United States of America, until duly exchanged by proper authorities.
>
> Sworn to and subscribed before me, at Vicksburg, Miss., this 7th day of July, 1863.
> [Signed]
> Paroling Officer

One by one, the commanders said good-bye to their men. Colonel Winchester Hall addressed his men this way,

Louisiana Volunteers:

Comrades—Again you have met the enemy. For over forty days you have withstood triple numbers armed with every missile known to warfare, and expended with the utmost prodigality. Your undaunted courage and intrepid bearing has drawn admiration even from your antagonists. Whenever the bravery and fortitude of her sons is called in question, our own dear Louisiana may proudly point to the historic pages gilded by your deeds, in the swamp of Chickasaw Bayou, and on the fortifications of Vicksburg.

Though circumstances not in your control have forced you to surrender your riddled and battle-stained flag to the foe, the proud consciousness that you have done your duty should take away the sting of defeat . . .

General Moore stated, "I cannot speak too highly of the conduct of the officers and men. None ever endured such hardships with more cheerfulness . . . many remained at their post in the trenches who were fit subjects for the hospitals."

Grant expressed the hope that many of the Rebel parolees were through with fighting and the war and would simply go home. From July 7 to 11, the Yankees gave free passage across the Mississippi to any Rebel who wanted it. Grant and Porter were making it as easy as possible for their former opponents to return to civilian life. It would now be doubly difficult for the soldiers from Texas, Louisiana, Arkansas, and Missouri to return to action east of the Mississippi even if they wanted to, and Grant knew this is where the war would be decided. Although perfect evidence is lacking, there is enough to conclude that Grant was absolutely correct. The 2nd Texas Infantry Regiment, for example, went into the siege with 468 men.[6] It lost 38 killed, 73 wounded and 15 missing, and 11 men died of sickness. After being exchanged, only 29 men remained. The rest went back to Texas. The 21st Louisiana Infantry was exchanged in December 1863. Only 69 men rejoined the army. It was not reorganized. The men were merged into the 22nd Louisiana Consolidated

Regiment, along with the remnants of seven other regiments. Some of the parolees violated their paroles and played a major role in the massive Union defeat in the Red River campaign the following year, but this only occurred after the Yankees burned their homes.

Other units had a greater ratio of returnees. The 42nd Alabama had 566 men when it surrendered. Three hundred and seventy-four returned.

Meanwhile, Lieutenant Sterling Fisher of the 2nd Texas was fighting for his life. He had been seriously wounded on May 30 and now lay in a tent, where he had been exposed to flies, whose eggs hatched into maggots. Nurses removed them one by one with forceps, but his three larger wounds would not heal because of a lack of medication and nutrition. Bones in some of his wounds were exposed and his hair and beard both fell out. His friends hardly recognized him. Now that the city had surrendered, he was moved to the Vick Mansion, but he was still in critical condition.

As he was lying on what might be his deathbed, Fisher heard a Yankee demand if any of the men here were from the 2nd Texas. Fisher acknowledged that he was. The Yankee showed him a worn memorandum book with names written on one page. Fisher recognized his name, written in his own hand.

Fisher and the bluecoat had met before. At Shiloh on April 6, 1862, just after Union resistance in the Hornet's Nest had been crushed, the regiment stopped for a rest. Fisher and Dan Smith, another Texan, had been sent to the rear to fill canteens. They passed three wounded Yankees who were in a bad way. The Southerners took care of them, made them beds of leaves, and gave them canteens full of water and some haversacks full of rations, which had been abandoned on the battlefield. After a short time, they hailed a Confederate ambulance, which picked them up. The bluecoats were profuse in their gratitude and asked the Rebels to write their names and their regiment identification in their memo books. The astonished Northerners read their names and asked incredulously if they were really Texans. They had been told that Texans showed no quarter. The Federal now declared that he and his two comrades had searched every battlefield since, so they could return the favor that Fisher and Smith had done them at Shiloh.

The Yankee left but soon returned with the surgeon in charge of the hospital (a colonel) and several other officers (probably doctors), and repeated the story to them. From that moment, Fisher and the other wounded men in his ward were favored guests. They received constant attention, as well as better food, canned fruit, fresh sheets, new blankets and pillowcases, and the best medical attention Uncle Sam could provide. As a result, Lieutenant Fisher survived his ordeal and made a full recovery.

At 4:00 a.m. on July 11, all of the Confederates that signed paroles and were fit for duty marched out of Vicksburg and headed for Enterprise, Mississippi, 120 miles to the east. The last Rebel left the fortress at 11:30 a.m. The Yankees lined the road to watch them go, but there was not a single taunt, although Cantrell recalled that each man was searched by the Union officer before he left.

General Martin Luther Smith remained in Vicksburg to care for the sick and disabled and to have them transported by boat to New Orleans. There were about thirty-six hundred of them, mostly in private homes which served as hospitals.

July 11 was a hot day, but the army nevertheless marched fourteen miles and encamped on the east side of the Big Black. There was no longer officially any regular organization by companies or regiments, and a large number of the men simply went home, just as General Grant had hoped. The next day, they walked twenty-one miles, to Raymond. The ladies lined the streets and provided refreshments, and as usual welcomed their warriors with joy and encouragement. They crossed the Pearl River on July 13, where they contacted Johnston's outposts. They continued marching another twelve miles that day.

Pemberton's men now had a new phenomenon to adjust to: silence. For forty-seven days, they endured the constant drumbeat of musketry and cannon fire. "We became so used to the noise that it was hard for us to sleep a few nights after the surrender," Private Bachman recalled. "We missed the cracking rifles and the roaring cannons."

A good number of men left the main body on July 13. General Pemberton personally called on them not to, but they ignored him. The remnant of the 3ʳᵈ Louisiana camped near a corn field. The regiment only had one frying pan as a cooking utensil, so they took turns, using it squad by squad in succession. One Georgian ate nearly two dozen ears of corn and died.

The march began again at 3:30 a.m. The men suffered from a lack of drinking water and half rations issued by the Yankees. The column reached Brandon at noon after marching twenty miles in half a day. There were now only fifty men left in the 3ʳᵈ Louisiana. All day long they heard the roar of artillery to the west—Sherman was bombarding Jackson.

On July 16, all of the Confederate generals captured at Vicksburg were exchanged for Federal prisoners captured by Lee and Jackson at the Battle of Chancellorsville, May 1–6.

The column reached its destination—Enterprise, Mississippi—on July 21. Pemberton gave them all a 30-day furlough, beginning July 23. Jefferson Davis did not want him to do this, because he was afraid many of them would not return to the army. He was right, of course, and Pemberton knew it, but he let each man make that call for himself. I suppose he felt that he and the South owed them that.

The Confederate Army graveyard at Vicksburg. General Bowen's grave is on the far right.

CHAPTER XVIII

PORT HUDSON

And what was happening at Port Hudson while Vicksburg was under siege?

He has never been given much credit for it, but Confederate Major General Franklin Gardner, the commander at Port Hudson, was a tactician of the first order. After Farragut's failed attack in March, he used his time wisely. Jefferson Davis had ordered them to hold the place at all costs, and he intended to do so. He enhanced all aspects of the fortress. He improved the water defenses, strengthened the artillery positions, built new and better entrenchments, constructed abatis, cleared fields of fire, and pre-registered artillery fire. Constructed largely by slave labor, the defense featured a parapet about twenty feet thick, with a fifteen foot deep ditch in front of it. It also had twenty heavy guns and four small forts, defended by thirty pieces of field artillery and three infantry brigades, led by Brigadier General William Beale, Colonel William R. Miles, and Colonel Dr. Isaiah G. W. Steedman.

Gardner also had the 11th/17th Arkansas Mounted Infantry Regiment, commanded by Colonel John L. Logan. Gardner sent them out of the fortress before Banks could seal it in. Logan was ordered to roam the countryside, seeking targets of opportunity. This wise move forced Banks to keep a good number of his troops in the rear, guarding headquarters and vital installations from Rebel raiders.

Outnumbered five to one, Gardner could not have held the fortress unless his counterpart was incompetent. Here he was very fortunate. Gardner faced Nathaniel P. Banks, who was one of Lincoln's political generals. He was a masterful politician and a former speaker of the U.S. House of Representatives, but was a subpar military commander. He was nicknamed "Commissary Banks" because, in 1862, Stonewall Jackson smashed his army and captured so much equipment and so many supplies that it kept the Rebels provisioned for weeks. The nickname crossed the lines.

Banks' Army of the Gulf, which was also known as the XIX Corps, began to invest Port Hudson in May 1863, just as an order arrived from Johnston to abandon Port Hudson. Gardner sat down to plan the move when he received word from his scouts that Banks was closing in. It was too late to evacuate.

Gardner had about seven miles of breastworks to defend, as compared to Pemberton's eight and a quarter miles. Unlike Pemberton, who had more than twenty thousand men, he barely had six thousand. He would have to use his tactical genius and the advantage of interior lines to the maximum possible extent. He did. For example, he took a huge 10-inch Columbiad gun from the river battery and mounted it on railroad tracks. This allowed the gunners to fire in any direction, blasting whatever Union emplacements they desired with 102-pound shells. Fittingly enough, the Yankees dubbed it "Old Demoralizer." His field artillery was positioned so that it could also easily shift its fire from point to point and deal with various threats much more quickly than could the Yankees. His men also improvised, creating shot from ball bearings, nails, railroad spikes, nuts, bolts, broken bayonets, and even rocks and spikes made from sugar cane.

Old Demoralizer.

Union General Banks also had a plan. He intended to capture Port Hudson, march to join Grant at Vicksburg, assume command of both armies (he was senior to Grant and thus had that right) and then capture Vicksburg. With these victories under his belt, he would defeat Abraham Lincoln for the Republican nomination and be elected president of the United States the following year. But first he had to defeat Franklin Gardner. He should have been able to accomplish this, given the fact that he had 30,000 men and 116 guns, not including the naval flotilla which supported him.

The siege began on May 25. Two days later, Banks launched a major assault with four divisions, led (north to south) by Brigadier General Cuvier Grover, Brigadier General Halbert E. Paine, Brigadier General Thomas W. Sherman, and Major General Christopher C. Augur. Brigadier General Godfrey Weitzel's Brigade on the far (Union) right flank functioned as an independent command. Banks' men had massive artillery support, including the heavy naval guns of Farragut's fleet. The attacks were supposed to be coordinated but devolved into a piecemeal attack, in which one unit at a time struck the Confederate front, rather than all four divisions at once. This gave Gardner time to shift his forces and his artillery fire, enabling him to defeat one Union attack and then another.

Weitzel's Brigade started the battle with a strike against the northern flank. Here he opposed Colonel Steedman, who was described by one soldier as "utterly fearless, but never reckless." Dr. Steedman only had sixteen hundred men, which meant that he only had one man for every five feet of frontage. Even worse, they were mostly armed with smoothbore muskets that fired buckshot—which was deadly, but only at close range.

To confuse and disorganize the Yankees, Steedman posted five hundred men about half a mile from his main line of resistance. The Rebels had cut down the trees here but had not burned them, so they made perfect ambush positions. For some reason, the Northern commanders had not reconnoitered this section, and thus walked into what one survivor called "a huge bushwhack." The Confederates waited until the blues were right on top of them and then unleashed a devastating volley. Weitzel's men were fiercely resisted by the Rebel skirmishers, who finally gave way. Then, about two hundred yards from the main Confederate line of resistance, the Yankees were stopped by concentrated volleys and artillery fire from the Rebels. To make matters worse, the dry brush caught on fire and burned several wounded soldiers to death.

All along the Union advance, the men noticed white crosses nailed onto trees. They were puzzled as to what they meant and thought they might have a religious significance—until the Rebel artillery opened up with a devastatingly accurate bombardment. Then they realized that the crosses were pre-registered range finders for the Southern guns.

Grover's men struck the 15th Arkansas and met the same fate as Weitzel's soldiers. Their attack stalled about two hundred yards in front of a Rebel position aptly named Fort Desperate. Both Union forces went to ground. Weitzel waited for Grover to advance and Grover waited for Weitzel to move forward—and so nobody advanced. Meanwhile Augur's troops were also checked and then ran away.

Thomas Sherman, a West Point graduate and a professional soldier who knew his business, opposed the idea of a frontal assault against such fortifications from the beginning and did not advance at all. A furious Banks rode to his headquarters and demanded that he do so. Sherman protested that such an attack would be suicidal. Banks fired him on the spot and replaced him with Brigadier General George Andrews, the army's chief of staff.

It took some time for Banks' couriers to find Andrews, further disrupting the Union timetable. When he arrived at 2:00 p.m., Andrews found Sherman and his staff mounted and ready to lead the charge. Sherman also appeared to be drunk. Andrews decided not to assume command. He let Sherman lead the charge—which turned out to be a very wise decision.

Thomas W. Sherman and his staff advanced even in front of the color guard. Gardner, of course, had already shifted his defenses, and Sherman ran into a wall of fire. Sherman himself was hit by a large ball of grapeshot, which killed his horse, shattered the bones in his right leg, killed two members of his staff and wounded another. One of his brigade commanders, Brigadier General Neal S. Dow, also went down with a serious wound and was replaced by Colonel David S. Cowles, who was promptly killed. Two regimental commanders were also killed or mortally wounded. They never even got close to the Confederate trenches.

With their general down, Sherman's men retreated in disorder. Carried to the rear, Sherman was not expected to live, but he did. His leg had to be amputated, however.

Ironically, the ground over which Sherman advanced was called Slaughter's Field, after the local farmer who owned it.

Late that afternoon, a desperate Banks threw in the 1,080 men of the 1st and 3rd Louisiana Native Guards. (He was not planning to use his black soldiers at all, because of the overall prejudice against Negro troops in both the ranks of the Union Army and its higher commands.) It was the first time black units were used in combat. They faced Colonel William B. Shelby's veteran 39th Mississippi—which had been fighting Weitzel all morning and was down to about three hundred men.[1] They were extremely well supported, however, by the heavy guns of the river battery, which had pre-registered its fire along the exact route the African Americans advanced. They tore huge gaps in the Union ranks. Then, two hundred yards from the main line of resistance, the Rebels rose from their trenches and delivered a concentrated volley. Shelby had three field guns of his own, loaded with grape and canister. The 1st and 3rd Louisiana suffered 20 percent casualties in two minutes. They "hit the dirt," seeking whatever cover they could find. An intrepid group of forty brave men pushed forward, only to find their way blocked by a stream forty feet wide and six to eight feet deep. They were cut to pieces. Only six out of forty returned. The rest of the two regiments retreated in disorder. They had lost more than two hundred men. There were no Confederate casualties. The attack was nevertheless a milestone in American history, because the black Yankees had proven that they were just as brave as white Yankees—not that it did them any good on May 27. When troops are badly led, courage often doesn't matter very much.

Furious, General Dwight demanded that the attack be renewed. His officers were horrified. Then they realized that Dwight was drunk. They refused to obey his order.

Banks' first attempt was a total failure. He lost 1,995 men (293 killed, 1,545 wounded, and 157 missing). Gardner suffered 235 casualties.

A section of the Confederate trench line near the Old Demoralizer.

Three days later, Banks named William Dwight permanent commander of the 2nd Division—Sherman's old command.

Over the next two-and-a-half weeks, the Union army dug and moved closer to Gardner's lines. Much of the hard work was done by impressed ex-slaves, but there were not enough of them to do it all, so white soldiers were also used. The heat in Louisiana is merciless in summer and most of Banks' army was from New England. Literally hundreds of them suffered heat stroke and dozens of them died.

Banks attacked again on June 14. Things went wrong from the beginning. A huge artillery barrage began at 2:45 a.m., but that was too early. It was still dark when the cannons finished, so the Union infantry was unable to take advantage of the bombardment. All they accomplished was to alert the Rebels that something was up.

The main attack began at dawn. It concentrated on the northern sector. But once again Gardner anticipated them. As they neared Rebel lines, the men of the 1st Mississippi rose up and delivered a fierce volley at almost point-blank range. The Union divisional commander, Brigadier General Halbert Paine, was shot through the leg and could not rally his men, some of whom fled in disorder. Others pushed on and actually reached the Confederate works, where they were driven back after some hand-to-hand fighting.

General Paine himself spent most of the day between two cotton rows in the hot Louisiana sun. He was afraid to even shade his eyes, for fear that a Rebel sharpshooter might notice him. Several of his men tried to rescue him but were cut down. Late that afternoon, one of them did reach the general and dragged him back to U.S. lines. But it was too late to save his leg.[2]

Improvised Confederate housing at Port Hudson.

Some of Paine's Wisconsin troops actually breached the Confederate line. Gardner quickly threw in his reserves. One Mississippian recalled, "About one hundred of the bravest men I ever met came over our works. Here we had a hand-to-hand fight with the butts of our guns, the officers using their swords." But the Wisconsin attack was not supported and was also thrown back.

Meanwhile, Grover's division also struck Gardner's northern flank, which the Yankees considered Gardner's Achilles' heel. Like Paine's men, they reached the Mississippi breastworks but could not breach them. Private Samuel Townsend of the 91st New York planted the Union flag on the works but was shot dead, reportedly by his own brother.

Later that morning, Augur's division launched a frontal attack on the Confederate center while elements of Dwight's division tried to sneak under the great bluff and attack the fortress from the rear. The result was a miserable failure. They found a ditch full of abatis and sharpened wooden stakes, which they could not negotiate. Banks lost another 1,792 men (203 killed, 1,401 wounded and 188 missing). Gardner lost only 45 (22 killed and 25 wounded).

The Union wounded lay exposed in the hot sun, but when the Rebels tried to go out and help them, they were fired upon. This was at the order of General Banks. When Gardner asked for a truce to assist the wounded and bury the Union dead, Banks replied that there were no Union dead. Gardner was astonished.

Several subordinate Confederate commanders asked for a truce. Some of the Union commanders in their sectors accepted with thanks. Others did not. General Dwight, a West Point dropout, responded, "No, sir, I'll stink the rebels out of the citadel with the dead bodies of these damned volunteers if I cannot make the cowards take it by storm, as I have ordered them to do." They remained there until the siege was over.

A year later, General Dwight was arrested for cowardice during the Battle of Winchester in Virginia.

General Gardner had stockpiled more food per man than Pemberton and he had once had a larger garrison, but during a bombardment on June 9, Union shells burned down his warehouses and, after that, his men also suffered hunger. Soon they were eating peas, corn on the cob, molasses, and cows. When they ran out of cattle, they ate their mules. When almost all of the mules were gone, they ate dogs, cats and rats. Near the end of the siege, they were down to eating three ears of corn per day, along with horse or mule meat, if it was available. Like the defenders of Vicksburg, they preferred mule to horse. They were also inadvertently helped by the Yankees, who brought up 13-inch mortars and fired at the town and the river batteries. Often they would miss altogether and the shells would land in the river. Rebels would then row out in skiffs and gather up hundreds of stunned or dead fish. Other people had less desirable dishes. One Southern lady recalled, "Uncle Pat was in the artillery. He was surrendered at Port Hudson where he and his companions literally starved. He had a Negro boy, Monroe [,] who caught rats and cooked them for him to eat without telling him they were rats. He taxed Monroe about what this meat was, but Monroe replied, 'Never mind Marse Pat, what it is—it is good for you to eat.'"

Prior to the war, U.S. Brigadier General Neal Dow was known throughout the country as the leader of a temperance (prohibition) movement. When the war began, he volunteered, even though he was fifty-seven years old. (Abolition was another one of his causes.) Named colonel of the 13th Maine, he did not allow any of the common soldiers' vices in his camp, including liquor, gambling, profanity, and ladies of the evening. The troops did not appreciate this and took delight in slipping alcohol into his lemonade. Apparently, his scruples did not extend to theft, as he would confiscate anything he wanted, whether it belonged to a pro-Confederate or not.

Dow was shot twice on May 27. The second wound, a rifle ball to the left thigh, was serious. He was sent to the rear and, following surgery, to a local plantation, where he could recover. On June 30, however, he decided to move, because of rumors that Confederate cavalry were in the area.

A few minutes later, C.S. Captain John McKowen, Jr., of the Louisiana cavalry arrived. He and his men were disappointed at just missing Dow. As they were leaving, however, they ran into the Union general.

He was returning to the plantation alone to pick up something he had forgotten to pack.

Dow ended up in Rebel prisons for the next eight months, mostly in Libby Prison, Richmond. The Rebels treated him as someone special. They allowed him to receive guests and even to make temperance speeches, for which he was famous. Eventually he was exchanged for Robert E. Lee's son, Rooney.[3]

On July 7, word reached the Army of the Gulf that Vicksburg had surrendered. The Northerners cheered and celebrated, but most of the Rebels refused to believe it. The next day, Franklin Gardner was sitting on the portico of his headquarters, smoking a pipe of dried magnolia blossoms, when a courier brought an official copy of the surrender document, signed by General Grant. The general called a council of war and decided to capitulate. Although not as bad off as the Vicksburg garrison had been, the men of Port Hudson were running out of food. Gardner knew there was no hope and Grant would soon be down to finish him off if he did not run up the white flag.

After a siege of forty-eight days, General Gardner surrendered to Banks' chief of staff, General Andrews, the next day. Andrews declined to accept Gardner's sword as a "proper compliment to the gallant commander of such gallant troops." He then remarked that such gallantry "would be heroic in any other cause."

"This is neither the time nor place to discuss the Cause," an offended Gardner snapped as he sheathed his sword. Thus ended the longest siege in U.S. military history.

Banks agreed to parole both officers and the enlisted men, and about fifty-four hundred Confederate soldiers were paroled. About five hundred of these were wounded and two thousand were sick. After the surrender, however, he changed his mind and sent the officers to prison, mostly on Johnson's Island, Ohio. Franklin Gardner would be in prison for more than a year.

During the forty-eight-day siege, the Confederacy lost 188 killed, 483 wounded and about 200 who died from disease or sun stroke. Banks reported 978 men killed in action, 3,228 wounded and 418 missing.

Another 4,000 Yankees had been felled by disease or sunstroke. How many died from these causes was not reported, but they probably totaled 1,000 or more.

Apparently because they felt that the spirit of the original terms of the surrender had been violated by General Banks, the Confederate War Department seized upon a legal pretext and declared its paroled soldiers on furlough. They were ordered to report back to their units on September 15. (Paroles at that time had to be approved and signed by a certified parole officer, and this Banks failed to do.) Some of Banks' officers were furious, but Henry Halleck, the Union general-in-chief, admitted the Federals were in error concerning the paroles. He let the matter slide.

How many furloughed Rebels reported for duty on September 15 is not known, but it was well under one-half and probably less than one-quarter. Like their counterparts in Vicksburg, many of them had had enough.

Gardner's surrender marked the end of the Confederate hold on the Mississippi River. All of the food, supplies, equipment, and manpower west of the Mississippi were now lost to the Southern Confederacy, and the entire Trans-Mississippi Department was on its own. Coupled with Gettysburg, it was the turning point. The South could no longer win the war militarily.

CHAPTER XIX

AFTERMATH

A day or so after the surrender, Mrs. Mary Bowen and her husband reunited in Vicksburg. She barely recognized him. He was bedridden with dysentery.

General Grant liked Bowen from before the war. He offered the Confederate general medical treatment from the best U.S. surgeons, as did his former West Point classmates, McPherson and Brigadier General Eugene Carr, but he was too proud to accept. This cost him his life.

Early on the morning of July 6, Bowen was carried to an ambulance, which headed for Jackson. He was accompanied by his wife, Chaplain Bannon, and members of his staff, who provided protection. (Mrs. Bowen was an accomplished nurse. She was also a devout Catholic and the general had apparently converted.)

The trip was a nightmare. They spent the night of July 12–13 at John Walton's farm near Fourteen Mile Creek, about six miles west of Raymond. Bowen died early the following morning. He was thirty-three years old. They placed him in a homemade coffin, and he was first buried in Mr. Walton's garden. Father Bannon conducted the funeral in the Catholic tradition. That fall he was reburied in the nearby Bethesda Presbyterian Church Cemetery. When he heard the news of Bowen's death, John C. Pemberton lamented the loss of "one of the best soldiers in the Confederate Army." His passing was undoubtedly a terrible blow to the South, which needed every good general it could get, now more than ever.

General Bowen was reburied in Vicksburg's Cedar Hill Cemetery in 1877.

On July 16, 1863, President Davis signaled Pemberton and informed him that he and all of his general officers had been discharged from their paroles and could return to active duty. Meanwhile, much of the army, many Southern editors, and some of the officers viciously attacked Pemberton for surrendering on July 4, which was humiliating to the South. Pemberton, however, was stoic and quietly confident. "I am content to wait for the vindication of my military reputation," he said.

He would have a long wait.

Joseph E. Johnston and members of his staff were sitting on a cleared knoll on a moonlit night. Coming up the hill, Johnston saw "a tall, handsome, dignified figure." Suddenly he recognized him. Johnston jumped up, extended his hand, and declared, "Well, Jack old boy, I am certainly glad to see you!"

The feeling was not mutual. John Pemberton ignored the outstretched hand. He saluted and said, "General Johnston, according to the terms of parole prescribed by General Grant, I was directed to report to you, sir!"

Both men stood motionless and silent. Then Johnston slowly lowered his hand. Pemberton saluted again, turned on his heel, and walked away. They never saw each other again.[1]

Vicksburg underwent a harsh military occupation, but it was not as brutal as some other places experienced. Martial law was imposed immediately. Freedom of speech was not tolerated by the Unionists, and both men and women were arrested by the conquerors for the most minor offenses. Only citizens who signed Union loyalty oaths were permitted to operate businesses, hold jobs, or leave town without a military pass. Speaking ill of Lincoln or any Yankee politician or Federal officer could get a citizen expelled from the city for a year. Preachers who failed to pray for Lincoln and his cronies were arrested. Five women were exiled because they left their church one Sunday, rather than pray for Abraham Lincoln.

A typical incident happened to Margaret Lord, the wife of the minister. She was in her own yard, minding her own business, hanging out her laundry, when several Northern soldiers walked up and turned over her laundry basket, which was full of clean clothes. She heatedly reprimanded the soldiers for their rude action. They laughed at her distress and, pointing to the battered church rectory, which had been ruined by Yankee shrapnel, accused her of being a poor housekeeper.

"It is all you have left to us for a home," she snapped angrily. "And I will tell you now that I have lived for months in the midst of thirty thousand Confederate soldiers and this is the first insult I have ever received!"

Other Vicksburgians had similar or worse experiences. Lawless Federal soldiers thoroughly looted Mr. Bowie's home, for example. They filled up sheets with silverware, clothing, and anything else that struck their fancy, tied up the sheets, and hauled off their plunder. They ripped out the floor boards of his kitchen, to check for hidden valuables. They cut his shutters, just for meanness, leaving the windows open, as there was no longer any glass in Vicksburg.

Hester Bowie was engaged to the colonel of a Louisiana regiment and had prepared her trousseau, which was lying in her trunk. Yankee soldiers cut out the lock and stole everything, even her veil and orange blossoms.

Shortly thereafter, the Lincolnites drew up "Black Lists" of Confederate sympathizers. They were subject to exclusion, arrest without charges, confinement without trial, and special harassment. All of this turned the most pro-Union city in Mississippi into the most ultra-Southern.

Vicksburg slowly recovered after the war, but it never forgot the siege, the brutal military occupation that followed, the oppression of Reconstruction, and the subsequent post-war poverty. It was World War II before the city celebrated the Fourth of July again on a regular basis. Prior to that, all businesses—including the banks—remained open.

In May 1863, as Sherman approached Jackson for the first time, Pattie Pemberton and her family boarded a freight car and escaped to Gainesville, Alabama. There they rented an unpretentious house. In late July or early August, Pemberton returned home. His oldest daughter, Pattie, age thirteen, was playing in the yard, but she did not run to him. He had changed so much in five months that she did not recognize him. His black hair was now gray and he looked like an old man.

If Joseph E. Johnston was slow to rescue his colleagues, he moved with lightning speed to protect and defend his own military reputation. His staff officers wrote articles that appeared in Southern newspapers, placing sole blame for the Vicksburg debacle on Pemberton. They obviously had access to documents in General Johnston's possession. President Davis denounced Johnston for this vehement criticism and told Pemberton to keep them in mind when he wrote his own report. Pemberton himself refused to respond to these attacks. His adjutant, William H. McCardle, did. He blamed the disaster on Pemberton's lack of cavalry, on Johnston's orders forcing him to advance beyond the Big Black River, and the total lack of help from outside once the siege began. An offended Johnston immediately protested to Richmond, but President

Davis ignored him. He knew who was to blame. He had a private, unofficial investigation conducted, and wrote to Robert E. Lee, "[Pemberton's] force is [was] much less than half that of the enemy but I have the most favorable accounts of his conduct as commander."

In October 1863, Braxton Bragg suspended Lieutenant General Polk as a corps commander in the Army of Tennessee. Davis hoped Bragg might choose Pemberton to replace him and called Pemberton to Richmond to discuss the matter. General Bragg was not opposed to the idea. He liked Pemberton and they had been classmates at West Point but, after consulting with his officers, Bragg decided his appointment "would not be advisable." Because of Pemberton's tarnished reputation, the men in the ranks would not stand for it.

Pemberton was hoping for the assignment, although he loudly declared that he would not serve under Johnston again. He also hotly declared that, if he had it to do over again, the only thing he would do differently would be to ignore Johnston's orders.

Pemberton moved to Boydton in Mecklenburg County,[2] Virginia, and remained unemployed for another six months. On March 11, 1864, Davis wrote to Pemberton, "I thought and still think that you did right to risk an army for the purpose of keeping command of even a section of the Mississippi River. Had you succeeded none would have blamed, had you not made the attempt few if any would have defended your course." He later wrote a letter to Senator Phelan of Mississippi and blamed Johnston for the loss of Vicksburg and Port Hudson.[3]

Because it was obvious that he would never be reemployed as a lieutenant general, John C. Pemberton sent his resignation to General Cooper on April 19, 1864. He simultaneously requested another commission—as a lieutenant colonel of artillery. This selfless act silenced many of his critics.

Pemberton's resignation was accepted on May 9 and he was granted his new commission the same day. He was given command of the Richmond Defense Artillery Battalion, which was concentrated on the Bottoms Ridge area, north of the James River, and the Chaffin's Bluff sector, south of the river. He also consulted with Robert E. Lee and his son,

Major General Custis Lee, about General Grant. Every time they met, Lee addressed Pemberton as "general."[4]

Lieutenant Colonel Pemberton was promoted to inspector general of artillery and ordnance in January 1865, but without any advancement in rank. His headquarters was in Charleston and he visited Fort Sumter, among other old haunts. He recommended his former chief of artillery, Colonel Ambrosio J. Gonzales, for promotion to brigadier general, but the war ended before this was confirmed.

After Richmond fell, Pemberton escaped to North Carolina with some of his guns and had hopes of joining Jefferson Davis; however, during a skirmish with George Stoneman's cavalry near Sailsburg, North Carolina, the Yankees captured all of his artillery. Pemberton himself barely escaped. He made a hard ride to Charlotte, during which his horse threw all of its shoes. When he got there, he found that Davis had left the day before. It was impossible to get horses reshod, so Pemberton gave up and went to Newton, North Carolina, where Pattie and the children were staying.

Meanwhile, public hatred against General Pemberton was mitigated. Because he had accepted a demotion without complaint and served with dignity, his loyalty was no longer questioned by a majority of the people. Writing in 1866, W. H. Tunnard declared, "That General Pemberton was not altogether blameless, is a fact . . . yet that he should be made to bear the whole of that disaster is wrong."

Pemberton and his family lived in poverty in Newton until February 1866, when his mother came to his rescue and bought him a 200-acre farm near Warrenton, Virginia. The farm, "Harleigh," cost $5,000. It had suffered a great deal during the war and was a mess. Bacon had been hung from the rafters and had soaked through the pine flooring. There was no glass in the windows. The fences were down and the barn was overrun with rats. The entire family—John, Pattie, and the five children—pitched in and rehabilitated the place. Even the U.S. government contributed. Pemberton wrote a letter and asked that his furniture be returned to him. It had been in storage since he left Fort Ridgely, Minnesota, in early 1861. Remarkably, the government sent it to him free of cost. It included a square, out-of-tune piano. The entire family played it and sang every night.

John C. Pemberton thus entered a new phase in his life, in an area for which he was totally unprepared and in an economy which was a basket case. He really had no place in life at all now, except with his family.

Pemberton was very cultured and would often read and recite poetry. Reading aloud on a long winter evening was soon a family staple. A friend gave the general a bookcase full of old books, running from Shakespeare to Dickens to Dumas, as well as Gothic tales of horror that the children loved but which scared them to death. His grandchildren later remembered him as two things: a soldier and a scholar. They also recalled that he liked oatmeal covered with cayenne pepper.

He loved Latin and read it continually, especially Virgil. Once Anna, his youngest daughter, was irked by her father's reading Virgil. She said to her mother, "Come on, Mama, let's go to bed and leave Papa with his virgins."

John C. Pemberton later in life.

Pemberton's religious faith had deepened during the war. Now, the family had prayers every morning and then the general read a chapter from the Bible. He had always had acting ability. He made the readings very dramatic and the kids were thrilled by it.

He made a great many friends in Warrenton, including Brigadier General Eppa Hunton, who had led a regiment in Pickett's Charge; Brigadier General William H. Payne, formerly of the Black Horse troop; and Colonel John Singleton Mosby, the "Gray Ghost." All three lived within a town of twelve hundred. Nearby fellow farmers included Major General L. L. Lomax, who rode with Jeb Stuart, and Brigadier General "Extra Billy" Smith, a brigadier general and Virginia's last Confederate governor. Captain North, C.S.N., who helped construct the *Alabama*, lived nearby.

For all of his efforts, John C. Pemberton was not a successful farmer. At the end of 1875, with his health failing and at the urging of his family, he sold the farm and returned to Philadelphia. The City of Brotherly Love was too expensive for him, however, so he moved to Allentown, where he was associated with the Allentown Furnace Company. He reportedly attended Grace Episcopal Church there. He also made a couple of good friends. One was U.S. Brevet Brigadier General Robert McAllister. They were both cigar aficionados and frequently met at a tobacco store.

Another friend was Ben Zellner, who was one of the few survivors of the 47th Pennsylvania. He recalled that Pemberton was always well dressed and carried himself well. There were plenty of former Yankee soldiers around who were willing to start arguments, but Pemberton always had good comebacks for them. He took their teasing good-naturedly "but didn't back up an inch," Zellner recalled, and he was such a good sport "you really couldn't get mad at him."

By now, Pemberton had heart trouble. His health failed badly in the spring of 1881, so he moved back to Penllyn, near Philadelphia. He passed away peacefully at 5:11 p.m. on July 13, 1881. Shortly before he died, he told his wife and children, "Except for leaving you, I am not sorry my time has come."

He was buried in an isolated corner of the Laurel Hill Cemetery, Philadelphia, where he now lies next to his wife and near his mother.[5] A plain marble marker records only his name and the dates of his birth and death, and those of his wife. A flat bronze marker, identifying him as a Confederate lieutenant general, was later added at the base of his tombstone.[6]

CHAPTER XX

CONCLUSIONS

Why did Vicksburg fall?

Napoleon once said that victory has many fathers; defeat is an orphan. So why did Vicksburg fall? There are many reasons. As with the loss of the *Titanic*, several factors contributed to the disaster, and several men are responsible. To give credit where credit is due, praise must be given to Ulysses S. Grant. Pemberton had defeated him five times by force of arms and Grant had to "up his game" to the genius level to beat him—and he did. Henry Halleck, the Union general-in-chief, must also be given credit. He put petty jealousies aside and lavished reinforcements on Grant and his army. There was, I believe, a window of opportunity during which Grant was between two Rebel armies and they could have crushed him. By sending all of the reinforcements he could, Halleck closed this window as rapidly as was humanly possible.

In the court of public opinion, John C. Pemberton has borne the onus of failure for Vicksburg and he did make some serious mistakes. His biggest mistake, according to his own chief engineer, was that he tried to harmonize orders from President Davis and General Johnston that were diametrically opposed to each other. Depending upon Joseph E. Johnston to at least try to rescue him was another serious mistake. In addition, his holding a council of war on May 14 shows that he had lost confidence in himself. Things would likely have turned out much better if he had relied on his own judgment and issued orders, rather than soliciting opinions. But it must be kept in mind that Pemberton was groping in the dark—much like Lee during the Gettysburg campaign. Without cavalry, he was blind. "Had my earnest requests, often repeated, for the return of Van Dorn's cavalry been complied with, Grant would never have reached Jackson," General Pemberton wrote later. I believe him. In December 1862, when Pemberton did have cavalry, he used it very effectively to sever Grant's supply line and check his invasion of northern Mississippi. Is there any reason to believe that he would not have done the same thing in southwestern Mississippi in May 1863, when Grant's supply line was even more exposed? I, for one, don't think so.

Additionally, Pemberton should have sent the habitually insubordinate W. W. Loring packing, and long before May 16. Pemberton's failure to get rid of the uncooperative, insubordinate and irascible Loring—as Robert E. Lee and Stonewall Jackson had done earlier—was a major contributing factor to his defeat in the Battle of Champion Hill.

I believe General Joseph E. Johnston was primarily responsible for the disaster that overtook the Army of Mississippi at Vicksburg. That he should have provided it with adequate cavalry is, in my opinion, both an inexcusable and indisputable fact. But after Vicksburg was isolated, could Johnston have saved Vicksburg if he had acted quickly and aggressively? I tend to think so, but we do not know for sure. And that is precisely the point. We should know. Together with Gettysburg, Vicksburg was the turning point of the war. Johnston should have moved heaven and earth to save it. We do not know if he could have saved it because, for all intents and purposes, Johnston did nothing to rescue the Army of Mississippi when he had the chance. Difficulties or no, he should have at least tried.

In the early 1940s, Colonel Matthew F. Steele wrote that Johnston was "of practically no assistance" to Pemberton and his army. He never seemed to want to attack, preferred to retreat and avoid battle when at all possible, and did not listen to those in authority above him, including Jefferson Davis and the War Department. "A devouring egotism caused him to reject and scorn all ideas and strategy not his own," Colonel Steele concluded.

U.S. Marine Corps Colonel John W. Thomason, Jr., the author of several books, would agree with Colonel Steele. He wrote to John C. Pemberton, III, in 1941 and observed, ". . . it is obvious that Grant's success depended upon an absolutely supine attitude in Joe Johnston—who by every standard ought to have pitched into him. But Johnston wasn't a fighter . . . If Jackson or Lee, or even Longstreet—any of the killers—had been sent out there, Grant wouldn't have been free to starve out the fortress." He added that he had never been able to understand why Johnston had such a high reputation.

Johnston has a higher than deserved reputation among historians for two reasons.[1] First, the Atlanta campaign. Conventional wisdom has it that Jefferson Davis made a huge mistake when he fired Joseph E. Johnston on July 17, 1864, and replaced him with John Bell Hood. I believe conventional wisdom is half right. I believe that placing Hood in command of the army was a huge mistake;[2] I do not believe sacking Johnston *per se* was in any way a bad decision. Atlanta was undoubtedly Johnston's best campaign but, as before, he had retreated to the very gates of a vital city without fighting a decisive battle. Worse still, he would not communicate with Jefferson Davis and refused to promise that he would not abandon Atlanta without a fight. A frustrated president, in my view, had little choice but to remove Johnston. I also believe that he had retreated so far, and the Union armies were now so near Atlanta, that few generals could have saved the city. Robert E. Lee or P. G. T. Beauregard might have been able to do so, but certainly not John Bell Hood, who was clearly promoted above his ceiling. Johnston's reputation definitely benefits when he is compared to General Hood.

The second factor in Johnston's undeservedly high post-war reputation was the fact that he was the first to get his memoirs to press. In 1874, his *Narrative of Military Operations Directed During the Late War*

Between the States came out. In it, he placed the blame for the fall of Vicksburg and the loss of the Army of Mississippi squarely on the shoulders of John C. Pemberton and Jefferson Davis. He thus managed to frame public opinion.

Right after the fall of Vicksburg, Sarah Dorsey stated that she wanted to "crucify" General Pemberton, as did many other Southerners. Dorsey was a highly respected "Lost Cause" author and, in her biography of Henry Watkins Allen, she chose to investigate the Pemberton-Johnston controversy, even if it was off-topic. Johnston provided her with a written explanation of his conduct, while Pemberton produced the actual correspondence. "I believe," she concluded, "that General Pemberton has been greatly wronged by us all. Until this close examination of unimpeachable testimony, placed in my hands most frankly by General Pemberton, I, too, shared the popular prejudice against him." But Dorsey's work appeared in print too close to the end of the war. Because it defended Pemberton, even one of her best friends refused to look at it.

Pemberton himself wrote an answer to Johnston's self-serving criticisms and submitted it for publication in the *Official Records of the War of the Rebellion* in 1878 or shortly thereafter. The editor of the Confederate papers, Brigadier General Marcus J. Wright, decided not to include it in the *Official Records*, but he did not return the manuscript to General Pemberton, who died in 1881. The Pemberton manuscript then disappeared, only to reemerge in the 1990s, when it was purchased at a Loveland, Ohio, flea market. Historian David M. Smith edited the manuscript and published it in his book, *Compelled to Appear in Print: The Vicksburg Manuscript of General John C. Pemberton*. It opened the eyes of several historians, even iconic historian Edwin C. Bearss. In my view, the *Official Records* and *Compelled to Appear in Print* provide pretty convincing evidence that Joseph E. Johnston deserves the lion's share of the blame for the loss of Vicksburg.

Jefferson Davis must bear part of the blame for the loss of the city. To his credit, he stood by Jack Pemberton and made it clear that he also held Johnston responsible for the disaster. Davis, however, still deserves a measure of blame. He set a confusing command structure, in which neither Johnston or Pemberton could compel the Trans-Mississippi commander to cooperate with the commanding general of the Army of Mississippi. Grant took advantage of this fact by marching down the eastern edge of Louisiana and crossing the Mississippi south of Vicksburg. His supply line was completely exposed, but the Confederates did not take advantage of it. Had they done so, they would have cut off Grant's army and perhaps could have compelled it to surrender. It was that exposed.

Davis also made two unfortunate appointments. He named his friend Theo Holmes commander of the Trans-Mississippi after he failed in Virginia and kept him in command far too long. He also appointed Joseph E. Johnston commander of the Department of the West.

W. W. Loring also deserves out-and-out censure. He was a good regimental commander on the frontier but his talents as a general were largely wasted because he could never bring himself to cooperate with superiors he disliked, and these included John C. Pemberton. His disobedience of Pemberton's orders at Champion Hill cost the Confederacy dearly, as we have seen.

With the benefit of hindsight, Robert E. Lee must also be assigned a measure of blame. After his historic victory at the Battle of Chancellorsville, he successfully opposed the idea of sending one of his corps to Pemberton in Mississippi; instead, he advocated invading the North. This operation, of course, ended in disaster at Gettysburg. He has been voraciously attacked by Lieutenant General Daniel Harvey Hill and others for his strategy in 1863.

In closing, I would like to quote Douglas Southall Freeman, who wrote, "General Pemberton was one of the great men of the Southern Confederacy . . . a gallant and gifted man who paid as great a price for his devotion as circumstances ever exacted of an American." I believe that Pemberton was a good general but not a great one. Grant had to perform at the genius level to defeat him, and genius defeats good most of the time—especially when genius has a navy and good doesn't, and genius outnumbers good two to one. I believe that Pemberton was treated unfairly by public opinion at the time and has been unfairly treated by history. I hope that this book, in some small way, helps to balance the record.

One final thought. Pemberton defeated Grant four times out of five by military action and yet has been depicted as some sort of inferior, bumbling, incompetent idiot. But answer this question. If, despite heavy odds against me, I beat you four out of five times and I am a bumbling idiot, what does that make you?

CHAPTER XXI

A HISTORICAL FOOTNOTE

The fall of the city did not completely end Vicksburg's military prominence. It became a major U.S. base and a staging area for several Union operations. Almost two years after the siege, it was the starting point for the greatest maritime disaster in American history—a catastrophe greater than the *Titanic* in terms of the loss of human life.

On April 23, 1865, two weeks after Robert E. Lee surrendered, the northbound *Sultana* docked in Vicksburg. She was a wooden four-deck side-paddlewheel steamboat with a crew of about eighty-five. She carried around the same number of passengers and a cargo of more than one hundred tons of sugar and some livestock. She put into port because one of her boilers was leaking.

Union Lieutenant Colonel Reuben Hatch, the chief quartermaster at Vicksburg, approached the boat. He had a problem. More than twenty-one hundred Northern prisoners of war, recently liberated from Confederate prisons at Andersonville, southwestern Georgia, and Cahaba, near Selma, Alabama, had been dumped on him, and he had to get them transported back to their home stations in Ohio, Indiana, Michigan, Kentucky, east Tennessee, and West Virginia. From there they would be discharged from the army so they could return to their homes.

Hatch met with Cass Mason, the captain of the *Sultana*, and offered him $5 per enlisted man and $10 for each officer he carried north; furthermore, he offered the financially strapped Mason a substantial kickback if he took 1,400 passengers. Even though the *Sultana* had a maximum rated carrying capacity of only 376 passengers, the captain immediately accepted the mission.

Meanwhile, a mechanic inspected the leaking boiler and reported that he wanted to cut off and replace the leaky seam, but Morgan knew that that would take days and likely cost him his cargo and his bribe. He ordered the mechanic to patch it instead. The bulging boiler patch was fixed by beating it back into alignment with a hammer. At the same time, the former POWs boarded the vessel. Instead of 1,400 men, however, the Vicksburg authorities emptied their entire parole camp. They were packed in like sardines. Counting the passengers from New Orleans and the crew, there were 2,427 people on board when the *Sultana* departed Vicksburg during the night of April 24. She was so top-heavy that she listed severely when she navigated each of the many bends in the river.

The men were packed in so densely that every available space was filled. The boat was so crowded that the decks began to creak and sag. They had to be reinforced and supported by heavy wooden beams.

The Mississippi River was at flood stage in the spring of 1865. In places, it was three miles wide, and only the tops of the trees lining the banks were visible. The grossly overloaded paddlewheeler struggled mightily against the powerful river, but it reached Helena, Arkansas, on April 26. After a brief respite, she stopped at Memphis at 7:00 p.m. that night, off-loaded her sugar and took on more coal. She now weighed so much that it required a lot of fuel to propel her forward. It was nearly midnight when she started northward again.

The 1,719-ton *Sultana* was 260 feet long and forty-two feet at the beam. It featured four boilers, which were located side by side. Apparently, the boat's engineer mismanaged the water levels in the overworked boilers.

It also appears that, because the *Sultana* was struggling against the powerful flood, the operators exceeded the steam-pressure safety point. In any case, seven river miles north of Memphis, just before 2:00 a.m. on April 27, 1865, a boiler exploded, followed immediately by two more. With the supporting structure blown away, the forward sections of the upper decks collapsed, and a number of men fell into the exposed furnace boxes and were incinerated. Within moments, most of the boat was a blazing inferno.

The majority of the former prisoners who were not killed immediately jumped into the water; but the Mississippi River is not a place to go swimming, especially at flood stage. In addition, after months in Confederate prison camps, the men were very weak. Most of them did not get far. Many of them grabbed each other, clung together, and went down together.

About 3:00 a.m., the southbound steamer *Bostona II* appeared on the scene and began rescuing survivors from the burning hulk, which did not sink until 9:00 a.m.[1] Some of the survivors were swept seven miles downriver to Memphis. Here, around 3:00 a.m., the half-drowned men screamed for help. Crewmen from three steamers heard their cries and quickly began rescuing people. They were joined by the tinclad *Essex* and the gunboat USS *Tyler*. Other half-dead victims succeeded in reaching nearby submerged trees and clinging to the tops until morning, when they were picked up and saved. But more than seventeen hundred people, including all of the ship's officers, died in the explosion, or of burns, or drowned, or perished from exposure or hypothermia. Many of the bodies were never recovered.

The Sultana *on fire. From* Harper's Weekly.

Seven hundred people—many of them near frozen, suffering from severe burns and/or shock—were taken to the hospitals of Memphis, which were later highly praised by Northern newspapers for their selfless efforts to save their former enemies. Around two hundred of them perished nevertheless, many from burns or scalding.

Bodies of the victims continued to wash ashore for months, some as far south as Vicksburg. The final death toll easily exceeded 1,700, and the U.S. Customs Service put it at 1,800. The *Titanic*, which sank in 1912, resulted in 1,512 deaths—almost 300 less than those lost on the *Sultana*. About 710 people survived the *Titanic's* sinking, as compared to 550 from the Union steamboat.

No one was ever punished for the disaster. Colonel Hatch realized what was going to happen so he resigned almost immediately upon hearing of the disaster, placing himself beyond the reach of military justice. Captain Morgan was dead. The boarding officer, Captain George Williams, was a United States Military Academy graduate. Apparently, it was he who decided to place everyone from the parole camp aboard the *Sultana*, but he was shielded by the West Point Protection Association. Eventually, U.S. Army Captain Frederick Steele, the officer-in-charge of the parole camp, was selected to be the scapegoat.

Captain Steele was convicted by a court-martial for grossly overloading the *Sultana*. This author is too obtuse to understand why he was found guilty, because he spent the entire day of April 24 in the parole camp, and he apparently never laid eyes on the *Sultana* in his life. The judge advocate general of the army obviously felt the same way, which is why he overturned the verdict, set aside the conviction, and released the captain.

The Sultana. *This photograph was taken at Helena, Arkansas, on April 26, 1865, the day before she sank. Most of the men seen in this photograph would be dead within twenty-four hours.*

EPILOGUE: WHAT HAPPENED TO THEM?

Pattie Pemberton, the widow of the general, never remarried. She died in New York City on August 14, 1907, at the age of 81. The city had been her home for many years.

Pemberton's mother, Rebecca, died in Philadelphia on August 17, 1869. Her remains lie only a few feet from those of her son.

Francis W. Pickens served as governor of South Carolina from December 14, 1860 to December 17, 1862. After the war, he was elected to the South Carolina Constitutional Convention in 1865, where he introduced a resolution repealing South Carolina's Ordinance of Secession. It passed, 105 to 3. This was Pickens' last public office. He died at home in 1869.

John Summerfield Griffith, the cavalry commander who spearheaded the Holly Springs Raid, was asthmatic and resigned his commission for reasons of health in May 1863. He returned to Texas, where he was immediately elected to the state legislature and was made chairman of the Military Affairs Committee. In March 1864, the governor appointed him brigadier general of Texas State Troops. He commanded reserve forces in central Texas for the rest of the war. Left in poverty after the surrender, Griffith rebuilt his fortune selling orange seed. Reelected to the legislature in 1876, he won the sobriquet "Watchdog of the Treasury." He died in Terrell, Texas, in 1901.

Governor John J. Pettus of Mississippi was not eligible to run for a third term so he left office on November 16, 1863. He accepted a commission as a colonel in the Mississippi militia and served until the end of the war. He relocated to Arkansas after the conflict and died in present-day Lonoke County, Arkansas, on January 28, 1867.

James Zachariah George, brigadier general of State Troops, rejoined the Confederate Army after regaining his health in the fall of 1863. He was elected colonel of the newly formed 5th Mississippi Cavalry Regiment. He had more courage than discretion and was captured near Collierville, Tennessee, because he got too far ahead of his men. He was a prisoner at Johnson's Island, Ohio, for the rest of the war.

George became known as the state's top lawyer after the war and became chief justice of the Mississippi Supreme Court in 1879. He was elected to the U.S. Senate in 1880 and served until his death in 1897.

Major General Franklin Gardner, the commander of Port Hudson, was not exchanged until August 1864. He served under Richard Taylor in Mississippi until the end of the war. He was a planter in Vermillionville (now Lafayette), Louisiana, post-bellum. He died in 1873.

William Wirt Adams was promoted to brigadier general in September 1863. He fought with Forrest in the last weeks of the war and lived in Jackson, Mississippi, thereafter. He became state revenue agent in 1880 and postmaster of Jackson in 1885. In 1888, on a Jackson sidewalk, he exchanged pistol shots with a newspaper editor with whom he had argued. Both men were killed.

After being captured at Vicksburg, Brigadier General William E. Baldwin was exchanged. He briefly served in the Army of Tennessee and was then sent to Mobile with his brigade. On February 19, 1864, his stirrup broke and he toppled from his horse. The fall killed him.

Emma Balfour remained in Vicksburg and died in 1887. Her husband, Dr. William Balfour, had been dead for ten years. He was unreconstructed (i.e., he refused to take the Oath of Allegiance to the United States. As a result, his civil rights were never restored).

After Vicksburg, Brigadier General John Gregg and his brigade were assigned to Hood's Division and fought at Chickamauga, where Gregg was severely wounded. He later distinguished himself in the Battle of the Wilderness. General Gregg was killed in action on October 7, 1864, on the Charles City Road, below Richmond. He was buried in Aberdeen, Mississippi.

After the war, Rev. C. K. Marshall continued to visit hospitals, in which discharged Confederate soldiers could still be found, and helped them. He went to New York and collected several thousand dollars from generous citizens for that purpose. He spoke at the Cooper Institute and said, "Southern soldiers fought well because they deemed themselves the soldiers of God. Never was an army more thoroughly imbued with the idea that their cause was just—that it was the cause of religion, civilization, self-protection and essential to the preservation of the Republican principles as elucidated by the Fathers of the Country for the North as well as for the South." Dr. Marshall died on January 14, 1891.

In 1902, Lloyd Tilghman's body was exhumed on the orders of his two surviving sons (successful New York City stockbrokers) and was reburied in Woodlawn Cemetery in the Bronx.

After he was exchanged, Brigadier General John C. Vaughn commanded a cavalry brigade in the Shenandoah Valley in 1864 and drove on Washington, D. C., with General Early. He was wounded at Martinsburg, Virginia (now West Virginia) and, upon recovery, was sent to east Tennessee. He later joined Joseph E. Johnston in North Carolina and formed part of Jefferson Davis' escort in the last days of the war. He was paroled at Washington, Georgia, on May 9, 1865, and returned to the business world in Georgia and Tennessee. Later he served in the Tennessee Senate, which elected him presiding officer. The state had no lieutenant governor, so Vaughn was *de facto* lieutenant governor. He died in Thomasville, Georgia, in 1875.

After his exchange, John H. Forney commanded a division in eastern Mississippi from October 1863 until May 1864. He was sent to the Trans-Mississippi Department in July and was given command of the Texas Division (1st Division, I Corps, Army of the Trans-Mississippi) in September. He directed a division in west Texas from March 1865 until the end of the war. Post-bellum, Forney was a farmer and civil engineer in Alabama, and ran a small military academy. He died in Jacksonville on September 13, 1902. He was buried with full military honors and his funeral procession was a mile long. Forney left behind a widow and five children, four of them girls. His son Jacob was a professor at the State University of Alabama.

Sergeant William Henry Tunnard of the 3rd Louisiana was paroled at Natchitoches, Louisiana, on June 7, 1865. He moved to northwest Louisiana, where he became an editor of the Shreveport *Times*. He became a major general in the United Confederate Veterans in 1899. He died in Shreveport in 1916.

Colonel Thomas P. Dockery, the commander of Bowen's 2nd Brigade, was paroled and soon promoted to brigadier general on August 10, 1863. Returning to his home state, he was given an Arkansas brigade and fought at Jenkins' Ferry and Marks' Mills. After the war he was impoverished, but became a civil engineer and moved to Houston, Texas. He died in New York City in 1898 and was buried in Natchez, Mississippi, the home of his two daughters.

Francis Marion Cockrell was promoted to brigadier general on July 18, 1863. He reformed his brigade and fought in the Atlanta campaign and Hood's invasion of Tennessee. He was severely wounded at Franklin on November 30, 1864. Sent to Mobile after he recovered, he was captured when the city capitulated on April 12, 1865. General Cockrell returned to Missouri and resumed his law practice. He was elected to the United States Senate in 1874 and served there continuously for the next thirty years. Finally declining to run for reelection, he was later named a member of the Interstate Commerce Commission by President

Theodore Roosevelt. He died in Washington on December 13, 1915, and is buried in Warrensburg, Missouri, which was the town of his birth.

Mary Ann Loughborough wrote a book, *My Cave Life in Vicksburg*, which was published in the North in 1864. It was a great hit. She had three more children (her two-year-old survived the siege) and established *The Southern Ladies' Journal*. She lived in St. Louis (then a Southern town) and Little Rock post-bellum. She died in 1887. Her husband, James, survived the war and became an Arkansas state senator. He died in 1876.

Edmund W. Pettus, the commander of the 20th Alabama and brother of the governor of Mississippi, was promoted to brigadier general on September 18, 1863. He was assigned to the Army of Tennessee and fought in all of the major battles from Chattanooga to Bentonville and was wounded in the Carolina campaign. He returned to his successful law practice and headed the Alabama Ku Klux Klan. He did not run for public office until 1896, when he was elected to the United States Senate, and served until his death in 1907. He was the last Rebel brigadier general to sit in that chamber. He is buried in Selma.

Colonel Allen Thomas, the commander of the 28th/29th Louisiana, was assigned the task of collecting and organizing paroled prisoners west of the Mississippi. Promoted to brigadier general on February 4, 1864, he was given command of a brigade and later Prince Polignac's Division in Louisiana. He had a varied career after the war, including a professorship at Louisiana State University and an ambassadorship to Venezuela. He later owned a plantation in Mississippi, where he died in 1907.

Winchester Hall, colonel of the 26th Louisiana, moved to Pocomoke City, Maryland, after the war. He died there on December 10, 1909, at the age of ninety-one. His wife, Ruth Marie, who nursed him throughout the siege, died in 1915 at the age of ninety-two.

Despite being crippled for life at Baton Rouge, Colonel Henry Watkins Allen of the 4th Louisiana was promoted to brigadier general in August 1863 and was elected governor of the state later that year, despite the fact that he did not campaign for the office. He proved to be an incredibly competent administrator, leading Pulitzer Prize winning

author Douglas Southall Freeman to declare that, if the South had recognized his talents earlier, he was the one man who might have made a
difference in the outcome of the war. He fled to Mexico after the surrender, possibly because the Federal authorities ordered that he be shot
on sight. Allen nevertheless finished second in the gubernatorial election
of 1865, even though his name was not on the ballot and former Confederates were not allowed to vote. He died on April 22, 1866. Still
beloved by his state, he was later buried on the grounds of the Old State
Capitol—the only person to ever be so honored.

Brigadier General Francis A. Shoup, who commanded one of the
Louisiana brigades at Vicksburg, converted to Christianity that winter
and joined the Episcopal Church. He joined Bragg's army and was soon
named chief of artillery. He was chief of staff of the Army of Tennessee
under Hood, and ended the war as commander of the black troops in
Virginia. Post-bellum he was a professor of applied mathematics and
engineering at the University of Mississippi. In 1870, he married Esther,
the daughter of Bishop Stephen Eliot, resigned from the university, and
went into parish work in New York, Tennessee, and New Orleans. He
returned to the classroom in 1883 as a professor at the University of the
South. General Shoup died on September 4, 1896, leaving behind a wife
and three children. His great-grandson, David M. Shoup, earned the
Congressional Medal of Honor during World War II and was later commandant of the Marine Corps (1960–63).

W. W. Loring later commanded a division in the Army of Tennessee
under Johnston and Hood. He fled the United States after the war and
became a general in the army of the Khedive of Egypt. He returned to
the U.S. in 1879 and died in New York City in December 1886. He never
married.

Mary "Mitte" Bowen spent the rest of the war nursing Confederate
soldiers. She was captured at Atlanta and brought before General Sherman, who implored her to go home. She declared that, as long as there
was an injured Confederate soldier anywhere who needed nursing, she
most certainly would not. After the Southern surrender, she initially
settled in Raymond, to be near her husband's grave. She tried to set up

a school, but it failed to materialize. She eventually returned to Caron-delet, where she operated a boarding house. (The Yankees and Carpet-baggers had taken her original home.) She spent the rest of her life in Carondelet and raised her four children. Mary Bowen died on January 16, 1904, age seventy-nine. She never remarried.

Sergeant Edward J. Dunn of the 1st Louisiana Heavy Artillery and the 22nd Louisiana Infantry took the Oath of Allegiance to the United States in March 1865. He was transported to New Orleans and released on March 31, 1865. He returned home and died in 1891.

Brigadier General John Adams, the commander of the District of Jackson, later served under Leonidas Polk in eastern Mississippi in late 1863 and in the Army of Tennessee in the Atlanta campaign. He was killed in action at Franklin on November 30, 1864.

The Champion House was turned into a Union hospital. On or about July 7, after the patients were discharged, the Yankees burned it. Sid Champion, the owner of Champion Hill and a colonel with the 28th Mississippi Cavalry, was captured when Vicksburg fell. He was exchanged and seriously wounded in the 3rd Battle of Murfreesboro in December 1864. Severely weakened by the war, he died in 1868, at the age of forty-five. His wife Matilda fled her home on the morning of the battle. She died in 1907.

After his exchange, Brigadier General Seth Barton was given com-mand of Armistead's old brigade of Pickett's Division, which was then in North Carolina. Pickett censured him for lack of cooperation at New Bern and he was relieved of his command by General Ramseur in May 1864. Unemployed for some time, he was given command of a brigade in the Richmond defenses that fall. He was captured at Sayler's Creek on April 6, 1865. He returned to Fredericksburg, where he died in 1900.

Private William L. Truman of Wade's Missouri battery served in the Confederate Army until the end of the war. He married Cora Hadden of Alabama (1848–1916) and had three daughters. A farmer, he moved to Vermilion Parish, Louisiana, and to Gueydan in St. Landry Parish in 1900. He died there on July 30, 1933. He had been born on January 7, 1841.

Brigadier General John C. Moore was exchanged and commanded a brigade at Chattanooga. He could not get along with his corps commander, General Hardee, however, and resigned his commission on February 3, 1864. He almost immediately accepted a commission as a lieutenant colonel and was named commander of the Savannah arsenal. Later he commanded the arsenal at Selma, Alabama. After the war, he taught school in Texas for many years. He died in Osage, Texas, on December 31, 1910, at the age of eighty-seven.

Lucy McRae grew up and lived in Vicksburg until she married. She then moved to Lewisburg, West Virginia, where she raised a daughter and lived the rest of her life. She died in 1930.

Major Samuel H. Lockett, Pemberton's brilliant chief engineer, became a colonel and the chief engineer of the Army of Tennessee. After the war, he taught in Louisiana, Alabama, and at the University of Tennessee. After a tour with the Egyptian Army, he was the principal assistant engineer in the construction of the pedestal for the Statue of Liberty. He worked on a major project in Chile in 1888 and died in Bogota, Columbia, in 1891.

After he was exchanged, Brigadier General Louis Hebert spent the rest of the war as officer-in-charge of the heavy artillery at Fort Fisher, North Carolina, and as chief engineer of the Confederate Army in North Carolina. After the war, he returned to Iberville and St. Martin's Parishes, where he was a newspaper editor and a teacher in a private school. He died on January 7, 1901, and is buried in Breaux Bridge.

Dabney H. Maury only served briefly in east Tennessee. He was soon transferred to Mobile, which he successfully defended until April 12, 1865, when it finally fell. After the war, Maury founded the Southern Historical Society, whose *Papers* are invaluable to historians of the war. He was also ambassador to Columbia for four years and wrote a wonderful autobiography, *Recollections of a Virginian*. General Maury was in financial stress much of the post-bellum era. He died at a son's home in Illinois in 1900 and is buried in Fredericksburg, Virginia.

Joseph E. Johnston replaced Braxton Bragg as commander of the Army of Tennessee on December 16, 1863, and was relieved of the command of the army on July 17, 1864. He was restored to command in February 1865, when his old friend, Robert E. Lee, became general-in-chief. He surrendered the army to Sherman on April 26, 1865. Postwar he wrote his memoirs, served two years in the U.S. Congress (1879–81), and was U.S. commissioner of railroads (1885–91). He contracted a cold while marching in the funeral procession of General Sherman, which led to his death on March 21, 1891. He was eighty-four years old.

Colonel William T. "Theo" Withers, the commander of a provisional brigade at Chickasaw Bluffs and commander of the 1st Mississippi Artillery Regiment at Vicksburg, later fought at Mobile. He was invalided out of the service in March 1865. Colonel Withers lost everything during the war. He made his first dollars after the war selling buttermilk to Union soldiers who were heading home. He worked a "hardscrabble" farm in West Point, Georgia, for a time, and then became state agent to Washington, D.C. In 1874, he moved back to Kentucky and became a successful horse breeder. He died in 1889.

Private W. R. "Rollie" Clack of the 43rd Tennessee never returned to the Confederate Army. He married Sabria Caroline Newport after the war and raised a family. He died in 1919 at the age of eighty.

Captain Hiram M. Bledsoe, Jr., directed his battery for the rest of the war, serving as part of the Army of Relief, and fighting at Chickamauga, Missionary Ridge, Kennesaw Mountain, and the battles around Atlanta, Franklin, Nashville, the retreat from Tennessee, and in the Carolina campaign. He returned to Missouri after the war, became a farmer, married in 1869, and held a number of public offices in Cass County, including state senator. He died in Mount Pleasant in 1899.

Colonel William T. S. Barry, the commander of the 36th Mississippi, was wounded in the shoulder at Allatoona Pass. After he recovered, he fought at Mobile and was captured at Fort Blakely in April 1865. He returned to Meridian and resumed his law practice, but died of consumption on January 29, 1868.

Like their white counterparts, the Black Confederate soldiers went home but continued to be proud of their service to the Confederacy. On

February 11, 1890, an appropriation bill for a monument to the Confederate dead was introduced in the Mississippi legislature. The state had limited funds, so it met with some opposition.

John F. Harris, a Negro Republican from Washington County, rose to support the measure. He said to the Speaker,

> When the news came that the South had been invaded, those men went forth to fight for what they believed . . . Sir, I went with them. I, too, wore the gray, the same color my master wore. We stayed four long years, and if that war had gone on till now I would have been there yet . . . I want to honor those brave men who died for their convictions. When my mother died I was a boy. Who, Sir, then acted the part of a mother to an orphaned slave boy, but my 'old missus.' Were she living now, or could speak to me from those high realms where are gathered the sainted dead, she would tell me to vote for this bill. And, Sir, I shall vote for it. I want it known to all the world that my vote is given in favor of the bill to erect a monument in honor of the Confederate dead.

When the tremendous applause died down, the measure passed overwhelmingly. Every black legislator voted for it.[1]

Private Robert L. Bachman of the 60th Tennessee returned to his home, "Roseland," a plantation near Kingsport, where the Union cavalry robbed him and his family of all their food, horses, mules, and Negroes, who were compelled to go with them, whether they wanted to or not. In the summer of 1864, he was notified that he had been exchanged. He rejoined his regiment (now a cavalry unit) and served for the rest of the war, mostly in east Tennessee. He went to Hamilton College in Clinton, New York, and the Auburn Theological Seminary after the war and became a Presbyterian pastor. Bachman married May Rose of Saginaw, Michigan, in 1876 and fathered three children. He occupied several pulpits and was pastor of the Second Presbyterian

Church in Jonesboro, Tennessee, at the time of his death on September 12, 1921.

The town of Port Hudson no longer exists. After the war, the Mississippi River changed courses and left it high and dry. Port Hudson quickly withered away and died.

Colonel John Wesley Portis of the 42nd Alabama was exchanged but resigned his command in March 1864. Paroled in June 1865, he returned home to Suggsville, Alabama, and practiced law there for the rest of his life. He died in 1902.

Colonel Elijah Gates, the commander of the 1st Missouri Cavalry Regiment (Dismounted) was exchanged and led his regiment on the Western Front. He lost an arm while leading a charge in the Battle of Franklin. Gates was captured while in a field hospital and was put on a train headed for a prison camp in the North. He managed to escape again, despite his handicap and recent amputation, and reached Rebel lines. He commanded what was left of the Missouri Brigade in the Mobile campaign and was captured at Fort Blakely on April 9, 1865. After the war, he returned to Missouri and became a farmer, businessman, county sheriff, and state treasurer.

Dr. William Wilberforce Lord passed up an opportunity to go to St. Louis, but instead asked General Grant to give him a pass—he wanted to continue serving the Confederacy. Grant gave it to him. Lord served at Mobile and Charleston. He returned to Vicksburg, but later accepted a congregation in Cooperstown, New York, where he died.

Bowen's Missouri division was consolidated into a single brigade. The 2nd and 6th Missouri Infantry Regiments were combined, as were the 3rd and 5th Missouri. Colonel Cockrell was promoted to brigadier general and named commander of the new brigade.

Corporal Ephraim Anderson of the 1st Missouri Brigade fought in the Atlanta campaign, in Hood's Tennessee adventure, and at Mobile, where he was captured. He returned to Missouri and, in 1868, published his *Memoirs: Historical and Personal*. He died in 1916 at age seventy-four or seventy-five.

Major General Carter L. Stevenson commanded a division in the Army of Tennessee from 1863 to 1865. He was a civil and mining engineer after the war. He died in 1888 and, like Maury, is buried in Confederate Cemetery, Fredericksburg, Virginia.

NOTES

Chapter 1: Vicksburg: The First Siege

1. Ironically, this war was ended by Second Lieutenant Jefferson Davis, who personally captured Chief Black Hawk.

2. M. L. Smith had been named commandant of Vicksburg on May 12.

3. They included the 6th Mississippi and 8th Louisiana Infantry Battalions, and the 20th, 27th and 28th Louisiana Infantry Regiments. The 20th and 28th, however, had only 500 men.

4. Throughout this book, all army units are regiments, unless otherwise noted. A Civil War infantry regiment normally consisted of ten companies of sixty to one hundred men.

5. Colonel Statham, a Grenada, Mississippi, lawyer, died of fever in Vicksburg on July 30, 1862—twelve days after his thirtieth birthday.

6. Charles Kimball Marshall (1811–1891) was born in Maine and attended college in Cincinnati until his funds ran out. He then worked in a foundry in New Orleans while continuing his religious studies and leading a prison ministry. Ordained in 1832, he pastored a Methodist

church in Natchez. In 1836, he married Amanda Vick, the daughter of the founder of Vicksburg, and lived there the rest of his life. He heroically ministered to the sick and dying during the Yellow Fever epidemics and during the war. He set up a series of depots and hospitals for the Confederacy, constructed a model for wooden legs, and built up a factory for their manufacture.

7. The *Queen of the West* was originally a sidewheel steamer.

8. Columbiads were large-caliber, smoothbore, muzzle loading cannons which could fire shot or shell. They varied in size from 8-inch (203mm), 10-inch (254mm) and 15-inch (381mm). There were also 20-inchers which weighed sixty tons and could throw a 400-pound shell more than five miles.

9. The *Lancaster* was rescued by the *Queen of the West*. She was towed to Memphis for repairs, but was sunk at Port Hudson in March 1863.

10. Several of these wounded were so badly scalded that they subsequently died.

Chapter 2: John C. Pemberton

1. General Beauregard replaced Albert Sidney Johnston as commander of the Army of Mississippi after the latter was killed in action at Shiloh on April 6. Beauregard himself was relieved of command for going on medical leave without requesting permission from Richmond. He later commanded Rebel forces at Charleston, S.C. and south of Petersburg, Virginia.

2. These included Major General Sterling Price and Brigadier Generals Dabney H. Maury and Lloyd Tilghman. Maury had been Van Dorn's chief of staff when the latter commanded the Trans-Mississippi Department.

3. The U.S. Army did not pass out medals in those days, so they rewarded exceptional performance by issuing brevet (honorary) promotions.

4. Francis W. Pickens was born in 1805, the son of a former governor and a cousin of John C. Calhoun. He attended Franklin College (now the University of Georgia) and South Carolina State. Elected to the South Carolina legislature in 1832, he was an ardent supporter of nullification

and states' rights. He served eleven years in Congress but was defeated for the U.S. Senate in 1850. He was U.S. minister to Russia in 1860, when he was elected governor by the state's General Assembly via secret ballot.

5.   Colonel John R. Waddy (1834–1903) was a Virginia Military Institute graduate. Commissioned in the artillery, he was a second lieutenant when he resigned in July 1861. He was chief of staff of the Army of Mississippi (1862–1863). After Vicksburg, he was a special commissioner for prisoner exchange. He and his wife had five children. He is buried in Norfolk.

6.   Boggs (1829–1911) was an engineering genius. An 1853 West Point graduate, he worked for General Beauregard in Charleston in 1861. Later he was Bragg's chief engineer (1862), Georgia state engineer (1862–63), and chief of staff of the Trans-Mississippi Department (1863–65), where he played a major role in the Confederate victory during the Red River Campaign of 1864. He was promoted to brigadier general in the spring of 1863.

7.   Ripley (1823–1887) was a native of Ohio, but married into a Charleston family. He was given a brigade in D. H. Hill's division of the Army of Northern Virginia. He was an able field commander, but could not get along with any superior. He was seriously wounded at Sharpsburg, giving Hill an opportunity to get rid of him. Ripley returned to South Carolina in 1863, but couldn't get along with Beauregard either.

8.   Secessionville was a cluster of summer homes. It got its name because young planters "seceded" from their parents and went there to be on their own when not needed on the plantation. Its name had nothing to do with the sectional crisis.

Chapter 3: Northern Mississippi, 1862

1.   Pemberton officially assumed command on October 14.

2.   John J. Pettus (1813–1867) was a plantation owner and a "fire-eater" (i.e., a secessionist) who believed that secession was the only way to save the institution of slavery. Elected to the legislature in 1844 and to

the state senate in 1848, he was president of the senate in 1854, when Governor John McRae grew angry and resigned five days before his term ended. Mississippi had no lieutenant governor, so Pettus was governor for five days. He was elected in his own right in 1859 and reelected in 1861.

3. After Brigadier General Lloyd Tilghman was killed, John Adams was given command of his brigade. He was killed in action at Franklin on November 30, 1864.

4. Like Pemberton, Lovell (1822–1884) had been born in the North. A West Point graduate (1842), he resigned from the army in 1854 and became deputy street commissioner of New York City. His boss was future Confederate Major General Gustavus W. Smith. He was unable to prevent the capture of New Orleans in April 1862. He also performed poorly in the Battle of Corinth, but conducted a skillful retreat. He returned to New York after the war and worked as an assistant city engineer until his death.

5. Theophilus Holmes (1804–1880) graduated from West Point in 1829 and spent thirty-one years in the U.S. Army. After failing in the East, he was sent to the Trans-Mississippi, where he was relieved by Edmund Kirby Smith in March 1863 and was demoted to the command of the District of Arkansas. Unsuccessful there as well, he returned to his native North Carolina, where he ended the war organizing reserve forces. He was a farmer after the war and died in Fayetteville, NC.

6. William Henry Tunnard was born in New Jersey in 1837 but grew up in Baton Rouge. He was a newspaper man. His father was the regiment's major, but W. H. was a sergeant in Company K, before he became a commissary sergeant.

7. John S. Griffith was born into a prominent Maryland family in 1829. He moved to Texas in 1839 and prospered, raising cotton, livestock, and Irish potatoes. He became a company commander in the 6th Texas Cavalry when the war broke out and personally killed an Indian with his saber in a skirmish at Chustenahlah, Indian Territory, in late 1861. He refused to run for colonel of the regiment because of his poor health

but was nevertheless named acting commander of Sul Ross' cavalry brigade in 1862.

8. The 12-pounder was there to repel Rebel boarders, not for naval combat.

9. The wreck of the *Cairo* was discovered by noted Civil War historian Edwin Bearss in 1956. It was raised in three pieces in 1964 and was eventually hauled to the Vicksburg National Battlefield, where it was partially reconstructed and is now on display.

10. Freeman won the Pulitzer Prize twice for biographies of Robert E. Lee and George Washington.

11. Some people gave Johnston credit for winning the First Battle of Manassas, because he was the senior officer in the area when the battle was fought, and Johnston did funnel reinforcements to General Beauregard. Beauregard, however, actually commanded the troops on the battlefield and ordered the charge which carried the day. In my opinion, he and Stonewall Jackson deserve the lion's share of the credit for this victory, but historians will be arguing this point long after we are dead.

12. Matthew 6:24.

13. Carter Stevenson (1817–1888) was an 1838 West Point graduate. Commissioned in the infantry, he served on the frontier and in the Mexican War. He became the colonel of the 53rd Virginia in 1861. Promoted to brigadier general in early 1862, he compelled the Yankees to withdraw from the Cumberland Gap, leading to his promotion to major general on October 10, 1862.

14. Grant blamed Murphy for the disaster. He was cashiered without court-martial for cowardice and disgraceful behavior.

Chapter 4: Chickasaw Bluffs

1. Estimates of Holmes' strength vary from 35,000 to 50,000.

2. A "tinclad" was a vessel of light draft with thin armored plating, which only protected it from infantry weapons.

3. The 17th Louisiana only lost two men killed, ten wounded, and one missing during the Battle of Chickasaw Bluffs.

4. William T. "Theo" Withers (1825–1889) was a native of Kentucky but moved to Jackson, Mississippi, where he became a lawyer. He was wounded in the Mexican War and never fully recovered. He was an acting brigadier general of Kentucky State Volunteers in 1861 when the Confederate secretary of war asked him to raise an artillery regiment. He raised the 1st Mississippi Artillery, which he led at Vicksburg. He distinguished himself commanding the provisional brigade on the Confederate far right flank at Chickasaw Bluffs. He was described as "a thorough Christian gentleman."

5. Allen Thomas was the commander of the 28th Louisiana when not commanding a brigade.

6. Edward Higgins was born in Norfolk, Virginia, in 1821, but moved to Iberville Parish, Louisiana, as a teenager. Appointed midshipman in 1840, he resigned from the navy in 1854 in order to run the mail steamship service between New York and New Orleans. Commissioned lieutenant colonel in the 21st Louisiana Infantry (also a heavy artillery unit), he defended Forts Jackson and St. Philip south of New Orleans in April 1862. The fall of New Orleans doomed these forts, and he surrendered. Higgins was exchanged and sent to Vicksburg, where he later commanded the 1st Louisiana Heavy Artillery Regiment.

7. Andrea Warren, *Under Siege* (New York: Farrar, Straus and Giroux, 2009), 25.

8. Perhaps the most famous black Confederate soldier was Holt Collier (c. 1848–1936) of the 9th Texas Cavalry, which was part of Van Dorn's command. He fought throughout the war. During Reconstruction, he was arrested for murdering a Union officer who insulted his former master and commanding officer. Although he never denied it, the military tribunal did not have sufficient evidence to convict him. A renowned hunter, Collier was Theodore Roosevelt's guide and was instrumental in the creation of the Teddy Bear. See Minor Ferris Buchanan's *Holt Collier* for an excellent biography.

9. Robert Lucky Bachman was born on his family's plantation, "Roseland," near Kingsport, Tennessee, on June 14, 1844. He enlisted in the Confederate Army at age seventeen.

10. Commander David D. Porter was promoted to acting rear admiral in the fall of 1862. The ranks of captain and commodore he skipped altogether.

11. Confederate majors wore one star, lieutenant colonels had two stars, and full colonels had three stars. All generals wore three stars, enclosed by a wreath. The middle star was larger than the other two. Colonel Hall was born on November 12, 1819, in Jefferson County, Kentucky, and married Ruth Marie Carr in 1849. They had five children. In 1861, he was a partner in a law office in Thibodaux, Louisiana. After the fall of Forts Henry and Donelson, the citizens of Thibodaux formed the Allen Rifles with Hall as captain. It became part of the 26th Louisiana in April 1862.

Chapter 5: The Canal, the Lake, and the River

1. Ethan Allen Hitchcock (1798–1870) served in the army from 1817 to 1855. Following a dispute with Secretary of War Jefferson Davis, he retired but returned to active duty at the request of Winfield Scott when the war began. He was a close friend and an adviser to both Abraham Lincoln and Secretary of War Edwin M. Stanton.

2. Whistling Dick was disabled on May 22, 1863, and was replaced with a 32-pounder. Whistling Dick was later repaired and posted behind the Railroad Redoubt.

3. Turpentine balls were musket balls wrapped in turpentine-soaked flax or hemp fibers.

4. Carroll Parish was divided into East Carroll and West Carroll parishes in 1877.

5. See Linda Barnickel, *Milliken's Bend* (Baton Rouge: LSU Press, 2013) for further details.

6. To protest this discrepancy, several black regiments refused to accept any pay whatsoever. In 1864, the embarrassed Lincoln regime equalized the pay scale.

7. One of these lessees was Lewis Dent, the brother-in-law of U.S. Grant. He was later captured by the Confederates and handed over to General Kirby Smith, who treated him with kindness and then released him.

8.   Later redesignated 51ˢᵗ USCT Infantry Regiment.

9.   See Barnickel, 74–77.

Chapter 6: The Yazoo Pass Expedition

1.   Another man was killed later.

2.   Howitzers fired large projectiles with higher trajectories than guns or rifled cannons but lower than mortars.

3.   Buffalo gnats are blood-sucking flies which attack both humans and animals. There are more than one hundred species in North America alone.

4.   James Zachariah George (born 1826) served with Colonel Jefferson Davis' elite 1ˢᵗ Mississippi during the Mexican War. He then studied law and became very successful. Elected to the Mississippi Secession Convention, he voted to leave the Union. As a captain and company commander, he was captured at Fort Donelson and imprisoned for seven months. After he was exchanged, Governor Pettus appointed him brigadier general of State Troops, to serve until his health improved. He commanded a small brigade during the Bayou Expeditions and did very well. Lloyd Tilghman arrested him because he refused to obey an order which he felt disrespected State Troops, but the charges were soon dropped.

Chapter 7: The Steele's Bayou Expedition

1.   Maury was subordinate to Stevenson at this time. He was transferred to Tennessee on April 19, to the great regret of his men.

2.   William N. R. Beall (1825–1883) was a Kentuckian, who graduated from West Point in 1848. He joined the Confederate Army as a captain in 1861 and served under Van Dorn in Arkansas. Promoted to brigadier general in April 1862, he led a mixed brigade of Louisiana, Arkansas, and Mississippi troops at Port Hudson.

3.   A steam-screw ship was driven by a propeller, rather than a side paddle wheel or a stern paddle wheel.

Chapter 8: To Grand Gulf

1. Benjamin Stoddert Ewell (1810–1894) was the older brother of Lieutenant General Richard S. Ewell. An 1832 West Point graduate, he was a professor at various universities before the war began. He commanded the 32nd Virginia before joining Johnston's staff. He transferred to his brother's staff in 1864, but resigned his commission because of illness in March 1865. He was president of the College of William and Mary after the war.

2. Buckner did send the 2nd Alabama Cavalry to northern Mississippi in early May—too late!

3. Holmes became commander of the District of Arkansas.

4. Both battalions were under the command of Brigadier General Paul Hebert, the commander of the Subdistrict of North Louisiana. A former governor of Louisiana (1853–57), Hebert urged Kirby Smith to attack Grant's supply line but without success. Hebert (1818–1880) was a West Point graduate who finished first in his class, which included William T. Sherman and George Thomas. He headquartered in Delhi, Louisiana.

5. William Wirt Adams was born in Kentucky in 1819 and served in the Army of the Republic of Texas. Moving to Mississippi, he was a successful planter and banker, and a member of the legislature. He turned down an offer from Jefferson Davis to become postmaster general. His brother was Brigadier General Daniel W. Adams, who commanded an infantry brigade on the Western Front.

6. The John Ford movie *The Horse Soldiers* is loosely based on this raid, although the strongly Christian Benjamin Grierson was nothing like the hard-drinking, brawling, and unsophisticated character played by John Wayne.

7. Daniel Ruggles (1810–1897) was a native of Massachusetts who, like Pemberton, married into a Virginia family. He graduated from West Point in 1833, fought in the Seminole War, and won brevets to major and lieutenant colonel at Churubusco and Chapultepec in the Mexican War. He resigned his commission in 1861, after twenty-eight years of service, and became a Confederate brigadier general on August 9, 1861.

He distinguished himself at Shiloh, where he was instrumental in forcing the surrender of Prentiss' Division. He commanded various districts and departments until he was named commissary general of prisons on March 30, 1865.

8.   In February 1863, Bowen was already an acting division commander, directing his own Missouri brigade and Brigadier General Martin Edwin Green's Arkansas/Missouri brigade. This division ceased to exist when Bowen's brigade was sent to Grand Gulf. Green's brigade remained at Big Black and became part of John Forney's division.

9.   Colonel William Wade was a short man who wore a new uniform of Confederate gray, trimmed in red. Because of his flashy appearance, the men dubbed him "Red Woodpecker." W. L. Truman called him "a great society man, a remarkably fine conversationalist, good dancer and very popular with the ladies."

10. Grand Gulf was already in decline. Once it had 76 blocks and a population of almost 2,000, with saloons, hotels, warehouses, churches, etc. But the Mississippi River had gradually moved east and had eaten away 51 blocks. Cholera and yellow fever epidemics also contributed to the population exodus and it was further damaged by a tornado in 1853. There were only 158 people living in the town when the war began.

11. Grand Gulf was never rebuilt.

12. The 1st Missouri Cavalry had fought at Pea Ridge, Iuka and Corinth.

13. Bowen had previously commanded this brigade himself. Colonel Francis Marion Cockrell was a devout Christian and a fierce warrior.

14. Cockrell now controlled the 1st, 2nd, 3rd, and 5th Missouri Infantry Regiments, but he had no artillery and no cavalry, other than Harrison's battalion. He operated out of Hard Times, Louisiana.

15. Haynes, 27.

16. According to Ephraim Anderson, 303. A former U.S. congressman, Perkins (1819–1885) had been chairman of the state's secession convention in 1861.

17. He did this on April 20 and 22.

18. Edward D. Tracy was born in Macon, Georgia, in 1833 but moved to Huntsville, Alabama, in the late 1850s. A lawyer by profession, he commanded a company in the 4th Alabama in 1861 and fought at Bull Run. Named lieutenant colonel in the 19th Alabama, he fought at Shiloh (where his horse was shot from under him) and then in East Tennessee. On the recommendation of Kirby Smith, he was promoted to brigadier general on August 16, 1862.

19. General Baldwin was a Columbus, Mississippi, businessman. Elected colonel of the 14th Mississippi, he was captured when Fort Donelson fell. Exchanged in August 1862, he was commissioned brigadier on September 19.

Chapter 9: Port Gibson

1. The town of Bruinsburg was established in 1796 at the junction of Bayou Pierre and the Mississippi River. Future President Andrew Jackson established a trading post there and it was a thriving community until the Mississippi River shifted three miles to the west. By 1863, it was a ghost town. The former site of Bruinsburg is now on private property.

2. Elizabeth Meade Ingraham Diary, May 8, 1863.

3. Elizabeth Meade Ingraham (1805–1872) was ten years older than George (1815–1872).

4. Edward Duffield Ingraham was a West Point graduate and a member of General Van Dorn's staff.

5. Major General Banks was senior to Major General Grant.

Chapter 10: Raymond

1. General Gregg believed that he was striking the far right flank of the Union Army and would meet only a couple of regiments or a brigade at the most.

2. Colonel McGavock was born in Nashville, Tennessee, on August 10, 1826, graduated from the University of Nashville and Harvard Law School, and traveled extensively in Europe. He was elected mayor of Nashville in 1858. He became the captain of Company H, 10th Tennessee in May 1861, and was promoted to lieutenant colonel less

than three weeks later. Captured at Fort Donelson, he became regimental commander after he was exchanged in August 1862.

3. The 3rd Kentucky (Lloyd Tilghman's old regiment) fought at Shiloh, where it lost 174 men, and was then posted to Port Hudson. It was on its way to join the Army of Tennessee when it was diverted to Raymond.

4. Judge Dabney had ten children.

5. Mary Ann Webster Loughborough was born in 1836 in Phelps, New York. She married James M. Loughborough of Kentucky *ante bellum*.

Chapter 11: First Battle of Jackson

1. Colonel Vilas (1840–1908) was later a law professor at the University of Wisconsin, a member of the Wisconsin State Assembly, and a United States Senator. He was Postmaster General and Secretary of the Interior under President Grover Cleveland.

2. John Adams was born in Ireland in 1814 and immigrated to the United States in 1825. He graduated from West Point in 1846 and served in the dragoons in the Mexican War. He resigned as a captain in 1861 and was promoted to colonel and was named commandant of Memphis. In December 1862 he was promoted to brigadier general and was given Tilghman's old brigade of Mississippi regiments.

3. Grant reported capturing seventeen guns, but since Gregg only had three batteries of four guns each, this estimate is obviously in error. See Russell K. Brown, *To the Manner Born: The Life of General William H. T. Walker* (Mercer University Press, 2005), 150–51.

4. Thompson was the assistant inspector general of the Army of Mississippi.

5. Dillon's Plantation was a small settlement on the main road from Raymond to Port Gibson, nine and a half miles from Edward's Depot and seven and a half miles below Raymond.

Chapter 12: Champion Hill

1. Most of Champion Hill is gone. It was taken away by trucks after the gravel rights were sold in 1930. The rest of it is on private property.

2. These figures exclude Colonel Alexander W. Reynolds' Brigade of Stevenson's Division, which guarded the northern (main) wagon train until the Army of Mississippi retreated into Vicksburg. Pemberton also had Wirt Adams' cavalry regiment. Reynolds' Brigade included the 3rd, 31st, 43rd, and 59th Tennessee Infantry Regiments.

3. Drennan was the acting adjutant of Winfield S. Featherston's brigade. Barksdale was Featherston's assistant adjutant general.

4. Colonel McConnell recovered from this wound and resumed command of the regiment. He was killed at Missionary Ridge in November 1863.

5. Seth M. Barton was born in Fredericksburg, Virginia, in 1829. He graduated from West Point in 1849 and served almost exclusively in the West. He became the colonel of the 3rd Arkansas in 1861 and was Stonewall Jackson's chief engineer during the winter of 1861–62. He was promoted to brigadier general on March 11, 1862, and was sent to Mississippi.

6. Wesley O. Connor (1841–1920) later became principal and then superintendent of the Georgia School for the Deaf and is known as the father of education for the deaf in Georgia.

7. Bowen seems to have lost confidence in Pemberton after Port Gibson.

8. Thomas P. Dockery was born in North Carolina but grew up on his father's large plantation in Columbia County, Arkansas. He was instrumental in building the first railroad in the state. He was colonel of the 5th Arkansas State Troops and later colonel, 19th Arkansas. He had fought at Wilson's Creek and Corinth, among other places.

9. Private A. H. Reynolds ended up at Point Lookout, Maryland. He was exchanged at the end of 1863 and later rejoined his command in Arkansas.

10. Captain Ridley was a rich Madison Parish planter and a hero of the Battle of Chickasaw Bluffs.

11. Private Moore later became a medical doctor in Texas.

12. Command of the regiment devolved on the senior captain, George E. Brewer.

13. Temple Franklin Cooper was born in South Carolina on July 19, 1805, and died on February 2, 1864. He died on Johnson Island, Ohio, and is

buried there, in Erie Cemetery. His great-grandfather was William Franklin, the Royal Governor of New Jersey. His regiment, the 52nd Georgia, was part of Barton's Brigade, Stevenson's Division.

14. Watkins had gotten up out of a sick bed to reach his regiment before the battle. He commanded it throughout the siege, even though he could not walk without crutches.

15. Lieutenant McLaughlin settled in Florence, Alabama, married, and had a child. His brother, the Union colonel, moved to Topeka, Kansas, and became a gunsmith. It is not known if they ever met face-to-face again.

16. J. F. C. Fuller (1878–1966) was chief of staff of the Royal Tank Corps in World War I. The author of forty-five books, he is considered a great military theorist and was one of the fathers of the Blitzkrieg.

Chapter 13: The Big Black River

1. John C. Vaughn was born in Roane County, Tennessee, in 1824 and became a merchant. He served in the Mexican War as a captain in a Tennessee regiment and, despite living in a Unionist stronghold, recruited the 3rd Tennessee Infantry Regiment, which did good service at First Manassas. Promoted to brigadier general in September 1862, he was sent to the Western Front.

2. The east Tennesseans had played a minor role in the Battle of Chickasaw Bluffs.

3. Elijah Gates (1827–1915) was born in Kentucky. After taking part in the California Gold Rush, he moved to Missouri and became a hemp farmer. He was a captain in the Missouri State Guard when the war began. He became colonel of the 1st Missouri Cavalry on December 30, 1861.

Chapter 14: Into Vicksburg

1. Smith was later chief engineer for the Army of Northern Virginia and the Army of Tennessee.

2. Major James M. Loughborough (1833–1876) was born in Kentucky. He and his wife lived in St. Louis, where they were converted to the

Southern Cause. Mr. Loughborough joined the staff of Sterling Price and was now on the staff of Colonel Francis Cockrell.

3. Berwick Bay is near Morgan City, Louisiana.

4. Father Leray later became Archbishop of New Orleans.

5. *Hardee's Tactics* was written by William J. Hardee, who became a Confederate lieutenant general. It was the standard battle manual for both sides.

6. In the South, there were three meals: breakfast, dinner and supper. In many parts of the country today, the three meals are breakfast, lunch and dinner. According to the Bible, the South was right. Jesus had a last supper; he did not have a last dinner.

7. Frances J. "Frank" Ingraham was a member of the 1st Mississippi Infantry. He was the only man in the regiment killed in this battle.

Chapter 15: The Assaults

1. A redan is a V-shaped earthwork projecting from a fortified line. A redoubt is an independent earthwork, usually roughly triangular in shape, built forward of a fortified line. Unlike a redan, it is usually fully enclosed.

2. Witherspoon (c.1832–1865) was "a brilliant young officer" when he was sober and would have become a general officer except for his propensity for the bottle. He often led a brigade, but was cashiered for drunkenness in 1864. The sentence was voided, however, because of irregularities in the proceedings. He was mortally wounded at Franklin on November 30, 1864. He was a graduate of the University of Mississippi and was practicing law in Napoleon, Arkansas, when the war began.

3. This unit was formed when the 1st and 4th Missouri Infantry Regiments were consolidated.

4. Colonel Hall was replaced by Lieutenant Colonel William C. Crow.

5. Andrew Jackson, III (1834–1906), was the son of Andrew Jackson, Jr., the president's nephew and adopted son. He graduated from West Point in 1858 and joined the Confederate Army as a first lieutenant in 1861. When not a POW, he served in the heavy artillery throughout the war.

6. The 22nd Louisiana Infantry Regiment had fought as a heavy artillery unit at New Orleans and Fort Pemberton. Its A and B Companies were now attached to the 1st Louisiana Heavy Artillery, while C and D Companies were just behind the trenches with the 21st Louisiana Infantry Regiment.

7. Some of the eastern Tennesseans did, in fact, abandon the works.

8. Maury had been transferred to east Tennessee on April 29. Forney assumed command on May 4.

9. Mrs. Forney's great-grandfathers included Arthur Middleton and Edward Rutledge, signers of the Declaration of Independence.

10. Isaac W. Patton (1828–1890) later led the 22nd Louisiana Regiment (Consolidated) and commanded part of the Mobile garrison (1864–65). He was recommended for advancement to brigadier general several times but was never promoted. After the war he was adjutant general of Louisiana, mayor of New Orleans, and city treasurer. He is buried in New Orleans.

11. Part of Brigadier General John C. Moore's brigade, Forney's division. A lunette is an earthwork consisting of two flanks at angles to each other and meeting in the center and open in the rear.

12. Private Higgins was released from prison when Vicksburg surrendered and served for the rest of the war. He was awarded the Congressional Medal of Honor in 1898.

13. John W. Portis (1818–1902) was a native of North Carolina but moved to Alabama, where he became a planter and a lawyer. A state legislator and a trustee of the University of Alabama, he lost a race for the Confederate Congress in 1861. Undeterred, he joined the 2nd (later 42nd) Alabama as a lieutenant but was elected colonel in May 1862. He was wounded at Corinth.

14. Pettus had taken command of the 46th Alabama, which had lost all of its field officers at Champion Hill.

Chapter 16: Siege

1. The main XVI Corps Headquarters remained in Memphis. Since it controlled more than one division, Washburn's headquarters was, in

essence, a corps headquarters. I have labeled it "XVI Corps Detachment" for the sake of clarity and convenience.

2.   W. H. T. Walker was promoted to divisional commander on May 21, on the strong recommendation of General Johnston, who declared he was "indispensable" and the only officer in his command competent to lead a division. His new command included five infantry brigades: his own (now led by Colonel C. C. Wilson), Gist's, Gregg's, Ector's, and McNair's. He also controlled John Adams' weak cavalry brigade and eight batteries of artillery. All totaled, Walker had almost 12,000 men. He was promoted to major general on May 23 and confirmed by the Senate on May 30.

3.   Dr. William Wilberforce Lord was an Episcopal minister and rector of Christ Church. He was a Princeton graduate.

4.   W. R. "Rollie" Clack was a member of Company B, 43rd Tennessee, and was apparently a native of Strawberry Plains, Tennessee. He was twenty-four years old in 1863.

5.   The Cincinnati displaced 512 tons and was 175 feet long and 51 feet wide. It included six 32-pounds, three 8-inch guns, four 42-pounders, and a 12-pound howitzer, which was not considered a heavy gun.

6.   Both A. M. Paxton and A. B. Reading owned companies that made shells for the guns of Vicksburg. Paxton's foundry made shells for 6-pounders, and Reading produced ammunition for bronze 6-pounders, 3-inch rifles, and others.

7.   Major Gillespie was chief commissary for Stevenson's division but was acting chief commissary for the entire army during the siege.

8.   Colonel Lieb was among the seriously wounded.

9.   McCulloch was replaced by William R. "Dirty Neck Bill" Scurry.

10. Part of the XVI Corps Detachment was posted on the northern flank, relieving some of Sherman's XV Corps. The rest was held in reserve.

11. Edmund Pettus was born in Limestone County, Alabama, in 1821. He was a successful lawyer before becoming a lieutenant in the Mexican War. He went to California during the Gold Rush but returned to Alabama in 1853 and became a judge in 1855. An enthusiastic secessionist, he was instrumental in forming the 20th Alabama. He was

captured during the battle of Murfreesboro in December 1862 but was quickly exchanged. Pettus was also captured near Port Gibson on May 1 but managed to escape. Pettus was acting commander of the 46th Alabama until June 17, when command passed to the senior captain, George E. Brewer. Pettus was the brother of John J. Pettus, the governor of Mississippi.

12. Denton was born about 1839 in Strawberry Plains, Jefferson County, east Tennessee.

13. Andrew Eugene Erwin was born near Lexington, Kentucky, in 1833. He attended the Kentucky Military Institute and worked in New York and California before becoming a farmer and merchant in Jackson County, Missouri. He was a major in the Missouri State Guard in 1861, became lieutenant colonel of the 6th Missouri in 1862 and was named colonel on August 26, 1862. Historian Bruce S. Allardice said his men "all loved him like a brother." He was wounded at Pea Ridge and Corinth.

14. Leon D. Marks was born in Bayou Sara, West Feliciana Parish, in 1829 and, after graduating from law school, moved to Shreveport. He fought in the Mexican War, was a delegate to the Louisiana Secession Convention, and joined the Confederate Army as a second lieutenant in 1861. He was promoted to colonel on April 19, 1862. Marks was married to a relative of Julia Dent Grant, the wife of Ulysses S. Grant.

Chapter 17: The Surrender

1. Allen Thomas was born in Howard County, Maryland, in 1830 and graduated from Princeton in 1850. He married into a Louisiana planter family and, in 1861, organized an infantry battalion. When it was expanded into the 29th Louisiana, he became its colonel. He had distinguished himself at Chickasaw Bluffs. After the surrender, he carried Pemberton's report to Richmond. He was a brother-in-law of Major General Richard Taylor. Both Taylor and Thomas were brothers-in-law of President Davis.

2. Apparently this took place at an old house known as the "Rock House."

3. Tunnard, 274–75.

4. W. L. Faulk "Diary," McCardle Library, Old City Courthouse, Vicksburg.

5. Estimates of civilian casualties vary widely, but they are all less than one hundred dead.

6. The 2nd Texas had already fought at Shiloh, Corinth, and Snyder's Bluff.

Chapter 18: Port Hudson

1. Shelby (1827–1873) was born in Tennessee but grew up in Texas and Mississippi. A Mexican War veteran, he was a lawyer in Brandon, Mississippi, when the war began. He was elected colonel of the 39th Mississippi in May 1862. Captured when Port Hudson fell, he was a POW at Johnson's Island for the rest of the war.

2. General Paine (1826–1905) was a strong Abolitionist and later a Radical Republican congressman. He refused, however, to make war on women and children. When General Benjamin "Beast" Butler ordered him to burn Baton Rouge, he refused to do so. Later, as Commissioner of Patents, he introduced typewriters to the Federal bureaucracy.

3. Because of pain from his wound, Dow resigned from the army in November 1864. He resumed his prohibition activities and ran for president in 1880 on the Prohibition ticket, where he received 10,000 votes. He died in Portland, Maine, in 1897.

Chapter 19: Aftermath

1. Taken from an eyewitness account by Dr. L. Minor Blackford of Atlanta.

2. Located in rural Virginia, on the North Carolina border.

3. This letter was dated March 1, 1865. The paper he enclosed blaming Johnston was dated February 18.

4. Lieutenant Colonel John C. Pemberton is not to be confused with Lieutenant Colonel John Pemberton of the 12th Georgia Cavalry, who invented Coca-Cola.

5. His mother, Rebecca Pemberton, died in 1869.

6. His childhood friend, George G. Meade, the Union commander at
    Gettysburg, is buried in the same cemetery. He died in 1872. The
    Meade family reportedly objected to Pemberton being buried in Laurel
    Hill, but to no avail.

Chapter 20: Conclusions

1. Just for the record, I have always believed that, after the war, Joseph E.
    Johnston's reputation as a general was much higher than he deserved. To
    me, he was the most overrated Civil War general ever.
2. Among others, Robert E. Lee, Hood's former commander,
    recommended against it.

Chapter 21: A Historical Footnote

1. Caught in the current, the *Sultana* sank about six miles south of the site
    of the explosion, near the west bank, near the present day town of Marion,
    Arkansas.

Epilogue: What Happened to Them?

1. Newspaper article posted in the Confederate Room, Old Courthouse
    Museum, Vicksburg.

BIBLIOGRAPHY

Abbott, John S. C. *The History of the Civil War in America.* New York: 1873.

Alison, Joseph D. "Old Times in the South." Unpublished diary located in the McCardle Library, Old City Courthouse, Vicksburg, Mississippi.

Askew, Samuel L., III. "An Analysis of Unit Cohesion in the 42nd Alabama Infantry." Thesis, Master of Military Art and Science, Auburn University, 1988.

Anderson, Ephraim McD. *Memoirs, Historical and Personal, including the Campaigns of the First Missouri Confederate Brigade.* St. Louis: Times Printing Co., 1863.

Arnold, James R. *Grant Wins the War: Decision at Vicksburg.* New York: John Wiley & Sons, 1997.

Atkinson, Matt, ed. *Lieutenant Drennan's Letter.* Gettysburg, PA: Thomas Publications, 2009.

Ballard, Michael B. *Pemberton: The General Who Lost Vicksburg.* Jackson, Mississippi: University of Mississippi Press, 1991.

Bachman, Robert L. "Reminiscences of Childhood and the Civil War." Unpublished manuscript located in the McCandle Library, Old City Courthouse, Vicksburg, Mississippi.

Bankston, Marie Louise Benton. *Camp-fire Stories of the Mississippi Valley Campaign.* New Orleans: The L. Graham Co., 1914.

Banner, Nicholas Paul. *Banner Family History, 1723 to 1990.* Odessa, Texas: Privately published, 1990.

Barnickel, Linda. *Milliken's Bend: A Civil War Battle in History and Memory.* Baton Rouge: LSU Press, 2013.

Bassett, Thom. "Van Dorn's Wild Ride." *The Opinionator.* A New York Times Blog, 2012. Accessed 2016.

Bearss, Edwin C. "Grand Gulf's Role in the Civil War." *Civil War History* vol. 5 (1959): 5–29.

———. *Grant Strikes a Fatal Blow.* Dayton, Ohio: Morningside Press, 1986.

———. *Hardluck Ironclad: The Sinking and Salvage of the Cairo.* Baton Rouge: L.S.U. Press, 1980.

Bevier, R. S. *History of the First and Second Missouri Confederate Missouri Brigades, 1861–1865.* St. Louis, Bryan, Brand and Company: 1879.

Bogle, Jos. "Some Recollections of the Civil War, by a Private in the 40th Georgia Regiment, C.S.A." Dalton *Daily Argus,* 1911.

Booth, Andrew B. *Records of Louisiana Confederate Soldiers and Commands.* New Orleans, n.s.: 1920.

Bowie, Aquila. Untitled. Unpublished Manuscript in the McCandle Library, Old City Courthouse, Vicksburg, Mississippi.

Bradley, George. "Diary." Unpublished Manuscript in the McCandle Library, Old City Courthouse, Vicksburg, Mississippi.

Brown, Russell K. *To the Manner Born: The Life of General William H. T. Walker.* Macon, Georgia: Mercer University Press, 2005.

Buchanan, Minor Ferris. *Holt Collier.* Jackson, Mississippi: Centennial Press, 2002.

Burton, E. Milby. *The Siege of Charleston, 1861–1865*. Columbia: University of South Carolina Press, 1970.

Calkin, Homer L. "Elk Horn to Vicksburg." *Civil War History* vol. 2, no. 1 (March 1956): 7–43.

Cannan, John, ed. *War in the West: Shiloh to Vicksburg, 1862-1863*. W. H. Smith, Publishers, 1990.

Carter, Arthur B. *The Tarnished Cavalier: Major General Earl Van Dorn, C.S.A.* Knoxville: University of Tennessee Press, 1999.

Catton, Bruce. *Grant Moves South*. Boston: Little, Brown and Company, 1960.

Chambers, William Pitt. "Diary." Extract in the Confederate Room, Old City Courthouse, Vicksburg.

Chance, Joseph E. *The Second Texas Infantry: From Shiloh to Vicksburg*. Fort Worth, Texas: Eakin Press, 1984.

Chesnut, Mary. *Mary Chesnut's Civil War*. C. Vann Woodward, ed. New Haven, CT: Yale University Press, 1981.

Civil War Trust. "The Third Louisiana Redan." https://vimeo.com/57142460.

Clack, William R. "Rollie"; "Diary." Dotcw.com/category/civil-war-diary-kept-w-r-clack/. Accessed, 2017.

Connor, Wesley Olin. "Diary." Special Collections Library, University of Georgia. http://fax.libs.uga.edu/Ms3102/If/W.O. Connor Diary.pdf.Connor Diary.pdf.

Coulter, E. M. *Confederate Receipt Book*. Athens: University of Georgia Press, 1960.

Crute, Joseph H., Jr. *Units of the Confederate States Army*. Gaithersburg: Olde Soldiers Books, 1987.

Cubbison, Douglas. *The Entering Wedge: The Battle of Port Gibson, 1 May 1863*. Danville, VA: Blue and Gray Educational Society, 2002.

Cunningham, H. H. *Doctors in Gray: The Confederate Medical Services Corps*. Baton Rouge: L.S.U. Press, 1993.

Cunningham, S. A., ed. *Confederate Veteran*. Various editions. Volumes I-XXXI (1893–1923).

Daniels, Jonathan. *A Southerner Discovers the South*. New York: Macmillan, 1938.

Darst, W. Maury, ed. "The Vicksburg Diary of Mrs. Alfred Ingraham (May 2-June 13, 1863)," *Journal of Mississippi History*, vol. 44 no. 2 (May 1982): 148–179.

Davis, Varina. *Jefferson Davis by His Wife*. Chicago: Belford Company, Publishers, 1890. Two volumes.

Davis, William C. *Look Away: A History of the Confederate States of America*. New York: Free Press, 2003.

Davis, William C. *The Orphan Brigade: The Kentucky Confederates Who Couldn't Go Home*. New York: Doubleday, 1980.

Dawson, Sarah Morgan. *A Confederate Girl's Diary*. Boston and New York: Houghton Mifflin Co., 1913.

Dorsey, Sarah A. *Recollections of Henry Watkins Allen, Brigadier-General Confederate States Army, Ex-Governor of Louisiana*. New York: M. Doolady, 1866.

Downey, Fairfax. "Field and Siege Pieces." *Civil War History*, vol. 2 no. 2 (June 1956): 65–74.

Drake, James and Rebecca. "The Battle of Raymond." http://battleofraymond.org.

Dunn, Edward J. "The Life of Edward J. Dunn." Unpublished manuscript, McCandle Library, Old City Courthouse Museum, Vicksburg, Mississippi.

Eisenschiml, Otto. *The Hidden Face of the Civil War*. New York: Boggs-Merrill, 1963.

Elson, Henry W. *The Photographic History of the Civil War*. New York: The Review of Books, 1911.

Estes, Claud. *List of Field Officers, Regiments and Battalions in the Confederate States Army, 1861-1865*. Macon, Georgia: The J. W. Burke Company, 1912.

Evans, Clement A., ed. *Confederate Military History*. Atlanta: Confederate Publishing Co., 1899.

Faulk, W. L. "Diary of Capt. W. L. Faulk, Co. B, 38th Mississippi, from May 18 to July 9, 1863, inclusive." Unpublished Manuscript in the McCandle Library, Old City Courthouse, Vicksburg, Mississippi.

Fremantle, Arthur J. L. *The Fremantle Diary.* Walker Lord, ed. Boston: Little, Brown, 1954.

Fuller, J. F. C. *The Generalship of Ulysses S. Grant.* London: 1929. Reprint ed., Boston: Da Capo Press, 1991.

Gallagher, Gary W. and Joseph T. Glatthaar. *Leaders of the Lost Cause.* Mechanicsburg, PA: Stackpole Books, 2004.

General John G. Forney Historical Society. Various unpublished documents in the McCandle Library, Old City Courthouse, Vicksburg, Mississippi.

Giambrone, Jeff. "A Terrible Storm Will Overwhelm Us: Secession Sentiment in Vicksburg, Mississippi." Mississippians in the Confederate Army, July 12, 2011. https://mississippiconfederates.wordpress.com/2011/07/11.

Grabau, Warren E. *Ninety-Eight Days: A Geographer's View of the Vicksburg Campaign.* Knoxville: University of Tennessee, 2000.

Groom, Winston. *Vicksburg, 1863.* New York: Knopf, 2009.

Grant, U. S. *Personal Memoirs of U. S. Grant.* New York: Charles S. Webster & Co., 1892.

Hall, Winchester. *The Story of the 26th Louisiana Infantry in the Service of the Confederate States.* CreateSpace, 2012.

Hartje, Robert George. *Van Dorn: The Life and Times of a Confederate General.* Nashville: Vanderbilt University Press, 1994.

Haynes, Malcolm G. "A Reevaluation of Pemberton at Vicksburg." Fort Leavenworth, Kansas: School for Advanced Military Studies, U.S. Army Command and General Staff College, 2012.

Henry, George. *The History of the First Kentucky Brigade.* Louisville, Kentucky: C. T. Dearing, 1911.

Ingraham, Elizabeth Meade. "Leaves from the journal of a Lady Near Port Gibson, Mississippi, Kept During Grant's March Upon Vicksburg via Grand Gulf and Port Gibson," in Sarah A. Dorsey, *Recollections of Henry Watkins Allen, Brigadier-General Confederate*

States Army, Ex-Governor of Louisiana. New York: M. Doolady, 1866.

————. *Leaves: The Diary of Elizabeth Meade Ingraham.* Rebecca Blackwell and Sue Burns Moore, eds. Edwards, Mississippi: Champion Hill Heritage Foundation, 2000.

Johnson, John. "Story of the Confederate Armored Ram Arkansas." *Southern Historical Society Papers,* vol. XXXIII (June–Dec 1905): 1–15.

Johnson, Robert U., ed. *Battles and Leaders of the Civil War.* New York: The Century Co., 1884–1886.

Johnston, Joseph E. *Narrative of Military Operations Directed During the Late War Between the States.* New York: D. Appleton & Co., 1874.

Jones, John B. *A Rebel War Clerk's Diary.* Philadelphia: J. B. Lippincott & Co., 1866.

Kaiser, Leo M. "In Sight of Vicksburg." *The Historical Bulletin,* vol. XXXIV (May 1956).

Kennedy, Frances H., ed. *The Civil War Battlefield Guide.* Boston: Houghton Mifflin Co., 1998.

Kidd, J. T. "The History of J. T. Kidd, March 18, 1862–May 23, 1865." Unpublished Manuscript, McCandle Library, Old City Courthouse, Vicksburg, Mississippi.

Kirwan, A. D., ed. *Johnny Green of the Orphan Brigade: The Journal of a Confederate Soldier.* Lexington, KY: 1956.

Kountz, John S. *Record of the Organizations Engaged in the Campaign, Siege and Defense of Vicksburg.* Washington: United States Government Printing Office, 1902.

Lanier, Elizabeth Ann. "Recollections." Unpublished Manuscript, McCandle Library, Old City Courthouse, Vicksburg, Mississippi, 1911.

Leon, Mrs. Arthur. "Confederate Letters, Grace Dudley Shelby." Unpublished letter in the McCandle Library, Old City Courthouse, Vicksburg, Mississippi.

Lindsley, John Berrien. *The Military Annals of Tennessee: Confederate.* Nashville: 1886.

Lockett, Samuel H. "The Defense of Vicksburg," in Robert U. Johnson and Clarence C. Buel. *Battles and Leaders of the Civil War.* New York: The Century Co., 1884–1886.

Long, E. B. *The Civil War Day by Day.* Garden City, N.Y.: Doubleday & Co., Inc., 1971.

Longstreet, James. *From Manassas to Appomattox.* New York: J. B. Lippincott and Co., 1896.

Loughborough, Mary. *My Cave Life in Vicksburg.* New York: D. Appleton & Co., 1864. Also Project Gutenberg, www.gutenberg.org/files/35700.

Lowe, Richard. "Van Dorn's Raid on Holly Springs, December, 1862." *Journal of Mississippi History*, no. 61 (1999).

Mahin, John Lee and Martin Rackin. "The Horse Soldiers, or Grierson's Raid." *Civil War History*, vol. V (1959).

Marshall, Dr. C. K. Published File in the McCandle Library, Old City Courthouse, Vicksburg, Mississippi.

———. Untitled. Unpublished letter to his brother in the McCandle Library, Old City Courthouse, Vicksburg, Mississippi.

Martin, Bessie. *Desertion of Alabama Troops from the Confederate Army.* New York: Columbia University Press, 1932.

Martin, David G. *The Vicksburg Campaign, April 1862–July 1863.* Conshohocken, Pennsylvania: Combined Books, Inc., 1990.

Maury, Dabney H. *Recollections of a Virginian.* New York: Charles Scribner's Sons, 1894.

McDonough, James L. *Shiloh—In Hell Before Night.* Knoxville: University of Tennessee Press, 1977.

McMorries, Edward Y. *History of the First Regiment, Alabama Volunteer Infantry, C.S.A.* Montgomery: 1904.

Miller, Dora Richards. "War Diary of a Union Woman in the South." Dotcw.com/category/war-diary-of-a-union-woman-in-the-south/page/9/.

Miller, Francis T. ed. *The Photographic History of the Civil War*. New York: The Review of Reviews Company, 1911.

Moore, Dr. W. T. "A Thrilling Experience." Unpublished manuscript in the McCandle Library, Old City Courthouse, Vicksburg, Mississippi.

Mumford, William T. "From a Confederate Diary." Unpublished manuscript, McCandle Library, Old City Courthouse, Vicksburg, Mississippi.

Norris, L. David, ed. *With the 18th Texas Infantry: The Autobiography of William Hill King*. Hillsboro, TX: Hill College Press, 1996.

Northern, Charles Swift, ed. *All Right Let Them Come: The Civil War Diary of an Eastern Tennessee Confederate*. Knoxville: University of Tennessee Press, 2003.

Oldroyd, Osborn H. *A Soldier's Story of the Siege of Vicksburg*. Springfield, Illinois: privately published, 1885.

Owen, Richard and James Owen. *Generals at Rest: The Grave Sites of the 425 Official Confederate Generals*. Shippenburg, PA: White Mane Publishing Co., 1997.

Pemberton, John C. *Pemberton, Defender of Vicksburg*. Chapel Hill: University of North Carolina Press, 1942.

Pirtle, John B. "Defence of Vicksburg in 1862—The Battle of Baton Rouge." *Southern Historical Society Papers*, vol. VIII (June–July 1880).

Porter, David D. *History of the Civil War*. New York: 1886.

Pratt, Fletcher. *Civil War on Western Waters*. New York: Henry Holt & Co., 1956.

Raab, James W. *A Dual Biography: Lloyd Tilghman and Francis Asbury Shoup*. John McGlone, ed. Murfreesboro, Tennessee: Southern Heritage Press, 2001.

Raab, James W. *W. W. Loring: Florida's Forgotten General*. Sunflower University Press, 1996.

Reynolds, Donald E. "Arkansas and the Vicksburg Campaign." *Civil War History*, vol. V (1959).

Richard, Allen C., Mary Richard and Terrance J. Winschel. *The Defense of Vicksburg: A Louisiana Chronicle.* College Station: Texas A & M Press, 2003.

Robertson, Phil. Personal communication, 2017.

Robuck, J. E. *My Own Personal Experience and Observation as a Soldier in the Confederate Army During the Civil War, 1861–1865.* Leslie Print and Publishing Co., 1911.

Ropes, John Codman. *The Story of the Civil War.* New York: G. P. Putnam's Sons, 1907.

Rowland, Dunbar and H. Grady Howell, Jr. *Military History of Mississippi, 1803–1898.* Jackson: Mississippi Department of Archives and History, 1908.

Sanders, Mary Elizabeth, ed. "Diary in Gray: The Civil War Letters and Diary of Jared Young Sanders." *The Louisiana Genealogical Register.* Volume XVII no. 1 (March 1970) and no. 3 (September 1970).

Sherman, William T. *Memories of General William T. Sherman.* New York: D. Appleton & Co., 1875.

Sifakis, Stewart. *Compendium of Confederate States Armies, Louisiana.* New York: Facts on File. 1995.

Sims, L. Moody, Jr., ed. "A Louisiana Engineer at the Siege of Vicksburg: Letters of Henry Ginder." *Louisiana History.* Vol. 8, no. 4 (1967).

Smith, Bridget. *Where Elephants Fought: The Murder of Confederate General Earl Van Dorn* (Mechanicsburg, PA: Milford House Press, 2015).

Smith, David M. *Compelled To Appear in Print: The Vicksburg Manuscript of General John C. Pemberton.* Cincinnati, Ohio: Ironclad Publishing, 1999.

Smith, Derek. *The Gallant Dead.* Mechanicsburg, PA: Stackpole Publishing, 2005.

Smith, Timonty B. *Champion Hill. Decisive Battle of Vicksburg.* New York: Savas Books, Ltd., 2004.

Smith, Timonty B. *Corinth 1862.* Lawrence: University Press of Kansas, 2016.

Symonds, Craig L. *Joseph E. Johnston: A Civil War Biography.* New York: W. W. Norton & Co., 1992.

Truman, William L. "Memoirs of the Civil War." Unpublished Manuscript. www.cedarcroft.com/cw/memoir.

Turner, Dale Oliver. *"Six Flags to Glory:" The Story of Lieutenant Dabney Minor Scales, The Confederate Ram Arkansas, and the C.S.S. Shenandoah.* Unpublished manuscript, McCardle Library, Old Courthouse Museum, Vicksburg.

Tucker, Phillip T. *The Confederacy's Fighting Chaplain: Father John B. Bannon.* Tuscaloosa: University of Alabama Press, 1992.

Tucker, Phillip T. *The Forgotten "Stonewall of the West:" Major General John Stevens Bowen.* Macon, Georgia: Mercer University Press, 1997.

Tucker, Spencer. *The American Civil War.* Santa Barbara, California: ABC-Clio, 2013.

Tunnard, W. H. *A Southern Record: The History of the Third Louisiana.* Baton Rouge: n.p., 1866.

Urquhart, Kenneth T., ed. *Vicksburg: Southern City Under Siege, William Lovelace Foster's Letters Describing the Defense and Surrender of the Confederate Fortress on the Mississippi.* New Orleans: 1980.

Van Dorn, Earl. *Reports of Battles Embracing the Defence of Vicksburg.* Richmond, Virginia: Bailey & Co., 1863.

Vilas, William F. *A View of the Vicksburg Campaign.* Madison, Wisconsin: 1908.

Walker, Peter F. *Vicksburg: A People at War, 1860–1865.* Chapel Hill, N.C.: University of North Carolina Press, 1960.

Warren, Andrea. *Under Siege: Three Children at the Civil War Battle of Vicksburg.* New York: MacMillan, 2009.

Wesley, Charles H. "The Employment of Negroes As Soldiers in the Confederate Army." *Journal of Negro History,* Vol. IV (July 1919).

Winschel, Terrance J. "Chickasaw Bayou: Sherman's Winter of Despair." *Blue and Gray,* Vol. XXIV no. 3 (2009).

———. *Triumph and Defeat: The Vicksburg Campaign*. New York: Savas Publishing, 1999.

Winters, John D. *The Civil War in Louisiana*. Baton Rouge: L.S.U. Press, 1963. Reprint ed., Baton Rouge: L.S.U. Press, 1991.

Woodworth, Steven L. *Jefferson Davis and His Generals: The Failure of the Confederate Command in the West*. Lawrence: University Press of Kansas, 1990.

Young, Bennett H. *Confederate Wizards of the Saddle*. Reprint ed. Lanham, MD: J. S. Sanders and Co., 1999.

"Narrative History of the Alabama 37th Regiment of Volunteer Infantry." www.Alabama37th.com/History-a-htm.

"Capt. William H. Wiseman, Co. G 43rd Tennessee Infantry CSA." www.pricecamp.org/wiseman.htm.

Acadians in Gray. www.acadiansingray.com.

www.southernheritage411.com/be.php/nw=037.

ORDER OF BATTLE, ARMY OF MISSISSIPPI AT VICKSBURG

Army of Mississippi: Lieutenant General John C. Pemberton
Smith's Division: Major General Martin Luther Smith
Vaughn's Brigade:
Brigadier General John C. Vaughn

60th Tennessee
61st Tennessee
62nd Tennessee

Baldwin's Brigade:
Brigadier General William E. Baldwin

17th Louisiana
31st Louisiana
4th Mississippi
46th Mississippi

Shoup's Brigade:
Brigadier General Francis A. Shoup

26th Louisiana

27th Louisiana

28th/29th Louisiana

Forney's Division: Major General John H. Forney

Hebert's Brigade:

Brigadier General Louis Hebert

3rd Louisiana

21st Louisiana

36th Mississippi

37th Mississippi

38th Mississippi

43rd Mississippi

7th Mississippi Battalion

Moore's Brigade:

Brigadier General John C. Moore

37th Alabama

40th Alabama

42nd Alabama

1st Mississippi Light Artillery

35th Mississippi

40th Mississippi

2nd Texas

Stevenson's Division: Major General Carter L. Stevenson

1st Brigade:

Brigadier General Seth M. Barton

40th Georgia

41st Georgia

42nd Georgia

43rd Georgia

52nd Georgia

2nd Brigade:

Brigadier General Alfred Cumming

34th Georgia

36th Georgia

39th Georgia

56th Georgia

57th Georgia

3rd Brigade:
Brigadier General Stephen D. Lee

> 20th Alabama
> 23rd Alabama
> 30th Alabama
> 31st Alabama
> 46th Alabama

4th Brigade:
Colonel Alexander W. Reynolds

> 3rd Tennessee
> 39th Tennessee
> 43rd Tennessee
> 59th Tennessee

Waul's TX Legion

River Defense Artillery:
Colonel Edward Higgins

> 1st Louisiana Heavy Artillery
> 8th Louisiana Heavy Artillery Battalion
> 22nd Louisiana
> 1st Tennessee Heavy Artillery
> Remnants, 54th Alabama

INDEX

A

Adams, Wirt, 116, 118, 152, 173, 175, 178, 191, 346

African Americans, 55, 60, 64, 83–85, 111, 119, 208, 218, 246, 261, 303, 315

Alison, Joseph D., 59, 205, 251, 265, 282

Allen, Henry Watkins, 7, 16, 336, 349–50

Army of Mississippi, the, 17, 183

Army of Relief, the, 171, 173, 191, 194, 245, 259, 270, 272, 297, 305, 353

Army of Tennessee, 17, 44–46, 73, 104, 113–14, 118, 120, 275, 305, 327, 346, 349–52, 356

Army of the Cumberland, 120

Army of the Gulf, 107, 312, 320

Army of the Tennessee, 17, 96, 112, 137, 166–67, 170, 178, 222, 259

Ashwood, 146, 150, 218

B

Balfour, Emma, 56, 204, 212, 253–54, 288, 347

Balfour, William, 56, 347

Banks, Nathaniel P., 105, 113, 148, 244, 312–18, 320–21

Bannon, John B., 192–93, 323–24

Barry, William T. S., 59–60, 353

Baton Rouge, Louisiana, 5, 15–16, 118, 349

Battle of Corinth, 124

Bayou Baxter, 78, 80

Bayou Pierre, 126, 137, 143–45

Beale, William, 311

Bearss, Edwin C., ix, 167, 336

Beauregard, P. T., 17, 22, 29, 31–33, 57, 138, 147, 164, 220, 245, 335

Big Black River, 123, 125–26, 145–46, 148–49, 151–52, 164–66, 168, 170–71, 180, 191, 194–95, 198–201, 205, 212, 214, 227, 259–60, 277, 297, 305, 309, 326

Black Bayou, 99, 101

Blair, Francis P., Jr., 231

Bledsoe, Hiram M., 59–60, 353

Bowen, John Steven, 19, 117, 119, 122–29, 131, 133–35, 138–39, 141–46, 148–49, 152, 175, 178, 182–83, 185, 187–89, 193, 196, 198, 200, 212–13, 217, 282, 285, 287, 295–300, 310, 323–24, 348, 355

Bragg, Braxton, 17, 22, 36–37, 44–47, 69, 73, 104, 114, 120, 162, 164, 226, 245, 249, 275, 327, 350, 352

Breckinridge, John C., 8, 15–16, 255, 259, 305

Brown, Isaac Newton, 11–12, 15, 43, 92

Bruinsburg, 137–39, 142

Burbridge, Stephen G., 298

C

Camp Hall, 207–8

Chalmers, James R., 34, 120, 122, 129, 152

Champion, Sid, 177, 351

Champion Hill, 174–75, 177, 179–80, 182, 184–88, 192–95, 199, 212, 227, 281, 334, 337, 351

Champion House, 177, 183, 351

Charleston, SC, x, 27–32, 41, 57, 89, 138, 253, 329, 355

Chesnut, Mary, 45

Chickasaw Bayou, 59–61, 67, 152, 200, 307

Chickasaw Bluffs, 38, 55, 57, 62–64, 69–72, 90, 112, 137, 206, 209, 214, 226, 248, 353

Cincinnati, 250–52, 257

City of Vicksburg, 81, 275, 306

Cockrell, Francis Marion, 128, 131, 142–43, 183–84, 198–200, 217, 233–34, 294, 348, 355

Coffeeville, MS, 40, 42

Cole's Island, 30–31

Confederate River Defense Fleet, 17

D

Daily Citizen, 275

Daniels, Lee L., 56

Davis, Jefferson, 4–5, 10, 18–19, 27, 29, 32–33, 33–36, 39, 44–48, 53–55, 58, 69, 73, 89, 104, 114–15, 120, 124, 127, 129–30, 138, 146, 152, 163–64, 172, 174, 220, 260, 272, 275, 304–5, 310–12, 324, 326–28, 334–37, 347

De Soto peninsula, 8, 259

De Soto Point, 56, 75, 80

Deer Creek, 99, 101–3, 119–20

Department of South Carolina, Georgia and Florida, 27, 29–30

Dewey, George, 107

Dillon's Plantation, 171, 173–74

Dockery, Thomas, 183–85, 287, 348

Dorsey, Sarah, 7, 131, 271, 336

Dow, Neal, 319–20

Dunn, Edward J., 37, 351

E

Edward's Depot, 164, 166, 170, 191

Ellet, Charles R., 81–82

Erwin, Eugene, 143, 284–85

F

Farragut, David, 5–6, 8–9, 14–15, 104–6, 108, 113, 126–27, 130, 311, 313

Fisher, Sterling, 308–9

Forney, John H., 124, 152, 198, 200, 212, 217, 226–28, 231, 233–37, 266–67, 285, 296, 302, 304, 348

Forrest, Nathan Bedford, 18, 37, 47, 51, 114, 122, 147, 161, 164, 346

Fort Donelson, 153

Fort Henry, 97

Fort Hill, 217–19, 223–25, 232–33, 250

Fort Pemberton, 92–94, 96–99, 102, 126, 137

Freeman, Douglas Southall, 44, 287, 337, 350

Fuller, J. F. C., ix, 187, 193

G

Gardner, Franklin, 34, 104–6, 152–53, 311–13, 315–18, 320–21, 346

Garrott, Isham W., 143, 238, 273

Gates, Elijah, 126, 198, 355

George, James Zachariah, 346

Gillespie, G. L., 256

Grand Gulf, 108, 117–19, 122–23, 125–29, 132–33, 137–39, 142, 146, 148–49, 167, 195, 218, 248, 259, 263

Grant, Ulysses, ix, 5, 17, 24–25, 35–42, 47–49, 51, 54, 58, 61, 66, 71, 75, 77–78, 80, 83, 86, 97, 99, 102, 104, 109, 112–14, 116, 118–20, 122–24, 127, 129–33, 135, 137–39, 142, 144–49, 151–52, 161, 166–75, 178, 182–83, 187–88, 192, 194–95, 198, 200, 210, 212, 217–18, 222, 227–31, 233, 239–41, 244–45, 247, 250, 257–61, 263, 266–67, 270, 272, 281, 285, 290, 296, 298–3, 305, 307, 309, 313, 320, 323–24, 328, 333–35, 337–38, 355

Grant's Pass, 91, 94

Green, Martin, 183, 239, 287

Gregg, John, 65, 152–59, 162, 167–70, 245, 347

Grenada, MS, 15, 40–42, 49, 54–55, 58–59, 90, 96, 117, 146, 148

Grierson, Benjamin, 116–19, 126, 138, 154

Griffith, John Summerfield, 41, 48–49, 51, 345–46

Gwin, William, 61

H

Haines' Bluff, 42, 55, 70–71, 99, 133, 198, 200, 249

Hall, Winchester, 6, 60, 62, 66, 69, 71, 206–8, 222–23, 257, 259, 289, 306, 349

Hankinson's Ferry, 148–49, 221, 280

Hatch, Reuben, 339–40, 342

Hebert, Louis, 152, 211, 221, 233–34, 266–67, 278, 284, 304, 352

Helena, Arkansas, 54, 87, 90, 129, 340, 343

Herron, Frank, 160–61, 266

Higgins, Edward, 57, 61–62, 65, 130

Higgins, Thomas J., 236

Hill, D. H., 36

Holly Springs, 40, 48–51, 112, 151, 345

Holmes, Theophilus, 36–37, 53–54, 115, 220, 337

hospitals, 1, 32, 40, 57, 97, 147, 160–61, 173, 178, 207, 223, 265, 277–78, 307, 309, 342, 347, 351, 355

Hurlbut, Stephen, 38, 119–20, 122, 127, 129

I

Indianola, 82–83

Ingraham, Elizabeth Mary Meade, 146–47, 150, 218

ironclads, 9–12, 55, 75, 87, 91–94, 101–3, 130–31, 133–35, 229–30
Louisiana, 11
Mississippi, 11
Tennessee, 11
Arkansas, 11–16
Carondelet, 12–13, 124, 130, 351

J

Jackson, Andrew, 20, 40

Jackson III, Andrew, 128, 221, 286

Jackson, MS, 36, 38, 41–42, 44, 49, 58–59, 69, 89, 103, 117–18, 126, 130, 137–38, 146, 148–49, 151–54, 162–64, 166–73, 177–78, 183, 190, 206–7, 211, 237, 259, 266, 268, 273, 275, 283–85, 305, 310, 323, 326, 334, 346, 351

Jackson, "Red," 42, 49, 258–59, 305

Jackson, Stonewall, 44, 89, 177, 312, 334

James Island, 30–32

Jews, the, 38–39

Johnston, Albert Sidney, 226

Johnston, Joseph E., 22, 26, 44–47, 53–55, 58–59, 69, 73, 103–4, 113–14, 118–20, 129, 132, 138, 147–49, 152, 163, 167–74, 190–91, 194–95, 213, 227, 229–30, 245, 247, 249, 253–56, 258–60, 264–65, 267–69, 270–72, 274–75, 278–79, 281, 289, 297, 305, 309, 312, 324, 326–27, 334–37, 347, 350, 352

Johnson's Island, 320, 346

K

Kennon, Beverly, 43

Knox, Thomas, 63

L

Lake Providence, 71, 78–80, 112, 116, 123, 290

Lanier, Eliza Ann, 244

Lee, Robert E., 4, 22, 27–29, 31, 35, 36, 39, 44–45, 53, 56, 58, 64, 66, 69, 71, 74, 89, 97, 147, 162, 164, 172, 177, 180, 244

Lee, Stephen Dill, 58, 143, 183, 217, 231

Lewis, Charles S., 224–25, 232–33, 267, 291

Lincoln, Abraham, x, 2, 4, 16–17, 37–38, 75–76, 84, 112, 193, 239, 285, 312–13, 325–26

Lockett, Samuel H., 15, 125, 176, 195–96, 199–201, 203, 214, 229, 284, 352

Lord, Margaret, 325

Lord, William Wilberforce, 246, 258, 288, 355

Loring, W. W., 42, 87, 89–92, 94, 96, 98, 117–19, 124, 138–39, 145, 148–49, 151–52, 164, 166, 171, 173, 175–78, 181–83, 187–93, 195–96, 200, 217, 245, 259, 305, 334, 337, 350

Loughborough, Mary Ann, 162, 166, 204, 229, 258, 274, 276, 304, 349

Lovell, Mansfield, 7, 19, 34–35, 207

M

Magnolia Church, 139, 141–42

Mallory, Stephen, 10–11, 43

Marks, Leon D., 222, 271, 289

Marshall, C. K., 9–10, 347

Mason, Cass, 340

Maury, Dabney H., 18, 420 58–60, 98, 102, 124, 226, 352, 356

McClernand, George, 75, 112, 127–29, 139, 141, 143, 150–51, 173, 178, 182, 214, 227, 237–39, 299

McDonald, Myra, 161

McGavock, Randal William, 97, 153, 156–57, 161

McPherson, James B., 80, 123, 127, 144–46, 148–51, 155, 159, 167, 169–70, 173, 214, 239, 266, 299, 303, 323

Meade, George G., 20, 22, 147

Memphis, TN, 9, 11, 17, 37–39, 42, 70–71, 120, 127, 129, 244, 248, 258, 340–42

Meridian, MS, 46, 117, 163, 169, 353

Mexico, 18, 23–24, 44, 104, 350

Miller, Dora, 204, 252, 269

Milliken's Bend, 71, 77–78, 83, 85–86, 116, 127–28, 133, 151, 261–63

Mobile & Ohio Railroad, 117

Moon Lake, 87, 91

Moore, John C., 98, 217, 231, 235, 252, 275, 293, 304, 306–7, 352

Morgan, G. W., 59, 65–67, 70, 72

My Cave Life in Vicksburg, 347

N

Narrative of Military Operations Directed During the Late War Between the States, 335

Nashville, TN, 17, 46, 357

Norfolk, VA, 22–25

O

Official Records of the War of the Rebellion, 336

"Old Demoralizer," 312–13, 316

P

Paine, Halbert, 313, 317–18

Parrot guns, 261, 296

Patton, Isaac W., 229

Pemberton, Rebecca Clifton, 20, 345

Pettus, Edmund, 239, 273, 349

Pettus, John J., 35–36, 45, 116, 169, 346

Pickens, Francis, 27, 29–33, 345

Pope, John, 17, 22, 112

Porter, David D., 9, 13, 61, 70–71, 81–83, 92, 99, 101–2, 126, 130–31, 133–35, 142, 148, 229, 228, 250, 256, 278–79, 282, 307

Port Gibson, 18, 115, 118–19, 127, 129, 132–33, 137–42, 144–46, 149–50, 171, 218, 298

Port Hudson, xii, 16, 34–35, 42, 53, 78, 104–6, 108, 113, 120, 122–23, 126, 130, 137–38, 146, 148, 152–54, 169, 244–45, 311–13, 317, 319–20, 327, 346, 355

Q

Queen of the West, 12, 81–82

Quinby, 96–99, 103

R

Raymond, MS, 115, 151–52, 154–55, 158–62, 169, 171,

173, 175, 178, 187, 190, 309, 323, 350

Red River, 15, 78, 82, 116, 308

Resaca de la Palma, 23, 96

Ripley, Roswell S., 31

Ruggles, Daniel, 34, 120, 122, 152

S

Scott, Winfield, 26, 44, 98, 112

2nd Texas Lunette, 231, 235–36, 238, 298

Seddon, James A., 162–64, 168, 260, 271

Seminole Wars, 44

Sherman, William T., 2, 22, 397– 39, 42, 47, 52, 54–55, 58–61, 64–67, 70–72, 75–76, 80, 99, 101, 103, 119, 127, 129, 133, 137, 145, 147, 149, 151, 169– 70, 173, 200, 214, 217–18, 223, 225, 232–34, 237, 239, 250, 305, 310, 313–16, 326, 350, 353

Shiloh, TN, 21–22, 29, 30, 38, 105, 124, 141, 220, 235, 308

Shoup, Francis, 219–22, 232–34, 264, 265, 270–71, 274, 350

Smith, A. J., 61, 178, 298–299

Smith, Edmund Kirby, 44, 115

Smith, Martin Luther, 6, 34, 56, 59, 203, 207, 212, 217, 219, 225, 234, 287, 309

Snyder's Bluff, 35, 70, 87, 198, 206

Snyder's Mill, 55, 57, 61, 98, 137, 152, 200, 206–7, 210, 214, 255, 278

Steele, Frederick, 54, 59, 61, 119, 163

Steele's Bayou Expedition (Deer Creek Expedition), 99–101, 112, 209, 222, 302

Stevenson, Carter, 46, 59, 69–70, 73, 102, 114, 122, 124, 133, 138–39, 149, 152, 164, 171, 175, 177–78, 180–82, 185, 187–89, 192, 194, 200, 211– 12, 217, 227, 230–31, 238–39, 245, 267, 280–81, 296–97, 356

Sultana, 337–41

Swords, J. M., 273–74

T

Thomas, Lorenzo, 84–85

Thompson, Martha ("Pattie"), 23

Third Louisiana Redan, 270, 275, 283–85

Tilghman, Lloyd, 22, 42, 90, 93, 96–97, 104, 138, 145, 176–78, 187, 189–90, 347

Tracy, Edward D., 46, 133, 141–43

Truman, William L., 127, 134, 145, 198, 351

Tunnard, William Henry, 40, 143, 207, 211, 248, 255, 260, 267, 276, 279, 286, 290, 296, 306, 328, 348

U

USS *Benton*, 13, 61, 130, 133–35

USS *Cairo*, 43, 55, 77

USS *Chillicothe*, 93, 95, 97

USS *Choctaw*, 209, 262–63

USS *Hartford*, 13, 105–6, 108, 127

USS *Mississippi*, 105–7

USS *Monongahela*, 105–7

USS *Richmond*, 105–7

V

Van Dorn, Earl, 14–15, 17–19, 33–35, 39–40, 42, 47–51, 73, 103, 113–15, 124, 147, 203, 334

Vaughn, John C., 65–66, 152, 196, 198–200, 219, 223, 347–48

Virginia, 4, 18, 23–26, 28, 32, 44–45, 89, 147, 172, 177, 226, 229, 318, 327–28, 330, 337, 340, 347, 350, 352, 356

W

Walnut Bayou, 109

Walnut Hills, 53, 55, 59

Warrenton, MS, 35, 53, 127, 132–33, 138, 166, 217, 280

Warrenton, VA, 328, 330

Washburn, Cadwallader Colden, 41, 112, 243, 258, 264, 267

Weitzel, Godfrey, 313–15

West Point, 15, 18, 20–21, 36, 44, 57, 65, 80, 96, 104, 123–24, 219, 226, 235, 314, 318, 323, 327, 342

Williams, Thomas, 5–6, 8, 15–16, 75, 342

Willis-Cowan House, 279

Windsor Plantation, 139

Withers, Theo, 8, 57, 60, 65, 182, 221, 353

Y

Yalobusha River, 40, 42, 47, 49, 58, 90

Yazoo City, MS, 11, 92–93, 95, 114, 206

Yazoo Pass Expedition, 87–88,
90, 99, 112
Yazoo River, 11–12, 35, 42–43,
55, 58, 60–61, 70, 78, 87, 92,
98–100, 133, 149, 207, 209–
11, 213

Z

Zellner, Ben, 330